Tickets To Ride

Tickets To Ride

The Journey of a Yorkshireman

Phil Hart

Published by Phil Hart

A CIP catalogue record for this book is available from the British Library.

ISBN 978-0-9933516-0-0

Book layout by Clare Brayshaw

Prepared and printed by:

York Publishing Services Ltd
64 Hallfield Road
Layerthorpe
York
YO31 7ZQ

Tel: 01904 431213

Website: www.yps-publishing.co.uk

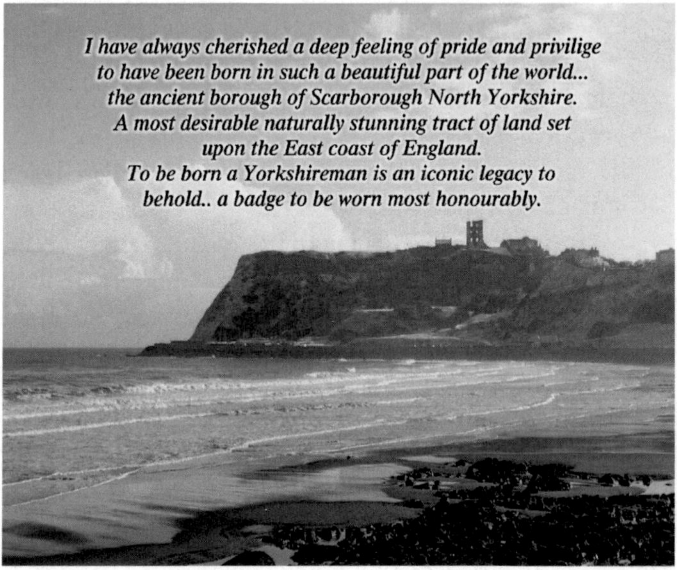

I have always cherished a deep feeling of pride and privilige
to have been born in such a beautiful part of the world...
the ancient borough of Scarborough North Yorkshire.
A most desirable naturally stunning tract of land set
upon the East coast of England.
To be born a Yorkshireman is an iconic legacy to
behold.. a badge to be worn most honourably.

Phil Hart ... wit, raconteur, entrepreneur and passionate about Scarborough and all things Yorkshire and more importantly my friend for over 20 years. I met Phil Hart when our two families were on holiday in Tenerife and since then we have enjoyed many happy times together and also a few sad occasions.

I am proud to have Phil as my friend and we have over the years enjoyed many healthy debates about the state of the nation, sport, politics, etc etc. This often being accompanied by a small sherry to help proceedings along.

It was on one such evening that I began to think about the colourful life Phil had experienced over the years and after the second small sherry of the evening I suggested that he ought to recount his life in words by producing a book. This caused some hilarity that evening but the following morning, in the cold light of day, Phil thought it might be a good idea.

From then on I was bombarded with page after pages of handwritten text which took hours and hours to type as my skills on the keyboard amount to just the two fingers!!

After many months of effort by Phil and I, a final version of his story was produced. As I hope you will find out Phil Hart has indeed led a very eventful and colourful life and his yarns make a great read.

Good luck my friend

Phil Wiggington, Family friend and good egg!

I first met Phil or Harty as everyone called him around 1970, at North Marine Road on the cricket field.

From the very beginning, playing for Scarborough C.C. his enthusiasm and great love for the game was obvious for all to see.

He had a natural talent for cricket, as his games for Yorkshire proved in later years. He had the canny knack of taking vital wickets, and scoring runs when they were badly needed.

Phil has been a great example to all our young players and I know for sure that his enthusiasm and will to win rubbed off on them.

Throughout life he has been the eternal optimist, always a smile on his face.

He became in later years, an excellent coach and mentor for many young cricketers who are always still delighted to see him when he attends games.

This book has been written with the same enthusiasm and love for life with many funny stories along the way.

Phil has written this book with family in mind, which records the great love he has for Helen, Katie and the grandchildren, and how proud he is of all his family.

I wish him luck with this first venture in writing, I hope after reading this one their may be more to follow.

Tony AJ Moor
First XI Skipper 1972-79–82, 84

In many ways Phil Hart is a remarkable man. I am proud to say he is my brother-in-law. He was instrumental in arranging a blind date with his wife's sister and the rest is history as they say.

Phil is a kind, generous man who is always thinking of others. He has been a regular visitor at the old people's home in Scarborough where he entertains the residents with his brand of humour and energy.

He has been at the forefront of life in Scarborough for many years and is a well known figure in the town as a result of his sporting prowess at Scarborough Cricket Club and in many fundraising activities in the area.

His life has been varied to say the least. He left home at 15 to join the army, remarkable to think of that train journey from Scarborough to Dorset on his own when he had never been out of Scarborough before. It shows his courage and thirst for adventure, this has continued throughout his 67 years.

I really got to know Phil when he was selected for the Yorkshire Cricket team in 1981. He was brought out of League cricket at the age of 34 due to an injury to Yorkshire's spinner at the time, Phil Carrick. It was an incredible opportunity for him and although his professional career didn't last long, he enjoyed and made the most of every minute. It is something we still talk about to this day and he rightly has great pride in having represented his county.

This book exemplifies what Phil is about. A man full of enthusiasm, a thirst for adventure but with a truly loyal and caring personality.

I hope you enjoy reading the story of his life as I believe it is a story that should inspire us all to make the most of our time on this planet.

You're a good man Phil and I'm proud of you.

Martyn Moxon, Director of Cricket YCCC

"You"ll never get anywhere if you keep running on your heels young North" the infamous words that still haunt me nearly two decades on!!

I first met Phil around 17 years ago, … he's 67 now you know … sorry Phil! Now in these 17 years, through my brief foray into the world of cricket, followed by my pursuit of an acting career, I have met some scary characters, but no one has managed to strike fear into my bones like Mr Philip Hart!! It was worth it though because he was the best cricket coach I have ever known.

Looking back, Phil was responsible for some of the most talented cricketers I have had the pleasure of playing with including one side in 2001 which boasted no fewer than five "U15" Yorkshire players all the product of his expert coaching prowess. One notable member of that team was a certain Adam Lyth who as we all know has gone onto greater things (and he was battling at no 5!! … Phil's idea no doubt)

I recently came out of cricket retirement to turn my arm over for the team where it all began … the Scarborough 3rd XI. I came on to bowl praying everything would come back to me as I attempted to tweak down a few leg spinners. As I got to the end of my mark to turn and run in something caught my eye on the boundary edge that made my blood run cold. It was Phil with arms crossed and a broad grin on his face. My knees immediate turned to jelly as he barked that my fielders were in the wrong positions. Somethings never change!!

Anyway, it was great to see him again after all these years and it gave me the opportunity to express my thanks and gratitude for all the help and guidance he gave, not just me, but all the hundreds of young cricketers, that he brought on during his coaching career.

No one was more passionate and wanted us to succeed more than Phil. Hopefully, we did him proud.

To a top cricketer, coach and above all, a top bloke. Cheers Phil.

Mikey North alias Gary Windass

It gives me great pleasure to write a few words about Phil. I first met Phil when he came to my primary school, Airy Hill, in Whitby, when I was about 10 years old. He came to show us how to play Kwick Cricket. This lead to a few of us going on to play for Whitby juniors. Tom and Bob Spedding, Ricky, James and Roseanna Hall, Ashley and myself (quite a family affair really!) Also in the team were Andrew Wood, Chris Batchelor and Chris Shardlow.

While Ashley went on to play for Scarborough 1st team, the rest of us spent many a happy Saturday playing with Phil for Scarborough 3rd team. Great times Phil and so many lovely memories. You encouraged us all so much and we were all given chances to perform. Your time spent with the juniors was for me, the kickstart to my professional career. Thanks to you I went on to represent North Yorkshire, Yorkshire CC, The North of England and of course England right through the age groups from U11 to U19.

You are the nicest person I have ever met, a great family friend, and I can safely say Phil, if it wasn't for you, I wouldn't be where I am today. Thank you Phil.

Adam Lyth, YCCC

Dedication

This book is dedicated to our three beautiful grandchildren, Jessica, Louie and Archie Post, who with luck and good fortune throughout their lives, will aim to contribute their adventures and fond memories to the continuation of the journey.

Chapter 1

Being Born....school and Mum and Dad

My arrival on Planet Earth coincided with one of the coldest harshest winters in living memory, 12 January 1947. My entrance was slightly flawed as I had a problem with my belly button, which after investigation by a doctor was diagnosed to be a leakage within that orifice. To counteract this slight impediment, a unique form of treatment was put in place – three penny pieces were stacked on the wound then held in position with gaffer tape. This advancement in medical science amazed the family. What must I have looked like? They obviously knew what they were doing as, after a couple of days, I was healed up and watertight (well, sort of) and ready to set sail. My first port of call was to a bungalow named Hazel Dean, which stood in a field close to Cayton Village. It was built of wood and quite basic with no electricity. An orchard of apple and pear trees surrounded my new home,with outbuildings housing the dog, chickens and family pig.

After his demob, Dad found work employed by a Mr Newsome, who was an ex Oxford University Don. He owned the land and kindly offered Dad the accommodation at a reduced rate. It would be a temporary agreement as Mum and Dad had put their names down for a new council house being built in Seamer village, a couple of miles west. Mr Newsome employed Dad to help him run his new business venture at Osgodby, a small outcrop on the coast along from the South Cliff side of Scarborough. He was in the fur trade, breeding and rearing foxes at Silver Fox Farm, as fox furs were the height of fashion at this time.

During that bleak winter of 1947, life and times for ordinary families had been demanding and hard to bear, resilience being the key word. There were tales of hardship which became folklore and legend all being played out throughout all corners of our land. These stories were bandied round dining tables as we tucked into our meals, conscious of the fact of how lucky we were. The winter developed into what resembled an arctic whiteout with temperatures plummeting way below zero. It was so cold that, according to Mum, the mice came to lodge with us. With all the apples picked and stored in boxes under the beds there would be apples all over the floors in the morning, thanks to the scavenging mice. This used to irritate Mum no end; she became concerned for my welfare and I ended up with a mosquito net attached to my cot. With no electricity on hand in the bungalow, oil lamps would be lit which fizzed and flickered, casting long eerie shadows up the walls. With a blazing log fire in the hearth, Mum and Dad enjoyed their long winter evenings. One particular Sunday they invited some friends over to supper. After the meal, they were relaxing and catching up with the gossip when from under the floor an unusual quacking sound was heard … "What could it be" cried the excited guests. Dad took up a couple of floorboards and with a torch in hand went hunting for the uninvited guests. "Up yer come!" dad shouted and produced a very bewildered hedgehog. After a lengthy debate, the consensus around the room was to put him back under the floor where he appeared to be warm and dry to allow him to sleep, oblivious to the freezing conditions outside.

Probably the most dramatic account of our time at Hazel Dean came from Mum. She recalled the day they came to kill the family pig. This ritual would usually take place in the Autumn before the onset of Winter. Up and down the land, rural communities would gather to witness this gruesome act. It was an essential part of community life and gave a much needed boost to the family larder. Mum found it hard, particularly as she tended to feed the pig on a daily basis, creating a bond. So much so she even gave the pig a name, but to have it put down in such a savage manner upset her. But a good pig would feed a family for months.

Babies were booming, being born every hour according to the media, which coined the phrase "Baby Boomers". William (Bill), my little brother arrived on 19 June 1948... another mouth to feed.

Dad was born in Ruston village on 22 January 1921. Ruston was a tight knit community close to the village of Wykeham, standing alongside the A170, Scarborough to Pickering road. He was the only son of Elizabeth and Richard Hart, with his sister Dorothy arriving shortly after. His parents were ardent Methodists and Richard was in fact a parson or preacher. They were well known throughout the area making their way to Sunday service on Richard's tricycle, Grandad peddling and Grandma standing on the back praying for guidance I shouldn't wonder. Dad was christened Richard after his father, but he always preferred Dick.

They lived in a small family cottage on the Main Street in Ruston. Dorothy, Dad's sister would inherit the cottage when she married. I never met Grandad Richard as he died before I was born. Grandma I do recall vaguely, but unfortunately she passed away when we were young.

Dorothy or Auntie Dot married Danny Ferguson, an amiable friendly Scotsman. They had two children, Ann and Peter. I remember with affection spending many a happy hour chasing around their massive back garden dressed in my cowboy outfit, re-enacting scenes of my hero at the time 'Roy Rogers'. Auntie Dot baked the best scones ever, with real butter and golden syrup…Roy Rogers never had them!!

Dad always used to instill in us as kids how important school was. He had been a bright spark as a youngster at school and would have loved to have had the opportunity to further his education. He loved to draw and sketch but like thousands of other gifted students up and down the land, his future lay in working. The family were in no position financially to support his hair brained ideas so he left school at fourteen and started work, as in those days, employment meant food on the table. The 1930's were austere another world, when compared to the throw away society of today.

The one positive aspect of those days was that manpower was in constant demand, which meant that employment was readily available. Dad started his working life planting trees for the Forestry Commission up above the village of Ruston. The Commission managed hundreds of square miles of forestry and woodland throughout the UK. Timber was required in vast quantities, for example for pit props to shore up the coal mines. Today, machines rather than manpower plant and harvest the trees. It was back breaking hard graft according to Dad. All aspects of the work in the forest was 'hands on', but he loved the fresh air, the outdoor life, seeing nature close at hand and recognising the different diverse species of plants, wild flowers, trees, birds and mammals. Years later when we were growing up he enjoyed nothing more than taking us up above Sawdon village, brambling, filling our buckets from natures garden whilst passing on his rustic knowledge (priceless).

Now was the coming of age of the combustion engine, transport was changing 'big style" it was now the beginning of the end of horse drawn vehicles. Dad had become obsessed with motor cycles, they were his passion. Triumph, BSA, AJS, Matchless, Rudge, these machines left him drooling, his favourite being 'Norton'.

When World War 2 broke out in 1939, Dad was too young to join up therefore he enlisted in the local Wykeham Volunteer Force. The initial few months of the so called War, nothing really happened and it became known as the 'phoney war' Then as September dawned, the rumours were rife that Hitler's Nazi thugs were preparing to invade Great Britain sending in paratroopers to soften us up. Dad loved to tell us this account of his actions. People were tense and concerned,. Imagining the dreadful scenarios about to unfold. It was Sunday afternoon, the volunteers were assembled within their HQ. According to Dad the tension was unbearable. He was sent forthwith with his mate, on their bikes the guard the bridge over the sea cut between Ruston and Sherburn village. Armed with just a pick axe handle and torch, had the Nazi paratroopers dared to challenge them they would have certainly met their match!! They did take their duties very seriously, keeping their eyes peeled until well after dark. We make light of those scary days now, but if Germany had indeed decided to invade on that lazy Sunday afternoon, nothing much would have stopped them and I would not have probably been writing this account of events.

Eventually Dad got his chance to prove his worth and serve his country. He joined the Royal Artiillery attached to the Eighth Army led by General Montgomery or 'Monty' as he was affectionately known. Dad got the chance to live his dream as he became a dispatch rider astride his beloved Norton 500...how bizarre. He landed in North Africa as part of the axis force, and would help push the enemy back towards the sea. I guess he revelled in his role, delivering his orders at full throttle across the Libyan desert, ginger hair ruffling in the breeze...Bless Him!!

His exploits and stories of his life in the desert probably planted a seed in my sub conscience as I would follow his Norton tracks a few years later.

Dad's war ended in Italy when he contracted a serious bone infection to his right ankle which hospitalised him for over a year. He was eventually repatriated back to blighty no worse for wear. His love of motorbikes continued and he would take Bill and myself up to the race circuit at Oliver's Mount. This track is renowned throughout the bike racing world, standing majestically above the town of Scarborough, sending its roar of the engines sweeping throughout the Borough. Dad's favourite rider was the great Geoff Duke. No doubt these were very special times and a real treat. Looking back now I realise being a parent and grandparent, how much pleasure Dad must have gained, the warmth and love he generated was more than enough for the two of us.

Baby Winifred Dobson was born into this world on 5th August 1923. She was the third child to be born to Frederick and Laura Dobson in the village of Weaverthorpe up on the Yorkshire Wolds. Her two elder brothers, Leslie and Maurice made up the trio. Tragically just after the birth of Mum, Fred, her father passed away from that dreadful disease TB, which wiped out families in their thousands throughout the country. It was devastating for the family especially Laura, losing her husband and the family breadwinner at such a young age of 23 years. Bringing up three young children single-handed was I am sure her worst nightmare. As time passed, Laura found new happiness with Arthur Armstrong. She recalled years later how lucky she had been to find such a kind and loving man who became her new family rock. Arthur had endured the physical hardships of the Great War, joining the West Yorkshire Regiment as a waggoner, he reached the rank of Sergeant. I was too young to have been interested in his exploits during that horrendous War. I guess he would feel both lucky and blessed to have survived the carnage and sheer barbarism committed by both sides. I cannot imagine the horrific sights and sounds those men must have witnessed during that pointless struggle.

Laura and Arthur married and within a year had another daughter and little sister for Winnie, Joan Armstrong entered this world a strong healthy child to enjoy the love and security of family life.

Winnie enjoyed school in Weaverthorpe and was a popular student. At the tender age of 14, as was the norm in those days, she left school. She felt her luck was in as she took the opportunity to become a cook's assistant within the noble walls of Brompton Hall, the ancestral home of the Cayley family.

The family dynasty began its reign in the year of 1642 when the first baronet was installed. Sir Kenhelm Cayley was the head of the household when young Winnie embarked on her new career. How scary it must have seemed for this young girl, leaving the security and warmth of her family home, bidding farewell to her mother and father, brothers and sisters. She was nervously starting life below stairs, we have all witnessed the hard work, as screened by the dramas Upstairs Downstairs and Downton Abbey.

Young Winnie had no need to worry, she was welcomed with open arms, the household staff and family were so helpful and friendly during her settling in period. Mum used to talk affectionately about those days, and really cherished the memories even though their work was hard and demanding. Sir Kenhelm and Lady Cayley, were in her eyes, the perfect employers. They were firm but fair and all the staff below stairs were proud of their house and all it stood for. There was determination and teamwork with total commitment and trust within the workforce. There was always lots of healthy food on the table which provided all the nourishment needed to work so hard. Winnies day would begin very early at 06.00hrs to be precise. Her first job was to rake out the ovens, then clean them and black them. This was largely achieved by serious elbow grease with a bit of spit and polish thrown in. Next laying out the kindling then firing up ready to satisfy the keen eye of Cook before the onslaught of another gruelling day. Compare the technology of today with what Mum had to endure and it seems like they were living centuries ago!! Mum felt privileged to be given the knowledge and expertise to enhance her own culinary skills by helping to prepare banquets for the palates of the rich and famous.

Brompton village nestles a mile west of Ruston and Mum would ride her bike the short distance on her days off. She had met a young man at the local dance, a Mr Richard Hart. Winnie used to love to reminisce recalling these liaisons. She would often chuckle as she explained how she fell in love with his wavy ginger hair. The romance blossomed and they became inseparable, meeting at every opportunity, until war intervened. Dad enlisted into the Royal Artillery and like thousands of similar couples this parting would have been extremely difficult to handle mentally, him going away to fight in the war, not sure of the outcome. Life had to be lived from day to day. For Winnie it was more difficult as she was now pregnant. She was only 17 and the father of her unborn child was somewhere in North Africa doing his duty for the country. These were strange days when comparing with the norm and was not a time to be judgemental.

The local Seamer Charter is still read during the month of July, the local schoolchildren are herded down to the village Green by the Church and decaying Manor House. Here they assemble to listen to that same script, a graphic reminder of bygone days and centuries past. To be brought up within these historic surroundings and rituals, I was convinced would broaden my outlook as I moved forward.

Our new house was on Denison Avenue, No 4. The Avenue was named after Lord Denison who was around during the hundred years war in the 1400's. The avenue is taking shape with a few houses still to complete. Our nextdoor neighbours are also just settling in, they are the Dawson family, Toby and Phyllis and baby Paul. Toby is the son of the local shopkeeper Jack Dawson, a lovely friendly man who was another ardent Methodist. Our house is built very solidly, with two sitting rooms, kitchen, and pantry, with three bedrooms and a bathroom upstairs. It had an outside loo and coalhouse next to the shed. The garden was ample, with plenty of space for two young boys to play plus an area for Dad to grow his veg and potatoes.

Dad is still employed at the Fox Farm, he cycles to work everyday, a good five miles in all weathers from Seamer to Osgoodby. On occasions as I recall he sometimes brought the old Jowett van home from work, he called it the kipper cart. It had a bright red steering wheel. I sometimes went with Dad to work in the van, usually on a Saturday morning. I was only three or four at the time, he used to let me steer the van across the field to the farm sitting on his knee. Mr Newsome lived across the main Scarborough road from the farm in a massive fancy house which in my eyes was a mansion, with Labrador dogs which we fed in their kennels adjacent to the house. He was softly spoken with a strange flowery accent. Dad said he was a good natured type and would help in any way if he could.

He would go shooting with his dogs, a crackshot by all accounts, being mentioned in dispatches during the war.

On my christening, he presented Dad with a solid silver mug, engraved with my name and date of birth, obviously a good egg as they say in Oxford!!

My first sight of the Foxes took my breath away. I was a little nervous at first as I stood by their run. Dad used to go in to feed them and to check their welfare. Some were more friendly than others, but they were incredibly beautiful looking creatures, with their silver coats shining in the sunlight. Their diet consisted of week old chickens, cockbirds in fact who arrived in tubs from the breeders.

Occasionally dad would open a tub and the first lair of chickens would still be alive. He would bring them home where we tried to rear them, keeping them warm in the hearth of the fireplace. Apart from the foxes, pigs were also reared on the farm, sows laid with umpteen piglets vying for position to feed. The boar pigs were enormous to a young chap like me, and they were really scary. Dad used to let me know how dangerous and destructive a boar pig could be, creating havoc if harassed. The pigs played second fiddle to the foxes, it was deemed the height of fashion to be wearing a fox fur, designers would pay top dollar for prime furs. Dad got really upset when the day came to kill those beautiful creatures, the vet would arrive and carry out the evil deed. It was Dad's job to hold the foxes while the vet injected them with a lethal dose. It was a shame to destroy such pristine animals in their prime. He was so incensed with the fur trade and all it stood for. I recall the particular day when he arrived home early. He told Mum that he had resigned and this was met with tears and thoughts of how were they to manage with no money coming in. Bill and myself sat nervously in the front room awaiting the outcome. It must have been hard for Dad to actually go through with this action, but as the years rolled on we all admired him for sticking to his beliefs and ideals.

Dad was soon on his bike and found a job driving a cattle truck for a local butcher, Mr Fred Humble. He did not have to travel far to his work and he enjoyed driving for a living, and with an increase in his salary Mum once again had a smile on her face.

The Downes family in Weaverthorpe were primarily farmers, but also ran a local bus service to Scarborough on a Thursday. This particular Thursday Mum, Bill and yours truly were catching the bus to Weaverthorpe, it was a special occasion. Grandad Arthur was retiring from his work. He would leave home at 05.30 to cycle the three miles to work, in all weathers he would prepare his horses for the days work. Tending his charges on that final day must have left him feeling a little sad after all those years, going through the same routines each morning. I wonder how the horses reacted the following week when Arthur did not show, a tad confused to say the least. I guess as long as they were fed and watered Arthur would soon be a fading memory for the horses.

We were taking Grandad Arthur home with us, he was coming for a weeks holiday, and would visit the Scarborough Cricket Festival and the best bit of all ... he was taking me with him!! I was five years old now, soon I would be starting school. Grandad and me caught the local service bus to Scarborough, we were making our way to a place called North Marine Road, the home of Scarborough Cricket Club and its world famous Cricket Festival. I felt so grown up at the side of Arthur, as we plodded the streets finally reaching our destination. Mum had been busy since early in the morning preparing our packed lunches, complete with the thermos flask for our tea. Grandad paid at the entrance, and we had to slide through a weird contraption to enter the ground. It was a 'turnstyle', it clicked many times as the crowds flooded in to the ground. I was a little bewildered to say the least, the atmosphere was electric with what seemed to be thousands of faces milling around, some seated, some standing, some on the playing area inspecting the arena, generally a buzz of anticipation and excitement. This was my introduction to cricket. Trueman, Close, Benaud and Miller would become etched into my mind. At first I did not understand the rules too well, but just to be there, together with my Grandad and my tomato sandwiches and bottle of pop was simply magical. I often thought of Grandad Arthur throughout my career in cricket, I am sure I got his nod of approval, a wry smile and the customary wink of the eye, the apple of his Grandads eye. Arthur passed away when I was 10 years old, he had suffered for many years with his breathing, which he always felt was caused by being caught in a gas attack during the Great War. The mustard gas had affected his lungs, leaving him permanently short of breath. He was sadly missed by all who knew him, and came into contact with him, a true hero.

As a five year old, waiting for Christmas seemed to be a never ending period of time, but it was the most magical time of the year. The weeks building up to Christmas week were hectic, Mum and Dad saving and working many hours to earn a bit of extra cash to help to fill Santa's sack to struggle down our chimney. Dad and Toby from next door would go plucking poultry most evenings after work, and at weekends too. Hens and geese were on the menu in most homes in those days. It was a long hard slog, wringing the birds neck before ripping off their feathers. Dad would earn something like a shilling for hens, and two shillings for geese. He would arrive home by 10 o clock, covered in fleas from the birds. He would jump straight in the bath, Bill and I would sneak out to check on Dad and his new friends, which were in the seams of his shirt collar and cuffs, horrible little things.

On Christmas Eve, Toby offered me a chance to accompany him in his coal truck, to help him deliver Christmas presents to his sister in the next village. I recall on the return journey, it was a clear frosty night with stars twinkling all around. "He's there in the sky" shouted Toby... I strained my eyes hoping to spot Santa, Rudolph and the boys, but to no avail. I felt quite despondent at not getting to spot him, Toby just laughed and told me to check next year!!

He did arrive, very early next morning. I bet Mum and Dad would have relished a lie in, no luck for them as we were up and at em!!

Those early Christmas days were really special, the warmth, the love and the true feeling of community at our new house in Denison Avenue.

The next adventure on the horizon was waiting ... SCHOOL.

I remember as a boy of five, I had gone with Dad to Sonny Lownsboroughs to pluck chickens, it must have been later in the year closer to Christmas, when Dad got the call, it meant a little extra money, for the family coffers which were always in short supply. This particular day it would have been a Sunday, the boss Sonny arrived with half a dozen men with terrier dogs. The buildings we occupied whilst plucking chickens were quite dilapidated old wooden framed horse box type, housing sheep, goats, geese all the usual livestock fit for trade. As you could imagine the place was crawling with long tails or rats, there was evidence everywhere. As a young lad this was going to be exciting, they were going to put hose pipes down the holes, then force the rats to the surface where the dogs would be waiting. All the blokes were characters from villages, crusty old buggers, with pipes full of baccy, and hazel sticks ready to beat the walls, creating confusion within the rat population. The stage was set, I stood on a chicken coop making sure I could see all the action, Sonny turned on the taps, it took a few minutes, then all hell let loose, rats squealing, dogs yelping, men cussing and shouting it was total mayhem, I remember hopping up and down, imagining rats up my trouser leg, they were running up the walls through holes in the roof. The dogs were piling in no wonder there known as terriers, one snap at the back of rats neck job done, it took thirty minutes to clear the sight, and what a sight. The men called off the dogs tied them to fences, then set on to pile up the dead vermin, hundreds of them in a heap in the yard, petrol was poured over them then a match was thrown whoosh!!! Another memorable experience.

When everyone had gone and the excitement died down, Dad grabbed another bird wrung its neck sat down, and started to tell me of the day when he and Mum started courting, they had met at a village dance. A week or two after they had met, Dad was cycling over to spend some quality time with Mum, it was dusk as he neared the top of a rise in the road, he saw up ahead what he thought was water crossing the road, as he cycled closer he got the shock of his life, what he thought was water turned out to be a whole migration of rats moving from one farm to another, thousands of long tails a chilling sight as you could imagine. Nothing stopped them, in those days, when life was very rustic, it was not uncommon to witness this evacuation as Dad explained it would take more than a horde of rats to stop him from meeting Mum.

During the afternoon of this memorable day, something just as breathtaking was about to appear before our very eyes, Dad was busy hands full of feathers moaning about the bloody fleas, when in the distance emerged this droning sound, it got louder and louder, then above us from the

South East at around 2000ft, they came into view, Dad calculated at least 100 of those dark ghostly machines. Lancaster bombers he shouted, he too was excited I could tell. He was then explaining in no uncertain terms, what roll they had played in the last war. All their crews were heroes, he was stating with great enthusiasm, he then went on to mention the thousands of young airmen who had sacrificed their lives for a better future, and that I should never forget that fact. These bombers he thought would be probably taking their final flight, showing all the people like us below, the might of Bomber Command before they faced the scrapheap. A sad end to such a majestic beast.

What a day full of incident, when we eventually got home, Mum had the Yorkshire puds and the beef waiting for us two, I never stopped talking over the meat, I couldn't't wait to get to school in the morning, such interesting times for a young lad to take in.

The day had arrived I was now five Mick Wharton who lived opposite and myself were walked to the village primary by our Mum's and signed in, Miss Leeman was our teacher, and the class was full of our friends mostly, but some boys and girls we did not know. It didn't take long before we all mingled in, this was the start of a new era. I remember we had to take to school an old shoebox, this was to put all your pens and pencils, rubbers, rulers and stuff then it was neatly stacked with the rest. Those early days at school don't register too much I'm afraid, but I do remember the outside loos freezing up, but we still had to use them, the lad who sat next to me in class didn't bother going, he just did it in his pants. Another memory of that time was of the Coronation of Princess Elizabeth to Queen, we had a big party at school, then got presented with a mug with her picture on, I'm pleased to see the Queen has lasted longer than my mug, I broke it on my way home.

After primary school we moved next door to the junior school, this is where I met my first cricketing mentor, the Head Master, Mr Eddie Wilson. Eddie, or Mr Wilson was a Lancastrian, but I forgave him for that, he was a lovely man, very funny, great storyteller, just as I imagined a good teacher to be, but most of all he opened the batting in our village 2nd XI and to get his practice we had to bowl at him at playtime. This was the start of my cricketing career.

I'm growing up quickly now, I'm almost nine, but I did enjoy school, everyone knows everyone in the village and both girls and boys lives were exciting, learning different skills, never in the house, always on the move, bird nesting, minnowing, football, cricket. Winter seemed to be more severe at this time, I recall central heating was for the rich and we certainly didn't possess it, waking up on a winter morning, ice had formed on the inside of the windows, getting dressed in bed. I remember too playing outside in the snow, we wore short trousers with wellingtons and after a while that red ring from the boots round your legs became very sore. We used to go sledging to a place called the Maram, everyone from the village young and old were there making big fires. Dad's old boss Mr Newsome gave him a Swiss sledge for us as a gift, we WERE LIKE THE VICAR'S KNICKERS when we arrived with that. Great times were had there, and I can't recall anyone getting hurt.

Miss Beatie was our Maths Teacher in Junior School, one morning she stood me up in front of the class, for me to explain how decimal points worked, I had no idea, and this was the end of our beautiful friendship. She harassed me up hill and down dale after that, my maths suffered I just couldn't take it in, or I think what it really was, I would show her the 'battle-axe' I wouldn't take it in.

Mr Wilson's son Mike, would visit us from University where he was studying Marine Biology, and he organised a trip for our class to study the rock pools in the South Bay in Scarborough. This was so exciting, right up my street I loved nature and everything connected with it. We set off on the local bus and had to walk the ten minutes to the South Bay. Mike was amazing; there were the species in the pools that we had read about in the books, sucker fish, blennies, star fish and hermit crabs. We carried a selection of these up to the bus and had some funny looks from passengers on our way back to Seamer School. Back at school we put them all in a pickle substance in big jars, and they are probably still there educating a new generation. During the summer after my tenth birthday, most evenings I would be at the Seamer Cricket Club, practising with the teams.

This was the Locke and Laker era, two great spin bowlers for England, I was a slow left arm bowler and I spent hours copying the action of Tony Locke, honing the skill of spin bowling. Then one day George Wellburn, a committee member of the club approached me with a challenge, now he said we picked you as 12th man on Saturday for the 2nd XI to play at Harwood Dale, and if or when you play, the first time you get double figures, or 3 wickets, I'll give you sixpence. 'Thanks George,' I said and ran home to tell my Dad. Saturday arrived, I didn't possess white trousers, but I had a white shirt which Mum had washed and ironed and white canvas shoes or pumps as we call them, and short grey trousers, we had to meet at the school, I was first there. Eventually the team turned up, I travelled with Mr Wilson in his new Ford consul, very posh I thought this is how Tony Locke would travel. We arrived at the ground I was very nervous, even though I was only 12th man. We were knocking up before the game when I got the call, I was playing, wow what a feeling. We went onto win the game, but I didn't get a bowl or a bat, that's cricket. I kept my place in the team from that week, and it didn't take long before old George presented me with a sixpence, I've never forgotten that little challenge, and the encouragement it gave me to succeed.

Dad played for us some weeks when we were short, he used to borrow the old van on weekends, and he would taxi the team kit and all, and on one Saturday we were coming back after a game at Deepdale, there would be at least 5 players in the van plus the kit bag, we were crawling up Edge Dell, it's quite steep when the front wheel fell off, it was hilarious, what a performance putting the wheel back on, but eventually we got on our way.

At this time a new family had arrived in the village, they took over the farm in East gate, they were the Hill family, they had come from over in the Dales, the two sons Malcolm and Tony, joined us at school, and I used to spend a lot of time on their farm helping out. In July we used to get an influx of travellers or gypsies, sometimes they would send their kids to our school for a few weeks, they were a rum lot. We were having P.T one day and Mr Wilson asked us to strip our shirts off, these lads said they couldn't because they'd been sown up for winter.

These gypsies used to frighten my mother to death, they used to come up the avenue selling their wares, knocking on doors, many a time mother, Bill and I would be under the bed until they left. They used to camp down long lane, with their small green caravans and horses tethered, the older lads used to tell us they ate young lads in pies, so we then got on our bikes and went like the wind through their camp looking for the evidence, then we would go home and have nightmares.

Mum and Dad were friendly with a couple who lived at the top of our avenue, and they arranged during the summer holidays that we would all go to Blackpool for a week. They owned a car and we hired a car for a week, off we went to the other side of the country, it could have been a million miles away for all we knew. We stayed in a typical B and B, with a typical land lady, once you left in the morning you weren't allowed back until the evening. I remember it was a brilliant week, we went to the baths, Dad showing off with his diving and swimming skills. Then up to Fleetwood to watch the trawlers come in and unload their catches. We went to a show on a pier starring Hilda Baker and Ken Dodd, Doddy was making his first appearance as a 21 year old, but was still very funny. Then the illuminations, as young boys we were overly impressed, and talked about that trip for years. In fact that trip would be the only trip we ever made as a family group.

Another surprise awaited my brother and myself, the introduction of our eldest brother Peter Derek, it was explained to us that Derek had been born during the war while Dad was away, as young lads we just accepted it, didn't bother us he had been brought up with Grandma in Weaverthorpe he was a few years older than us, but no matter we were all together now as a family. Derek would be quite inspirational to me later down the line, but that's another story.

I had to go to Scarborough with Mum on the bus this day to pick up my new school uniform, as I was soon to be starting George Pindar Secondary Modern, three miles up the road in Eastfield, it was quite a new school opening in 1957. The Headmaster, Mr Roland Davis had a liking for the great outdoors, after exploring Antarctica with Sir Vivian Fuchs, these were the kind of people who ticked my boxes, and therefore I relished the start of a new adventure.

We used to cycle to school when the weather allowed, and a mini bus took us during the winter months. I quickly made new friends at school, expanding my boundaries so to speak. I enjoyed the diversity senior school offered, lessons like Science, Woodwork and I really took to the sports representing the school at Soccer, Cricket and Badminton, the gym was great, a totally new environment for us. It was around this time when my eldest brother Derek decided on his future. He had been working as an apprentice butcher and slaughter man, but had decided it was not for him. He and his good friend John Watson built themselves two racing cycles from scratch, then cycled down to Cornwall, Penzance to be precise and joined the Merchant Navy, the next time we heard from Derek he was in Rio de Janeiro. This was a real Alf Tupper moment for me, the fact that my brother had shown such grit, determination and courage to better himself, he deserved all the accolades good luck to him.

My Mum at this time was suffering with her health, she was such a hard worker, not just with bringing us up that was bad enough, but holding down a job in Scarborough at Cooplands in the café, she loved the job, but it was beginning to take its toll. She'd had a major operation a few years previous in the infirmary in Leeds for a Thyroid problem, and now her eyes were letting her down, we all mucked in to help, the neighbours were great rallying round to help Mum, popping in for a fag and a chat keeping her abreast with the local gossip.

I began my first love affair about now, a girl in my class Pauline Roper, our first date was the Scarborough Fair. I can't remember how we finished or why but I still see her, she hasn't changed still as bubbly as ever. During the half term holidays I spent a week at my Auntie Joan's on their farm, Uncle Tom was the farm manager for Arthur Johnstone a local butcher and horse breeder, I needed some cash, and therefore I was going potato picking for a week. You certainly earn your money, bending your back picking spuds into wire baskets, and then into four stone bags. I earned I remember to this day £6.31 for the week, with an aching back, but my head held high I returned home with my fortune. As I was entertaining the opposite sex, I had to look the part, there was a clothes shop in Scarborough Swinneys, young menswear from Italy and my hard earned cash accounted for a sweater, slacks and a new style in shoes the winkle picker. It was school speech day the following week, and with much posturing I got permission to wear my new clothes, my mother was actually furious, that I wouldn't wear my school uniform, but young boys seem to know better, I had won a prize for an English Essay I had written, I seemed to have a gift for storytelling. Mum was right like they always are, the Deputy Head Mrs Grey took one look at me, and if looks could have killed ZAP!! I got detention for a week, and became the butt of everyone's jokes for ages after.

I had become very interested in a new hobby at this time Steam Engines, with two friends Alan Henderson and Frank Berriman from school. We would embark on the first train from Scarborough to York on a Saturday morning, and spend the day on the platforms of York Station. Steam Trains are the epitome of Great Britain at its best, amazing engines, I absolutely loved those days, collecting the numbers then transferring them into a combine, until you had the lot, the hairs on the back of your neck used to rise when an A4 Pacific appeared round the North End. In those days it was a popular pastime, hundreds of anoraks assembled on platforms with cameras and notepads. It was a sad day when they started phasing out the steam loco. Can I also mention that never once did our parents question our wellbeing, words like pervert or paedophile hadn't been invented then, even though I'm sure they existed?

A new decade was born, 1960 appeared on the calendar, and I was now a teenager with all the baggage to boot. My poor Mum who was still struggling to care with a myriad of health problems, spent hours having to sew the name of Tommy Steele in shocking pink stitching on a pair of new jeans I had acquired. Then the greatest advance of the technological age arrived at Number 4 Dennison Avenue, the television set wow!. All the kids from the street were sat in our house, when the man switched it on, what a piece of kit, a Bush 12inch, we had the world in our house. Things seem to improve on all fronts. Mum's health seemed to improve, her eyes regained full vision. Dad had changed jobs again, he now was a full time driver for Stockdale's potato merchants. My Dad loved driving, he was in his element behind the wheel of a big artic, and spent hours on the road. In fact things were going really well for Mum, she had gone into business with a friend, Mum loved cooking and they opened a little café down Eastborough selling lunches and teas to holiday makers during the summer season. It proved a big hit and after the season, they could afford to go on holiday, they went to Austria for a week.

Money was always tight, it must have been a struggle for Mum and Dad, but we as young boys would never have known, it's only now as a grown up, how much you appreciate the hard work and commitment, that went into keeping the family unit going. Dad would be away for most of the week driving around the country delivering and picking up his bags of potatoes. Mums week was no picnic, Monday was wash day, and it was all done by hand, clothes would be soaked in the copper, then she used to rub all collars and cuffs, then it was put in another tub to be ponched with a peggy stick, to be then rinsed, followed by putting it all through the mangle releasing the water and at last if the weather was kind hanging it all on the line, that would take all morning, her hands would be red raw. No forty minute cycle there then!! Tuesday hopefully if the weather had been kind would mean it all had to be ironed, and the beds changed. Mum had the luxury of an electric iron, but they hadn't been on the market long. Wednesday was bottoming day cleaning, polishing, sewing and mending, during the afternoons at 3ish. Mum would knock on the wall in the kitchen and that was the signal to next door that the kettle was on, this ritual was played out most days. Thursday was the day Bill and I enjoyed the most, baking day.

Mum loved her baking, devising new recipes and skilfully creating mouth-watering dishes. She would prepare pies of every description, sweet loaves, cakes with all the fillings that you could imagine, we did not own a fridge at that time, everything went onto the pantry shelf, it looked superb when it was completed, but then we just set on and ate it, and the following week the whole process had to be repeated. Friday was the day the butcher called, I mentioned at the beginning of this chapter; how tight money was, but we never went without meat, as it was an important part of our diet.

I guess we were no different from all the other families in the avenue, as time went by we became a very close knit community. Sunday we enjoyed as a family, Dad was back home, he would probably catch up with his garden, in the early days he did grow most of the vegetables we consumed, Sunday lunch was always a pleasure, Forces Family Favourites, The Billy Cotton Band Show, with Archie Andrews bringing up the rear, then it was off to Sunday school for Bill and myself, looking back I realised now why we were sent to worship. But I can honestly say it didn't do us any harm. I do believe in the guidelines the scriptures set out for people to lead their lives, I've tried to follow the code, and plough my own furrow so to speak.

The families living in the Avenue were an average working class cross section, the Wharton's opposite, were a large family, we became good friends and solid neighbours. Then there were the Greenwoods, who kept themselves to themselves a bit aloof if you know what I mean. On our other side we had the Kelds, Jack the Dad had been in India during the war, which left him with malaria. Tim

Thornham was opposite the Kelds his Mum and Dad, Tilly and Cyril were good fun. Last but not least we had the Sunleys next to the Thornhams, Doug and Betty, Doug opened the batting for the 2nd XI, and he was a great story teller used to have us in stitches. They had a daughter Elizabeth who I had a crush on during this episode which I'm sure was pre puberty.

Mick Wharton was, and still is a good lad, your typical hunter, gatherer, he was never happier than when he was with his dog, gun or catapult, stalking his prey in the bottom fields of Seamer. My brother Bill was of the same thinking, he also loved to hunt; he and Mick go on shoots even today. In these early days, no one owned a car or very few did, I think there was probably three up the avenue at this time, this allowed us to play cricket in the street, this became a popular past time, a few window panes took a hit, but on the whole the cricket in the avenue helped to cement a camaraderie. So did the winter when it snowed, we used to create a slide outside our house; I recall one day we had at least twenty people gathered, a great atmosphere. I remember there was the odd negative side to the street, Jim Graines who hadn't been here to long, kept pigeons he was quite renowned, we found out afterwards, he had won the prestigious News of the World race with one of his birds, he was having problems with the local cats, so he poisoned them, ours was one of them that became ill and we had to have her put down. The only problem in those days we couldn't prove it. Next door to Jims were the latest arrivals, Mrs Coy and Sid Lawty, she had lost her husband tragically I think, and Sid found his way into her life, they became good friends of mine, Sid was a good man, strong as an ox, he loved his football and would organise games up on the cricket field, great fun, we spent many hours kicking the ball about. We certainly had a childhood in those far off days, I believe we have been the luckiest generation of all.

I was selected to play for the North Riding schools under 15's, I had success on the cricket field this summer culminating in the receipt of my North Riding Colours, I felt very proud, it's a very smart badge, and sits well on a navy blazer. This particular morning when we arrived at school I noticed army vehicles parked in the car park. Our form teacher Mr Edwards informed us of the presence of the Royal Artillery, they would be outlining their role in the service, with demos of their weapons, vehicles etc. I had never imagined myself as a soldier, I'd not been involved with the cadets not even the boy scouts, but something inside me, in my head was sending me positive signals, Dad used to embellish his war stories for us, and made it sound far more macho than it probably was and since Derek left to travel the world, something inside me was saying this is a chance, a challenge you only get one, never refuse an opportunity. Six weeks later I went to York to Strensall Barracks to be assessed. I would be joining the Junior Leaders Regt RAC. Bovington Camp in Dorset on the 1st May 1962. I'd never travelled further than York on my own, what had I done? ... was I up for it? ... was I fit enough? I wasn't very big, quite scrawny really all these negatives filled my head then the day arrived. Dad was leaving at 3am so he came in to see me to shake my hand and wish me good luck. I remember vividly stepping out of the door with my suitcase, and Mum telling me to look after myself, and if I didn't like it to come home. She then told me as I was a big lad now, I could have ten fags and she stuffed them into my pocket. I wished Bill all the best and he likewise then I made my way down the avenue to the bus stop. The neighbours were out to say good luck lad, I turned round once and saw Mum waving and there was a little tear, it wouldn't have taken much for me to run back home, but I was nearly a man I was 15 years old. I caught the 7.30am bus to Scarborough Station George Morley was the conductor whom I knew quite well and he wished me well.

Chapter 2

The Army and Growing Up ... Fast

I checked my pockets before I boarded, the few quid and fags mum had slipped me and my travel warrant were very important. I bought a copy of Ring magazine, I thought if people saw that, they would think I could look after myself, funny the things that go through your head, the guard gave us an 'all aboard' and that was it, the 8.10am train from Scarborough to York got the green light. I took in the local landmarks shuffled to a seat, feeling excited frightened and very alone. From York I was to travel to Southampton via the Black Country and the potteries, arriving at the said destination at 17.30pm, from Southampton take the train to Dorchester, alighting at the village of Wool, where transport would be waiting, here's to the next two and a half years that was the plan. It was now 9.30am, I kept thinking I wish I was trainspotting for the day then going back home on the last train, but that was not the case, tonight I would be in a strange bed, on what could have been the moon for all I knew. My train was due in twenty minutes, I had a quick coffee and slice of mum's homemade meat pie that cheered me up.

It was a long boring journey to Southampton, being inexperienced at all this travel malarkey, it got to a point where I started to panic, thinking we had passed Southampton as I'd fallen asleep for a while, I was reassured by a kind old lass, who I think realized I was a bit green around the gills and offered me some comfort, when I explained I was from Yorkshire and going to join the army we got on like a house on fire.

As we entered Southampton the train travelled right alongside the dry docks, and low and behold right below was the 'Queen Elizabeth' in all her glory, fantastic it certainly was turning out to be an interesting day. The train to Wool was full of army types in their uniforms and as we approached our destination, we all seemed to get off together. I felt very small and inferior, everyone knowing where they were going, me not sure, quite surreal. Everyone vanished I was left just me, no transport. I sat on a seat with my suitcase quite tired now I had been travelling 12 hours, I remember looking up and wondering what everyone would be doing at home in Seamer, then the transport arrived!! 'you there to me on the double, move yourself!' I ran and got on the bus, no one else just me was I the only one joining today, we were passing acres of sports fields with old tanks in each corner, quite breathtaking really, then we were at the gates and there in front of me must have been 100 lads of my age who like me had been travelling all day from every corner of our country. I was soon ejected off the bus and told to go and join a queue and check in. I was wearing my blazer proudly portraying my North Riding Cricket colours with the Cricket badge attached, when this officer in his fancy uniform, spied my attire quickly made his way over, this was Simon Smail Captain in the 11th hussars, and he would become another cricket mentor. We were quickly herded into groups of eight, and sent to a barrack room, found a bed, threw your belongings on it then headed to the cookhouse for a meal...what a day!

After a hasty meal it was back to the room, and introductions which took an age. You can imagine eight fifteen year old lads meeting for the first time from every conceivable town or city, it was who could talk the loudest, who could tell the dirtiest jokes, to who could fart the loudest, you would have loved to have been a fly on the wall but eventually after all the banter the lights went out, I laid for what seemed hours, going over in my mind, contemplating my future, had I done the right thing, when at least two or three lads started sobbing absolutely heart broken, what had this little tyke come to.

Let me explain how the junior leaders works, lads come in at fifteen and they leave at 17. They learn basic skills, driving tanks, radio operating and tank gunnery. You are brought up in a vigorous environment and you are taught how to become leaders of men, during the final term you choose the cavalry regiment you would like to join. Apart from the army training there is a lot of emphasis on sport and fitness. Discipline and team work, are key elements in a successful organization, and after 2 and a half years the raw recruit is transformed into a confident well mannered young man, they do lose a few on the way but that applies to all competitive institutions.

6am lights go on, a maniac explodes into the room. 'Hands off cocks, hands on socks.' What's happening, where am I, then it sinks in, I'm in the army now!!! It's truly 50 years ago since this happened, I apologise unreservedly but I only remember the name of the lad in the bed opposite me, Brian Limbert, he was a scouser from the Pool, that's Liverpool! He was a laid back young man as I remember, for my first contact with a scouser who had a very broad accent, quite nasal and he was telling me to look out for this new pop group from Liverpool. The Beatles, had a good chance of success. All the other boys as I recall were Southerners, with a Welshman thrown in he was a pain, Delamare was his name thought he knew everything, he had been everywhere, down the coalmines up the chimneys, what a twat!

That first morning our room corporal gave us the run down on what was expected, he was a good mush, as they say. I was learning the jargon already. First up was our bed blocks, every morning we had to fold our sheets into a small oblong, then wrap the blankets round them, this creates as you can imagine a block with square edges, you placed the block at the top of the bed with your pillows above it. We had to make sure our own bed space was tidy as that was your responsibility.

Our corporal then takes us into the ablution block, to the uninitiated the wash rooms, showers, and toilets, as we were young adolescents shaving was soon going to become the morning ritual, further he explained how to use a razor without taking half your face off. Breakfast next on the agenda, down to the cookhouse, it was heaving with young men in their uniforms, denims, boots and gaiters. Breakfast over then back to the room. We were now going to the barbers, then onto the MO to be checked out then to the QM's for our lovely kit. Every soldier will remember this ordeal as he queued for his kit, they glance at your size, then throw you the item simple as that, no measuring it, left up to you to fit into the garment, everything into the kit bag and back to the room.

As I look around the room when we return, all the boys are a shadow of their former selves, it seems losing most of your hair has this Samson effect on young men. All kit is then emptied onto bed, and our corporal explained what everything is and what everything does, and when folded to perfection where everything is stowed in your personal locker. I look down at the two pairs of boots that need work on, belts that need polishing, brasses that need attention, how am I going to cope, the next and quite poignant operation is parceling up your civvies and sending them back home. Next morning will be fun we will parade at 0800hrs in working kit, but before that the ordeal of breakfast. Having not had the experience of the cadet force, everything was new to me, can you imagine what I looked like heading down to breakfast. I believe it's the most embarrassed I've ever been, the ridicule and abuse we received, apparently this is par for the course and no doubt we will be howling at the next new intake.

Our second morning, how time flies we were to meet the commanding officer, and all commissioned and non commissioned officers attached to our squadron. Four squadrons make up a regiment. A regiment would consist of around 1 thousand men, each squadron of about 200 men; you would have the HQ or admin troop, LAD or mechanical engineers making up the numbers required. Our pay was next on the agenda, we would earn three pounds 7shillings and 6pence per week for our first year, you would receive 10shillings and 6pence in your hand, the rest would be split between admin charges and holiday credits, which I guess was a good idea as you would have money to take on leave when the time came. The paymaster issued you with a regimental number that would stay with you for all time. I'm 23905063 JNR Trooper Hart PR. Any old sweat will tell you that number goes to the grave with you. Pay day came round on a Wednesday lunchtime, the Sqn leader officiated the ceremony accompanied by the paymaster, clerk and the Sqn Sgt Major.

The third day was to become a rude awakening; we had to muster in the gym in our new pe kit, all the intake was on parade. We were then sized up in pairs, same height approx and weight, we then had to put the boxing gloves on step in the ring and knock seven bells out of each other. I had never seen a boxing ring, never mind stepping into one, the bell rang and we were at it. I landed a punch but sprained my thumb in the process, we huffed and puffed, through a few more punches kept moving, my opponent glanced a few blows off my head, then I caught him with a straight left on the nose, blood oozing, I was left handed and I knew it was a good shot as they say in the game, and the bout was stopped. I couldn't continue into the next stage as my thumb was shot, but one of the organisers from the boxing team took me to one side, he thought I showed promise, had a decent left jab and would expect me at the next training session. My opponent, a lad from Morcambe in Lancashire, Burt Lawson who would become one of my best mates in the regiment, he was army through and through loved all the history of the cavalry regiments, an expert on the peninsula wars, was to join the 11th Hussars or the cherry pickers as any cavalry man will tell you.

We then made out a timetable for the week for the first term a bit like school. We would in fact for the first term be going back to school, Maths, Map Reading, English, History and German. Wednesday afternoon would be free for hobbies as well as Saturday afternoon. Sunday morning was a church parade with the afternoon free.... Wow!!! I selected sailing as my hobby, even though I came from the coast, I had never been in a boat. We spent a month rubbing this yachts keel down, and then sand papering until your hands bled. and eventually it was ready for the water. We took it to Poole Harbour on the Saturday, the skipper forgot the Centre Board, the thing that keeps it upright, off we go into the briny, haven't been in two minutes when we capsize, luckily we didn't forget the life jackets, what a bloody fiasco fishing us out, I said bollocks to sailing and played hockey instead. I've shown a lot of detail within the first week of my military career, this is to give the reader a flavour and prepare a base as we move forward.

The first week was a survival course not for the faint hearted, lads were going home, leaving after a few days not really giving it a chance. People were given a month to make their minds up, I was finding it difficult in some respects, but exhilarating in others, I think I saw the bigger picture quite early, and recognized the opportunities on offer, there was no going back for me. Our first major task as recruits was to learn the art of drilling, or marching as a unit in quick time. Our drill instructors were grisly old sergeants who pleasured themselves by having us running around the regimental square in formation of threes not knowing our left from our right, bollocking us left right and centre, it must have looked hilarious, but if I am brutally honest I enjoyed it, ok it took a while to knock us into shape, but after a few weeks of hard slog the fruits of our labors began to show. We began to look like soldiers marching in squads in time. As a soldier marching behind a band to the great regimental tunes, it gives you a definite buzz, the green shoots were just sprouting, a long road ahead to the finished article.

As I mentioned earlier discipline within the ranks is paramount, lads who broke the rules were punished and I mean made an example of, in all walks of life there are a minority who live on the edge, bad apples so to speak, the lads who steal off their mates, or bully the vulnerable, this would not be tolerated. I remember a lad who was found stealing from a buddies locker in his room, he was taken to the guard room after the CO had sentenced him to three weeks hard labour, this entailed drilling every day for an hour, with pack full of bricks, I saw this lad suffer the consequences of his actions each day, he would collapse in a heap after thirty minutes, it was nothing short of brutal, but in my mind necessary, he was thrown out of the regiment after his ordeal never to be seen again.

On another occasion a nutter from London who thought he was Reggie Kray, he was picking on young lads and abusing them physically, he was soon put in the picture, the CO who loved his boxing put him in the ring with the regimental champion. It was a pleasure to witness the bawling and bleating of this bloodied cockney, it took two minutes before he was carried out never to be seen again.

This was the army getting their message across, it no doubt wouldn't be allowed in today's society, with human rights and health and safety issues being of paramount concern, its such a shame we in this country make rods for our own backs. Our first term was now up and running a month had passed and very quickly. We were never allowed time on our hands, cleaning kit, keeping the rooms spotless these were the objectives, the first term was proving to be a challenge but three troop A squadron was up for it. Bovington Camp was the head quarters Royal Armoured Camps, apart from our organisation, the regular army had units there also, Bovington although we had only marched through it on our way to church parade on Sundays consisted of the usual buy anything store, I remember there being a C of E club and a R C club it would be the next term before we had the pleasure of frequenting these dens of inequity. I was beginning to settle down to the tasks put before me, it was pleasing to think I was coping, not struggling to find my way. I had a role to play, involvement within a team this was the way forward.

School work came exams passed, I got grades required to take me to the next stage, but that was next term, we were now going on a great adventure, to Plymouth onto Dartmoor outward bound training this was what I joined the army for, bring it on. We arrived in Plymstock after travelling by rail, the camp was a relic of the last war, old Nissan huts bunk beds with a stove in the centre, it was situated on a cliff over looking Plymouth sound and the breakwater, it was an idyllic location, with great views over the bay, its probably a touristy hotel complex now. We were going to be here for a fortnight with weapons training, orienteering, pot holing, rock climbing, canoeing and the dreaded 30 mile trek across the moor to complete wow!! Time to sleep lights out.

The three tonners were waiting for us next morning, but first we had to face the two PTI's who accompanied us to Plymouth. Physical Training wasn't a problem for me, I relished the running stretching and warm ups got the day off to a positive start. After breakfast our troop were off to the live firing ranges at Tregantyl just over the causeway in Cornwall, we were going to be firing the old 303 rifle used by the infantry in the Second World War, and the Bren gun or general purpose machine gun with its own tripod. This was going to be our first live firing sortie and we were all quite excited. Firing the rifle was an experience not to be forgotten, the kick in the shoulder on firing was frightening as well as bloody painful, we all ended up with bruises, I appreciate we were only young boys, very inexperienced, not fully developed, physically, but those rifles were quite heavy, and infantry guys of the last war in the desert campaigns deserved every medal going, it was then when I appreciated the fact I was going to be riding everywhere rather than walking, long live the cavalry. Next up the Bren Gun, I remember vividly my attempt to hit the target from 100 yards, the Bren has two sights, one that flips up by your hand known as the foresight and the other at the end of the barrel you line these two up together on the target then squeeze the trigger bingo!! You should find it difficult to miss, I finished off a magazine of ammo in seconds made the weapon safe, then strode with our instructor to the target, very sure I had done well, not a sign of a strike, what a bloody shambles the instructor ranted on that the shipping was in more danger than the target, then we realised I hadn't flipped the foresight up, I got it in the neck again I repeated the process and shredded the target what a relief, it was an interesting rewarding day full of incident, plenty to discuss at the de brief.

Next day we were going to the Abbey at Buckfastleigh for some pot holing, this would be a first for most of us. What I remember fondly about that trip to Devon all those years ago, was the beautiful countryside with weather to match, if I hadn't been a Yorkshire man then a Devonian I would be. We arrived at the Abbey mid morning, our troop leader was a Lieutenant Blake, he was around 6'5" in his stocking feet pencil thin, he was organising and briefing us on our descent down the pot hole, it would take us two to three hours to negotiate the narrow paths down to a cavern 400 ft below, there would be water too, the feeling among us all was of dread. I remember one of the lads screaming absolutely terrified, he pleaded with the instructors that he suffered from claustrophobia, it fell on deaf ears, I was relieved he was not in our group, I can hear that terrifying echoing scream even today. I'm not sure the management got it right that day, but to their credit he did make it down and probably overcame his demons. We set off down the pot hole, our long leader in the front. We were wearing hard hat type helmets, with a bicycle lamp attached, not the ultra modern kit of today, and also we were attached to each other by rope.

I was last man in line as we struggled in this very narrow trench. How the mind plays tricks, I was sure someone was behind me quite unsettling really, we turned our lamps off it was scary then, you could not see a bloody thing, I've never known such dark ever, then the fun began our illustrious leader got wedged in the trench what a dip stick, some of the boys were becoming very nervous, I also didn't see the funny side of the operation. Eventually through good luck rather than judgment he freed himself, but it put us a long way behind the rest. Next came the water, it was certainly becoming a character builder, we had to take a deep breath go under and up into a small cave, we were now wet through and fucking freezing. Eventually an hour later than planned, we arrived at our destination like drowned rats, dejected, hungry, totally pissed off, then what we discovered was unbelievable, half a dozen young lads about ten years old all having a fag and a laugh as they saw us, this was their den and it only took them ten minutes to run down, there was motorbike frames, old tyres, mattresses, I've never forgotten that day it brought a smile to my chops as we battled to beat our demons.

After a week we left the camp at Plymstock, and made our way onto the Moor. We would be now residing under canvas, two men bivouacs we carried and my mate Burt Lawson was my buddy, we were both enjoying our adventure in Devon, what was next to be thrown at us. We were heading to the River Dart, this is the main artery through Devon and it ran onto Dartmoor. A stretch of the river had been recced and found fit for our next task, as a troop we had to carry a tree trunk down the river, the tree trunk was simulating a tank barrel, and we had to get if from point a to point b. This would require team work, organisation, preparation and leadership. This was a million miles away from my home in Seamer, we were beginning to work as a unit, developing skills I couldn't have imagined a few weeks earlier. The instructors were playing the enemy, throwing thunder flashes into the river; these were extremely noisy quite frightening it would give us a little taster of what being under fire was like! One of our boys got tangled up by a rope whilst heaving on the trunk, we had been in the river a long time by this stage and Rob was becoming cold a little panic set in, then low and behold I remembered the knife my dad had given me the night before I set off for Bovington, it had a knife fork and spoon attached to it a little like a swiss army knife. I had it in my pack back up the river, I set off with great haste, and it took about ten minutes to cover the ground there and back. Rob was suffering by this stage, the trusty blade got to work and we had him out and wrapped in blankets in no time at all, after a hot brew inside him Rob was as right as rain, we carried on to complete our task. At the de-brief we were praised for our teamwork under pressure, the trusty old knife got mentioned in dispatches.

The canoeing and rock climbing passed without incident, we were left with the two day slog over the moor, this would be a challenge as we had to do all our own navigating by compass bearings, Burt and I set off on our first leg of fifteen miles, Dartmoor can be quite daunting, the mist comes down in seconds, we had to trust our judgement with the bearings, our route took us through Princetown where the prison stands, I remember having a pee in the public toilets and inscribed on the wall Foxy Fowler was here, he was a notorious criminal who escaped from custody a few years earlier. We pressed on, making short work of the distance, it was a joyous feeling arriving at the camp site smelling the stew simmering on the stoves.

After our evening meal, we then set on scrubbing our bodies of the days toil, we then had to organize guard duty, this was new to us another learning curve, Burt and I would have two stages to complete, two hours on and four hours off. I was on guard at two until four in the morning, the mist had come down. I was stood alone in the mist, when in front of me I could hear steps and movement but could see nothing, I had a torch and pickaxe handle, and was about to wake up the whole camp when this shape came into view, it was a bullock. I was sweating with bloody fright but relieved when I saw the big ugly bugger. We achieved our goal the next day quite knackered, now it was back to Bovington back to camp and a shower.

On the standing orders board the notice read cricketers wanted, practice after duties, I turned up on time there was about a dozen of us all eager to impress, Major Simon Smail was in charge, with corporal of horse Tom Singleton, the coach. There was going to be inter-squadron matches in the coming weeks and I became our Squadron skipper. The standard was pretty poor really, but that didn't deter A Squadron, we won the competition and I was presented with a stunning trophy by the CO's wife. I could only look forward to next season and probably regimental colours who knows.

The first term was nearing its conclusion and my first leave was on the horizon, we were not allowed to write letters home in the first term therefore it will be great to catch up with all that's gone on. My suitcase weighed what seemed like a ton as I was taking all my kit home to show the family it was Christmas leave two weeks at home, then back early January 1963. Catching the train from York to Scarborough never felt better, the walk from the bus to home with my case, I felt like a millions dollars. I had rang Mum and Dad to let them know when I would be arriving, Bill my brother was there on his bike to meet me in the street, I think when he saw me knocked him for six. Mum couldn't believe how well I looked, how fit and how I'd grown, I must admit I felt I had made the right decision all those weeks ago.

Dad was there in the background quietly taking it all in, he knew how I was feeling. I caught up with my mates from home we hung around, they couldn't stop me talking about life in the army, but before you knew it, it was time to be thinking of returning which was a different feeling entirely. 1963 was turning out to be one hell of a winter especially down Dorset way, I thought I might get a message not to return for a while, but it was not to be. It was a hazardous journey, but I made the barracks on time. Some of the lads were very upset at having to return, in fact two boys went AWOL which was another learning curve. That January was the worst in Dorset in living memory, they were finding people dead in their cars stuck under snow, most of the regulars in the Bovington HQ were on snow clearing duties for weeks.

The second term was upon us, that year we would be concentrating on Tank Gunnery for six months and Radio operating skills the other six, plus all the other incidentals like cleaning kit, polishing room floors, playing sport and yes a little free time, time to relax at the Friday night disco organised by the WVS or the Woman's Voluntary Service. Also this term we would be taking part in the passing out parade in the Autumn, this is the ultimate, where the boys passing out become men, and go on to join their respective regiments. A general will be there on the dias to take the salute all very grand, it's a lot to take on, but the boys of 3 troop A Sqn will be fit for purpose, I'll just touch on the bull aspect a little, and how much time it consumes, most evenings after evening meal, Time is taken up preparing for the next day. PREPARATION is the buzz word in any unit, if you kept on top of chores like bulling boots until your face shone in them, keeping leather belts polished, and supple webbing blancoed, clean tunics pressed, brasses shining. It was hard work with a lot of blood sweat and tears on the way, but once you were there in control life became a lot easier, time for a bit of leisure, relax a bit, write a letter home. Some would argue that a young man caught up in this rigorous controlled environment would turn out more robotic, not to question but do the job whatever, I'm sure there is a point to that argument, I can only state my case, I am very thankful to the army for the way it molded me into this person, and I wouldn't have missed it for the world. But enough of this rhetoric there's some growing up to be done, and some big guns to be fired.

Chapter 3

The Beatles...Love or lust and Foreign parts

Sergeant Brunton 17/21st Lancers or the death or glory boys, he was our chief instructor on the gunnery course at Lulworth Cove, a typical Scotsman full of charm and generosity I kid you, he was a right bastard hard as nails from the gorbols, but fair, with a dry sense of humor. I remember he was always borrowing fags off us, a right old sweat. Another of the instructors SGT Wilkinson, a Yorkshireman from Wakefield in the 3rd tank regiment, a totally different kettle of fish, quite human in fact. He became our troop instructor, and a brilliant teacher he was too. We would be working on centurion tanks with a gun of 105 mm, a very accurate weapon in the right hands. Our course was to take twelve weeks, quite intense a lot to take in. We spent the first two weeks on a simulator of the gun, like a model getting used to the range finders and other instruments attached to the weapon. A 105mm gun is made up of a breech mechanism and a barrel, it can be fired co-axley, which means on the move keeping on target whilst the vehicle is driven over all terrains, the ammunition or rounds are about a metre in length and weigh about 56lbs.

After the initial two weeks in the sim, we would travel everyday to Lulworth to the classroom by the actual range. Lulworth Cove is a beautiful part of the Dorset coastline, with magnificent views. The MOD has had a range there since the last war. I really enjoyed this course, in fact I was enjoying life in general, when one day I got a wake up call and circumstances were going to change that feeling for a while. We would be this day stripping the breech block of the gun, this was a tricky procedure which had to be tackled with care, there was a uniform pattern on how to do the job safely without cutting corners. We worked in pairs and my buddy that day was another Yorkshirman from Bradford Fred Sykes, I went first stripped the block then re-assembled it no problem. Fred then climbed aboard, he was a sullen young man, bit of a loner with scary eyes and ginger hair, he was about halfway through the operation when it went tits up, he had messed up big time and the mechanism nearly sliced his thumb off, he knew he was guilty of cutting corners, and insisted in no mean terms that I should keep stum or else. He was then rushed to the medics, we had de-brief. I guess I was very naïve, for I grassed him up, explaining how he had been negligent, that was my mistake, for Sykes was charged and nearly thrown off the course. I had never been in this position before I felt really bad, that I had let myself down, I'm sure all the other lads thought the same. Sykes arrived back from the medics arm in pot, it didn't make any difference, he hammered seven bells of shit out of me, and I let him, for I deserved it, both my eyes were closed and swollen, what a state the lads in the room couldn't understand why I didn't defend myself, but I knew I deserved this beating. Sgt Wilkinson the next day understood what had happened and turned a blind eye. Sykes became more and more aloof after this ordeal and eventually would leave the regiment. It took a week or two before the wounds healed, but I certainly learned from it. I had another run in with Sykes later before he left, this incident summed him up.

This morning we were going for P.T a cross country run, Fred didn't want to turn up, he asked me to shut the door on his fingers, I obliged with great gusto breaking three of his pinkies, when I slammed the door on his hand, he just looked at me with those scary eyes no screaming or noise nothing, he was a total nutter and today I sometimes recall those events and wonder what ever happened to Fred Sykes from Bradford. The final week of the course arrived with exams at the end, we had live firing at targets up to 1000yards, what a buzz seeing the target go up in a fireball great piece of kit the 105 mm. Exams arrived Jun Trooper Hart 96% third in the class, after all the drama of the previous weeks, this was a fair result. I was now qualified tank gunner, not much need for them in civvy street, but onward now to conquer the radio.

I was walking one day passed the adjacent block when the lad hung his head out of the window asking where I was from, "Scarborough" I replied. "Bloody hell" he came back I'm from Pickering, he came scuttling down shook my hand you'd have thought I was the prodigal son. Tony Wrey was his name, we became good buddies, he was a couple of years older, and going into the household cavalry the life guards, in fact the regiment I was to join but I didn't know this at the time. Tony after he left the army joined a petroleum company travelling all round the globe, he came to live in Staintondale close to where I live in Scalby, and sadly he passed away prematurely a few years ago.

Over the road from the barracks, where we did our original square bashing stands the impressive tank museum full of memorabilia from the last war, German Tiger Tanks as well as our own, really interesting place open to the general public. And just up the road out of Bovington there's the cottage of the late TE Lawrence, or as we know him Lawrence of Arabia, he died in a motorcycle accident; we used to pass his place on our cross country runs. Friday night, we were all getting our gear on after shave the business, going to the disco to check out the talent, not even sure if females were allowed. The drummer in the group Sid Eastman was in our troop, and a good mush. Sid would swap allegiances later and join the Regimental Band. He was also a decent cricketer and hockey player, and we played alongside each other in both. The club was run by a lady, Sheila in her twilight years but don't let that fool you, very elegant, passionate about her roll within the regiment, any lad who had a problem personal like, she would look after him like a surrogate mother. She was helped by a couple of Junior NCO's, they organized trips out and social events in general. We walked through the door aftershave wafting in our nostrils not a bird in sight apart from Sheila, what a disappointment, she did tell us the local army nurses had been invited, we grabbed a couple of cokes in anticipation. During the evening two boys from London appeared they were from our intake, real geezers or so they thought, here have butchers at these one of them shouted my first sighting of drugs. Small purple pills, purple hearts and they were on them, you could tell, they were known throughout the squadron as a pair of queens, limp wristed and always together.

A notice went up on the board, they'd organized a trip to Bournemouth the following month, I couldn't believe what I was reading, live in concert at the Boscombe Ballrooms, the Beatles, Brian Limbert had been bang on, this group were amazing, Bournemouth here we come! The bloody nurses never turned up so we trudged back to camp to listen to Henry Cooper take on Cassius Clay for the world Heavy Weight title. I got a letter and the local rag from home once a week, the local news from home was always welcome. Mum and Dad were working hard keeping the wolf from the door. Bill my brother was an apprentice mechanic at Stockdales of Seamer, a potato merchant of repute. I've been at pains not to mention girls too much, I love the opposite sex there's no doubting that, its just no opportunity has arisen yet, probably later who knows. Cricket nets have been running for a few weeks, I've been netting most evenings after duties, Simon and Tom have me penciled in for the regimental first team, and the skipper is the son of a cricketing legend Bill Alley who played for Somerset for years. Graham is in the pass out troop his final term he's a decent player, all rounder lively bowler who can bat. News came through which shocked all the lads to the core. Chris one of the Junior NCO's who worked with Sheila, for some reason had gone down to Wool station laid on the track and let the London bound express kill him, it was a gory business they reckon bits of him were scattered for miles.

I made my debut for the first team away in Somerset against an army apprentice outfit, it took us three hours in the back of a three ton lorry to get there, we won by seven wickets knocking off 170, didn't bat but got a couple of wickets with my slow left arm spin. The radio course went without a hitch interesting course using the new A sets. Remembering all the call signs and codes the phonetic alphabet, using the new equipment was a boost for when we joined our regiment. Tom Singleton was in the life guards and he was nudging me into joining them. He mentioned the Household Brigade cricket, they play the MCC and county seconds sides thought it might be an opportunity for me, I said I would think carefully before deciding. I passed the Radio course exams, I was now a gunner, radio operator, only the driving to pass but that will be next year. We had a great night in Bournemouth the Beatles were truly magical their music so vibrant, so new, and all the girls, beautiful girls going crazy. The

Beatles lit the match, which set the world wide music scene on fire. Four young good looking lads became an overnight sensation, raising the bar, creating an exciting vibrant new sound, setting the standards for thousands of song writers and musicians to follow in their wake. To be witness to the birth of the Beatles was up there with the Moon Walk... the 60's ...yeah yeah yeah...yeah!!!!!!!!

We were in full swing practicing for the passing out parade, our Kit has to be bulled to perfection, the parade is a week away everyone is getting anxious. The whole regiment on parade in their best number one dress for Officers, number 2 dress for us. I enjoy the pomp and ceremony, marching to the band those regimental marches are class. Sunday mornings were always full of dread, church parade. I was C/E as were the majority, which meant forming three ranks outside at 0900 hrs. This particular Sunday it was bucketing down with rain, we reckoned it was god having a laugh as we paraded there, with our military poncho's over our uniforms, it was three miles to the church, every Sunday an hours march, when we finally arrived, sweating wet through, the stink in the pews was something else, the service would commence at 1030, it was worth every mile marched to check out the talent on show, the Officers wives, girlfriends of different class, they knew it too, mincing up the aisle, their arses swaying, tits hanging out, not a good recipe for young virile boys who spent the next ten minutes altering their dress. After church the return trip then lunch, the meals in the cookhouse as I remember were excellent, it was a modern camp, with a varied selection of good wholesome food. Sunday afternoon was leisure time, catch up on letter writing etc, this particular Sunday we would venture up to the village and check the C/E club to our amazement it was a hub of activity pin ball machines, juke box, dart board, snooker table, everything a young man desired, to top it off girls wow!!! We didn't get too carried away, but it was a step in the right direction, the allure of perfume mixing with the cigarette smoke, we were growing up. The beans on toast with frothy coffee went down a treat. It was packed with regular soldiers, lads from camp and lasses from the woman's branch of the service the W.A.A.C.S, this would become a regular bolt hole for me, on a Sunday, the R/C club was close, we went for a nosey, it was almost deserted similar facilities, I asked if you had to be a Catholic to use the club "no" came the reply, so why was it empty, probably the beans on toast were naff!!.

The day of the parade dawned it was a beautiful clear day, we had moved out of our block, living in the gym, our rooms were taken over by parents of the lads passing out it was tradition, parents arrived to watch their sons pass out. I thought my turn next year, Mum and Dad would love it here. Time ticked away quickly, it was time to don the uniforms all of us looking splendid, dusting each other off, checking for blemishes as we were to be inspected by the C/O before we made our way to the parade ground. The parade ground for the passing out was our cricket ground, plenty of room for cars and spectators. It was a magical time, the colours of the different cavalry uniforms, the band was in three ranks in perfect formation, then the Junior RSM who was to control the action marched up to his spot, the General taking the salute arrived on the dais, you could hear a pin drop the tension was electric, PAR ---DE SHUN, we were on, it would last about an hour in total then back to the gym get the kit off a job well done. I couldn't wait for next years parade there is something about marching in unison to a military band, all the hard weeks of practicing perfecting the steps the different marches, slow quick, we all felt a bit special.

Apart from the cricket team, I had made it into the Regimental Basketball team, I'm not exactly 7 foot tall only 5”10”, I was recommended as my defensive qualities in the zone were awesome (as quoted). We were off down to Weymouth to play against a Borstal, scary or what. We arrived outside the gates of the so called Borstal. Someone somewhere had been fed misinformation, this was no Borstal but H.M prison, we were to play seasoned criminals and murderers. Discussions took place it was decided as we had travelled a long way the game would take place. We as a team were never consulted, not that we would have backed down, this was the army, good versus evil. We arrived on court, there was a viewing gallery packed with lads whistling, hollering, but I think they appreciated the fact, we had turned up to play. I remember we put up a decent show, but they were well drilled performers and big lads to boot, they beat us quite comfortably, we took it all in good spirits, at least we would be leaving, they had no option. The prison was actually situated at Portland strategically placed on a cliff overlooking Portland Bill, escape was out of the question then!!

November 22nd just an ordinary day, listening to the radio in the evening, whilst cleaning kit, the usual routine when the broadcast was cut, and returned to the BBC News. President Kennedy had been shot dead in Dallas Texas, the boys just stared in disbelief total shock, it had an effect on us rookie kids that evening, we knew that this was big. As the story unfolded he had been shot by a nutter, one of their own which eased world tension, it was a tragedy for the US and the world in general, as he was thought to be a forward thinker, set to unite the problem areas, it had turned into a day when everyone remembered where they were, but it doesn’t get my boots polished, or my pack blancoed god rest his soul!

We were ready for some leave by now, it had been a heavy year fitting a lot of work in, when I return it will be my final term, pass out troop what a thought a regiment to select, the Junior Army Cricket competition, a beer in the NAAFI, we were allowed as PASSOUT Troop, bring it on. As a young man in the senior troop, you are a law unto yourself. We are allowed to the front of all cookhouse queues, a couple of pints of mild in the NAAFI, a pass out on Saturday night until midnight and not forgetting verbally abusing the new intake, it takes your mind back to the morning I made my entrance as a rookie all those months back. I now proudly wear my regimental colours I earned for cricket and hockey, this is an elongated lanyard in yellow and red, where everybody else wears ordinary lanyards in white, we also carry white flashes on our tunics to display our status.

This term we have driving lessons in ¼ ton trucks. We took to the open road with our L Plates on show, unfortunately I failed to pass the test as I was too young to take it, you have to be seventeen, with me only sixteen, I will have to wait until I join my regiment. Hand brake Harry was our instructor, an old dinosaur who hated every minute of every day, a right miserable old sod, I can honestly say I never once saw him smile or show any joy, you have to have something to get out of bed for on a morning, poor old Harry. He probably wasn't getting his quota at home, he was an expert at doubling his clutch though!! I had made my mind up and I'd been accepted into the life guards household cavalry, the most senior cavalry regiment in the army, formed in the 1600's to protect Charles,the monarch of the age. They were based in Windsor, a lovely part of the country close to London. I met Tom at the cricket nets, I think his influence had helped my selection. He was a good steady bloke Tom, a top coach knew his cricket. Cricket was next on the agenda, I had been made skipper of the regimental first team and we were to play in the army championships.

I had been looking forward to driving a centurion tank from day one, it's the ultimate toy, the latest AFV the chieftain had been rattling up through Bovington to the trials ground for weeks and it looks magnificent, sleek, powerful packed with testosterone, pull the chicks with one of those I thought. We had three weeks on the tank tracks in the centurion, there's no superlative to match the buzz, ask anyone who has driven these beasts over multi-terrain created especially for these masters, this was the climax to all those months of anxiety, it was now I realised I had made it, beaten all the demons, through my own endeavours, it was an exciting time.

A lot to look forward to, our passing out parade with the rest of the boys was on the horizon. 2 and a ½ years we had been together how time flies. Our individual regimental uniforms had arrived with our new peak caps how proud we were as we mingled together, Burt Lawson looked very dapper in his 11th Hussars outfit with the crimson trousers, it will be sad to leave these lads after all we had been through together, we all felt a great sense of camaraderie. The Army cricket championship arrived, the summer was in full bloom, with hot weather making conditions ideal for scoring runs, and that's what we produced, blowing away the first two sides, it was a nail biting semi final at home against the Army apprentice XI from Kent, we scrambled over the line, nine ten jack taking us to the final, it was a fairytale, but that's cricket, we were going to Aldershot representing the Junior Leaders Regimented Armoured Corps in the final how good is that.

Our big day on the parade ground was creeping closer, invitations to parents had been sent. Mum and Dad were definitely coming taking their holidays hiring a car, having a week touring. We were kept occupied going through the service manuals of the centurion tank, changing a discarded track, sprockets and all. Our final net session before the final was in full swing, Simon Smail and Tom Singleton were more nervous about the game than us players. We were to receive brand new kit, white shirts and sweaters. Four coaches of supporters from the regiment were travelling to Aldershot, our success on the field had really taken off around the camp. We were to play the Electrical and Mechanical engineers Apprentice XI, from somewhere in the Midlands. We looked resplendent in our new kit, as we had our team photo, the C'O was there, Simon and Tom with our mascot, Simons golden retriever William. The sun was cracking the flags as we two skippers walked out to toss the coin. I won the toss, we were batting. It was a forty over per side game, and we amassed a total of 210 for 6 with the skipper unbeaten on 106, we bowled out opposition for 115 with the skipper's bowling figures reading 6 overs 1 maiden 3 wickets 6 runs ...not a bad all round performance, what dreams are made of. I was presented with the trophy a silver cup, we were the Army champions, a great team effort over the whole competition, and it was a marvellous trip back to barracks.

One evening the following week the whole regiment was seated in the gymnasium, the CO addressed us on the high and lows on how he saw the regiment going forward, we as young soldiers were gripped by this stern judgement of which it became clear, he without a doubt believed in the Junior soldier going on into their respective regiments as future leaders. This was a new concept, helping to create self-confidence and belief. We were young back then, it went in one ear and out the other, it's now when I look back how quite moving I find it, he was obviously a top man, who felt the need to give these young men his blessing as they fled the nest. He also paraded the cricket team in front of the audience, we were a very proud brick in his wall.

Mum and Dad arrived on the following Friday night, it was absolutely marvellous to welcome them to the Bovington Camp, during Friday I had to report to Simon Smails office immediately, I marched there smartly, halted gave a stylish salute and waited, Tom was there with him, I was to be presented with an outstanding award for Sport, at the parade tomorrow. It was there on the table a statue on a plinth it was engraved with Outstanding Junior Army Cricketer 1964 307 runs, AV 101.6 23 wickets AV 6.3,1 was in shock, this really was the icing on the cake. I didn't get much sleep that night, going over in my mind all the moves required tomorrow, marching out to receive my trophy from the General, don't want to cock it up with Mum and Dad watching. They had a splendid trip down on route via the Cheddar Gorge, Dad loved his driving, Mum looked radiant, her health issues were up and down but at this time no worries.

The crowd was building around the parade ground, as were our nerves, all the boys milling around before we were fell in shaking hands, patting backs, this was it. I've handed all my kit back to the DHS, paid for my deficiencies we were going to leave Bovington tomorrow on the Sunday. We were fell in, the Band who had entertained the crowd for an hour, struck up with a stirring number and the show began. Everything went to plan, the salute, my presentation, and incredible memories. I look back on those days with affection, it amazes me how I ever plucked up the courage to make that journey as a young lad, I feel it was probably the finest decision I ever made, I was going to the next chapter in my life in great shape, confident, smart and respected.

It's a crying shame that the Junior Leaders Regiments were closed in the Thatcher era. Although I realise the country didn't need the manpower, technology had arrived.

I believe in all honesty that our young people at sixteen years of age should spend some time away from home, not necessarily in the Army, but say for instance doing community service, utilising the barracks at Bovington or elsewhere. This country is missing a great opportunity to prepare our youngsters for adult life, give them something to aspire too, to achieve goals, parents are not always the answer, extreme pressures of today's society leaves a percentage of them wanting in that regard. Three weeks leave, before I join the life guards in Combermere Barracks Windsor, my buddy in Seamer David Tennant and myself decided we were going to France. Derek my elder brother, after his adventures in the merchant navy has changed his allegiance, and is now in the RAF. He is an office wallah, stationed at SHAPE HQ Fontainbleau, near Paris. He married a lovely Italian girl from Naples Veneranda, she is typically Italian, very passionate quite loud, but very genuine, what you see is what you get. Ven and I have always got on very well we have a similar sense of humor, they have two kids Leslie and Carmella and it will be great to see them all.

Dave and I took the ferry from Dover to Calais, where Derek met us with his mate Mick, we squeeze into the red mini, luggage and all, and off we roar, I have no idea how far Fontainbleu is from Calais, when Derek explained the drive would be four hours we were quite shocked. After an age in the little car we were there, wow what a beautiful part of the world. This is where Napoleon had his palace. You walked out of the gate and over the road was the River Seine. Tons of barges in long lines sailing from the great cities of Europe. Dave and I soon made ourselves at home, Derek and Ven were perfect hosts, taking us round the local sites. We visited SHAPE HQ had a look around where Derek worked, he loved his sport also, he was a javelin thrower at this time, and practicing for the

R.A.F championships. This particular evening friends were invited round for dinner, the beers and chianti wine were flowing and it was decided we would all go up to Paris, it was midnight when we set off, on the hours drive to the city. Derek explained midnight was the best time to see Paris nothing happens before then, I must say he was spot on, we were in Pigalle the red light area. Apart from the girls plying their trade, I was transfixed with the Algerians and how they did a deal on a watch.

Six or so watches up their arms "have a look at this" they would urge, and as soon as money changed hands they were nabbed by the secret police, also watching, amazing. But the girls stole the show, they wanted my trousers off and no messing, but they didn't account for my sister in law! It was back home for day break, the kids were staying with friends so we all got our heads down, dreaming of what could have been. It was the custom in the village to fish with a long pole, we used to make the bait of bread and fat rolled into a ball fastened to the hook, the one benefit of fishing was the box of miller light you took to sit on, this was a very refreshing way of relaxing, you knew when it was time to go home, when the beer ran out.

This evening we were going to the cinema and we were taking the next door neighbour with us, apparently this was a lady, Ingrid a German girl married to Pierre a chemist, who was away working. There was a knock at the door, enter Ingrid. She was the most stunning lady I had ever clapped my mincers on, it was love at first sight, she was beautiful, quite tall, vivacious, cheeky face and those eyes. I had no idea what the film was about, we sat together, she rubbing up against me I was on fire, I didn't want it to end. We got back to the house, had a drink then Derek asked me if I would walk Ingrid home, up like a shot I was placing her arms in her coat, she thanked everyone for a lovely evening. When we got outside she explained that her mother was staying with her, and that she would be expected quite soon. That didn't stop her taking me by the hand and leading me by the river, if this was seduction it was working, my legs were like jelly, my manhood had stood up like a blind cobblers thumb, I'd never been kissed like it, she was a vampire.

We arrived at her door with everything intact, I hadn't disgraced myself yet. I was in love, I got back next door luckily everyone had gone to bed, I don't think I could have bluffed my way through this one, another learning curve. We were due to leave tomorrow, Dave had to get back home, I decided to stay another week. Tragically Dave was killed in a car accident years later.

Pierre arrived back, he was a charming bloke, spoke brilliant English, very interesting, good company and enjoyed playing Tennis. Luckily for me he was going off again the next day. The following afternoon after Pierre had left, Ingrid took me to the woods to pick mushrooms, I was in paradise. I've never enjoyed the company of mushrooms so much in my life. Ingrid was also a very intelligent young lady, I think she was enjoying this little fling, I was hoping to spend more time at her gaff than next door. To their credit Derek and Ven made nothing of it. I had to leave the next day, we had a super party that evening. Ingrid gave me a photo of her in a bikini, it was very hard saying good bye, I never saw her again, ships that pass in the night and all that. It had been a magnificent holiday I was indebted to my brother and his lovely wife. Comber mere Barracks here I come.

Paddy O'Halloran and John Lloyd were buddies of mine from the Junior Leaders, we met up at Johns house in Windsor before making our way to the guard room at Combermere. John Lloyd was the son of John Bunker Lloyd R.C.M of the life guards regimental corporal major, he was a nobbly old dinosaur of a generation passed, quite pleasant when I met him in the house, but I could imagine a different kettle of fish on duty. He was a legend within the regiment the story goes, he was chairing a NCO's meeting in the mess, when under any other business someone proposed purchasing a chandelier for the mess, bunkers reply "that would be fine but who could play it." this story has entered the annuls of life guard folklore. We arrived with our suitcases, were met by the regimental police on duty at the gate. We were to be seconded into A Sqn. The only problem with that was A Sqn were in Cyprus under the flag of the United Nations. They had only a month left to complete, therefore it was felt not a viable proposition. They were there helping to round up General Grievas and his AOKA Terrorists. As it turned out it gave us time to acclimatise getting used to the camp, to the change in routine and last but not least the town of Windsor. I was still only seventeen, but I had relented to the smell of the barmaids apron. There was a skeleton crew within the barrack block, which were of modern brick design, two floors with a light airy ambience, eight to a room.

The life guards had a sister regiment, The Royal Horse Guards or the blues as they are known, they were in Germany, changed over from a reconnaissance regiment onto heavy battle tanks, this is what happens when the two regiments swap their rolls, as we the life guards are soldiering in England, we will therefore work with Ferret Scout cars and Saladin armoured fighting vehicles, with Saracen PCV troop carrying vehicles bringing up the rear. There are two wings to the Household Cavalry, most people recognize the life guards as those men on horseback with the red tunics, polished helmets and breastplates, this is the equitation arm of the regiment, they are stationed in Knightsbridge, where they guard Whitehall and protect the queen during state visits by leaders of other countries.

We are known as troopers in the regiment, it is possible to join both arms. I would say probably the majority of troopers opt for the mechanical wing rather than the horses, the regiment was initially formed in 1662 to protect the monarch and is the most senior regiment in the British Army.

As I familiarize myself with my surroundings I can pick out the HQ Sqn Block, the desk wallahs, LAD mechanics, the medical wing which is quite modern with a dental unit, the band block, consisting of obviously the band, the band one of the finest in the military, travel all round the country plying their trade, there's something about tradition in this country that we all find gives us a lift. C Sqn and B Sqn blocks make up the set, with the parade ground in the centre. The officers mess, NCO's mess and cookhouse behind the square, all I need now is the NAAFI. I was assigned to a room, there was the two of us John and myself, it felt weird with the place more or less empty it used to echo, I woke early, and spied the duty bandsman march up to his mark at the edge of the square, he then sounded reveille wow!! He would return at lunch and lights out, I thought this is the dogs bollocks.

Today we were to collect our kit and proceed to the tailors with our uniforms and great coats. It took most of the day sorting it all and folding it neatly into the locker. Just like the Junior Leaders it would take hard graft to get on top of the bullshit, the boots, the belts, were actually white had to be whitened, then left to dry, but we would overcome. It was imperative people read standing orders every evening, they gave you the run down on the following day's activities type of clothing to wear, boots etc.

It was middle of September, we had received a memo instructing us of our movements taking in the next three months, I was speechless how were we going to fit it all in.

The regiment was due back at the end of the month there would be leave but on a staggered basis, we were to be honoured with the freedom of Windsor, that would mean rehearsals and bullshit, we also had to take over Castle Guard duties in Windsor Castle, as the Scots Guards were going to Libya on manoueveres for two weeks. This would be the first time in the history of the Regiment that it guarded the castle. When the Scots guards returned it would be our turn to head for Libya. It was quite bewildering. Received a letter from home Dad had written to me, informing me that Mum had reached the District finals of the Glamorous Grandmother competition. She had entered the Seamer and Irton area of the competition for a bit of fun and won. The final was to be held at the Spa Ballrooms Whitby and a bus had been laid on, not that I was surprised by the result for Mum was a fine specimen of a woman. Quite tall, with straight black hair and long legs, a fine figure to be sure. She was of a fair complexion blue eyes, high cheek bones a real stunner. I made it up from Windsor just in time to catch the bus to Whitby, most of the village were making the trip to support Mum, I've never seen her look more beautiful, the girls from the village had done her hair creating a shower of ringlets, someone else had done her makeup, I felt really proud sat on that bus, it was a really warm pleasant atmosphere, among people I had grown up with. Mum's dress was black with what looked like diamonds sewn around the midriff with black high heels she looked an absolute picture. The beer was flowing with a buffet on display, I was starving, it was morning since I had eaten, chicken leg in one hand, a pint in the other, it was turning into another memorable night, on to the stage they swaggered, it was hard to believe these ladies were grandmothers, all were interviewed, made to saunter up and down, then it was up to the judges. In first place Mrs Winifred Hart, wow! The whole place erupted it was just incredible I wouldn't have missed this night, the cameras were clicking. Mum was milking it who could blame her. If anyone deserved to be treated like a film star, pampered made to look a million dollars it was my mother, to be in the limelight as her self, to become that self indulgent beast for a couple of hours, how good would that feel. We sang all the way back to Seamer, I can't recall the village ever topping that evening, very emotional good on you Mum.

The following Thursday I received another letter from Dad, I thought before I opened it, aye aye, after all the euphoria of the previous week, Dad's best mate his constant companion, Sherri his corgi bitch had been run over in the yard of his work. I could tell Dad was still distraught, he would miss that little dog, to make things worse it was one of Dads work colleagues that reversed into her, not his fault just a tragic accident.

John Lloyd was a big lad, he enjoyed his scoff, he fancied a ramble up to the new Wimpy Bar that had just opened, it was a quick shower out on the town, and the Beatles were still number one.

Windsor was very much the Military Bastion, the Scots Guard were occupying Wellington Barracks up towards the Castle by Peascot Street, with our mob in Combermere Barracks. Windsor was big enough for the two, no problems as far as I recall. There were plenty of public houses that I do remember, The Queens Head opposite the barrack gate. The Lord Raglan up on the corner opposite the General hospital, then another five minutes further up the main drag. The Trooper a favorite haunt, I found the beer down south inferior to the brews from home, I was still lawfully underage to drink. The fish and chips also left a lot to be desired, hake or skate wings in an insipid milky batter, they were clueless, bring on that prime chunky cod, or sweet haddock cooked in animal fat with golden brown batter no contest!! We made our way up the hill to the top of Peascot Street, Castle in all its glory straight ahead, we made a left passed the Theatre Royal down the hill into Eton, our next generation of leaders would be tucked up in their cots, bless em!!

John had told me about this new restaurant that had just opened over the bridge, it was one of them new Italian places, bloody hell I thought, and I explained that my sister in law was Italian, she was a brilliant cook. I sampled my first spaghetti Bolognaise ever and fell in love, I spent many an evening in that cafe drooling over their cuisine. We were having drill tomorrow, sword drill this would be another learning curve, it was obvious they were finding things to occupy us while the squadron was away in Cyprus, only a week then they would be back. A new lad had made himself comfortable in the room, Jimmy Harnett had travelled down from Consett County Durham, he had been a coal miner, worked with the pit ponies carrying coal to the top, he was an outgoing lad, very friendly and glad to be out of the mines and looking forward to a military career. We were allowed four free travel warrants per year, as I had no duties over the weekend I decided to make the journey home, I took the 16.30 train from Windsor to Waterloo, one of the office wallahs had given me a set of instructions regarding the underground, off I went up the Northern Line eventually arriving at Kings Cross. People in there bloody thousands like ants running hither and thither, climbing the stairs into the daylight.

With my ticket I shot through the barrier, up along the platform to board the 1805 stopping at Peterborough and York. What an adventure, I would get used to this stint.

The journey time to York was three hours 15 minutes quite smooth. I only just claimed a seat as the train was packed, I noticed there were many service types travelling, matelots mainly, in their uniforms when I got off at York. I ran to the front of the train to check out the engine that had pulled us, it was to my delight an A4 Pacific, brilliant, the memories of being a kid on this platform with Frank Berriman and Alan Henderson all those years ago, weird!! The last train to Scar borough pulled out 21.20hrs arriving at 22.15, then the bus home, a very hectic few hours but enjoyable all the same.

Life at home was no different to how I imagined it would be, Bill was still at Stockdales, he was now developing an interest in cars, mini's were the rage, he and his mates were into the rally scene. Dad was a bit concerned about Mum's health, she had never been the fittest being on the planet, but to me she was the strongest. She was going for a lumber puncture, it meant sod all to me, but it would have an effect big time, in the future. Saturday night got the bus into town went to the SPA with Simon Barningham, had too much to drink, sick in the toilets, never again!!

The journey back to camp was another learning curve, last bus to York 20.30hrs arrive in York 23.00 hrs train to London 0100 hrs manage to find an empty compartment to stretch out, arrive London Kings Cross 0430hrs, then it's a matter of legging it down the platform to the taxi rank, a queue of matelots heading for Waterloo, into a cab through town to Waterloo, a quick wash a brush up in the public loo, all the cubicles were filled with vagrants coughing and spitting. First train to Windsor arriving 0700hrs half an hour hike to barracks, into boots denims and gaiters for parade 0800hrs spend the day like a zombie, can't wait for bed time.

Combermere Barracks is situated right under the main flight path into Heathrow or London Airport as it was, you have to hold on to your hat when one of those VClO's accelerates away overhead. Talking of aircraft the squadron is due back to barracks today, will make a difference, John and myself have been sent to the Cookhouse to prepare for the invasion, we both feel a little nervous wondering how we will gel with battle hardened individuals. We need not have worried, the boys were just glad to be home, back to their families, the consensus and feedback we got was that they all thought Cyprus a magical place.

It was Saturday tea time, we were on the razzle early, had been to a local soccer match, Brian Smith one of our LAD boys had been representing Windsor and Eton, as we were downtown, we decided to have some Italian food again, I introduced the boys to the new restaurant they were impressed, that spag bol is delicious can't get enough. I was dressed to impress had my new chalk striped suit on with brown suede loafers, looked the business after tea a few beers, then a few more, as we were walking beside the River Thames, I noticed these exotic looking river boats moored by the static pole about ten metres from the bank, being under the influence, I decided to board a boat by using the leopard crawl method along the pole pulling myself along. "Police" was the cry with that I lost control and fell into the river, luckily still hanging onto the pole. The current was racing, I heaved myself along back to the riverbank where the boys fished me out. My new suit didn't look new anymore I was shivering, shaking like a shitting dog what a prick, as it was dark we flagged a cab down. Back at Combermere as I exited the cab, I noticed the water swilling around the foot wells, the boys quickly sorted the fare, we legged it, I never heard anymore about that incident, but I know I never used that firm again. One of the characters based in Combermere, a Geordie lad, pudding Heed Knowles, a portly chap loved his food, he also loved his Newcastle Brown ale, this particular Sunday he had been celebrating his birthday most of the day. Early evening Knowles had been arrested on the M4, riding a stolen push bike, on his arrest, he explained he was looking for the M1 and then on to Newcastle. He was charged with being drunk in charge of cycle and riding the fast lane of the M4.

The squadron was quickly re-structured, I was to be moved to two troop, which meant moving into another room. My troop leader would be Roger Levitt B.E.M. he was a legend within the regiment, an ex SAS trooper earned his gong seeing off communist guerrillas in Malaysia, I would become his driver. Blondie Woodlands, corporal, another good mush, knew all the there was to know about soldiering within this environment, I learnt a lot from him. We spent the first few days familiarizing ourselves with our vehicles the Ferret Scout car, a two man vehicle built for reconnaissance, four ton in weight with 30 Browning machine gun armament capability, we also met the LAD light aid detachment or mechanics who would be our pit crew when or whenever we needed their assisatance. I passed my driving test in the scout car, it has a pre-select gear box quite different from your usual family run around, we were preparing for the freedom of Windsor bash, which would entail driving in formation through the town taking the salute from the Queen ...WOW!!! We spent the next week bulling up the cars if it moved grease it, if it stood still paint it, the parade went without a hitch, in the evening it was time to sample the Watneys Red Barrel. Gerry Clark a lad from Morpeth another buddy in the troop, he had decided to have a crack at the SAS selection course, he was a fit young man, good footballer, felt he needed to challenge himself, urged me to accompany him on this course, I declined. To become an SAS operative took 110% commitment, and I felt it was not for me, Gerry went on and got selected into the SAS, had a coloured career I believe.

Castle Guards were next up, we would be drilling everyday for this daunting operation. A drill sgt Blood had been drafted in to put us through the wringer. As I mentioned earlier it would be the first time in the history of the household brigade that the cavalry would take over the infantry's roll in guarding the monarch. We were briefed in the guard room, the castle guards are privy to the public, for obvious reasons, plain clothes police operate within the castle perimeter 24/7.1 vividly remember being on duty, patrolling the garden verandah it would be 02.30 crunching along. I remember seeing a small light in a room above wondering who would be in there, then as you notice the statues in the garden the mind plays tricks you have this feeling, I'm sure that statue is moving. When from nowhere a hand pats you on the shoulder, "Everything ok son?" when I landed back down to Earth I replied, "No problem officer." Smug bastard I thought did that on purpose. It was quite a novelty but I was pleased when the duties ceased and the Scots Guards returned, each to their own I thought.

Csqn had gone to Libya, as part of Operation Archangel, 29,000 troops, the 14" 20" Hussars were based in Tripoli had been there for five years, therefore they were going to be tested to see how desert hardened they had become. We would be taking over from C Sqn in three weeks, in the meantime we were heading to Salisbury plain to hone and practice our reconnaissance skills. The work was intense a crash course on survival. Salisbury plain is a long way from the Western Desert, as we would soon be finding out. In the evening sat round the fire having a beer, the old sweats would recall their adventures, try as we could, there was nothing forthcoming from our troop leader regarding his heroics, a great bloke all the same. We had five days simulating life in the desert, got back to Combemere in the early hours, we were having our first flight later in the day. I had never flown, I was excited at the prospect. We were to drive two land rovers and two Scout cars to the airfield of Abingdon, load up the vehicles into a Blackburn

Beverley heavy transport aircraft, I stood and gawped at this giant, thinking it would never lift off. We precisely parked the vehicles and took to our seats high in the Gods of the plane. I remember a small window looking out onto the wing, the Beverley had four engines, as the pilot increased the power to the engines the wings seemed to flap slightly, then he took the brake off, it seemed to take an age to leave the ground but eventually we did, this was my baptism of fire, flying, scary!!

We were only going down the road to RAF Benson, the landing was probably more dramatic than taking off down a bit, a bit more, ears popping clear nose, down a bit more, bang bang engines, roar in reverse thrust, what a commotion we are down, taxi to a halt. I only recently returned from Dubai, travelling business class a board the nearly new A380, four hundred people on board, to recall that initial flight forty seven years ago brings it home how we take progress for granted, great memories.

It would be my last chance for a few weeks for a weekend at home, so I packed a bag and endured the rigours of the railway, arriving in Scarborough at the usual 22.15hrs.

Mums health was still giving cause for concern, she was to have more tests as her legs were affecting her mobility some what, this was affecting Mums temper as she wasn't one to sit around moping. On Saturday Simon Barningham and myself went to a dance or disco as it is now, at the Cricketers pub in Scarborough. As we entered the bar I spotted a young lady I had been at school with, Pauline Davis she was a lovely girl, we had a little thing going whilst at school, seeing her now sent my heart all a flutter. We spent the whole evening together, reminiscing, I explained how I had joined the army, the fact that I would be away for the next few weeks, I gave her my address, we would keep in touch.

We flew to Libya from R.A.F Brise Norton, Libya was ruled at this time by their Royal family, it was pre General Gadhafi, Libya during the war had been the epicenter of the North African campaign, the German Army cutting off the axis forces at Tobruk, then General Montgomery rallying the troops in a counter attack, with the climax at El Allamein. We were going to re-enact some of the rolls played out there twenty two years previously. My first impression as we arrived at our holding camp was total and utter bewilderment. We landed at the RAF base of El Adum, we then dispatched along the metal road to the village of Timimi, where we hung a left onto a desert track for another four miles into our holding camp. I remember the sun was on its way down and the sunset was amazing, a vehicle appeared which disturbed me, it was a flat bed truck with three or four Arab men stood on the back with rifles. They were running down an antelope of some description, the animal was trying to dodge the vehicle, it was obviously a regular past time for these people, eventually the animal collapsed and that was the end, how I wanted to turn a 30 browning machine gun on that truck, I had only been in Libya two minutes and I was at war with the natives.

We took our vehicles from C Sqn wished them bon voyage, we were then briefed on the do's and don'ts, being especially vigilant where scorpions were concerned. Everything had been abandoned in the desert since the war, the mine fields were as they were left. The enormity of the place, the heat during the day, the cold at night and frost in the morning, the incredible views of the universe using binoculars, especially the moon its craters so obvious without the interference of light. After a few days acclimatising, navigating by using a sun compass, learning all the other skills to survive in this hostile environment, we were ready to take our first patrol into the desert;

our vehicles had been ferried from Blighty, they were painted olive green, whereas our enemy for this exercise the 14th/20th hussars their scout cars were in desert camouflage, they had the drop on us as we stuck out like a sore thumb, I remember we were patrolling along a dry river bed or wadi, from out of nowhere the enemy pounced it was quick, embarrassing, but they were up for it, took all our ammunition- Henry Boyt one of our troop leaders, the eccentric Henry he was a Jack the lad, dressed like John Wayne in his suede boots a red bandana,. He was up in front of the colonel, as he had led his troops through a mine field, luckily they had lived to tell the tale. Not so fortunate was a party of four lads on a swimming day out, they got into difficulties and drowned, the body bags were filling up. We had brought out our cooks from Combermere to provide the scoff, it was interesting observing their improvised ovens, and how they quickly adapted to life on the beach. We could be miles from civilisation in the middle of nowhere, it would be blistering hot, then you would here the cry, 'one eggy one jam' a local lad from nowhere appeared carrying a bucket of eggs, it was good fun bartering our compo rations that we disliked for his eggs, to this day I have no idea where they came from. But the omelettes were welcome.

Another wonder which affected me, was the shifting sand as we found our bearings within the area you became accustomed to objects like rock formations small bushes etc., the next day in the same area would be boots, helmets, gas mask holders and flimsy fuel cans by the score all abandoned from the last war, becoming visible by the shifting sand, not all small items, one area unearthed a three ton truck that had been straffed from the air, full of bullet holes. What stories these objects could tell. Ken Whalley, my commander on this particular patrol, was learning the sun compass. We travelled for an hour keeping on a bearing, the terrain was soft sand which made you very wary, Ken came over the inter com telling me to stop, we got out of the car to the side of the track, there laid in the sunshine was a skeleton, can you imagine how we both felt, it had what looked like material attached to the upper leg when I touched it, it turned to dust, there was a helmet above the skull, Ken thought he had been an Italian lad, there was no id attached therefore we thought he must have been put there in a shallow grave, we stayed there glued to the spot, it was really moving to think his mother had said goodbye never to see him again. When we got back to camp we informed the powers that be of our gruesome find we included the grid references and we also inserted a recognition marker to assist recovery, I never heard a thing regarding the incident, one can only hope that a relative had been informed of their loss. Our camp covered quite a large area, a part from the usual requirements within a military compound, we also stocked our petrol in Gerry cans and tyres within a separate fenced area. The latrines were dug downwind of the main camp they consisted of six cubicles or thunder boxes, these were cleaned out everyday. An Arab used to come with his pre war Bedford every morning from the village.

You could hear this truck for miles as it had very high revs it like screamed its way along, I was on guard duty this particular evening 2 hours on 4 hours off, it was freezing on a night, we had to wear full combat gear to keep out the cold, I had the stag 0200hr, 0400 hours the nights were beautiful, so dark with a magnificent sky, I was admiring all the beauty, when down the road I could hear the Bedford heading this way. The heart started racing, my mind was working overtime again. All the lads were asleep around me by their vehicles under camouflage nets. The Bedford got louder closer now, then all went quiet, scared I moved over to a land rover turned my torch off put my back against something solid, and waited. I didn't have to wait long, for a minute or two later there was a whistle and a muted shout of 'Johnny Johnny'. I didn't move they knew someone would be on duty, so I played them at their own game, they started to throw pebbles at the compound, I was crapping myself should I wake up the boys. I hung on for a while longer not giving my position away all went quiet, then I heard the Bedford start up and head back down the road all was well. I explained the incident to my troop leader in the morning, he agreed with my course of action, I left that meeting with a spring in my step.

The next day had all the ingredients of being quite hairy, we were to make for a designated area where we were going to test our radios, we were also going to be attacked by the RAF, wow!!! We arrived at the said grid reference, created sixteen feet of aerial, Ken then sent information back to HQ who then sent it on to the other units, I was left with time to reflect, and there had been no time up to the present. We had all been totally focused on our tasks at hand. My mind began to wander back to Fontainebleau and Ingrid, that sexy beautiful lady, I had a pang of guilt then, and wondered if Pauline was still as keen as I was, she was lovely. I then thought about Mum, hoping her test had gone well, home felt like another planet compared to this majestic wilderness.

Then they appeared out of nowhere, Ken hurried me out of the drivers seat, we both clawed our way under the vehicle, as it was a land rover rather than a ferret scout car in reality it would have stood little chance against the firepower of the Hawker Hunter. I had not prepared for the next five minutes, this plane came in at low level, I mean low level flicking the top of the ariel, the noise, screaming noise was absolutely deafening, when we thought it had returned to base if came again this time from height straight down, then it straightened, then it lifted up and away the heat from the down draught, I can say that I've never experienced anything as scary as those five minutes, this was only an exercise, what it must be like for real, god forbid. This was turning into one hell of an experience this trip to Libya, men of the Highland DIV were marching in the mid day heat making for their destination to attack the enemy, as we rode by them they would give us the thumbs up or the V sign, I thought those poor buggers in the last war with those horrible heavy 303's, they deserved every medal going, we were given the following day off to relax, do some doby, write a letter, or to catch up with a bit of maintenance on the cars, the sand really takes its toll on bearings etc., therefore keeping oil levels topped up was paramount. We learnt a few tricks from the sweats from Tripoli, strapping your tin of stew to the manifold an hour before camp, it would be piping hot when you arrived. Keeping tea bags dry after use, a tea bag should last a week if dried in the sun.

We had a night operation finding our way using the stars, an incredible skill, we were heading through the desert arriving in Tobruk at daybreak, we travelled in convoy with each commander taking over the lead, you had to be on your mettle, luckily it all went to plan. Another memorable moment was our arrival in Tobruk at the birth of a new day as the sun began to rise out of the sea, words fail to describe how that affected me. The harbour was then just as it was after the German bombardment, masts of stricken vessels sticking out of the water as they were sunk. So tranquil now on that beautiful morning. I felt quite privileged to be part of this trip, to bear witness to historic events in this part of the world and yet there was more to come.

We headed back to camp after a gruelling twelve hours, we were driving down the coast road back to Timimi, this is the road the legendary SAS hero Paddy Mayne had used to attack the German airfields in 1942, he and his team with their improvised jeeps and Lewis guns, rode back and forth on this road causing havoc, stuff legends are made of. Another day, another dollar as the proverb^ states, today we were going to visit the area known as Cyrenaica, we were going to be moving as a troop four scout cars, it was going to be interesting, as we had to map read and use the sun compass to find a certain Oasis, as in every oasis there will be a well, it would be a full days patrol plenty of miles to endure, we had stocked up with an adequate amount of supplies including extra fuel and water as those were very important commodities within a desert situation. It got quite monotonous driving for hours at a time, therefore we were spelled after two hours, the commander taking the wheel for thirty minutes good call!!!

At last after eight hours the landscape began to change, more greenery appearing we had found our oasis, in the distance we could make out what looked like camels. We made our way down very slowly to within fifty yards of the beasts then cut our engines. The troop leader told us to stay put by the vehicles whilst he and Ken Whalley approached the gathering. It turned out to be a caravan a family of Bedouins. These people are travellers, and the desert is their home, they were also keen to find the well. We were sent for as they had invited us to take tea with them, after paying our respects we sat in a circle and enjoyed a lovely glass of tea, accompanied by pastries. They were the most hospitable people, no one spoke English but through signs we understood. Wearing black robes with daggers in their belts was a little intimidating, we collected all the camps rations we did not need and offered them to our new friends, they accepted our gifts with genuine heartfelt thanks. Whilst we sat round in the group my mind flashed back to Bovington and the cottage, where the legendary Lawrence of Arabia had lived. He spent years living the life of a Bedouin. As we went our separate ways, I reflected how blessed by good fortune we have been, long may it continue. Cyrenaica at last and the town of Cyrene, it was like stepping back in time, this was a working town full of locals plying their trade. You could feel a slight tension as we stepped out of the vehicles.

We decided to leave a couple of lads guarding the cars, they said they didn't mind, to them it resembled a right shit hole. The locals were a little guarded to say the least, we were in the local bazaar and hanging up on coat hangars, were uniforms from the last war, English, German and Italian. How bizarre, I realised why the traders were a little nervous and I wondered if they knew the war was over, I couldn't help wondering whose side they had been on. All of them" I guess. This town boasts the finest Roman Amphitheatre outside Rome, we rounded a corner and there in all its glory, magnificent pillars inscribed with murals, dating back thousands of years. We made our way to the stage in the centre of the seating, the acoustics were amazing, I could only imagine all the beautiful voices of yesteryear that had graced this building, another highlight on this memorable visit to Libya courtesy of her majesty. After savouring the sights and smells of this quaint but not too friendly town it was off again, we were now heading for the Derna Pass. This was where many allied forces landed from the sea, many lost their lives trying to escape the German onslaught, when we arrived we understood why.

The pass is a road down to the beach and rocky outcrop, it must be at least three hundred feet high, and the road winds itself down with hairpin bends similar to a ski run. We decided to drive down to get an idea of what it must have been like for those unlucky men marooned there. We had made a plan earlier to be spending the night on the beach, after a recce of the surroundings it was felt safe enough. We set up camp built a massive fire from driftwood, had some scoff a couple of beers, my stag on the guard roster was 0400hrs head down lights out. The sun came up around six as I took pleasure in waking the camp, we cooked breakfast full English. Around the perimeter of our camp, must have been a dozen wild dogs, vicious looking buggers, we left them the remains of our meal then set off back up the pass. Our three weeks would soon be up. Our final mission sounded hands on!!!

The task was to follow without being detected a regiment of enemy battle tanks. The patrol would take place through the following night, the object was to link up with our friendly tanks and guide them onto the enemy. This was going to be hard work for the Radio operators, using deciphering codes, interesting times ahead. Vehicles maintained oil levels topped up, equipment stowed and a new commander. He was a young man very nervous, he had been seconded to us from Tripoli for the experience. I hadn't reached my eighteenth birthday yet, but I felt I had a lot more experience than this young man. As the sun went down it soon became dark, we weren't moving off until around midnight when we would receive the signal from HQ that the enemy had been sighted. It was quite poignant, sat there imagining how it must have felt, waiting to go into action, we were just playing, twenty odd years ago, the anticipation the dread the raw fear, I guess the great camaraderie and friendship within the troops must have helped ease the stress levels, plus the training and professionalism with terrific leaders of men.

I was asleep on the side of the vehicle, when the SQN leader patted my arm, "We're on," he whispered, I was in the seat in a flash, no lights to be used, we were to be invisible. Using goggles to drive, you cannot imagine how difficult it is travelling behind a regiment of tanks in the desert. The bloody sand gets everywhere, just one thick cloud non stop. Driving using a periscope only would have helped but at night with no lights we felt we would have to suffer the sand. The night seemed endless, on and on up top the young commander was in full cry non stop on the radio passing on co-ordinates receiving coded grid references, he was put in at the deep end so to speak. Eventually the sun made an entrance, as dawn arrived, I tried to take in the enormity of the event unfolding around us, there were vehicles as far as the eye could see, all shapes and sizes, infantry dug into their foxholes, I wondered if we were winning or not, my man up top had no idea either, we were halted, I was busting for a pee, so I nipped out, quick leak. The message then came over the headsets exercise ends, you could hear the cheers all around us. We got out of the vehicle and I set about making a brew. My new buddy was checking the map, he was sure we had gone round in a massive circle and that camp was only a few miles up there he said!!! As I had been driving all night, my buddy offered to drive back to our HQ, I was quite happy to sit up top, enjoy the view, thats when it all went belly up!!

About fifty yards dead ahead was an abandoned infantry fox hole 6x3 and 2feet deep, I had the intercom at hand, but I didn't want to undermine my new driver. We were in line with this hole in the ground, Ferret scout cars were not the stable lest of vehicles, quite high, made them a little top heavy. We had lost a young man the previous year, when a car had rolled, killing him in the most gruesome fashion. It was too late the blind stupid bugger had driven straight into the hole, like I mentioned earlier I had been blessed with good fortune, was it to end here. The car toppled from side to side, lurching down then up as it reared out of the hole, my leg around the outer thigh was bleeding profusely caught on something sharp, what a bloody fiasco, I climbed down he was in total shock, shaking like a leaf, I radioed for assistance, a no duff message which the operator would realise was a genuine problem.

We tied a belt round my leg to stem the bleeding, the cars suspension was knackered, we called the lad boys out to recover it. After I had calmed down, had a fag. I went over to my buddy he was in a state, "it was an accident nothing else, not easy to spot those bloody fox holes, I should have warned you from up top." it seemed to settle him down. There was a thorough investigation into the cause of the damage to the car, my new buddy got a massive bollocking a right dressing down, he went back to Tripoli with his tail between his legs. I got exonerated and patched up, had nightmares for a few nights, but felt lucky to be alive, the lads thought I had a guardian angel looking over me, scary. We had a couple of crates of booze sent from the HQ Sqn with a message job well done, our last night in the desert, we built a fire with all the crates and discarded junk, the chefs roasted what they thought was a goat, and the party began. After a while a few old sweats were reciting a couple of legendary stories connected to this part of the world. The Tank commander during the desert campaign of the last war, who needed to move his bowels sharpish, unzipped his tank hood, legs akimbo and with great delight relieved himself.

After tidying himself, he set too with great haste to climb back into his tank suit zipped up, without delay pulling on his hood, only to find that he had crapped in it, the boys were howling pissing their pants, I was thinking actually it would be an easy mistake to make.

Another tank commander with the same problem got his suit off, then squatted to do the business, as he lifted himself up from the ground, he noticed attached to his scrotum a scorpion, legend has it he fainted with this creature dangling from his bits, he apparently recovered unharmed, I guess he would eat out on that story for a year or two.

And finally the SAS lad who got cut off behind enemy lines, after their patrol took a hit, he legged it, all he had was the clothes on his back, he went for days travelling at night, living off the dew among the shrubs, he made it back over one hundred miles, sat there it was difficult to imagine, how he would have managed. The endurance, fortitude, fitness levels, mental strength, all those qualities that make the SAS the elite of elite. A memorable evening, the end of a most rewarding three weeks, the memories I've stored in my head for my dotage a time to reflect, probably write them down on paper for my grandkids who knows!

Back to Combermere, back to the miserable weather, dark nights all the stuff we really love about dear old blighty. Even the beer, the warm beer here in Windsor we have to get used to it all over again. Christmas not far away, I check the orders board the guard rostas for crimble, I'm off for Christmas but on duty on New Years Eve, that's a bummer, but someone has to do it. Went home for the weekend, Pauline was pleased as punch with her present from Libya a pair of green pyjamas Arabian style, Mum was still spending a lot of time at the doctors, Dad said they had no idea what was causing her problems, she had lost the sight in one eye again which was a worry. I had a Regimental soccer trial the following weekend, we were to play the mounted regiment from London, for the Household Brigade trophy. It was the first round, it would be a grudge match against our sister regiment. We had also begun our trade tests, we were being tested and upgraded on our radio skills, this technology was always updating, therefore we had to keep pace with all the advances. The day of the game arrived, we looked the business in our new kit.

There was a definite needle between the sides, I thought it must have history and go back to encounters past. I was on the left wing, I got into a ruck with their right full back, we were both on our knees on the deck, I was behind him when he lashed out with the heel of his boot into my mouth. I can still picture that scumbag as he turned and smiled, smirking as my two front teeth were lying next to me on the pitch. I was rushed off to hospital for a tetanus jab. The nurse who applied the three injections was some butch klepto maniac, who pleasured herself at the thought of me screaming whilst at her mercy. I had to have three injections into my thigh, I'm not kidding when I say I had a bruise there for a month. I was then transferred back to Combemere to our own medical unit, my mouth was a bloody mess, my two front teeth missing, the gums shot, apparently gums are made up of tiny bones, my tiny bones were even tinier now crushed in fact. The dentist was summoned as I had become an emergency, he arrived I think he was quite shocked at the state of the injuries, jelly was rubbed onto the gums which acted as a numbing agent, the dentist proclaimed he couldn't do much more until the swelling went down, I was tucked into a bed given something to ease the pain. I remember wondering at nearly eighteen years of age in my prime, how was I going to manage without front teeth. It was a shock, I had always had great teeth took pride in them, now as I looked in a mirror reminded me of some clown in a circus. Being blessed with good fortune had certainly come to an end. I could only swallow liquids. My buddies were allowed to visit, which helped a little, you can imagine the song on all their lips, all I want for Christmas is my two front teeth. I completed my radio theory in hospital. I spent ten days in dock, the dentist could take the impressions for my false teeth, it sent shivers down me at the thought, it would be six weeks before they arrived. Six weeks without laughing or smiling and that is definitely not in my make up. I rang home with the news, Pauline was sorry and wished me well. I would see her at the weekend, put my looks to the test.

As I look back and recall the scrapes I got into this had to be the most devastating. But there's always someone worse off, that was my philosophy so move on!!! Six weeks took an age, but eventually the day dawned when my dental appointment took centre stage. The old dentist was a flaky old geezer, he would stand over me stinking of garlic bloody garlic, I think my loathing of garlic stems from him.

He fitted my new dentures they felt massive in my mouth. The dentist made some adjustments, he said they would bed in after a day or two, I looked hideous, Christmas came and went all jolly and merry, onward into 1965 all going to plan, bullshit here bullshit there, schemes on Salisbury plain and Righteous Brothers were number 1 with – Unchained Melody, things were going well, my teeth stood up to the rigours of an 18 year olds eating habits. Pauline was as lovely as ever, we enjoyed each others company, similar sense of humors, that was in Scarborough, in Windsor another lady came into my life, that is when every thing went tits up one more time.

Our troop was leaving for Melton Mowbray Leicestershire, we were going to test our radio's on a sky wave exercise, stayed for a couple of nights enjoyed the local pork pies, with a few beers, do all the necessary with the wireless, then started for home. We were driving through Aylesbury, I was tailing this Austin shooting brake for miles, I spied a young lady mincing up the footpath, she was gorgeous after a second or two of friendly banter, eyes back on the road, oh shit the car in front had stopped suddenly, and I couldn't, and into him I went, blondie up top was as much to blame as me as he'd been drooling over the skirt also. I started remonstrating with the driver of the Austin, when he turned around to face me with his dog collar in full view, a bloody vicar, his wife turned to him and said, 'we don't want any trouble,' which I thought at the time was strange. Blondie insisted we head for the nearest police station to report the accident, we instructed the vicar to do the same. He had a slight dent, we were unscathed, we left the cop shop after filling out the appropriate forms, no sign of our crash victims. Something odd about them two, not all they seem, I reckon I would have got away with it, if we had kept stum. Back at Combermere after the report I was sent for, I was to go up in front of the CO. he laid it on thick how important whilst being in charge of an AFV it was to be b'"" vigilant, I had obviously been distracted, therefore fined twelve pounds, and seven days confined to barracks, bugger it!! The Lord Raglan Pub was on the corner by the hospital, one of the nurses a bonny petite lass had come on strong, and we were seeing each other. When confined to barracks it meant just that, fatigues in the cookhouse. Followed at 10.30pm. by Parade at the guardhouse in best kit, best boots, the works, inspected by the orderly officer, after the inspection, it was back to the room at full gallop civvies on, then out the back gate up to the pub, I had got a message to Jane, saying I would be late. As we met I explained what had happened I told her I would have to be careful, didn't want anyone seeing me out, the following evening we followed the same pattern, lust conquers all I thought, eighteen years old you think your invincible, it would be around two in the morning when I left Jane, I straddled the back gate, when all hell broke loose. Spotlights came on a belligerent voice telling me to halt, on my knees down on the ground, I squinted could see rifles pointing at me it was an ambush someone had grassed me up, the whole guard were there to apprehend me, lads I knew well, silly bugger, daft prat, they whispered 'how did you think you would get away with it,' I spent the night in the cells, next morning guess what the CO wanted to see me again, twice in as many days, that bloody stupid vicar had set all this off. The CO was very disappointed in my actions, nothing for it but close arrest for a week march out. I was marched out double time, my tie, boot laces, and belt were taken from me in case I hung myself, straight to the barbers to be cut to the bone, then it was double march up to my room to collect all my kit, the lads were in my room, I wasn't allowed to speak or acknowledge them in any way, back down to the guard room into my cell I'm now a criminal, a convict.

My cell had a bed and a chair, I had to be escorted to the toilet, the loo had no doors all very basic. My kit had to be laid out and a full inventory carried out, any deficiencies had to be paid for, I was allowed two cigarettes per day. Everything had happened so quickly, someone had seen me with Jane. Corporal Bill Johnson was the regimental policeman, he was from Hull, not a bad lad I got to know him well and work with him later in my service. It was the degradation you felt the most, letting yourself down, letting your peers down, on reflection I look on this incident as an accident waiting to happen, young men irrational decisions, all part of the male process, but if you come out the other side a more rounded person then that experience is advantageous. The lads were in the room to greet me on my release, they were great took me out for a beer, it gave them the greatest pleasure to inform me that Jane had met a lad from the PARA's bollocks!!! I never let on at home, about the incident couldn't bring myself to spill the beans.

Chapter 4

England win World Cup...sex, but not as we know it and Civilian life

The year was moving on at a pace, a few of us went up to London one Saturday to watch Arsenal v Man Utd. enjoyed the game. I can't remember the score but I do remember George Best had a magical match what a player he was. Getting out of the ground was a nightmare 57,000 people my feet never touched the ground, if anyone had stumbled it would have been curtains.

We used to go up the smoke, or London quite often when not on duty, up to the Kings Road, Carnaby Street, wonderful clothes, 1965 the designs, colours, I bought all the mod gear, bell bottom trousers, tank tops, paisley shirts with amazing collars, high heeled boots, I had a pair of plum suede shoes loved em. The cricket season was upon us, Lt Petherick had taken cricket nets and I had caught his eye, I was selected for the regiment to play in London, had a successful day did well, a fortnight later the household Brigade were to play the M.C.C at Burton Court in London, home of the Chelsea Pensioners. I would be at home on leave, Lt Handbury sent for me, I had been selected, I explained my position, but I made it clear I would return to London to play in the match, he gave me the date, I would see him there. My dad was chuffed to bits, I was playing against the M.C.C and Colin Cowdrey would be taking the field as skipper.

Charlie Booth a lad from Scarborough a buddy, also in the regiment was on leave also, my dad would take the day off work, hire a car and Charlie would come too. We set off for London at 04.30am on the day of the match in a little black Ford Anglia heading down the M1. We arrived in plenty of time, the game was scheduled to start at 11.30am, arriving at the ground, the grounds man was busy rolling the wicket, dad and Charlie sat in the car as I made my way over with my kit, I met the groundsman,

"Lovely day for it," I said,

"For what" he said,

"Well the game." I said.

"The game" he said, "that was yesterday, had a great day."

You could have knocked me down with a feather, how was I to explain to dad. The grounds man couldn't believe I'd travelled all the way from Yorkshire, Dad shrugged it off like I knew he would bless him, we all burst out laughing. We decided to take a walk around the ground, get some air, Dad opened a gate for a lady with a small poodle, it was Katie Boyle my Dads favourite lady, it made his day he honestly felt it was worth the trip just to get that close to Katie Boyle. How do you make a mistake over a fixture, Lt Handbury had some explaining to do.

I never did get to the bottom of the cricket debacle, one blames the other.

Another incident I remember one you can relate to the 60's scary, Jim Edgar a buddy from the regiment and myself had met two girls at a club in Hackney Wick, East End of London. We arranged to meet them the following week a Friday. Jim borrowed a standard eight car off his mate, then onto London we did go, we hit the club at around nine, met the girls who were waiting for us, had a pleasant evening few beers, some food, good time all round, started out on our journey back to barracks, keeping to speed limits, gently making our way through Bethnal Green when this 3.2 litre Jaguar roared past, cut us up and his rear bumper got locked onto our front bumper. Two big guns in camel coats jumped out of their car, Jim to his credit eased himself out of the standard, it was a commotion f-ing and blinding, whose fault was it. Jim kept calm claiming he was innocent, the heavies were huffing and puffing, their mates in the car were chiming in "don't want no trouble, get it shifted" so we all got onto the Jag heaved, and it was off, they got straight in the car, gone just like that. Both of us white as sheets, it took some believing we were sure we had come upon gangsters, hoodlums, whatever I had a wager with Jim, I reckoned they would have known the Krays, how do we prove it. Another memorable episode could have gone tits up that one!!!

I have a confession to make, this incident would make it onto the Simon Mayo's radio programme, unfortunately I would be on guard duty on Christmas Day, pay back time, I thought for my extraordinary year, not to worry knuckle down keep my nose clean, clear my slate so to speak.

All my kit is bulled, polished ready for my duties, most of the boys have left for their jollies just a skeleton staff keeping the barracks ticking over, luckily for me Jimmy Harnett is on duty rosta too. Christmas Eve we thought we would walk up the town together call in the Lord Raglan, the Trooper, and get into the mood, join in the celebrations. We had a few in the Lord Raglan, lovely warm atmosphere, moved on up to the Trooper, over the road opposite the pub was a house full of hippies, junkies, Jim thought we should go round the back of the house for a nosey, we arrived at the back door it was open, there was no one around deserted, we had a quick shufti, mattresses on the floors, candles in bottles, the place stank of stale smoke a typical commune. On the cooker in the kitchen were all the vegetables Prepared for the lunch tomorrow, with the bird in the oven. We just looked at each other then set about ruining their efforts, washing powder in the veg, washing up liquid inside the bird what a bloody mess. We legged it, quickly through the gate, forget the Trooper went back to the Raglan. I've often recalled those events with utter dread, the next day we both were ashamed of our actions, I was on the main gate on Christmas day, never got any feed back relating to the incident. I was pleased to see the back of 1965 it had proved to be a difficult year all round, growing up quickly would be my resolution for 1966. In the middle of the January we were sent a memo that sent shivers down the back.

At the end of May we were going overseas, B Sqn to Hong Kong, C Sqn to Malaya, Borneo and A Sqn to Singapore, we were to be away from England for two and a half years. It took some time to sink in, I got engaged to Pauline and set a date for the wedding 7th May, we would get married quarters in Serenban Malaysia exciting stuff. It was all hands on deck for the regiment a great deal to organise, we would be taking over from the Queens own Hussars who were coming home. We spent a lot of time on Salisbury Plain, I was now driving a Saladin armoured car 76mm gun.30 browning machine gun mounted, six wheels go anywhere vehicle great to drive, nothing much argued with you on the open road. We were learning new skills, we would be heading for a jungle environment totally new to us. C Sqn would be heading for Borneo, Sarawak, which was still an active Theartre of War, this was going to be the real test, we would be working alongside the Royal Marines 40 and 42 Commando giving protection and support, therefore it was back to the drawing board on Salisbury Plain. There was a buzz about the squadron.

There would be five troops of Saladin AFV's and Ferret scout cars, with a 6th troop who would take an infantry roll. After a full day in the field it was time for some scoff and beer round the fire. The mail had arrived from HQ and I had two letters from Pauline which I thought a little odd. I opened them in sequence, and the flowers for the church had been ordered, everything was in place, I opened the second letter and a sledgehammer hit me, it was all off, she couldn't go through with the wedding, I was mortified, devastated to say the least. The boys in the troop kept out of my way for a while, Tommy Alderson my corporal helped to calm me down, what was I to do, I eventually got to a phone but it was no use there was no going back. It took a long time to get over that Dear John another learning curve. As I recall those days, I guess it was a daunting time for a young girl leaving home, not sure of the future I was only a trooper the money not substantial it was probably my ego that suffered the most, I guess Pauline made the right call.

We left London airport on the 29th May travelling in a Bristol Britannia, or the whispering giant as they were known, three legs stopping off at Abadan, Bombay and Colombo, all the boys were sat together, I remember China, crockery, steel knifes, forks and spoons how the other half lived. Eventually we arrived in Singapore after a tiring flight, we were taken to Neesoon, a garrison where all the new guys arrive. To be checked out and sort out the provisions of jungle kit, olive green shirts, shorts and long jungle boots, we were issued with everything jungle. A company of Ghurkas guarded the garrison, it was a sight to see them making their way to the guard room for inspection, walking stiff legged so as not to ruin the creases in their uniforms, great little fellas a credit to their species. After duties that first day in Neesoon, we tried out the local brew, at a bar outside the gates, Tiger Beer or Lion Beer with a drop of lemonade known as a pint of tops. The temperature at night was also quite impressive very humid took some getting used to. After the initial acclimatisation in Neesoon, it was off to the jungle warfare school Kota Tingi just South of Jahore Baru. We were going to learn how to survive in the Jungle or Ulu as it is known in local circles. Also doing the course were young American boys on their way to Vietnam. These young lads not quite sure, a little anxious still full of American swagger, with long cigars and shades. I definitely would not have swapped venues with these yanks, and I wondered how many would be going home zipped up inside a bag. It was a very interesting 10 days.First up playing hide and seek against the Ghurkas no contest.

They would go off and set an ambush, we would learn the hand signals required then set off in patrol mode taking turns as leading scout. They would have seen us in no time at all, but they enjoyed baiting us. We got within a few feet of them without realising, not until they showed the whites of their teeth with laughing, one of our lads a bit thick at the best of times, fired his rifle from about ten feet even with blank ammo this was a foolish act, the Ghurkah was definitely not laughing when he appeared from the ambush lifted the young man by the scruff of his neck. The other Ghurkhas stepped in to rescue our man, not for the faint hearted. We learnt how to build our own sleeping quarters or bashers out of attap, a long local grass from the dense undergrowth. Mosquitos were a real problem, these little buggers were the cause of many problems for the rookie squaddies, Paladrine a pill was the antidote, taken once a day, this would hopefully stave off the malaria. After duties one evening we organised a barbi and soccer match against the yanks, it was a great success, and seemed to relieve a lot of tensions, the strain was telling on some of the Americans as they were getting news of all the casualties coming out of Vietnam. We had an interesting morning listening to an Australian guy, a doctor, he enlightened us to the fact we could live off most of the plants and trees around us, if you were constipated, had the runs, a sore throat, all those kind of symptoms there was a cure at our fingertips. The problem was remembering the right leaf or grass, it would be a problem taking the cure for constipation or the runs or vice versa. He also brought with him a jar of leeches, he explained that eight of these left on a human body overnight would kill the poor sod, they are strange creatures, but in the right hands could be quite useful. It had been an informative course very useful to have the information stored, hopefully we wont need to bring it to our attention, we had a few drinks in the NAAFI with the Yanks, wished them all well and a safe tour, God be with them.

I was part of four troop, L/CPL Dave Moss-Norbury my commander up top in the Saladin, we were to fly to Kuching compliments of the New Zealand Airforce part of the ANZAC contingent in Sarawak. We landed in Kuching the capital, this is where the fun will kick in. Our troop climbed aboard a three tonner, we were going to be travelling down a black road, the itinerary suggested the black road could become a war zone. Our personal weapon was a sterling machine gun and we had been issued with a magazine of ammo, we were heading to a camp known as Wong Padong or 'Wonkers', it was 90 miles down this bloody road, we were shitting ourselves. Every bend, it was the most terrifying trip ever. The reason we were here in Borneo was to do with a General Sukharno who was head of the Indonesian Communists, he had tried in 1962 by military means to extend his borders into Sarawak.

The British with their interests in the area intensified their forces including those of Australia and New Zealand.

The SAS and Ghurkas followed by the Royal Marines had bared the brunt of these attacks, repelling the Communist regime, by the time we arrived it was a case of mopping up the Communist threat and displaying hearts and mind skills. We arrived inside the perimeter wire drained but relieved, Captain Petherick gathered up the troop, COH Fincken gave us the run down, with immediate effect we would be taking over our vehicles signing for them equipment and all. The Saladins were full of live rounds a poignant reminder this was no joke, with all the vehicles and stores, we made our first patrol to our new home the observation point 30 minutes down the road from wonkers, this would be our home for a month. We were to be armoured protection and cover to 40 and 42 commando, they were living dug in underground over the way from our camp. They were observing the Indonesians every move. We parked up the vehicles ensuring each gun had an arc of fire, so we covered the whole perimeter, we had to stand our own guard that first evening it was quite scary but hilarious too. COH Fincken posted me by the side of this banana plantation, explaining my route; I was there in this godforsaken hole imagining all kinds of scenarios, when the Banana palms started swaying. Bloody hell I thought its them the enemy, my heart was racing keep calm I kept saying to myself, I had a full magazine, then from behind the palm looking at me full of wonder a bloody big grey monkey, I picked up some stones and let fly laughing out loud.

Our camp was quite basic, the living quarters had a few chairs and a couple of tables, small kitchen area where our chef Smudger Smith hung out making up his gastronomic delights. Sleeping quarters, mosquito nets, camp beds small lockers. Captain Petherick and COH Fincken had small rooms adjacent very five star. Ablution block outside across from the main quarters, and in between the two, was a badminton court made out of used browning ammunition belts, with racquets and shuttle cocks on sight. As the days passed, we got into a routine no worries, our supplies were brought up from Wonkers, the weather at this time of year June was warm, beginning to get a decent tan. The marines made contact and invited us to their bunkers for a darts and dominoes evening. They had every facility, amazing, it was very cozy they had a bar with everything laid on, we made a couple of trips, socially a great bunch of rough buggers. They were using the new armourlite rifles, their arsenal was unbelievable.

The Indonesian border ran parallel to our camp, the Marines sent patrols out every day, they invited us to join them on a patrol to a border crossing, a couple of the boys tagged along, setting off before dawn, they were totally knackered on return, branding the marines as total nutters, they doubled all the way to the border four miles, all quiet no commies so they doubled all the way back, very memorable one lad took his camera got some terrific pics. After a couple of weeks a little Chinese fellow turned up on his bike, he'd been sent from Wonkers to cut our hair, it was really hot now, so I told him to take all my hair off, he hadn't come prepared, but he persevered. I got one side off without much trouble, he couldn't strop his razor to sharpen it. He took as much off with his scissors he then finished the rest with my battery operated Philishave what a bloody fiasco, my head was bleeding in places really sore, it felt strange having no hair, after a couple of days I was pleased to have had it done quite refreshing a lot cooler.

I was cleaning the ablution block this particular morning, singing and whistling away not a care in the world, with my bass brush going ten to the dozen, when glancing up I spied, looking down at me a bloody snake, I dropped the brush shot out of the bogs to get the lads, 'come and see this!' I screamed, they gingerly followed me in, there it was about 6 feet long, shiny black with yellow rings wrapped round its body, the boys were impressed, keeping our distance we were deciding our course of action. After hearing all the commotion into the block strode COH Fincken resembling John Wayne, 'stand back lads, let the dog see the rabbit' as he slid his machete out of its sheath, 'can't be too careful with these reptiles,' this reptile was curled up on a section of the framework in total command, our intrepid leader went for the lunge, hack option, the snake with complete nonchalance ducked his head under the weapon. COH Fincken then dropped his weapon ran out of the block in total panic, some lads followed him in total disarray, the rest who stayed found it hilarious, it was only a snake after all.

I picked up the bass brush and with careful aim did for the poor beautiful creature. We found out later after examination of the remains that it had been a tree snake, harmless lived on small birds and rodents, it was a sad end to what was a disturbing but funny incident. On one of the days we took the AFV's on to live firing exercises to keep our gunnery up to scratch, we arrived at an abandoned quarry, with extremely high cliff walls, made an excellent target area. We had not been there long before a crowd of locals had turned up and there was a slight problem keeping them from the target, the moment we started firing those 76mm shells at the rock face, that kept them back, they had never experienced anything like the sheer ferocity those shells displayed, it was great fun practicing the gunnery skills it had been a while, after obliterating the quarry we drove to camp to clean all the gunnery equipment. A few days before we were due to leave our O.P, I was sent on a dashing mission, Paddy McIvor had been brought up from Wong Padong, I had to get him to

Kuching Airport for him to catch a plane home, his mother was dying. Dave Moss-Norbury and Paddy were up top as we set out in my Saladin.

We were on the limit to catch the plane, it was foot down, don't spare the horses. Exhilarating stuff powering along in a twelve ton AFV, we were approaching a river suspension bridge I could see this car approaching, I was flashing my lights but the bugger kept coming, it was going to be close, it was one of those moments, shut your eyes, hope for the best, I heard a scrape of metal as we passed each other, onward we thundered, arrived at the airbase they had kept the plane ticking over on the tarmac as Dave had kept in contact by radio, Paddy shook my hand, "Great piece of driving man, wouldn't have missed the buzz of that drive for nothing." Dave drove it back, I was knackered.

The newly formed Malaysian Army took over the O.P. we wished the marines well and motored back down the road to Wonkers. Wong Padong our new home, the camp stretched upward and onward the Troop huts at the top, were wooden rectangular buildings, taking in two troops of men to one building, they were airy comfortable beds with mosquito nets attached. Our AFV's were parked strategically above us, concentrating on an area of fire through the perimeter fence.

Down the hill we had the armouries, stores and workshop, the dobi wallahs, and Mr Abdul Ghani, his famous Tea shack became the focal point of the camp, Abdul gave us tick, he stocked Heinz baked beans and soups, home from home. The OP's room was keeping us posted regarding the World Cup back home in England. Come on England was the cry. Along from the troop huts to the left was the NCO's Mess, shrouded under a massive tree, to the unsuspecting visitor this could prove to be a scary experience, perched high up in the tree attached to a long rope was Charlie, a grey monkey, quite large about 3' tall he would jump down and scare the living daylights out of you. Out of the blue you would hear a scream or a "get off you bastard monkey", an every day occurrence, we had taken him over from the last mob. I can't really imagine how many regiments he would have seen come and go.

In our particular hut we had a small monkey also, he was quite tame, in the roof of the huts were beams which stretched across the whole roof, he would spend his nights on those beams, living off the bugs, there was some amazing bugs, apart from mosquitoes we had the infamous flying frogs, they were hideous, hence the name they resembled the look of a frog, they had no mouth, only lived for a month living off their own body fat. How and why they ever evolved is a mystery, however as nightfall arrived so did these little buggers.

We would be tucked up under our nets, you would hear this buzzing very much akin to the VI bombs that blitzed London, Buzz Buzz then it would stop, and you knew it had landed on someone's bed, our little monkey bless him would catch these frogs in mid air, and start to eat them forthwith, chomp, chomp, finishing off his meal. I don't know which was worse the buzzing or the chomping. The mosquitoes obviously posed a far more serious problem, it was very important to take the paladrine tablets each day, for some of the lads who were restless sleepers they really suffered, boys with arms and legs stuck out of their nets were covered in bites the next morning, there was no escaping the odd bite which did irritate, but to be covered must have been purgatory, it meant M.O's and hassle.

Our days were filled with patrols, maintenance, soccer. We organised a game of soccer against our native trackers the Ibans and Dyaks, lovely people, loved the Brits enjoyed their rolls, very courageous hard working tough as old boots. We arrived at the ground or Padang, where they lived with their families, just down the road from Wonkers, we were kitted out in Adidas boots, shin pads, the works. Come on England, they took the field in bare feet, hard as nails could kick a ball with as much venom and power as us Puffs in our Adidas boots. A memorable day in prospect as we set off down the river in a flat bottomed assault craft, on paper this was a river patrol, in reality we were taking the medic to visit a longhouse to check out the families

A little hearts and mind operation, we had two Iban trackers front and rear, or bow and stern, armed with twelve bore pump action guns, we had SLR's or Self Loading Rifles. Our tracker at the front took aim into the river and fired, there was a splashing in the river then the gaff was applied and there it was this green monster being hauled aboard an iguana, then as we glided under the canopy, the Iban on the stern took aim and fired, two squirrels, we just sat in awe of these marksmen, they obviously knew where to find their prey, but hitting it is one thing, they also cut grasses from the river, by the time we arrived our boat was like a floating general store.

We were made very welcome by the chief of this particular tribe of Dyaks, we also were very respective, after making the vessel safe we headed to the long house. This structure measured 50 yards in length, built on stilts ten feet off the ground, each family had an area sectioned off along the whole building, with a communal area at either end. Pigs lived under the structure with hens strutting about also, we were led to a communal area made to sit cross legged on rush mats awaiting lunch, which would consist of the iguana, squirrel and lettuce from the river including pork, couldn't wait. Before the meal was ready, we were invited to partake in a drink, enter arak and tuak rice wine.

The meal arrived, prepared and placed into dishes we were asked to help ourselves, I can state categorically there was no great rush to finish the iguana, it would have been disrespectful not to have tasted what had been prepared, it was different not every day you get the opportunity to feast on lizard, compliments to the chef it tasted like chicken. More wine, a glow was steadily appearing, I had noticed some young boys with marbles, I introduced myself, then taking the marbles into the circle, set upon explaining the rules. Take one marble try to knock out marbles from the circle, the person with the most marbles is the winner. I added some spice to the proceedings by placing a dollar bill under each marble in the circle, the young boys were really excited now. I thought with it being a new game they wouldn't have much idea, the boys came haggling for which order they should go in, I made them queue, then off we went, the first young lad shuffled up to the line placed the marble on his fingernail, and flicked it at the target, to his delight and my astonishment he obliterated two marbles, like lightening he scooped up two dollars a smile from one side of his gob to the other. These young boys were obviously marble sharks, and within ten minutes had skint me, more wine, the medics were doing a good job, had a queue of patients, usual stuff runny eyes and noses, coughs, ointments for sores, tablets for upset tummies.

We were given a tour of the longhouse, in all the family bedrooms strapped to the bed was a fighting cock, the Dyaks favourite sport was cock fighting, apart from attacking and killing their neighbours. Outside the main entrance to the house hung a net full of skulls, these are from battles against other tribes, the chief did assure us that was in the past, many years had passed since anything untoward had happened, he showed us one of the blow pipes they use for hunting. It was a giant pea shooter, they were so accurate. To end our visit we went to the local cock fight, the men with their cocks, displaying sharpened knives tied to their feet, bundles of money changing hands before a fight.

The rules a large circle with a line through the centre, the cocks are held by their handlers goading each other until a bell sounds, then they let go, the loser either dies or turns its back on its opponent. We watched three fights didn't last long a few seconds, blood and guts everywhere. Not to be recommended. The medics had run out of medicines, it was time to leave, one more glass of wine, toast our very hospitable hosts. I made my way unsteadily I have to say, with kids hanging from me, I had made some friends, they must have thought I was an easy touch. I lifted myself into the boat, as it screwed round to leave immediately I fell out into the river, to this day I still have shivers thinking of the next few seconds, I felt the propeller shave my arm as they hauled me in, the slightest graze appeared, that incident soon sobered me up. I had been so lucky it could have been so different. The medics gave me a tube of antiseptic cream to apply to the graze on by arm, after being in the river not knowing what lurgies lurk in there.

I received mail from home, Mum had been diagnosed with an illness they call multiple sclerosis, sounds awful, Dad said the flying frog I had sent her through the post had nearly seen her off, a pang of guilt shot through me. Dad wrote explaining with difficulty how Mum's health had got worse, she was struggling to keep going to work, that wasn't the news I really wanted to hear.

The weapons from my Saladin were due for the amourers inspection, therefore we stripped them out of the vehicle taking them to the workshop. There had been rumours of people trying to break into the camp through the wire, how odd I could understand people trying to break out not in. That night after a beer or two it was under the net into the bed as usual. I had just dropped off to sleep, when I was awakened by an almighty explosion, followed by a starburst, fucking hell, people were bellowing outside Positions, in the event of an emergency like this personnel have to clear the huts, find their own designated space, I would be making for my vehicle, but first I had to get my kit on, panic total bloody panic two legs down one trouser leg, what a joke eventually make it to the AFV there's total mayhem. One lad has been run over by a Ferret scout car, there's firing onto the fence, people shouting orders, our crew all present and correct sir, in position over looking our arc of fire, then I remember our weapons are with the armourers.... bollocks, keep stum its only a practice.

At the debrief the next morning it turns out the local lads who cut hair break out of camp as they please, go for a shag down the road and break back in again, only this evening the troop were waiting for them. Put the fear of Allah up em! Us also, there was an inquiry into why the lad had been run over, over zealousness the cause, that wouldn't make the bugger in pot feel any better. It had been an interesting exercise however, showing up a few flaws. That evening everyone was having a beer we were all on edge, England were playing Germany in the World Cup Final we were expecting the result around eleven o'clock.

Great excitement as the news filtered through ... England 4 Germany 2, what a result, it put a spring in everyone's step, World Champions couldn't believe it, then to cap it all my Saladins gear box seized up. My vehicle and I were transferred by scammell heavy recovery vehicle to Simenggang a town about an hours drive away.

It was common practice that if a vehicle had to go to command workshops then the driver accompanied it, I was quite pleased and excited at the thought of seeing a woman again, it had been weeks, no months since I'd had the pleasure of a ladies company away from these hairy arsed squaddies. We left early the following morning, just as the kids from the Padangs were setting out to school. These boys and girls would pop out of the jungle absolutely spotless, Daz white shirts, with navy shorts or skirts, it always amazed me to see the urchins so happy and smiling, beautifully turned out a credit to their parents care and attention.

Simenggang was a bustling little town full of modern shops, we found the workshops got the Saladin parked up, the mechanic, Ted Drummond a Yorkie from Selby showed me to my quarters, very nice too, clean sheets and towels, we had a separate eating area, with bloody table cloths, this was the real McCoy five star service.

Life was relaxed within the compound, left to our own devices, no one with rank shouting the odds very civilized indeed. We had a dhobi wallah next door, two very fit young ladies, washing and pressing the boy's kit, these Asian girls were exotic, sexy everything a young trooper desired. I was hoping my vehicle would take a while to repair. I enjoyed the freedom of this place, being able to spend some quality time relaxing, swimming in the pool after work which started early and finished early. The gearbox was assessed, it was too damaged to repair, one had to be sent from the UK, which would take a week then two days to fit, what a bummer I thought, grinning like a Cheshire cat. We were having a beer after work, the sun was setting, beautiful sunset. I could hear live music coming from a bar up the street, it was quite visible from where we were in the compound, on the microphone with her back to us, was this female singer, her singing wasn't worth a mention. Its what she was wearing that caught the eyes attention. She had long black hair, wavy type down to the crack of her arse, a silky little number for a top, and leopard skin tights. From here after a few beers she looked like a million dollars, I thought to myself I'm going to have some of that. After consuming our meal on our lace tablecloths, quick shower, smelly on the shirt, jeans attached and zipped, I was off to investigate this mysterious being.

The boys had warned me about the local whores, a high percentage of squaddies had caught the clap or gonorrhea, with the odd unlucky sod catching syphilis. They also warned me about the local curfew, from 10pm until 7am, the local police often patrol these zones. I had my Johnnies or condoms in my pocket, stay cool, nothing silly, my motto, I entered the bar it all went out the window. It was 8.30pm, a few people sat round Donovan was playing on the juke box, 'mellow yellow,' I ordered a beer, sat down at a table breathing in the atmosphere, there was a couple of squaddies sat around with what I imagined to be the local girls, then the singer I had spotted turned up. I ordered another beer and whatever the singer was having the barman poured out a port and lemon, the lady accepted, sang a number Shirley Bassey I remember, then came over to my table thanking me for the drink. By this time, I had downed a few beers and was quite relaxed, up close she was actually a bit rough, the old complexion was suffering, and the teeth, if she had a white one she would have had a snooker set, but the ruby lipstick made up for it, it's the old adage the more beers I consumed the bonnier she became.

We had another couple of drinks, the time was creeping up to curfew.

I had this feeling she knew about my ulterior motive, I asked her where she lived, and could I walk her home, she mentioned the curfew and how dangerous it might become, with a gallon of Tiger beer inside me, I was thinking positives, faint heart never won the lady, who dares wins. The intoxication was winning the argument. Hand in hand we set off for her home, walking up a metal road one minute, then off into the dense jungle up a track, shit I was beginning to wonder if she was going to be worth all this covert stuff, in a clearing up ahead three or four huts appeared quite small, in we went and there sat in the small lounge was I presumed mum and dad. As I looked around this little room, my eyes were fixed on the fireplace, resting on it was bottle of Guinness, and above a picture of the Queen that's our Queen Elizabeth, how quaint, father was very nervous at the sight of me getting quite excited with his daughter, he could speak English and in no uncertain terms made it clear that the police could come at anytime during the night and everyone would be punished, I was sobering up at a pace, feeling like shit, should I go now, the girl thought no, and dragged me into her lair. I didn't even know her name, or she mine, it occurred to me probably that was a good thing.

In the tiny bedroom there was a mattress on the floor, a shelf with a curtain across, worked as a wardrobe. I looked into her eyes, Christ I thought she was ugly, what was I doing here with this, she undressed and climbed into what was nothing more than a sack, my mind went back to when I was a kid in Seamer, going to the threshing days watching the men carry sacks of corn up granary steps, I undressed leaving my socks on in case, and slipped inside the sack. She was ugly, god she was, ugly, she had her own aroma sweat, nothing sensual more like beetle juice, she was bony. I laid there plotting my next move, she was snoring when I made my decision, bugger the curfew, I couldn't stand this a moment longer, got dressed made my way to the door, thank goodness it opened, I checked the coast was clear, and made off, dogs were barking, I was shaking with fright, hoping the path I was following was correct, it was bloody dark in that jungle, my senses were straining every fibre, I kept on the track until I eventually reached the road, I know it wasn't far to the compound from here, I stooped down listened for a while, it all seemed quiet, I made a dash for it and reached the compound undetected. My heart rate was racing as I collapsed on my bed.

I went for a quick shower, I was sure there must have been lice in that bloody sack, I relived the evening as I laid having a fag in bed. I had got away with it; this process of growing up, the challenges, mine fields out there to fall into, and it's a demanding job. I was contemplating the next challenge, then well earned sleep intervened, what a night.

Captain Petherick and COH Fincken called in at the workshop to get an update on the gearbox, it should be here tomorrow, the chief technician informed us. I should be back up at wonkers within the week. I told Captain Petherick life here at the workshops had been an ordeal, quite boring really nothing much to do outside work, I would be with them by the end of the week. The young Dobi girl was getting braver by the day, very cheeky too. She was lovely, enjoyed having a coffee and a biscuit with me on a morning for her break, I knew time was of the essence, I asked her if she would fancy seeing a movie this evening showing over the road, "ok" she quipped "why not, you good man." she would be a little younger than me around 17yrs, long hair, lovely eyes, tucked into a chubby round face. We enjoyed the flicks, I escorted her home, it must be part of their culture, her mother a little old lady welcomed us into her living room, with a double bed and a cot at the end. Nothing of this nature had entered my head, she was an innocent young lass in my eyes, her mum brought us tea, after the ordeal of the other night, this was totally bizarre, her mum, I'm sure was wanting us to hook up. Being a young lad with everything in working order I found it confusing, but amusing, my friend then asked if I would like to stay the night, I had nothing else planned, then I had this uneasy feeling. Where was the mother going to sleep.

Mother then left us, so we undressed and got into the big double bed, I was uncomfortable with all this, the light went out, as I laid there the door opened, mother quietly entered the room slid into the cot at the end of our bed. Could you bring yourself to imagine this occurrence at home in England, you in bed with your girlfriend, and her mother. I can with hand on heart inform you all, nothing of a sexual nature took place that evening. I have fond memories of that young lady, she was hoping to become a hotel manageress one day.

Back to Wonkers, what an amazing few days, as I drove back I was recalling events, and thinking we only come this way once, make the most of all opportunities, life's too short, bollocks enjoy it. We were going to be leaving Sarawak shortly, it was time to hand over the reins to the Malaysian armed forces.

We had served our time in Sarawak, which meant we would be entitled to the General Service Medal with Borneo clasp, an active service gong, not that we had seen much action. My active service action was in that bloody sack. We were to drive the vehicles down the mountain to the ferries in Kuching. On the orders board was a memo that caught my eye. Anyone wishing to go on a months leave at Christmas apply within, it was going to cost me £400 for a month at home, I bit their hands off, I had saved most of my pay, but I realised that £400 was a lot of wedge, but money is not everything, seeing mother again in her condition was top priority.

Captain Petherick had been a brick on this tour so far, a top man held the respect of all the troop to a man, he must have friends in high places, he had arranged for the troop a weeks R & R leave on an uninhabited island off the West coast of Malaysia Tiomen. We would be flown in as this port of paradise had an airstrip, it was rumoured one white man lived on the island, it was also mentioned that parts of the musical South Pacific were filmed there. It had been arranged that we would smuggle our two monkeys into our next home Paroi Camp Seremban. They would spend the next few days inside the vehicles whilst on the ferry. One of the lads had dressed the small monkey in a khaki uniform he looked a picture, poor little bugger.

We thought this was the right course to steer as we knew that the Malays eat monkeys. It was the monsoon season when we started packing everything up rain, rain everyday you could set your clock by it. Eventually it was time to depart, when just out of the blue my hydraulics failed, the brakes and steering just as we left the camp. I decided I could manage the beast, our LAD sergeant said he would keep an eye on proceedings, what a trip my arms were shot by the time we reached the docks, I deserved another bloody medal, something else to tell the grandkids. Round hairpin bends down slopes a nightmare. We were to sail in the Empire Gannett a military ferry, there were tons of these ferries chugging around the oceans of the world all named after birds.

It took twenty four hours sailing to Singapore, the monkeys were being looked after they had survived this far. Another memorable sight, the flying fish landing on the deck, not that it did them much good. I spent ages throwing them back. My vehicle was taken to some local garrison workshops, this time without me, bugger. I had to cadge a lift with Roger Taylor, in his Saladin. Paroi Camp, Seremben 200 miles from Singapore, this would be civilization as we used to know it, but not yet, our troop under the guidance of our resolute leader were off on our jollies, swimming, sunbathing, snorkeling, Bali Hi.

We took off from Paroi camp in two chipmunks courtesy of the army air corps. We were carrying all our own food and booze to last us five days, R & R rest and recuperation, good old Captain Petherick or 'Feather prick' as he was affectionately known. It was amazing flying at around 1000ft, great views in the clear skies with our island in sight, the airstrip visible, down we went for a week of nothing to do but nothing. Tiomen was absolutely deserted, the airstrip ran parallel with the beach, there was a couple of decent sized cabins where we slung our beds and nets, we lit a fire which we kept going for the duration, the sea was just as you imagine it from the 'bounty' advertisement, plus just below the sea was one of the most beautiful corral reefs in South East Asia. I remember sitting on the beach on one of the days and remarking, 'I can imagine this place becoming a major tourist centre in the future, well today it hosts holiday makers in their thousands. We were like the pioneers checking out this virginal paradise, as I sat there with the rainforest creeping down to the beach, thinking it won't stay as idyllic as this, we had such a great time, words fail me. The days just flew by, the only downside to the week, Trooper Jock Ballsaille, a portly scots lad, whilst hauling himself back into the boat, the clasp of his new Rolex watch unclipped and the watch slid off his wrist into the briny, we hunted for that watch for days with no luck, £450 down the bloody drain was all Ballsaille would utter. I wonder if that Rolex is still ticking today. Back to the real world, Seremban, a bustling town about 40 miles from Kuala Lumpur the capital of Malaysia. There had been our two monkeys, firstly our little friend with his uniform, the boys put him on a long lead and took him outside their huts, he immediately climbed a pylon electrocuted himself fell back to Earth as a cinder, one down all that effort and heartache, Charlie, while we had been away, crossed the line, causing an international incident. On the camp in those days to keep the grass under control we, or the army employed young Tamil girls armed with sickles, Charlie being Charlie remembering his old antics, decided one day to jump onto one of these girls, to his credit I wouldn't have minded jumping on a couple myself. The girl hysterical, as you could imagine, was quickly whisked away rumour had it that to cause no further embarrassment a kangaroo court was established, Charlie was taken to a tree, blindfolded and with a cigarette between his lips shot. Relations between the Tamil population and the MOD quickly improved and they got back to normal. RIP Charlie.

Mick Folding was another mate, enjoyed his life in the regiment, he had the pleasure of being attached to 6 troop whilst in Seremban, one of the leading lights, or was that scouts. Mick arrived on a motor bike, a Matchless 500, I bet he still has it today, it had a really macho roar, turned heads that machine. This particular weekend Mick asked me if I fancied a run into Seremban, a few beers and a jump, 'go on then,' I said, 'anything to oblige a pal,' I had been looking after my hygiene, the MO had slipped me this tube of cream with a nozzle several inches long, it was to be used up to 24hrs after intercourse. Off we roared leaving Paroi in our wake. Mick said he'd been tipped off about these sisters who were up for a good time. We parked the machine, then Mick strode out to this address how bizarre, these two girls appeared they were twins identical in matching sari's, I don't like yours, I whispered.

After crossing their palms with silver they escorted us to an awaiting cubicle. Draped between this cubicle was a curtain, that's all that separated the four of us. As the saries hit the floor, we were both muttering adjectives 'what the hell are they?' came from the opposite cubicle as tears were flowing down my face at the sight of my dreamboat, Micks lady under her sari daintily flaunted a pair of men's Y front under garments, whereas mine looked quite fetching in a pair of England soccer shorts, keeping my mind on the job at hand was difficult enough, made even worse by the moans and groans next door. I appeared a few minutes after Mick, 'a bit premature were you mate?', 'something to work on' I quipped; he reckoned my bird was more of a turn on in her Bobby Charlton shorts. After our brief encounter (apologies for the pun) it was back to camp and to the shower block, this was going to be tricky, I thought eyes watering already, I hadn't mentioned the tube of cream to Mick, when he saw it in my hand his mouth dropped, I inserted the nozzle up the pipe of my 'willy' and gently squeezed the tube I didn't know whether to laugh or cry it was a severe burning sensation, Mick declined my offer, of the tube. Another memorable day.

The people reading the accounts of my life so far, must think especially at this stage in Seremban, that we were just a bunch of sex maniacs, yes it does appear that way, let me put your mind at rest, we were strapping young men, who worked hard and played hard, it's a totally different culture out in S.E Asia. What people took for granted out there, would be frowned upon at home, also the climate lends itself to this form of pleasure, warm balmy evenings, in the grey austerity of England People went out for a few pints, fish and chips. In Seremban it was a few beers and a cuddle. Who was I to try and change their ways.

I took a trip to the orderly room this day and paid for my leave to blighty for Christmas, apparently only four of us would be travelling. Something to look forward to, things were looking up, I had been selected for the next cadre course, promotion more money. I had to get my kit sorted out, back to bullshit. Jimmy Harnett and Charlie Booth were selected also. The married lads were looking forward to their wives joining them tomorrow, the married quarters were outside the camp, but very modern and tasty by all accounts. I was thinking Pauline would probably have been coming, wasn't to be move on. Pat Lundie a good mush, we became good mates whilst in Seremban decided we would check the town out give it the once over, the usual array of bars, shops, restaurant, the weather had cleared over the last few days, the monsoon giving way to sunny days with pleasant humid evenings. After a few beers we came across what was to become another bolt hole of mine. Anna's massage parlour, these premises were strictly off limits to M.O.D personnel, Pat bid me farewell took a cab back to camp, I could see his point his missus was due tomorrow, he had all his love saved up for her, I thought well it's a shame seeing I've come all this way crossed the road, opened the door signed 'welcome' inside it was like a doctors waiting room, a petite oriental lady popped into the waiting area, next please. As you entered the parlour, you had to book in and pay, ten bucks or £4.00 for a massage that's full frontal and back and a happy ending. I ordered a beer sat down checking out the clientele, mostly squaddies, with a couple of locals thrown in. This young thing came hopping and skipping over to me, 'would I please follow,' this is all new to me, but my back had been giving me some problems. I can recommend ANNA's parlour, my back clicked in no time.

Our cadre course began on the Monday, was to take two weeks, bloody marching, drilling the squad, inspecting the squad, addressing the course with a lecture lasting at least 30 mins, to be honest it was good fun, our instructor was brilliant a naturally funny man. I'm really sorry that I can not remember his name, he deserved to be remembered, for making that course the success it proved to be. Everyone passed, we had to watch this space. CambraI Day, arrived, it meant a day off, in remembrance of the Battle of CambraI 1917. 1918, when tanks were used for the first time in battle.

We went swimming, next to the married quarters in the public baths it was a massive pool, full of squaddies and their wives, Jimmy and Pat introduced us to their spouses, it hit me how white and anemic they looked, but they were looking forward to their new life in Malaysia, I decided after swimming, to head back, quick change, something to eat, went for a beer or two, nothing outrageous, I had this niggle in my back again and wondered if I should get it seen too. As I was waiting in the room, reading the Straits Times, my chaperone appeared a different lady, this chick had some class I thought, we walked into her own quarters, this was ANNA. She made me very welcome extremely welcome, after she had put my back right again, she cuddled up, she had noticed me on my last visit and hoped I would call again, she thought how young and handsome I was, I bet you say that to all your customers, no she was adamant, to her I was the best thing since sliced bread. We spent a very passionate hour together, when it was time to leave she insisted that I was her special friend, and when I returned I should make my way to her room. I have no idea how people will reconcile these memories only that they have been in my head all these years just waiting to be released. These are very personal memories, it has not been easy translating these.events. As a nineteen year old, a long way from home, the liasions I found very comforting, these people were so friendly, so obliging very genuine.

We had in the camp outstanding sporting facilities, the sports pitches were flat full size grassed arenas, I remember the squadron having a decent Rugby, XV who played many fixtures against military opposition, the games were of high quality. I was part of the raucous crowd of supporters who certainly got entertained. I played in the squadron soccer team against local opposition, these games were tough, the Malays love their sport, very passionate players. Not long now for my leave, looking forward to going home, seeing my family again, it will be an adventure no doubt. This evening I decided to check up on Anna, I hadn't seen her for a week, I must admit I enjoyed her company, she welcomed me with open arms, and we spent quality time together. I said my goodbyes telling her of my trip home to England, she wished me bon voyage, as I stepped into the lounge on my way out, a voice nonchalantly chimed, 'hello, hello, hello, what have we got here?' Military Police having a beer, I couldn't believe the girls hadn't given us the nod. Anna was giving them a right bollocking. They were very accommodating friendly lads, 'are you going to do me then?' 'I'm afraid so lad.' I explained about me going on leave, they said not to worry it would be after Christmas when it would come to a head.

They assured me I would get away on leave, they then very kindly proceeded to give me a lift back to camp, shit I thought here we go again. There was four of us travelling to the UK from Paroi, we had ordered a taxi to the airport in Singapore. Bags packed the lads had come to wave us off, they were wishing they were travelling, tight buggers I shouted and off we drove. It was an enjoyable journey home, Christmas is that time of year, warm friendly, arrived home very tired but pleased to be back. Everyone was pleased to see me. I was quite tanned compared to everyone, it was freezing. A month is quite a long time I thought. Mum did not look as bad as I had expected, she was on a lot of medication which helped to ease the pain, she was telling me of Tim over the road, it had struck him down also. Tim Thornham we had grown up together, good athlete, a talented cricketer, multiple sclerosis, the doctor explained the symptoms muscle wastage, nervous system affected, motion cells in the brain drying up, as far as he knew no cure to eradicate this terrible affliction, in fact the medical world was at a loss at this time M/S was very new to them.

I had met up with Simon Barningham for a decent pint of Roses Bitter in the Mayfield Hotel in the village. Life in the village was very much as I had left it, after I had been at home a couple of days, it felt as if I had never been away how strange. Simon enjoyed having me back, he was a bit of a loner, found it difficult making friends for some reason, his parents had been really strict with him, didn't have much of a childhood, his dad was the village bobby for years, my mother got on well with Simon he enjoyed the banter with a good meal thrown in. Christmas came and went again all very jolly, had some fun up at number 17 with Doreen and Frank Marr, she was a good friend of mums, always popping in to help, she loved the stories I brought back with me, had been into town a couple of times to the new cellar bar in Huntriss Row, all very tropical with the fishing nets hanging from the ceiling, lobster pots in the alcoves, a fishing we shall go!! Colin Frank a friend from up the avenue was courting an old school mate Kath Webb, he had been in the cellar bar when we were there, a friend of Kath's had seen me, Colin thought she had fancied me and would like to meet up, nothing to lose I thought why not, I put my suit on shirt and tie, the real deal, down the stairs into the gloom of the cellar bar. It wasn't gloomy for long this young cheeky looking girl with short cropped hair made her way over, that smile we introduced ourselves, her name was Helen Slack, it all seems a blur now but from that night we were inseparable. Helen was only sixteen, I was to be twenty next month, she shouldn't really have been drinking, she assured me she had been drinking since she was fifteen. Simon had a green van, so the following evening we met Helen and her friend Linda from Cayton in the Everley Hotel for another drink. I was besotted by this young cheeky imp, although only sixteen she was very street wise knew the score, quite mature for her years. She had left school because she couldn't stand the regime, thought it all a waste of time, needed to start work. On her own account she got a job at the local major store in town Rowntrees, she enjoyed it there but the money was rubbish, so applied to join the

National Westminster bank, being successful she was now a trainee counter cashier, what an independent young lady, we hit it off from day one. She was also very interested in my life up to date, not too pleased when I explained I was only here on a temporary basis. We enjoyed each others company for the next couple of weeks before I was due to make tracks back to the Far East.

She took me to her home to meet her parents, a lovely detached bungalow on the North side of town, Marjorie and Duncan, they both were very pleased to meet me. I think Helen wanted to show me off, there was Susan too, Helens younger sister, she would be about seven. Duncan had been a bit of a hero in the last war defusing bombs and such like. I had enjoyed meeting Helen's family they were very friendly towards me, I suspected Marjorie was giving me the once over trying to catch me out, I said my goodbyes, they wished me good luck and that was it. I was catching the last bus from town to York, the two of us were finding it very difficult, we sat in a bar for an hour before the bus, Helen was heartbroken poor lass, and I felt really sad. The bus arrived a quick snog and off I went, the joys of love and war. I had said my goodbyes to Seamer earlier, Mum was upset, it was hard for her not knowing what was round the corner. I can say going back was the worst journey I have ever endured. I met up with the other lads in London, they were feeling exactly the same.

Back to Paroi Camp Seremban, the results of the cadre course had come through, I was to be transferred to Selerang Barracks, Singapore, to join 5 troop A Sqn. I had a week before I left for Singapore, bloody hell I thought, its difficult keeping up with what's going on. I received a letter from Helen, what beautiful handwriting, she had enclosed some photos it was marvellous to see her again, if only on paper. I wrote a letter return post giving her the news of my new posting. I was counting down the days wondering if I had got away with the altercation with the MP's, with two days left before my transfer I was charged and placed on squadron leaders orders, it was embarrassing listening to the chaste old duffer Major Langley laying it on thick, regarding fornication in these parts with these Johnny foreigners. I stood cap in hand taking in all the drivel, I was thinking I bet he is jealous really. He fined me twelve pounds. About turn march out.

Selerang Barracks, Changi, Singapore, this was my new home. These barracks had been home to the Japanese army when they were over in Singapore in 1944. If my memory serves me well, they were built of stone blocks very sturdy, but also quite noisy, each block had two floors, each floor had a verandah which ran the length of the building. Each room held eight men, similar in design to most barrack blocks in England. The parade ground was in the centre of the surrounding blocks, apart from A Sqn the camp also played host to a detachment of artillery, plus we had attached to us a Sqn of the Royal Horse Guards, known as the Blues sqn. Selerang was in the parish of Changi. To the north end the notorious Changi Jail, to the south, Selerang Barracks, twenty five years previously it had been the home to the Japanese army, it was also a prison where allied prisoners were kept before shipping them north to work on the notorious Burma Railway and the bridge over the River Kwai. It was estimated that over 1700 prisoners went through Selerang Barracks. It was a formidable sight Changi jail, we passed it most days a very depressing situation, but a stark reminder of those shocking days, it's always been a lottery being in the wrong place at the wrong time.

I met up with my new troop, it was all very exciting, 4 Troop A Sqn was waiting for a troop leader, one was due any time, our troop COH Frank Fettes a down to earth Scotsman lovely man, had that quiet assured manner, which held the respect of the troop. Satch Rumbelow was corporal and I was L/CPL, tailend Charlie as I was known within the troop. I was to command a Ferret scout car with my driver TPR Brennan a 'Jina' from Liverpool, typical scouser full of life, full of fun, full of shit. Troopers Dave Balsaille John Moment, and Jim Lloyd made up the family. Satch Rumbelow was an interesting young man, he had been seconded from the Blues Sqdn. We hit it off from the start, he was a giant, a big lad who enjoyed life to the full, all the attributes required for fun in the military.

Our new Rupert or Troop Leader arrived, a dapper little fellow by the name of Captain Henry Fellows. He had transferred to the Life Guards from the 10th Hussars, he introduced himself to all the boys in a very forthright, keen, and up for the job manner, and to be fair to all the other officers in the Squadron were top blokes and Captain Henry would be no exception.

Selerang had much more to offer than Paroi Camp, Serenban, Singapore at this time was made up of Military bases throughout the island. Naval bases, RAF Squadrons and Army units, the MOD had thousands of men operating in this theatre in the 1960's. To facilitate all the personnel within our compound in Selerang, building had become paramount. Accomodation was an issue, Schools, Offices, all the paraphinalia required to house an Army and their families. The building was contracted out to local firms. The Chinese held the monopoly within the building trade, and they would rock up at the workplace, the majority being women labourers or coolies, grizzled, as hard as nails, enduring 12 hour shifts mixing cement, climbing up and down ladders and laying bricks. They showed incredible strength and stamina and some even brought their babies to work! At break times they would all sit around in a circle with their tea, unfolding their rice from banana leaf parcels, ranting in local dialect. They were totally engrossed in their work, and their toilet habits left nothing to the imagination, bobbing down anywhere and at anytime to relieve themselves. After their food had been consumed the fags or pipes took hold. The noise of the chattering and the spicy aromas from the smoke drifted throughout the commune. Amazing to imagine ladies taking on these challenges, but then again it was hard to imagine these beings as ladies.

The cricket season was upon us, I had been selected for the Army XI after doing well at the trials, we would play our home games at Neesoon, this was the garrison we initially stayed on our arrival in the Far East. When viewing the fixture list I was amazed how diverse the teams we would be up against were. I had no knowledge of the Chinese playing cricket, but the game in this part of the world was booming. Singapore is a multi-cultural island, Indians, Sri Lankans, Chinese, malays, which encouraged an interesting cricket cocktail. I recall the game against the Indian Association vividly, nothing to do with the actual game, the lunch interval was the problem, usually lunch would consist of a run of the mill salad with meat etc. The Indians invited us to share their speciality....bloody curry, served out of a round metal bucket. They ladled this vivid yellow mass on to my plate, all the boys were tucking in with relish. I tried a thimble full and I thought my mouth was on fire and I cried 'water water' ... nothing had prepared me for this. How can anyone seriously enjoy this food, leaves me both staggered and bewildered. To this day I still find the smell of curry repulsive.

Back to the cricket, which was a decent standard with all the teams producing good cricket wickets. I personally was having a successful season picking up wickets on a regular basis. In fact I was beginning to make a bit of a name for myself. Singapore Recreation Club played Selangor Cricket Club each year. Selangor is a province of Malaysia, Kuala Lumpur being the capital city. This year Selangor were hosting the match and the rivalry was apparently very keen with the media taking an active role in promoting the game on radio. I had been invited to a net session with a view to selection...how exciting!!

Satch Rumbelow and myself took a cab into the city to celebrate his birthday. Singapore is a twenty four hour city, another one that never sleeps. We were now becoming old hands around the bars and flesh pots of 'Singers'. Seeing is believing, its difficult to put into words how exciting and exhilarating the place is. The sultry balmy evenings, just a shirt and slacks, no overcoat scarf or gloves.The Union Jack Club full of soldiers, sailors and airmen, all with tales to tell. Just across the road, the infamous Raffles Hotel. The UJ Club being subsidised by the MOD enabling it to sell food and drink at discounted prices, therefore after a Nasi Goreng and a few bevvies it was along to the highlight of the evening, Bugis Street. There will a percentage of people who read this book who will be aware of the reputation of this street. For the uninitiated I will try to conjure up a typical evening. Early doors Bugis Street goes about its business in an organised chaotic manner as an outdoor eating area, hundreds of metres of tables and chairs lining the street. Early evening the restaurants are working flat out with communities and families enjoying their evening meal, hundreds of Woks and spatulas going ten to the dozen, creating mouth watering aromas, stir fries and rice dishes to die for. Then at midnight, the street comes alive.

The whole character of the place changes, long gone are the families, and a brand new atmosphere emerges as hundreds of drunken matelots, Airmen and squaddies converge together. Satch and myself arrive and find a table, we are both on good form, taking in the amazing sights and sounds with kids as young as five urging the blokes to play noughts and crosses. They come at you really strong...would you like my sister for a couple of hours, one young lad haggles. There are cats and dogs enjoying the scraps from the half eaten meals. A group of New Zealand squaddies are knocking hell out of each other just down the street, then from nowhere your eyes 'marvel at the beauty before you, shimmering dresses, exotic tastes to behold, hypnotic music, smiling faces lighting up the whole street. This is what the punters have come to witness the local transvestites strutting their stuff. A young blonde then sits upon my knee and looked the part until she opened her mouth and with a gruff northern accent ordered 'port and lemon'. She turned out to be an RAF Corporal, with the toe of my boot up his arse he buggered off. Satch fell off his chair with laughter, what a remarkable place. The 'Trannies' were renowned throughout the island for their shows. They are made up of lads from the services allegedly!! Satch enjoyed that birthday without a doubt, we rolled back to the barracks in the very early hours, fit for work I'm sure'!!

Singapore Recreation Club is situated in the main Padang or Park, a beautiful arena just along from the Parliament Buildings, close to the waterfront. The club members are predominantly Eurasion, well heeled young men from wealthy backgrounds. There was a wealth of talent on show at this final selection day. Jimmy Griffiths, a West Indian lad attached to the RAF Squadron at Seletar. He was a powerful all rounder, typically West Indian with the style and swagger to match. His claim to fame was that he reckoned he was a cousin of the legendary West Indian fast bowler Charlie Griffiths, and no one questioned that assumption as he set about the bowling in that wristy caribbean flamboyant way....Yeah man!!

We were both made up when the team was announced as the two of us had been selected. I was the only white man on board, no worries though, after all the introductions and back slapping we were handed the itinerary...Wow!!. A reserved carriage on the train to Kuala Lumpur. Then picked up at the station by a fleet of Jaguar Mk 7's and transferred to a country club on the outskirts of the capital. How bloody exciting was that...the trip would take five days and we were leaving next weekend. My inclusion in the side was relayed to the Squadron Leader, who was delighted and he wished me well, stating that it could only be good for morale and would help to cement relations between us the Military and the local establishment.

Captain Fellows, Frank, Satch and the boys in the troop gave me some stick for missing duties again eh!!... bloody cricket, but deep down they were solidly behind me. Saturday morning the team resplendent in shirts and club ties met at club HQ, then we travelled as a group to the station. Steve Allen, the skipper was then harangued to do an interview for the local radio station. Steve was a smashing bloke, he was a Captain with Singapore Airlines. He opened the batting and was a very steady player. Jimmy and myself took our seats in our carriage, we felt quite special, but you would wouldn't you. The journey took about two hours, the train actually stopped at Serenban en route, which was my old stomping ground. A picture of Anna entered my head but she didn't stay for long. Four majestic Jaguars stood purring on the tarmac, our luggage and kit were transferred by truck, such a luxurious journey to our next port of call, as our entourage stepped out of the limo's there before us another wonder to behold, a beautiful wooden building, polished with a modern façade of glass panels stretching the entire length. Jimmy and myself were speechless, the other boys were taking it in their stride, as we entered we were greeted by the Selengor officials who greeted us with a handshake and welcoming smile. After the speeches and formalities

We were asked to follow our hosts into the lounge area. Standing in line along the lounge was an array of beautiful young ladies of all shades, apparently it is customary in Malaysia that visiting guests facilitate themselves with a lady who will on all accounts look after her guest, tending to his every need. I looked at Jimmy, the colour draining from his cheeks, I was just 21 years of age and to be honest could only think of one thing!!!!!. It came to my turn to choose a lady, how scary, there in front of me, a girl, I assumed about the same age as me and she was as black as coal, with a lovely smile and friendly face. I recall she screamed when I chose her...I was hoping it was a scream of joy!!

Without wasting any more time she had my suitcase and kit bag under each arm, and I presumed her duties had started. The following morning after an early breakfast, it was down to the cricket ground for a practice session. The ground was situated in the centre of the city, the hustle and bustle of traffic and traders selling their wares. It was a modern arena with permanent stands erected on three sides, a real cricket ground, they really take their cricket seriously in this neck of the woods, a situation I had not been aware of. After our workout it was back to base and my girl who I named Molly, as I thought it suited her. She had my bath running and shirt ironed, as we had been invited to a banquet to cement more relations, and to honour the game. The restaurant was enormous, resembling a Cathedral with sparkling chandeliers, the works. It was top nosh Chinese fare with one hundred year old eggs, and all the trimmings. I was beginning to get used to this lifestyle, but we had to keep our feet firmly on the ground as we were here to win a cricket match. During the evening we were introduced to the Chief of Police who came over as being a 'bit of a lad', genuine rough diamond. He welcomed us to his city and looked forward to the game tomorrow. The adrenalin was pumping when we got to the ground the following morning and whilst knocking up a lively crowd had gathered, looking very excited and somewhat intimidating. Selengor won the toss and elected to bat. I recall the temperature was in the 80's, really warm. They got off to a decent start being 50 for 1 at lunch. It was a three day game we were playing, with 90 overs being bowled per day. I got a chance to bowl in the afternoon session, ending up with four wickets for not many as we bowled them out for 290. Jimmy also got a couple of wickets. I had some fun with the crowd on the mid wicket boundary and gave as good as I got!! They had not seen too many blonde, gobby Yorkshiremen before, or had they?

At the close of play Steve Allen had accumulated a dozen with his oppo, which probably meant we had a slight advantage going into the second day. Guess what happened on the next morning, it absoluteley poured down, stairods and it was only a short time before the ground was awash, and to top that thunder and lightening, it was like the world was coming to an end. The dreaded scenario....match abandoned for the day. After lunch at the ground, the Chief of Police took us on a tour of the city, the locals we encountered were really scared of this guy and it appeared he ruled with an iron fist. We visited an up market bar, very swish and after a couple of beers, he got the playing cards out...'stud poker gentlemen'. He tried to teach me the basics then proceeded to relieve me of all my cash... I wonder how many other victims this guy had sucked in!! After A few more drinks he escorted me to a room and said ' have this lady on me, Phil'. I declined. The poor girl, suitcase in hand was going to visit her family. You will entertain my friend he demanded of her striking the door with his riding crop just to enforce the order. The girl was in tears as we entered a room together and both sat down, I got the ciggies out and explained that we should have a smoke and then go back to the foyer. I assured the girl that I would tell the chief that we had a fabulous time and she nodded with a smile which was tinged with relief. She thanked me for that. It worked a treat, he was none the wiser as she trotted off. When I woke next morning stacked at the side of my bed was a pile of money, the money I had lost to the Chief. I presume he was teaching a lesson but his action made me alter my opinion of him, no doubt he was hard but also fair. Apparently in 1969 he was brutally murdered in Kuala Lumpur which when I read it shocked me to the core!!

The game was abandoned after lunch due to the storm, the cricket had become incidental, a kind of an anti climax you might say, we were all disappointed after such a positive first day. I thanked Molly for all her work and dedication to duty by giving her a bunch of flowers. I'm sure there was a tear in her eye as we parted. Back on the train and to the real world. It had been a fantastic experience for me personally, a trip to savour and a real privilege for a humble yorkshire lad. A few weeks after the trip I was feeling a little down in the dumps, Dad's letters suggested that Mum's health was deteriorating, and her illnnes had more or less left her bedridden. I was also missing Helen after our coming together last Christmas. She wrote letters to me at least twice a week. I had a word with Frank Fettes, my troop Commander, he was a fatherly figure and influence at this time and I told him how I felt regarding the army, he suggested that if I was not happy then I should do something about it as 'lifes too short'. With that I made another impulsive decision, and that was to buy myself out of the Army. The Squadron Leader was informed of my intentions and he put the plan into action.

After a couple of weeks I received orders to visit the Squadron Leader, to go over my application for dismissal from the Army. He informed me that I could leave the Regiment, but that it would cost me £400. He confirmed that the Regiment would be very sorry to see me go. They insisted that I had all the Attributes to make a first class NCO.. He then changed his tack and told me that his doctor in Taunton Somerset was on the board of Somerset County Cricket Club. He would be writing to him to see if they would be willing to offer me a trial. He then gave me a release date of 11 February 1968, three months to the day. I thanked the Squadron Leader, shot up a perfect salute, my knees were knocking, he then wished me well shaking my hand vigourosly....no doubt he was a top man.I was flabbergasted that the buy out was £400, in those days that was a fortune. The boys were in shock when I told them and they thought I was a 'lucky bastard. It took a little while to sink in, civvy street, a little unerving at the thought. I posted a letter to Helen and the family at home, I wondered whether Dad might be in a position to help a little with the cost ... kids eh! ... who would have em!!

Ray Cornish, another solid Yorkshireman, we played troop cricket together, getting on really well. After a particular match Ray asked me to do a favour, would I mind sitting in with his wife and kids, whilst he went with the NCO's mess darts team on a jaunt. I accepted as I saw baby sitting as a way of saving money. Margaret, Ray's wife was a lovely bubbly larger than life character, full of fun. She helped over the road at the Primary school with the kids, I would spend most weekends as part of their family, particularly enjoying Sunday Lunch. I really appreciated their warmth and freindship. One particular Sunday afternoon we were relaxing after a tasty lunch, Yorkshire Puds and all the trimmings, then from nowhere I got a pain in my stomach. Margaret was worried in case she had poisoned me!!, but that was rubbish. I decided to go to my room to try to sleep through it. It seemed to get worse, a general stomach ache. I summoned the duty driver who took me to the medical centre in Changi, a couple of miles up the road. The duty medic was quick with his prognosis, upset stomach and handed me some Milk of Magnesia. I tried to explain that I thought it might be appendicitis. It was like talking to the wall!! Back in my room, the pain concentrated in one area of my lower stomach. I then started to vomit like the proverbial 'dog'. Appendicitis, I had all the symptons, back to the medical centre forthwith. I was met by a different medic, who seemed to possess some degree of care and immediately called for a doctor. The doctor took about 10 minutes to arrive and was slightly perturbed as I had pulled him off the golf course. Without delay, he pulled on his rubber gloves and asked me to bend over as he was about to examine and explore my rectum with his fingers!! As I was in no state to object I obeyed and it appeared that the doctor became a little concerned about my appendix. I was hurried into a ward to face the knife, first thing in the morning. I recall a few seconds as the Anaesthetist looked in my eye, the next thing I remember was waking up, operation complete, with bandages inplace. Trying to remember the chain of events was almost impossible, it is a weird sensation. Pam Fettes, Frank's wife was a nurse in Changi hospital and she came along to assess my condition after a couple of days. By then I could get out of bed and take myself to the loo. After another few days I was going round the ward with the tea trolley feeling much more like my old self. Margaret visited me, she had been concerned but I told her it was just one of those things. The crew of a Halifax anti submarine kite had crashed into the sea, and they were being operated on, a couple of them spending eight hours in theatre. I felt like a fraud, until the doctor told me that my appendix was close to bursting and if that had happened I might not be here today!! Army life was coming to an end for me and as it got closer I began to realise how much I was going to miss the life, the teamwork and the Regiment. I take away wonderful memories and I remain convinced that growing up as a soldier had helped to shape me into a capable committed young man.

My adventure continued as the plane taking me home to the UK, had to make an emergency landing, coming down at Karachi airport. It was a technical fault, something to do with circulating air in the cabin. We were to be five days in Karachi, with the airline putting us up in a five star shithole in the suburbs. The MCC cricket team were touring Pakistan at this time and were staying at the same hotel, Micky Stewart skipper, how bizarre!!

Eventually we touched down in blighty. I had to travel to Knightsbridge, the home of the regimental barracks in London to hand in my documentation and receive my travel warrant for my train home.

Blondie Woodlands, my old troop corporal from Windsor, happened to pass by and he was really pleased to see me, but was shocked when I told him I was leaving the regiment. We shook hands and wished each other good luck.

That was it ... I was now a civilian ... FRIGHTENING!!!!!!!!!!!!!!!!!!!!

Chapter 5

Losing Mum … Helen

What a shock to the system, becoming a civilian overnight, life as I knew it was consigned to history. The real world for me was now here, back home in Yorkshire what a contrast, and the weather didn't help it was bloody freezing. I found it extremely difficult settling back to the drudgery of routines and I missed my buddies terribly, the camaraderie, the mischief, the trust, the crack that makes military life whichever the service the finest experience a young man could hope for. Each and everyone of us in life as the opportunity to make choices, I believe my life this far has hinged most certainly on impulse, someone somewhere deep in my subconscious triggers the next step forward then physically you implement that calling, therefore here I am on a wing and a prayer heading into the unknown about to take on the world as an old soldier and old soldiers never die they just fade away.

Mum had been in a bed downstairs for a while now, as her condition deteriorated she became bed ridden. Her medication as I remember was a cocktail of different types of drugs, the district nurse would visit most days followed by the home helps who were true heroin's and became close friends with all the family, then the neighbours would pop in to help keep Mums spirits up have a brew and a fag keep her abreast of the local gossip. To be honest our house resembled a world war one clearing station, it was manic at times but we wouldn't have wanted it any other way. This was community at its utmost, a common bond among friends all very humbling.

I had fallen in love with Helen she was and still is a gem of a person. I have Colin Frank to thank for the opportunity of that first meeting, through her determination to succeed she secured herself a job with the National Westminster Bank as junior cashier at the main branch in town, this was to be an inspirational move for Helen as she had taken herself out of school, the local convent, against her parent's wishes she felt she needed to be earning not wasting her time learning latin, it was a courageous step forward, but that's my girl such an impulsive little imp.

Tony Pyemen my ex squadron leader Selerang, had been true to his word, as a letter arrived from Somerset CCC inviting me down to Taunton for pre-season nets. I had to find my kit, make sure it was all serviceable. During these first few weeks back home, I was in the process of looking for employment, I was finding it difficult to organise and motivate myself, in the mob all the administrative chain of events were taken care of by others, in the big wide world it's a different kettle of fish, organising the money always having a few quid for the essentials was always a juggle, it sounds crazy but that's how it was, a total new learning curve, I thought how fortunate to have my junior cashier on-board to assist.

I made the journey to Somerset at the end of March arriving in the evening after a long day on the train. I was made most welcome and the first night I spent at the Orb and Sceptre pub sleeping in the skippers bed as he was at Lords on captains duties. That first night we all got introduced, a young lad had just arrived from Australia, Greg Chappell was his name, we hit it off became buddies, had an hilarious week. Greg went on to become an Australian legend scoring thousands of runs and captaining the side with aplomb. Bill Alley another legend of the county game turned up for nets the next morning, it was just another day's work for him, bat under one arm bait box under the other, a lovely man, I mentioned the time when I played alongside his son during my time in Bovington with the junior leaders, it was sad as Graham his son had been killed in a car crash which he said had affected him terribly, this was to be Bills last season playing before he took up umpiring. Fred Rumsey he was another character, funny man, useful left arm, medium quick bowler played for England. In those days indoor facilities were like rocking horse droppings, and the weather during that week kept us off the middle and out of the nets, therefore very little was achieved, apart from Greg and myself being ejected from an Italian restaurant for being too noisy, he was pissed, don't know any Aussie who can take his drink. Somerset offered me a game in their 2nd XII which would have meant moving down to Taunton finding digs, after discussing this with Helen, I decided to decline their offer, I didn't take the decision lightly, there was a lot happening inside my head, Mother's health, getting it on with Helen, settling down all these factors to consider. I took the lead from my head, another impulsive gamble, would it be the right one only time would tell.

My brother Bill was now working at the newly opened McCains factory at Eastfield, thousands of tons of spuds arrived into the place then left as oven chips the new phenomenon hitting the dinner table. Dad was still working for Stockdales as a driver nothing he loved more than hauling his load up and down the motorways, he seemed to be coping with Mums illness, he was a resilient character kept his feelings locked away. As the weeks passed the weather improved, I was now definitely back acclimatised the tan had long gone, the Seamer and Irton cricket club started nets just before the season started, there were lots of new faces which had appeared since the last time I played, the club was full of characters young men and not to young a healthy mix, a recipe for success.

At weekends Dad would wheel Mum up to the cricket ground in her wheel chair if the weather was kind, she enjoyed the banter sat with all the old sweats. Helen would get the bus out to Seamer and help in the canteen serving cups of tea, we became one big happy family. Village cricket played on village greens or enclosed fields up and down this beautiful country of ours, is one of the pastimes we are renowned for its more than a game, locally every game became a local derby, keenly fought contests bringing the best and the worst from each team. Total commitment was shown by club players, throughout the season, the evening league would mean journeys of up to twenty miles, starting at 6pm, avoiding on coming traffic, arriving at the ground feeling quite shell shocked as I recall these times, no major car accident comes to mind which on reflection was miraculous. Eddie Wilmore R/H bat fixture secretary, cricket fanatic extraordinaire lived and breathed the game, Graham Scruton left arm medium bowler R/H Bat, young farmer life and soul, lead a sheltered life up in the hills then he found us and then every father had to lock up his daughters. Paul Sullivan all rounder, married the village magnates daughter ex college lad, very entrepreneurial travelled the world flogging his stuff, very generous.

Reg Coward R.A bowler l/h BAT. Excellent opening bowler, marvellous action, lovely man, could have gone all the way as a player, great role model. These were just a mere cross section of talent we had on show, I apologise to the lads I have forgot to mention the list is endless great people and with all the wives, girlfriends and supporters,

Seamer and Irton cricket gave me some of the fondest memories of my cricketing career.

I'd been on the cricket committee the year we opened the new cricket pavilion, brick built with showers and a bar, this was luxury compared to the ancient green hut endured for years, John Welbourne and Tom Young these were the gentlemen responsible, hard working guys putting their efforts into serving their community, giving up hours of their time, chasing councillors to sanction this and that, planning permission was a problem. Organising a licence the red tape they had to break through, it seemed to take an age. Eventually everything came together, and the building was complete. I tabled a motion in committee to hold a gentlemen's evening, which would comprise of a couple of adult films, followed by pie and peas and a few beers, I got a seconder to support the motion, it took some doing persuading the rest, the evening was really a vote of thanks for all the hard work that had gone into the project.

The evening arrived it was a Friday, I had begged a couple of movies off an old lag who was a friend of a friend, the projector we borrowed, the problem we had was the electricity hadn't been coupled up at this time. Therefore we had to apply an extension lead into the new primary school in the far corner of our ground, we arranged for a window to be left open at the school. The leads arrived the equivalent of 250yds of cable, we set off for the school from the projector, we arrived at the open window plug in hand only to find it was the plug for the projector, what a bloody performance, we were curled up laughing. Eventually we got the bits and pieces hooked up, we were ready for action, Len Tennant and the older members were like cats on hot bricks, as the films were blue they were against the law, they were keeping a vigil outside checking for blue lights flashing up to the pavilion, we only had bottled beer to drink as the pumps were electric. After a lot of banter and leg pulling we got the evening under way, I had no idea of the content of the movie, then bugger me the people who had watched them last, hadn't rolled the things back, they were coming instead of going, 'bollocks' more raucous laughter piss taking, this certainly wasn't the Cannes film festival.

Here we go again and the old guard couldn't believe their eyes ladies engaging with their pets, horses, dogs and pigs, someone thought they saw a blue light flashing 'Turn it off,' was the call. 'Bollocks' cried the majority, total mayhem but hilarious worth all the snags. The final clip before the interval was of a lady trying to give her pet pot bellied pig a blow job riveting stuff. Then as the lights came on the gas lights, there was a call from the bar, 'hot pork pies and sausage rolls' you couldn't have scripted it to top that. The memory of that night is etched into my brain, I don't think I have ever laughed so much, even now when I recall the events tears are streaming down.

I had nailed a couple of jobs during this period first as a laundry van driver for Spencer's Dry Cleaners local firm based in Scarborough. The job was ok, the money was rubbish, £11.00 per week, it's difficult to comprehend in these affluent times, you wonder how people managed on those kind of wages, there again beer was 10p a pint ciggies 2/6 for twenty, Mum used to say when bread gets to 50p a loaf she would stop eating it, fish and chips were two shillings for one of each. This was the price in 1969. Brother Bill married a young girl Christine Lightfoot from Ebberston, a village on the way to Pickering. Christine moved in with us in Seamer we were one big happy family.

I played Hockey for Scarborough after the cricket season ended, hockey is a very physical game, I played full back enjoying the cut and thrust Mick Wilson Bob and Phil Stankiste were the guys who invited me to play. Socially it was very similar to the cricket scene, the girl friends would turn up after the match, we all enjoyed a pint with the banter thrown in, hot pants were the in thing all the lasses were wearing them Helen would turn up in hers looking a million dollars, they were very enjoyable times, and the Beatles were still number one. One incident from those days is worth a mention, we were playing hockey at Thirsk, the hockey ground is in the middle of the race course there, very pretty part of the world, the girls had travelled with us on this particular day, after the game finished we were all having a pint when it was suggested that if the girls could run around the race course within fifteen minutes we would reward them with a prize of five pounds, they were game and I thought we were on to a winner. I couldn't imagine Helen galloping round Thirsk racecourse in her hot pants under the specified time no way José, the flag dropped they were off, what a sight, four of them jogging away out of sight, the going was good to soft, time for another pint, there was a commotion over the far side of the course as the rooks took flight, obviously shocked at the sight of these four fillies, now blowing a bit. Then as we were downing our beer two minutes inside the time, the girls appeared, incredible, there had to be a stewards Inquiry!!

After a few minutes it was decided the girls had fairly won the bet, so we handed over our fivers in fact I was quite proud of Helen and I told her so, before I borrowed the fiver back to buy some more drinks. I left the laundry job, to become a car salesman selling Vauxhalls for Thompsons of Scarborough, being a young man of twenty three it was very difficult competing against old hands like John Owen and Fred Whittaker, they had been there for years building up their own clientele and lets face it at this time the Vauxhall brand was having its own problems finding a foot hold in a very competitive auto market. I didn't take to being the skivvy running after the old buggers, selling cars was not to be my vocation therefore back to the drawing board. Stockdales the local potato merchant were hiring staff, travelling to York to their plant each morning what's the saying beggars can't be choosers.

Helen's elder sister Christine had named the day for her marriage to Dennis Chapman a young plumber from Crossgates, they are to wed on the 22 August he had asked me to be his best man, why me I hardly knew him really, it meant missing cricket. Helen insisted I should fulfil the role, and as I liked Christine I accepted. The wedding was booked to take place at the Northstead Methodist Church with the reception at the Mayfield Hotel in Seamer.

It was so sad to see Mother wasting away in the bed downstairs it was now early March 1970, I arrived home early Friday afternoon from Stockdales Mother asked if I would slip down to Dawson's shop to collect her medication as this is where the doctor used to leave everyone's pills to save time delivering them to each and every household. I returned with her pills and she welcomed me with open arms, that evening I was out with the boys, Friday nights was boys night out. I remember arriving home pretty late around 0230am, it was customary for me to check in with Mum before I went upstairs, this particular time I just checked her from the door, she appeared so comfortable. As I was to be travelling to York that morning I was first to rise, as I made my way over to Mum I could see something was amiss, her face was the colour of stone, very grey, I felt her forehead it was as cold as ice, Mum had gone, she had died left us without a word, she didn't deserve this ending as she was only 46 years old. I sat holding her hand wondering how on earth she had managed to struggle to prepare a cup of tea, then swallow all those pills I had delivered to her the previous afternoon.

I felt a pang of guilt but realised after a few seconds, what a courageous act to prepare the ground then to actually end the suffering, she had a slight smile on her face enough to let me know this was a blessing in disguise, I woke the household, Bill was at work at McCains. Dad came down in total shock, poor man he had endured this nightmare disease with Mum, for it to end so tragically, he felt was a right kick in the guts. We alerted all the relevant services, they appeared in quick succession, I then went up to McCain to break the news and bring Bill home. Two days later Christine gave birth to a lovely daughter Becky, the old adage one door closes another door opens was never so apt.

The funeral service and burial took place at Seamer Church, it was a splendid turn out, family and friends thronging the church a fitting send off for Winifred Hart the most beautiful special mother and grandmother R.I.P. It took a while to get things sorted before life got back to some kind of normality. The cricket season got underway, I had a successful summer playing for Seamer CC, during the season I was approached by Scarborough CC offering me a chance to move to the next stage of my development, the East Yorkshire Cup and Yorkshire League.

Things were about to change on the jobs front too. Helens dad offered me work at the new factory Plaxton Builders were assembling at Cayton low road, in fact on the same site as that little bungalow where my story began. Duncan or 'Jack' as he was known in the trade began his life in Wadsworth near Doncaster he came from a family of butchers five brothers and four sisters. He was billeted in Scarborough during the war where he met Marjorie, he trained in demolition, bomb disposal and mine clearing, he went over the channel on D day and became a bit of a legend over in Germany clearing booby traps and mines. On one occasion he was in the middle of an apple orchard disconnecting a device when it got the better of him, he was blown into the canopy of the apple tree, both his lungs had collapsed, he spent sometime in hospital lucky to be alive. Before the war Jack took his apprenticeship as a stonemason, building was his preference rather than butchering.

When the war ended he purchased a motor bike and sidecar arriving back in Scarborough, he then married Marjorie, before taking up the position of foreman bricklayer with Plaxtons builders. Houses for the masses were top priority after the hostilities ended, building firms were inundated with contracts and Plaxtons were no exception. Jack made his way up the managerial ladder in quick time, he was a natural leader of men, and in 1970 he was made M/D of the building division and took his seat on the company board. It was a Monday morning, Jack drove me to the site he had sorted out some tools for me, tools I might need, we walked onto the site me with my tool box all the lads wondering who I might be. It was all a bit nerve wracking, they were all a bit wary of me at first, it took a couple of days before I was welcomed into the throng, a lot of piss taking when they found out I was courting Jacks daughter, after a few months, he had a new job lined up for me, Plaxton employed a mobile crane for hire the driver operator was leaving therefore a replacement was needed, I would travel with the operator for a fortnight learning how to handle this awkward beast. Arthur Spavin head engineer helped me tremendously to find my feet, this was no automatic hydraulic piece of equipment the jib had to be erected manually bloody hard graft. After a couple of weeks I was on my own. I had this feeling that Jack was testing me and my resolve, I was going to show him that this ex squaddie was up for it.

One job I got called for was to off load a sub station for the electricity board, this was in Sea Cliff road, up South cliff in Scarborough, I arrived on site quickly assembling one section of the jib pretty straight forward, when the sub station arrived, I realised I was facing in the wrong direction which meant I had to go down the road, turn around come in at the right angle, no problem, I arrived back at Beaconsfield Street our depot, job well done, it was then I was told to report to the office, apparently whilst travelling down Sea cliff Road to turn around my Jib had brought down all the telephone lines in the street, oh shit!!!

After a few weeks I began to get the hang of operating this heap of scrap, to be honest I thought the crane was dangerous, not fit for purpose I'm sure if it had been inspected Plaxtons would have been in trouble. The final nail came when I had to take it to Whitby to put a roof on a building, Arthur had warned me earlier that the crawler gear was knackered I was now approaching Ruswarp bank a 1-4 gradient, I was sweating cobs as I stuck it into first gear then gunned it up the incline, 'come on you bastard, more more!' I was beside myself the revs began to fade no I thought, then miraculously it slowly picked up and we made it to the top what a shambles, I arrived at the site finished the job then headed back to the depot. I'm in the same bloody predicament climbing out of Ruswarp up the bank when crash bang wallop, the whole shebang stops dead, there's oil all over the road, as I jump out of the cab and look under the vehicle there sat on the road is the bloody gear box. What a performance, luckily there was some farm buildings adjacent to the road and we managed with the help of a farmer and tractor to tow the bloody contraption into one of the buildings where it stayed for a month, until a farmer purchased it from Plaxtons to my utter delight, another interesting chapter came to a conclusion.

Chapter 6

Scarborough Cricket Club – An Institution

Scarborough Cricket Club's first ever fixture took place outside the old Queens Hotel. This hostelry stood just opposite the main entrance of the North Marine Road ground as it is today. It was 1849, John Bell, the landlord of the Queens encouraged young men to take up bat and ball and learn to play the new popular game of 'cricket'. It became a popular pastime amongst the local lads and a team was selected to take on a team from Filey, a local derby so to speak. The pitch or what resembled a pitch was no more that a meadow, common land where farmers brought their cattle to graze. The pitch was roped off, not totally ideal but it got the show on the road. John Bell, who opened the innings for Scarborough was also influential in promoting this important fixture, it became very noticeable how many visitors or spectators turned up to support the teams. Cricket was in the ascendancy taking off big time around the country. Clubs were being formed in most of the major cities and towns. Yorkshire was no exception, with Leeds, Sheffield and Bradford, all boasting strong interest and participation in the game

The Queens Hotel ground was deemed unfit for important matches that were now in the pipeline. A pitch was made available up on the Castle headland used by the Castle Hill Garrison, these facilities were far superior and ideal for the more experienced players. It also provided an opportunity for the newly formed Scarborough Cricket Club to raise much needed finance by charging an entrance fee. As the pitch was situated on the headland, controlling the crowds became much less of a problem. Even so, it was not all plain sailing, being perched up some 300ft above sea level brought new problems to bear. Such as hurricane style gales, which halted play on occasions. To the reader not familiar with Scarborough, the two bays that make up the resort, South and North, are separated by a rugged headland. The Ancient castle keep built by Henry II overlooks the two bays that have been there for a millennium or more. The South bay is where the harbour lies in the lee of the headland, the harbour was built and opened for trade in 1283. To build the original harbour, some 300 oak trees were drawn by horses from Pickering some 20 miles to the west. These amazing statistics appear from within the walls of the historical old town. Local wool was by far the largest exporter from the harbour, fishing has also played a major role, with families sailing their vessels to Iceland in search of cod during the 1400's.

Apart from the windy conditions during matches on the headland, the Volunteer Rifle Corps became a definite headache to the players and supporters, games had to be halted whilst the reservists practiced on the ranges next door, with live ammunition!!

An interesting fixture took place on the headland in 1869, a team of aborigines from the Australian outback arrived to take on a select local team. They were touring the country playing at all the important cricket venues. They were here thanks to sponsorship from a wealthy Aussie cattle rancher. The supporters flocked to witness this spectacle with 4,000 people paying at the gate. They certainly got their monies worth, the Aussie boys hammered the local lads by 10 wickets. After the game the aborigines threw down the gauntlet, challenging all comers to a spot of atheletics, involving sprinting, hurdling, jumping, vaulting with a pole, backwards running, throwing the boomerang and spear and finishing with who could throw the cricket ball farthest. The crowd hailed these flamboyant young men from afar, it was more a circus than a cricket match, they wiped the floor with all comers. They turned out to be highly tuned athletes, entertainers of the highest order, and sporting these names just added to their attraction –

Sherpherd
Two Penny Plain
Tiger Pink
Curzon White
Mullagh Blue
Red Cap Black
LaurencWe (Captain)
Peter Green
Dick a Dick Yellow
Charley Brown
Mosquito Magenta

These boys certainly left their mark that remarkable day on Castle Hill for many years, and their names are remembered with affection.

With the introduction of the railway into Scarborough around 1845, the resort was booming, it had all the ingredients on tap so to speak, the Music Hall theatre, plus stunning panoramic views of the promenaders taking their daily constitutional. The town enjoyed a remarkable up surge in tourism, not only for the lords and ladies, but the gates were now open to the working classes, the Millworkers, Coal Miners, Steel men and all their families taking advantage of this speedy new form of transportation, to allow them to enjoy their annual weeks family holiday in relative comfort within the new boarding houses springing up throughout the town

The wise men involved with Scarborough Cricket Club realising the potential of this influx acted accordingly, the original ground, or meadow used for those early matches outside the Queens Hotel was purchased. Tons of earth were removed before the ground was levelled and walls built around the perimeter, enclosing the ground. During the redevelopment of the North Marine Road, matches were still being played upon the castle hill. In 1871, probably the most important fixture in the history of the club at that time took place. Lord Londsborough XI v CI Thorntons Scarborough Visitors, which turned out to be the forerunner to the famous annual Scarborough Cricket Festival.

Yorkshire Cricket Club played their first fixture at the NMR against Middlesex in 1874, the game of cricket in Victorian England had now reached new heights. Clubs were becoming financially solvent by offering membership to the thousands of supporters of the game.. Scarborough Cricket Clubs annual cricket festival really came of age in 1865, with the star attraction being WG Grace, the most celebrated player of the day. Without exception, the receipts for this match rocketed and the great man did not disappoint, scoring 174 and entertaining the crowd with his forceful strokeplay. In 1896, a further development took shape, the building of the present pavilion at a cost of 2150 pounds, an imposing red brick design, with veranda, the building has developed and expanded over the years, though the original outline still exists. I would take a pee on numerous occasions in the home dressing room urinals, trying to imagine all the famous cricketing knobs that had hung there over the century and decades past.

The name Robert Baker became synonymous with Scarborough Cricket Club, he was the first Secretary and a real driving force involved in those early days of development, Lord Londsborough, Lord Derwent, Viscount Downe and CI Thornton, all these noble boys were the high rollers who put their own particular stamp on proceedings within the club, the pioneers who put the club on the pedestal where it remains to this day. In 1873, a man named John King took on the role of Scraborough's first professional player. He became a legend within the game. He lived in the village of Snainton on the A170 Pickering Road, some eight miles from the ground as the crow flies. John was a tall wiry character who would leave his dwelling in Snainton and proceed to the NMR. On arrival he would have his lunch and relax with his feet up before the start of the game. He opened the bowling and would regularly bowl in excess of 20 overs. He was noted as being a right handful with the ball, taking all ten wickets on one occasion without much fuss. After the match it would be all hands to the pump, rolling the wicket for twenty minutes. When John King left the ground it would be on foot, no other form of transport.

Another story involving a Scarborough CC player is a Mr George 'Curly' Watson. Just after the introduction of the railway into the town, the club arranged an away fixture against Leeds X1, the local boys would be travelling by train. On selecting the side, the committee were left with a problem as they were two players short. It was important to pick the strongest eleven as the Leeds club were very capable. George Watson was summoned to confront the committee, he knew where to find the two extra players, the two lads who fitted the bill lived in Malton. Without further ado, he saddled his trusty old nag and travelled 20 miles to Malton in search of the two players. It would take a day to ride the distance. Market towns were built 20 miles apart for that reason. After locating the two lads, they were delighted to oblige the club, being selected to play for such a prestigious club would give them the opportunity to impress. The following morning being Friday, George sent the message back to Scarborough CC HQ using his pigeon which he carried in his saddlebag, stating that the two players would meet the train at Malton to be united with the team ... (Priceless).

Chapter 7

Scarborough CC and Me ... Helen and Me and our second home ... Lords

Cricket training began in earnest Bill Pincher a young man I had got to know, a very good all rounder from Brompton was also joining Scarborough Cricket Club. We arrived together, my heart missed a beat as we walked through the gates into North Marine Road Scarborough's ground, it looked magnificent a natural amphitheatre, the ground was lush, the nets were erected the players were arriving we were both a little nervous as we were introduced to men I had read about, illustrious players with big reputations Geoff Dennis, (capt) AJ Tony Moor, Colin Oxtoby, C.W Bill Foord, Ray Bloom, Brian Rennard, Ken Stockwell, Chris Kirby and Malcolm Heath. I didn't grasp at that time but these lads and all the others within the club were going to have a great effect on me over the next decade. Net practise was well organised, I was asked to bowl in the first, XI net along with Bill, a good workout with fielding practise at the end of the session, after a shower we all had a chat, Geoff Dennis the xi team skipper made it plain what was expected of Scarborough CC Players.

Blazer shirt and tie was the dress code to all home and away matches, it was paramount that players attended club net sessions at least twice a week, club nights were Monday and Thursday. He stressed if people missed nets they would miss selection. The first XI travelled to away fixtures in a Wallace Arnold Coach provided by the club, plus the allowance for a silver service lunch. It all sounded incredibly professional. C.W Foord or 'Bill' was the senior pro at the club, a legend in his own lifetime, he was a highly respected seamer, opening the bowling for Yorkshire in the 50's taking over 200 wickets. He was now in the twilight of his career, a hive of experience with a wicked dry sense of humour. Colin Oxtoby a farm worker from Weaverthorpe the finest w/keeper I have played alongside, brilliant stood up to the quick's stumpings down the leg side were his forte, a real character never stopped talking and laughing, great lad to be around. Tony AJ Moor would become skipper after Geoff, solid opening bat L/H R/A swing bowler very competitive safest pair of hands in the game. Ken Stockwell opening L/H bat could break any opening bowlers heart, if it was his day no finer sight than watching him bat. These were just a few of the outstanding players on show at the club. The ground was full of committee men, ex players, all gave a welcoming nod. Waid Wood, Tommy Binks, Frank Winn, Len Halstead. These were the driving force behind the successful club and popular cricket festival.

After nets I got the bus home, Dad was keen to know how I got on, when I explained how it all worked at the club he was as excited as myself. I really did enjoy the net sessions, the standard was very high with the competition for places very fierce, after a few weeks the spirit among the players really began to gel we all enjoyed each others company plenty of banter and leg pulling with a few pints thrown in.

Ken Stockwell had arranged for us to visit the local Turkish baths situated in the crescent, after our final net session, this was an experience I was used to and I expected Anna to appear at anytime offering me one of her many delights. With the selection committee meeting on Monday, all players were contacted by post card which appeared on Wednesday, and sure enough on Wednesday the said post card lay snug on the welcome mat, Mr Phil Hart has been selected to the 1st XI for Saturdays game, I was over the moon, I really felt at home, the hard work was paying off as I had hoped it would, the army was now a distant memory, but a memory to cherish. Those days as I was beginning to realize had been so important, they had built me up to become a healthy strong character, harnessing a self confidence that hopefully would produce the rounded article, that was the plan. Helen's mum Marge was my judge, she had become my new surrogate Mum, whenever I got ahead of myself she would be there offering her own form of advice. I was spending more and more of my time with Helen and her family, that was no reflection on relations in Seamer, however I felt Bill Chris and baby probably needed the space.

It was customary in the 1970's to ask for the hand of the girl you were hoping to marry. Helen and Marge had been badgering me for weeks to ask Duncan for permission, as he was away on a regular basis finding the appropriate moment was difficult. Eventually we cornered each other in his lounge, the ladies were conveniently listening behind the door. I was nervous as I scratched around for the right words, setting out my agenda for the future. Duncan to his credit took it all in good faith and he was delighted that Helen and I were to be married, in fact he opened a bottle of bubbly and we toasted the forthcoming wedding. The date of 18 March was selected, which gave us six months to prepare. We found a small semi-detached bungalow in Stapleton Close round the corner from Denison Avenue in Seamer. It was on the market for £3250 and with the mortgage secured we were handed the keys. Wow our own property, what a fantastic feeling, really looking forward to married life. Jack was in his element now, adding this, changing that. It was the time of the power cuts in the early 1970's and I recall we were decorating the inside of the bungalow, with dad busy glossing the woodwork in the lounge and Jack papering the bathroom, when the power went off. Secretly I was delighted as I was knackered after a hard day's work. Without further thought however, Jack got in his car and drove to get his generator and within 45 minutes we had the light to carry on!!. As all the neighbours were blacked out they appeared a little puzzled as to how we had power for the lights. Two Thirty in the morning and I eventually crawled into bed!! ... Whatever Jack was on I wanted some!! Simon Barningham, my buddy for years, was selected as best man for the wedding, but after an altercation he decided that he did not want anything more to do with me or the wedding. Simon was a real introvert, very shy amongst strangers and on reflection I think he was looking for an excuse to pull out.

AJ or Tony Moor had become a good mate from the Cricket Club, and he kindly agreed to step into the breach and be best man. The day arrived, 18 March 1972, it was a beautiful sunny morning and we were to be married at 12 noon. I remember how nervous I was as I walked into Northstead Methodist Church, which was full of all our friends from Seamer, Helen's family who had come from far and wide. Standing next to my best man and waiting ... 10 minutes late she was, and I found out later that arriving a little late for most things is a family trait!! Wherever Jack had to be he would always be late, I recall the mumblings in church and it was a little bit frought, until the organ struck up and we were away!! It seemed to be over in a flash, as we exited the church as man and wife, the players from the club were forming a Guard of Honour with their bats, a novel touch. The reception took place at Scalby Manor, a very popular hostelry, ideal for a family gathering expertly run by the ever popular Shipley family

Family and friends gave us a terrific send off as we were whisked away to the railway station to catch our train to Manchester on route to the Airport. At Manchester Piccadilly we hopped onto a double decker bus, on route to the Airport. We were to enjoy our wedding night in the Excelsior Hotel, the only hotel at that time on the Airport site, a huge difference to the hustle and bustle of today. Up at the crack of dawn to catch our plane to Spain. We flew Dan Air or Dan dare as it was more popularly known at the time. The flight took us to Reus airport near to Barcelona. A coach would then transfer us to the san Marti Hotel in Lloret de Mar. There she was on the tarmac, a majestic looking De Havilland Comet, with sleek beautiful lines. The country's first jet airliner. Apart from Helen and I there were four other honeymoon couples on the flight all going to Lloret ... bizarre really!! We introduced ourselves to the other newlyweds and spent the week enjoying each others company. I wonder at times if they are all still together...I hope so. The whole trip for one week, including flight was a whacking £35, which today seems unbelievable, considering todays prices. We had a wonderful week together, just the two of us, it was certainly the start of a beautiful relationship and friendship. Back home in our little bungalow, our own to do with as we pleased. I took a while to get used to that fact. Helen had to adjust to catching the bus into town everyday, she felt a little isolated living out in the sticks and not having her family on hand.

The cricket season got underway, and I struggled to find any form in the season, the boys put it down to being married and on reflection I guess it may have had something to do with it. Helen's home cooking and such like, but I would work hard and get through the dip in form. The first XI reached the final of the cricketers cup to be played at Lords, a brilliant performance after the disappointment of losing in the semi final the previous season. The Cricketer Cup was established in 1969, a competition to be played out by local club sides at national level. An unbelievable chain of events occurred in the first season of the competition involving Scarborough Cricket Club and Pocklington Pixies. The Pixies were based at a public school in Pocklington. It was a first round match, the weather intervened on the scheduled start date with not a ball being bowled. Due to more rain, the game again failed at the second attempt but a result had to be forthcoming hence the toss of a coin. Due to the terrible stormy conditions, no one from either team turned up at the ground. Geoff Dennis, The Scarborough Captain, after a meeting with John Midgley, the Secretary, decided to ring the Pocklington captain, incredibly and people comment upon it to this day, the toss took place over the phone. Geoff's wife Margaret tossed the coin, the Pocklington skipper cried 'heads'. Geoff had the onerous task of informing the opposition they had called correctly and as such would progress through to the next round. I could not see that occurring in today's world.

We were to be playing Brentham in the final, another tough game in prospect, as their side included Graham Barlow who went on to play for Middlesex and England. I was to be 13th man on this occasion and obviously disappointed. Bill Mustoe was having a terrific season with the bat and ball and deserved his success. We travelled down to London by coach, staying overnight at the Clive Hotel in Hampstead. I recall exiting the coach on arrival at the hotel and making straight for the bar. I got the shock of my life when the beers I bought came to a staggering 50pence each. Ray Bloom our dapper left hand opener arrived in London earlier in the week, and had visited Lords soaking up the atmosphere, the following morning the Coach Driver was made aware of the situation to follow Messrs Bloom to Lords as he knew the directions. It was now 09.15 and the game started at 11.00. After passing and taking in the beauty of Swiss Cottage twice in each direction it was obvious we were lost. The coach then got stuck up a cul de sac. Team members and wives were beginning to panic, the driver was in a lather but eventually with the help of the local constabulary who travelled on the bus with us to direct us to St Johns Wood, we arrived with about 30 minutes to spare. Bill Foord, Malcolm Kirkland and myself, the three reserves so to speak, helped to soothe the players, organise the kit, establish an element of focus, the calm before the storm. As always happens in these situations Geoff Dennis lost the toss and Brentham decided to bat. On reflection we always inserted the opposition if we won the toss. Batsmen at this level were not used to playing in this type of arena and the pressure was far greater for them, as the fielding side had more time to get used to their surroundings. It was game on, the Scarborough support was amazing, with thousands making the journey by coach, train and car. As we scanned the ground, familiar faces came into view. Before the lads took that long walk down the steps and through the historic long room, Geoff had another rabbit in his hat, out came a bottle of scotch with a nip given to each player ... just to calm them down!! My old pal, Bill Alley was one of the umpires, Lofty Herman being the other. The game got off to a steady start, both teams handling the pressure until after lunch when the Scarborough bowlers with controlled line and length got their just rewards, helped by some first class catches taken by the fielders.

Bill Pincher angled a delivery down the leg side, the batsman got a faint nick, Colin Oxtoby showing his outstanding ability caught the ball as well as stumping the batsman, and the photo shows both umpires with their fingers up, all in the blink of an eye, great skill. The feeling at the interval was one of controlled euphoria, the supporters were enjoying the situation as well as the beer in the pavilion, Eddie Willmore my old mate from Seamer was trying to climb the flagpole without much success, Bill Foord was twelfth man and Malcolm Kirkland fourteenth, I must be truthful I wasn't enjoying being stuck in the dressing room like a spare prick at a wedding it was only that bottle of whiskey that helped ease the sorrow. We got off to a flier, Ken Stockwell and Ray Bloom putting on 50 for the first wicket. The crowd were sensing victory, then typically cricket was having its say, and before you could shout Bill Robinson we were four down. It was left up to Messrs Mustoe and Moor to see us home, they did so in style with Bill caressing a six over the tavern bar out of the ground into St Johns Wood, a great finale. It was as if we had won the ashes, I guess that's how I felt for the players. Our supporters were on the ground outside the dressing rooms chanting Scarborough, Scarborough, it was amazing, Geoff went up to collect the trophy presented by Mr ER Brown, the Derek Robins trophy and it was going to stand in our trophy cabinet at NMR, we were the club champions.

The Brentham team, assembled in our dressing room extending their good wishes to a great team effort. I thought that was a humbling gesture on their part which puts it all into perspective, it was the game that won the day. We as a squad enjoyed a few drinks with the supporters, then it was back on the coach and up the M1 back to gods country. We had been, seen, and conquered. On our way out of the gates, I looked back wondering if ever we could repeat this day. Personally I would have given my back teeth to have played but it was not to be, therefore on the coach trip home, I decided it was time I entertained, it was my turn now.

Up to the front of the coach, I took control of the microphone we were now flying, I introduced a rule that everyone on the coach had to sing a song of their choice, or recite a poem or monologue, the bus was in uproar, we had committee men and their wives who to us minions lived on another planet. They gave their all from The Old Wooden Cross. Onward Christian soldiers to living doll. It was one hell of a ride home, arriving back at around 03.30am truly magical day fond memories. About a week later the team and wives visited the clubs and pubs acknowledging their great support and showing off the trophy, but before this took place we were invited to the Town Hall for a Mayors Reception, Helen was enjoying herself, she loved a whiskey and dry ginger.

With all the speeches by the dignitaries exhausted it was off to shake some hands, the final stop on this rollercoaster of a night was the Rosette with landlord Ken Middleton, by this stage of the proceedings Helen was out of her tree she was passed redemption. I had never seen her in this state, I had to take her home, poor lass what a night I had with her, she has never touched a drop of whiskey since even the smell makes her heave. Geoff Dennis and Bill Foord announced their retirements forthwith, and Bill Pincher had been approached by Saltburn in the North Yorkshire South Durham league to become their professional. It was great for Geoff to finish on such a high, a little sad to be losing both Bill Pincher, who would take some replacing and Mr Foord what can one say, we wished them all well, as this chapter comes to a close. Mr AJ Tony Moor the new skipper of the 1st XI for the following season, I was looking forward to his professional ideals and leadership.

Plaxtons were turning out their new brand of luxury coaches, the new factory was now complete, twelve new spray bays had been installed and they were running to full capacity. The job of maintaining the bays was hectic, trying to keep them up and running, a bit like painting the Humber Bridge. Helen enjoyed her work at the bank, she worked full time putting in the hours helping to keep the wolf from the door. We enjoyed the winter having more time together, away from the hectic life style of summer with cricket practice and matches at weekends.

Helen never put any pressure my way regarding cricket, I could think of a few wives who might have tried it on, I believe Helen was pleased I was enjoying the game with Scarborough, she would have hated dragging me shopping on a Saturday God Forbid!! All in all as a couple we were very happy, loads of friends a busy social scene good fun!

Dad had really enjoyed the cricket he was my biggest fan, he had made new buddies on the coach as we travelled hither and thither, he also made for the rear of the coach to take part in the card school, he loved his cards no matter what they played. He seemed to have recovered from losing Mum, I know she was in all our thoughts but he had found a way to move on. In the winter months, he travelled far and wide to whist drives, rumour had it he had met a lady on his travels, no doubt the subject will pop up when Dad decides its right.

Marge and Duncan loved to celebrate Christmas, especially Duncan (Jack). He went to great lengths to provide the very best fayre for his family, this was our first Christmas married it felt very special. The lunch with us all present Chris, Dennis and little Sue. Family occasions tend to bring out the reflective mood, I raised a glass in honour of absent friends, I looked around the table and thought what a hell of a year.

In 1974 I moved jobs, Jack sanctioned the move into the factory semi skilled roll as a coach cleaner in the delivery bay, the wages were much better, it was hard physical graft climbing and stretching, ideal work for keeping me in good shape. We worked in gangs of four, there was no room for slackers it was all hands to the pump. Jack Smith was our ganger an ex military policeman, another character as you travel lifes highway you meet these extraordinary buddies, I can say with hand on heart, it was a pleasure to have worked alongside this exceptional talent.

I believe this was the year of the three day week, inflation topped 28% the country was stagnating, when I think back I wonder how we ever survived, I guess when your younger you just take it all in your stride.

We bought our first car, an Austin Somerset second hand from a friend of Jacks, I paid £40 after some bartering. It was quite big and bulbous, with leather bench seats at the front, the gears were on the steering column, and the indicators were those little yellow arms that shot out of the side by the doors. What fun we had in that car, I taught Helen to drive in it, the only drawback was the starter ring it had some teeth missing and it had a tendency to stall. It always seemed to stall at the most embarrassing times and places. The procedure went as follows stall, try starter button, no response have now to get the starting handle out, kicks the bloody car. Traffic lights were its favourable stalling points, Helen refused to drive because of this quirk, we laughed and cried over that Austin Somerset, great memories. It was with a hint of sadness we got rid and went a little up market, a popular family saloon the Vauxhall Viva, it was also second hand, and proved to be a winner all round.

1976 got off to a steady start, Plaxtons were introducing a new model of luxury coach to be displayed at Earls Court during the prestigious motor show. Helen and I were on the move also, we were moving to Scalby Village just to the North of Scarborough, a delightful rural community, quite posh. The property was a small semi bungalow on

Station Road and as luck would have it, it was next door to Christine and Dennis. Jack got started making plans for the makeover, we were busy again, changing old for new. It took us a couple of months to sell our existing property, and we moved to Scalby in April. Helen was delighted with the move, she was very close to Chris, typical sisters they had similar interests shopping, shopping and shopping. Jack and Marge were only round the corner which made life much easier, we enjoyed our time in Seamer, but Helen felt a little cut off. It was strange to be leaving Seamer personally after all the years, the village was changing, they were building hundreds of houses during this boom time and the old village was resembling suburbia, similar to all the surrounding villages.

Scarborough CC was heading in the right direction under the leadership of Tony Moor we were competing for more honours, becoming a force to be reckoned with, Bill Pincher was performing wonders in the North Yorkshire South Durham League, helping Saltburn win the title. We were drafting in new players, the pleasing aspect of this, they were coming to play from the local leagues

Martin Shepherdson, and Steve Glaves, from Forge Valley CC both Seam bowlers, Steve being left arm and deceivingly quick gave us a new dimension. I personally had the balls makers name imprinted on my forehead as I mistimed a hook from Steven during an evening league encounter. Also joining us Chris Clifford, he would become my spin twin. He bowled off spin with great success claiming over a thousand league wickets, he had been away with Warwickshire in the championship. Colin Oxtoby had retired to Bradford after meeting a lady, he had taken a job in a factory it seemed so sad, like a duck out of water. He was replaced by a young gun from Driffield, David Kneeshaw another character, success was built around self confident young men, and we had no shortage of them. Also into the frame arrived two lads from the York area, Richard Sherwood and Phillip Woodliffe, they were competent all rounders.

We had been drawn away in every round of the National Club Knockout, now known as the Haig trophy the whiskey company had snapped up the chance of sponsoring the competition. Sponsorship was now the buzz word around all sporting venues, clubs and teams were now becoming so reliant on multi national or national companies injecting enormous amounts of capital into whatever sport. Scarborough CC were no exception, in the past money was generated from membership and the successful Scarborough cricket festival. With the on set of agents representing players, Scarborough CC could no longer afford to stage the popular 6th test match, over the many years Scarborough CC festival played host to the touring side of that summer.

In 1948 Sir Donald Bradman scored a century before lunch, remarking that it was one of the better wickets he had batted on, North Marine Road, became renowned through out the cricketing world as a top venue, but with the reduction in first class fixtures, membership declined, it became plainly obvious that sponsorship was here to stay.

Fenners the engineering company from Hull became one of Scarborough CC initial major sponsors, it is to them we offer thanks and gratitude. Our performances as a team were looking good, all the practise was paying dividends. The skipper expected a full turnout at least once a week normally a Thursday night, for some it meant an hours travelling they were keen, it didn't put 'em off. We were top of the league by a mile hadn't lost a game, and after some close shaves we had reached the semi finals of the Haig trophy. It was turning into a marvellous season, the weather was amazing, the grounds were brown through lack of rain the team was excelling in all departments, every player had contributed in some way we were a bloody class outfit.

Malcolm Davidson was on the fringe of the team, and we have him to thank for us reaching the semi finals. Mally came in as a wicket keeper at the last minute, it got down to the last over up in Benwell near Newcastle, Mally caught the batter off the last ball, it was drama as they only needed three to win. Cricket has that tendency to put you through hell, your emotions are tested to the limit, you can be winning one minute then lose a couple of wickets, and before you know it backs to the wall. I look back in wonder on occasion how we got through some of those encounters. I have Helen to thank as she became my counsellor, we used to bounce off each other, grammatically speaking!!

The semi finals another away fixture down to North London, Southgate CC, if we were lucky to come out on top, then the following week we would be travelling again, to Lord's for the final. The wicket looked very green they had a couple of decent bowlers but there again so did we. Tony won the toss and decided to bat, the ball seamed around early on as we knew it would, the wickets began to fall I remember sitting next to Chris Clifford with my pads on we were 60 for 5. Someone had to come off, then I was in on my way to the middle, Phil Woodliffe met me I told him to play his normal game and let's look for some quick singles. The god's were with us we were nudging a few, I remember creaming a cover drive on the up, you have no idea the satisfaction and confidence that relays to you, we had a chat between overs, they were beginning to lose it, the tide was slowly turning.

I reached my 50 with a straight six, I was using Steve's Glave's bat, he was a gamekeeper and he'd drilled some lead shot into the toe, this enhanced its performance no end. I was out in the penultimate over for 64. Phil ended up with around 40 to take over total of 167 for7 I enjoyed my tea, the place was buzzing.

Malcolm Heath our gentle giant 6'6" he was the man for this occasion, Malcolm had played first class cricket with Hampshire trundling in and releasing the ball from the heavens to get the bounce and lift, in the season 1958 he took 128 wickets, Ken Stockwell with his variation, Tony Moor with his swing were far too good for the Southgate batsmen, these three intrepid performers saw us home bowling them out for 91. We had a drink or two after the game, the Southgate lads were in awe of our set up. One lad was explaining how much it cost him to play for Southgate for a season, £500 and that didn't include petrol we were dumbfounded, he nearly fell down when I laid out our costs, a membership at that time £4.75 with a Wallace Arnold thrown in for away games. We felt quite smug but the real picture told a different story. We all knew how difficult it was going to be for the club to afford another trip away, the big one. It was a marvellous trip home that night, very satisfying personally, getting a chance and taking it meant everything to me. I enjoyed reading the local newspaper that week, the town was gearing up for another assault on Lords. The clubs and pubs were ordering coaches, people were keen to shake your hand to wish you good luck. Walking out onto the hallowed turf as a player was another first, very exciting walking through the wicket gate, onto the ground, another marvellous turnout of supporters and beautiful day to boot.

We were playing another London squad, Dulwich CC, they looked a formidable outfit a real multi cultural mix, West Indians, Pakistanis, and an Aussie, they won the toss and elected to bat, after the 45 overs they only managed 136 for 9, all our bowlers really hit their line, and length from the first delivery, Ken Stockwell bagging three middle order scalps for only 13 runs, Malcolm Heath and Martin Shepherdson also picking up wickets. The crowd were in full voice as we began the run chase, it got off to the worst of starts as Dave Kneeshaws middle stump careered down the ground, in walked Brian Pedro Rennard a local fish fryer to stop the rot.

It was an anxious time sat on the balcony, the game was in the balance, Brian was still there as yours truly made his way to the middle, we were teetering at 70-5, and I was hoping my form of late with the bat would continue, the opposition were baiting me as I arrived at the crease.

I believe their sledging hardened my resolve, and it worked against them. Brian met me the middle, "it's six an over Phil!" wow I thought, "Well lets bloody go and get 'em!" My first delivery from the West Indian was a Jaffa, how it missed the stumps only him upstairs knows, the wicket keeper was the Aussie, he was questioning my ability in no uncertain terms, real Australian sledging. I kept talking to myself, don't make eye contact with the little shit, slowly but surely we were getting the run rate down. Brian played some big shots, he reached his fifty, I finished the game with a six into the tavern bar where apparently, I had hit a lady in a wheelchair.

I turned to shake the keepers hand but he had legged it, what a performance the two of us embraced in the middle to win a final at Lord's brilliant, the crowd were rushing onto the pitch they thought it was all over!!! I strolled back to the pavilion enjoying the moment friends slapping me on the back, shaking hands total delirium. After the prize giving it was back to the Hotel we were staying at the Westmorland just across the road, the club had booked us in for two nights we had a very enjoyable evening as you can imagine.

The next week we wrapped up the Yorkshire League, only losing the one game all season, a phenomenal performance, and during the following winter we went onto win the Yorkshire indoor championship 6 a side. The treble or full set, 1976 I believe was my most memorable season.

After the euphoria of 1976 it was going to take something extraordinary to top it in 1977. Early winter I was contacted by Normanby Hall a club in North Yorkshire, South Durham League, Bill Pincher had recommended me to them, offering me the job of club professional, this was a new direction and challenge, I mentioned it to the powers that be at North Marine Road explaining it would only be a short contract. They didn't want to stand in my way, and would welcome me back whenever. I would be paid for playing the game I loved, money had certainly entered the cricketing arena at this time, most league clubs were having to pay players. Normanby Hall was on the outskirts of Middlesbrough a bonny ground, the local supporters and players were very welcoming and very knowledgeable, they loved their sport, Dave Cooke w/k brother of Geoff, the Director of Cricket at Durham, he was one of the funniest men I have ever played the game alongside, he was a decent wicket keeper and batsman, but hilariously funny, not that the opposition always saw it in the same light. Kenny Thwaites, the skipper, lovely man stood a metre outside his leg stump and still managed to accumulate hundreds of runs, also a very talented musician the piano being his forte. We managed to be successful in two cup competitions that season beating Bill Pinchers Saltburn in one of them, I enjoyed that. I bought a Triumph 1500 before the season started as it was a bloody awful road to Middlesbrough. I needed something reliable. Dad enjoyed the change of venues, meeting new people visiting new surroundings. I was to play two seasons for Normanby

Hall very enjoyable. I honestly don't think the role of the club professional was what I was about. Building a spirit, creating an atmosphere of self-belief encouraging confidence in the young players, this was I believed the springboard to success within any club, all players equal, this had been Scarborough CC's policy over the years. But times were a changing.

Helen came to me during August of 1978, with the news that she was expecting. We had been trying for some time and it was wonderful news, she was so happy, everyone in the family were delighted, Christine had just given birth to a daughter Clare, to have two babies living next door to each other was going to change our lives forever, bring it on!

Chapter 8

Katie ... Lords Again ... the Caribbean and Jumping out of an Aeroplane!!

1979 all the talk as you could imagine was of nurseries, names for the baby, boy or girl, we had decided on the wait and see approach, as it was more exciting than actually knowing before hand. The baby was due in March, the weather that winter was very cold. I remember the week before the baby was due, we had a lot of snow, we were trying to get to Cloughton for a drink with friends, but alas the roads were blocked drifts higher than a car stretched across Burniston road. Helen was heavy with child people our friends were positive it would be a boy, she was pretty fed up and was ready for action.

Friday the 2 March, still no signs, Dave Burgess a good pal who lived further down Station Road, called for me as usual that evening to go for a pint into the village, it was the Friday night gang, friends from work we would have a few in the Rosette, the Nags Head and one for the road in the Plough. I arrived back home at around 11.30, Helen bless her was sat there her waters had just burst, don't panic Mr Mainwaring was the call, the overnight bag had been packed for days, into the car, I realised I was over the limit, but took the chance all the same, the hospital was only a couple of miles away, I drove with caution. On arrival Helen was quickly assessed, she was hurried away into the maternity ward. I remember it was a long night, helping to stay calm. I felt like a spare part. We had discussed the birth of the baby many times, it had become vogue, for men to assist at birth with their bloody box brownies to witness the event, it had never been my intention. I had the greatest respect for the mid wifery staff. They did not need some 6 foot awkward, over excited lad getting in the way, the day passed without interruption. I recall sitting outside with the husband of the young lady in the next room, they had just arrived. I was stunned when he explained that his baby had just died, the chord had got wrapped around the child's neck, and that she still would have the baby naturally, that pulled me up by my bootlaces, I couldn't imagine what that must have felt like, that couple were from Ganton, I often think back to those days and wonder in hope that they went on to have kids.

By tea time I was feeling a bit jaded, Helen suggested I should go home check everything was ok, she insisted she was fine and in control. I had a bath changed my clothes called on Marge and Duncan to keep them abreast of events arrived back to the ward, away about an hour, Helen had been taken into the delivery room, it was game on, then within minutes the door opened, and a nurse was holding a bundle wrapped in blankets, a little girl she said. Absolutely fantastic there she was my beautiful little daughter Katie Elizabeth had arrived. Mother and daughter were fine, I hugged Helen tears flowing from both of us, such a relief, it's now I was thinking of the couple next door some of my tears were definitely for them. This was an amazing time, a miracle, all the tiny fingers and toes were there the beautiful texture of the skin and those incredible little eyes, my mind was racing.

Bringing a new life into the world, being responsible it certainly was a sobering thought. She was born 20.15 on Sat 3rd March the most rewarding happiest day of my life. I stayed with Helen and Katie for a while until the mid wife suggested I should leave as Helen was tired. Marge, Duncan and Susie were ecstatic another granddaughter to spoil. The following evening I made it to the Blacksmith Arms Cloughton, and with my buddies Alan Readman, and Barry Wood, and wives Teresa and Pam we celebrated the arrival of Katie Elizabeth. The celebration carried on until the early hours. Helen arrived home after a few days of recuperation, I had everything organised at home for her return, cooked her a lovely meal, here we were at last our own little family. Dad and all the family were thrilled with the news, it had certainly been worth the wait. Helen took to motherhood, it was such a natural transition to her life, I enjoyed getting stuck in changing nappies, getting up to feed her at all hours. We had the cot in our bedroom it took a while getting used to the noises and snufflings that babies make, I wouldn't have changed it for the world.

It was exciting to be back at North Marine Road having had two seasons away, it was great to hook up with my old buddies again with more new faces, and competition for places would be as keen as ever. Chris Stevenson a farmer from Middleton on the Wolds, he was an experienced player and would form a reliable partnership with Tony Moor opening the batting, Chris was quite a dour character mentally very tough, owner of racehorses therefore enjoyed a good gamble, member of the back seat card school. Mel Brown wicket keeper batter arrived from local village side at Flixton, Mel was a flamboyant character in the haulage business, safe pair of hands, enjoyed his cricket very enthusiastic, Simon Dennis son of former skipper Geoff, nephew of Sir Leonard Hutton, left arm medium quick loads of potential would go on and play for Yorkshire and Glamorgan, lovely lad if not a little laid back, natural smooth action.

Not someone you rushed into the shower with as he would quickly intimidate you, as he had the nickname of 'donkey'.... very apt. John Precious, a young local player, good all round athlete, very quick between wickets, was very keen to learn. Amazingly the final new face in the mix was a cricketing legend Brian Close, England, Yorkshire and Somerset ...how good was that, it would be a privilege I'm sure for all of us to have his expertise on board.

Local business man Don Robinson had signed Closey to help promote Scarborough Football club gain admittance into the Football League. I was quite nervous about meeting the great man, the first Saturday we were at home, I arrived early to the dressing rooms on entering, there he was cup of tea in one hand, the sporting life in the other, and we made him very welcome.

Over the season it became very clear to me the effect Closey was having in the dressing room, he was always offering advice on all aspects of the game, a bottomless pit of knowledge. I'm sure the players who were willing to listen gained that quality information, which went onto enhance their performances. He was a tough task master in the middle, if he placed you in a particular fielding position and you moved you got a bollocking, no problem about that

He knew how a batsman was going to perform within a ball or two, and made the adjustment to suit, I remember he had this thing about batman's grips, we were playing in this particular round of the Haig trophy up in Tyndale, County Durham, these lads would come into bat, he would notice their grips and how they picked the bat up, after they had taken their guard, he would comment, "you won't score many With that grip lad, come and see me after the game." After the game which we won comfortably, he had a queue lined up, this was typical of the man, passing on his knowledge, he held court at most of the grounds we visited.

Brian loved his whiskey after a game, with a drop of lemonade, his language was a little choice at times, but this was a man's champion he reminded me of King Arthur or Sir Galahad. On one occasion we were playing Castleford away, Geoffrey Boycott was opening the batting for them, coming back after injury, he was his usual focused self at the crease, never looked in any trouble. Tony Moor, brought me on to bowl, in my first over I got one to move off straight, it caught the edge of his bat straight to Close at first slip, the safest hands in Christendom, he dropped the bloody thing I could have cried, he was an England selector at that time but surely that wouldn't have any bearing, would it?

Boyc's went on to make a hundred, but it wasn't enough, we knocked them off in true style. Mentioning Geoffrey Boycott, brought another story to mind, involving him. We were playing at Headingly against Leeds, back in 1972 again he was returning to the game after breaking a finger, Leeds won the toss and elected to bat, Geoffrey opened the batting alongside Richard Lumb, we had a young quick bowler who had just arrived to play for us from Hull C.C.

Barry Middleton, he came on first change there was a sizable crowd in, around 5,000, they obviously knew Boyc's would be playing. Barry or Bud as we called him ran in and bowled a beamer straight at Geoffrey's head he went down like a sack of spuds, as he climbed to his feet, adjectives were flying, 'You F***ing t**t, Bud who was a pragmatic character didn't seem to flinch he picked up the ball strode back to his mark. He ran in again and bloody hell, he gave him another straight at his head, the crowd became incensed, Boyc's was brushing himself down, then he called Geoff Dennis our skipper over, he'd never seen anything like this from Scarborough players he was definitely irritated by this confrontation. Bud was taken off after his over. Boycott carried on intimidating players of both sides, Bill Mustoe who was a little rotund to say the least was fielding in the gully, Boyc's played the ball square, through the hapless Mustoe's legs, two he called, he's only a pudding, we claimed the wicket, of Richard Lumb and in strode Jim Love another young tyke making his way up the rankings. Jim was a good timer of the ball, he played a lovely cover drive splitting the field, and immediately called for two, at the end of the over, Geoffrey confronted Jim in the middle, "Now lad this crowd has come to see me bat, I'll tell you when there's two." It was no joke out there, he was deadly serious, and ok he was an international star performer on the world's stage. Well he didn't cover himself in glory that Saturday.

I enjoyed the 1979 season, we had a lot of fun on the road, played some very good cricket, we were a top side, in fact we got to the final of the Haig trophy, going for a hat trick of victories, and it was the icing on the cake taking Brian Close back to Lord's. The competition had caught the imagination of the media, North, South divide, and with the inclusion of Close, they really gave it a boost in the national newspapers, another buzz around the town it would be unprecedented to win the trophy three times.

We were to play Reading CC in the final, we were obvious favourites which I believe adds a little more pressure to the situation, both sides were staying at the Westmorland Hotel, and each team had organised dinners for after the game, who would be dining as the winners, let the war commence!

We won the toss, and put them in, we discussed a different strategy, and it was decided that I would open the bowling with Steve Glaves quick's, my slow left arm might just unsettle them. After my eight overs, I had picked up a couple of wickets. I went for 17 runs including four maidens, Reading amassed 190 for 4 in their 45 overs. It was a quicker wicket than we were used to on our previous visits, it was surely going to make for an interesting finale, the supporters were a little restrained, they knew drama would ensue.

We got off to the worst possible start, both our prolific openers out for one a piece. Consolidate that was the buzz word in the dressing room, plenty of time, play yourself in, the boys did just that. Brian Rennard, with his experience helping Phil Woodcliffe through the initial crisis, putting on fifty. Close, got a rousing reception from the whole crowd as he made his way to the middle, love him or hate him at 49 years of age, striding out as if he were 18 years old, again no fear!!

He played his part keeping the board ticking over, he and Richard Sherwood, taking the total into the mid hundreds, Simon Dennis was next the young protégé, and he was shaking like a leaf, after he made his way through the long room, into the cauldron. It was now building up into one hell of a game. Reading were giving us a run for our money, John Precious added another dozen with Simon, I was now putting on my pads, on the drinks trolley in the dressing room nestling behind a jug was a bottle of lager, unbeknown to my buddies I quickly released the stopper and downed it, just what I needed to steady my old nerves.

John got out, and so did Mel Brown which left yours truly, it felt strange once I realised it was me, all my actions going forward were in slow motion. I started to make my way through the door of the dressing room, to the encouragement of the team, then ran back as I had forgotten my bat. We needed four to win, Simon would be facing, it was the last over.

He met me as I sauntered to the middle, poor Simon he had played ever so well, under tremendous pressure it would have been rough justice to fall short at this late stage. He then came out with the most profound statement, "What shall I do?" I gave him an icy stare before contemplating my reply, "do what you have to but try not to involve me." Without further ado, he went for the big one, and as a saving grace the ball struck his pad and scampered away for four leg byes, the finest leg byes I'd ever seen, it was pandemonium, the tears were flowing three wins out of three just champion. After the hilarity in the dressing room which honestly could have gone all night for me, we got prepared for our dinner. All the wives and girlfriends were in good spirits at the hotel as we arrived back.

After the dinner and speeches, Tony Moor's brother Brian an ex Scarborough player, who now worked in London for the Lyons group, would present three trophies, they were beautiful wall clocks. Sponsored by his firm. How exciting as I was presented with the bowling award, we had a fantastic evening, we were getting used to all this glitz, the Haig whiskey, dignitaries, were becoming old friends. Reading CC, all walked into the room and stood and clapped it was amazing, they were a good side, showing great character, I could see them winning sooner rather than later. Back home after a long journey on the coach, Katie Elizabeth was pleased to see us both again, Nana and granddad had enjoyed her company.

The following week after the triumph at Lords we were back down to Earth with a bang, we had to beat Barnsley away at Shaw Lane to win the Yorkshire League. Another double, I remember I was bowling we needed to dislodge one of the final pair to win. Closey pulled off an amazing piece of skill for a man of his years, he was very light on his feet, he was fielding very close to the bat silly mid off, as I ran into bowl he would creep closer undetected just like a lion going in for the kill, the batsman was obviously defending every delivery, this bounced a little and the batter had to defend higher up the bat, Close pounced and scooped the ball up, before it landed, brilliant I'd have paid to have seen it on camera.

Another double another great season, and to top it off at the Yorkshire Leagues Annual Dinner I was awarded the Yorkshire League bowler of the year award, I won it again in 1980, all the practice and hard slog was beginning to pay off. I thanked the lads for all the catches they caught to make it possible.

We had another important task to perform. The christening of Katie Elizabeth. Over the past year I had found another buddy, his name was Willy Maw, he was a friend of the local Blacksmith Alan Readman who also had become a good friend of mine. Willy was in his seventies and lived in the old folks dwellings in Cloughton Village with his sister, Millie. She was in her eighties, they were true farming people of a truly rural background lovely genuine Yorkshire Folk, Willy had come to live in the village after spending his life in a cottage up on the Moor, his family could be traced back through the generations to around the 1600's. To me Willy was living proof of times past, we would walk miles and he would recall his memories, tell his stories in his own dialect, a mine of information. He owned ten acres of pasture adjacent to the cottage, in the annual rotation of the crops, he knew when to cut the grass when the first swallow was sighted.

He married a dancer from the variety shows that performed in Scarborough throughout the summer season, they took up residence in the cottage, she wasn't too impressed and it was annulled after ten days, I remember sitting in his little bungalow at Cloughton when a letter came for Willy it was the decree nisi from 50 years previous, Millie was another inspirational character, she was church warden at the local church up at Stainton Dale, it would be close to a three mile hike, most Sundays she would walk to the church and hopefully get picked up on the way. Millie asked me if I would like to have Katie christened at Stainton Dale, our local vicar Chris Tubbs would like to take the service as it was part of his diocese. I said it would be perfect, and we set the date.

After the ceremony, we had arranged a buffet tea at Scarborough Cricket Club. It was a beautiful day for weather, the scenery up there on a clear day is a wondrous sight. All the guests arrived, the guest of honour arrived in her carry cot, and she was able to lift her head over the edge as she turned onto her tummy. She must have wondered what all the fuss was about.

It was all quite basic inside the little church, the tiny chairs that reminded me of my primary school days, the mobile keyboard on a stand played with enthusiastic dexterity sort of in tune to the hymns. The parents and godparents plus leading lady then made their way to the font at the rear, Rev Tubbs had relieved Millie of a jumbo flask of hot water, he then poured the liquid into the font as all who had gathered round stared into the abyss a cloud of hot steam rose with great effect to fog up his spectacles and cause a little panic amongst the flock. The reverend to his credit obviously through previous experiences, beckoned to Millie, "A little more cold water Millie." Within a blink of an eye, and a test with an elbow the ceremony was back on track, Katie played her part to perfection no tears or tantrums, it was a truly lovely family occasion, helped by the warmth of our many friends. I thanked Chris Tubbs for a memorable service, it still brings a smile to my face.

Another Mayors Reception at the Town Hall Tom Young, who I had known from my Seamer days he was the chairman of the committee when we built the new cricket pavilion, he had become the Mayor quite fitting really. He congratulated the team for helping to put Scarborough on the map. Chris Stevenson had arranged a cricketing tour to Barbados in November, he had been before, he felt we would all benefit from a couple of weeks in the sun, it would include wives or girlfriends, most of the boys were up for it, Helen was keen to go, but not too keen to be leaving Katie. Marge and Duncan agreed it would be a perfect break for us both, and they would love to look after the baby. Plaxtons sanctioned my request for time off, my buddies were giving me a hard time on the shop floor after I had broken the news about the tour. I kept singing the popular reggae song, 'We're going to Barbados' It would be the perfect end to a great season.

On a miserable rainy day in November, Helen and myself accompanied Tony and Joan Moor in his car, down to Tonbridge in Kent we were going to stay with his brother, Brian and wife Helen, before catching the flight to Barbados from Gatwick the following morning. Eight games of cricket had been arranged on the island against decent opposition, we were to be staying at the Sea View Hotel, whose owner Bobby Weatherhead was a cricket fanatic. Bobby met us at the airport he was very enthusiastic relishing our stay, attached to the hotel was a very highly rated restaurant 'Green Sleeves' where we were welcomed with champagne and canapés? As it was November that meant rain might intervene and spoil the cricket not to worry we would get over that small hurdle. We had 27 bodies in the party, Farmers, Fish fryers, Building society managers a cross section to behold, it was a truly convivial group who enjoyed each others company. We hired 7 mini mokes, which were small open top mini type cars to ferry us from A to B. Our initial excursion is worth a mention. Richard Sherwood happened to be the lead scout, he lead us off down into Bridgetown the capital, it was agreed that wherever he felt like stopping he should stop. All the ladies were in their finery, some much finer than others, I'm talking long dresses, matching diamond earrings, and necklaces, not forgetting the blue rinse, they were dressed for limo's not mokes.

After a few miles in convoy Richard had come across a shack or shanty with a liquor sign flashing in neon, the owner couldn't believe his luck, he had been in the process of cutting a man's hair, he soon showed him the door, and called us across, we took a vote and went for it this was basic bajan culture, not some overpriced commercial club, the ladies were a little sceptical to say the least as they entered this local fleshpot.

It was touch and go whether the party would stick together, I was enjoying the music, the ambience it was definitely a new experience for most, it took a couple of drinks before our party began to relax, the ladies began to sway to the beat of the intoxicating reggae, bottles of Banks to their lips, this was the real Barbados I'm sure the proprietor thought we were royalty as he sent out for more bottles. Sat wedged into a corner of the shanty was a white man, he looked a little dishevelled long white hair and beard, he asked us where we were from, then the story took an extraordinary twist, we mentioned we were a touring party from Scarborough Yorkshire, he became quite emotional, he was born in Hutton Buscel a village five miles to the West of Scarborough, as a young lad he attended the Graham Sea Training School in Scarborough, and then went on to gain his skippers ticket in Hull. How amazing that we had made this little bar our port of call, it was as if it had been meant to be, this old salt had gone to Primary school in Wykeham Village with our skipper Geoff Dennis, he explained after another rum and coke, that the devil drink had got the better of him and he had been stripped of his maritime status. He was delighted to make contact with us, he did mention the fact that if you ended up drunk in the gutter in Barbados.

There would be a good chance you would wake up with your wallet, no chance of that happening in any of the other West Indian Islands, in fact he stated you would probably not wake up. A very interesting evening and we had Richard Sherwood to thank for that. The weather became quite unsettled as the days flew by, it would rain just enough to put the cricket off then the sun would crack the paint, we used the beach facilities of the Hilton Hotel next door, very exclusive. One of the games organised, was slap bang in the centre of a sugar cane plantation, it had rained during the night the wicket to be honest was unfit, but both sides made an effort, we rolled about laughing after the first delivery was sent down it just plugged into the muddy wicket, both sides realising the futility of it all, lit the barbeque then invited us to a limbo competition.

Those Negro boys were incredible, they were lower than snake's bellies, reckoned to limbo under toilet doors, I don't think Helen used a public loo ever after that remark. The jolly roger was a must trip, the party assembled on the quay in Bridgetown. The little vessel was prepared for partying, most of our gang were on board, the boat was a replica of an old pirate ship which visited these waters regularly, before we sailed, the local lads entertained us, by diving into the harbour for coins, there was rubbish in there, dead animals, waste of all descriptions, diesel floating about, it didn't deter these hardy souls, I'm sure they would have sold there mothers for a few quid. This was Barbados before the influx of the elite with their posh villas and exclusive lifestyles. I remember vividly as the cruise ships docked, noticing all the rich flamboyant widows and divorcees mincing their way down the gangplank, all the Black lads hanging out of the trees flexing their bulging muscles waiting for the call.

We set sail for our day of raw fun, the music was blaring, the beers were hitting the spot, it wasn't long before we were all dancing and singing, not all our party had found their sea legs. Tony and Joan Moor were sent below, they were both suffering from the effects, their condition became a cause for concern therefore they were transferred to a ferry to take them back to shore. The rest of the gang stayed together on board, it was a magical day, there was a mix of nationalities enjoying the party. The climate made all the difference, I was trying to imagine the same deal, rocking and rolling in the North Sea it just doesn't have that same ring to it, partying in the Caribbean has all the ingredients you would imagine it to have sun, sea and how's yer Father.

A few days later just round the corner from our digs, there was a mugging, a young honeymoon couple who were actually staying at the Sea View had been attacked and a gun had been used. The girl as you could have imagined was in a distressed state, I never actually saw the couple as they were whisked away. That put a damper on proceedings people were very wary, some of the older members got quite scared.

Bobby Weatherhead to his credit, offered to stage a beach party for us at Bathsheba which is on the opposite coast, where it is naturally beautiful, the Atlantic coast where the sea is spectacularly rough, it would also fall on Independence Day, we had been invited to help the locals form a chain link round the island by all holding hands at a set time and break the record for this event. Another brilliant day. Bathsehaba lived up to its billing, breathtaking scenery, the chain link was successful achieving a record, the party with all the food and drink was just carnival, people singing and dancing we ended by giving the locals a rendition of On Ilkely Moor Bah Tat!! followed by Scarborough Fair. A most memorable tour the cricket became incidental, I think I managed one full game and the one recollection I have of that, was after the game teaching the locals how to bar dive, this was a new phenomenon devised at North Marine Road now sweeping the cricketing world.

Helen and I had never had a tan in November before, it was quite a novelty, and it soon vanished. It was a little odd when we arrived home, we rushed up to Marge and Duncans we were dying to see Katie, Helen rushed in to the lounge Katie was in her basket she didn't recognise either one of us. Helen was a little upset, Marge reassured her that it was a natural reaction, after a day, they were both reunited in smiles, and giggles.

Clare next door was six months older than Katie they were both blondes and looked just like sisters. It was now 1980 another decade, the seventies had seemed to fly by, it must be a sign of getting older I was the grand old age of 33. A friend Robin Atkinson had put his Labrador dog to Richard Hutton the local vets bitch, as a friendly gesture, he gave me pick of the litter, I took Katie with me to choose our pup we arrived home with Sally she was eight weeks old, a little yellow Labrador, Helen was over the moon with our new addition, it was like having another baby, up in the night settling her down.

Sally soon grew, as all puppies do finding their feet. Our kitchen table and chairs became her toy, as she chewed them to bits, the kitchen carpet next. I used to walk miles with her round the perimeter, pushchair in one hand and the dog in the other. As all dog owners will be aware the puppy stage seems to reach a crescendo with one almighty calamity. Ours started innocently enough, Sally was a typical lab, very inquisitive, intelligent and hungry. Helen, Katie and myself, were invited out one Sunday afternoon, we left Sally with the run of the bungalow. On returning early evening, we were met with tail wagging, barking, licking, look at me, how clever I am. She had nuzzled the fridge door open and devoured all the contents, eggs, lard, butter, milk, what a bloody mess it resembled a car crash, she looked at us with those eyes, Helen blamed herself should never have left her to roam. The problem Sally had was internal, it took days for her stomach to settle down, my lawn resembled a minefield. Sally after that traumatic day grew into a loving child friendly dog, she loved Katie and was very protective of her.

The buddies at work were keen to hear all the stories from the trip overseas they were impressed with the tan, but more so with the bottle of rum I bought them typical. Work was slowing down a little, orders for new coaches had dropped considerably, there was a despondent atmosphere rumours were rife as they can be in factories.

We were gearing up to another successful season at Scarborough CC, Brian Close was again on parade. Tony Moor had handed the captaincy over to Brian Rennard, Tony wanted to concentrate on his own game, and pass on the responsibilities to a younger pair of hands, he had been a very successful skipper.

Always leading by example, always giving 100% it had been a pleasure to have served under his leadership. Brian would also prove to be an excellent leader; his strategies called for bold decisions at times, his team would have run through brick walls for him. The Committee had submitted a plan to build another players suite and a bar under the existing bar, where the old stand at the back of the member's enclosure used to be. I had always wanted to do a parachute jump, ever since my days in the army, so I decided on a sponsored parachute jump to raise funds for the new bar and suite. To put more meat on the bones, I sidled up to Closey put the proposition to him, how would you like to jump out of a plane at two thousand feet, expecting a torrent of abuse, I was delighted when he turned to me and said, "I've always wanted to do that lad!". As he was an England selector his diary had limited free time, we managed to pencil in a date 12th September a Sunday. I rang Grindale the local parachuting centre near Bridlington, booked ourselves in. They would contact us a week or two before to organise the training course. I thought the media would love the idea of Captain Courageous doing a jump, it would give us extra publicity. As we travelled to all the Yorkshire league grounds, I took my sponsor form with me, the response was positive.

Brian Rennard was also making a positive start to his captaincy and we were heading the Yorkshire league again. Dad had left Stockdale's the potato merchants, he was now driving a little yellow truck around the local area carrying sand and gravel to building sites, he loved it! Bill and Christine had another daughter Nicki, he was still busy at McCain's.

We were into the Semi Final of the Haig Trophy again, we had some drama on the way, we were playing Moseley CC from Birmingham all was going to plan, we had amassed a total of 196 for 8, they were 137 for 5 with five overs left. I was fielding by the popular bank listening to Alan Rennard, Brian's Dad taking bookings for the coach to Lords. Another wicket and in strode their wicket keeper a little left hander, Martin Shepherdson our first change seamer was brought back for his final overs, Martin had bowled well in his first spell. It all ended in tears, credit to the batter, five sixes and a single, the Moseley supporters who had been non-existent all afternoon started unwinding their banners and flags it was all a bit surreal.

They went on to knock off the runs, then followed the de-brief trying to digest what had just occurred, poor Martin a nightmare for him, to be honest I don't think he ever got over that over. Tempers were a little frayed things were said that probably shouldn't have been, but at least we got it off our chests, it was time to move on and win it again next season.

September 11th dawned, I had to be at Grindale aero field at 0900 for jump training. Closey was travelling from Skipton, and I knew he would struggle to find the place, as its hidden away, I made my excuses for him, we were in the classroom learning about the technicalities of jumping from an aeroplane, 09.45 knock on the classroom door, in walks Closey wearing this Colombo style McIntosh sporting life in one hand, flask of tea in the other, the instructor ex SAS guy wasn't too impressed but back tracked a little to give the big fella some idea of the importance of getting prepared to jump. Brian then selected his horses, and then found a phone to place his bets with the bookie. Our final test before jumping was learning how to land properly, Close ignored that, said he would have no trouble landing, bloody falling out would be more of a problem.

The weather had deteriorated from the moment we had arrived; we had come prepared to jump if it was at all possible. Brian was available again tomorrow the 12th with no chance after that date. The problem with Grindale is that it is very exposed to Westerly winds and depressions, a young man we had met was doing a jump for the Hospice in Bradford, he had been trying for four weeks. It was decided by the powers that be, that the weather was too inclement we would have to return tomorrow.

It wasn't as easy as one realised jumping out of a bloody plane. Helen had been getting herself worked up about me jumping out from two and a half thousand feet, she was fed up of the media ringing every few minutes, and it really was getting to her. I woke early the next day, Sunday, I couldn't believe my eyes, I looked out the window and couldn't see a thing for fog, dense bloody fog, stupid thoughts start to appear inside your head, is someone trying to tell you something, what a shambles. I rang Grindale, they said there was no chance, but later looked more promising. Helen was beside herself by this time, I rang Closey and Viv his wife answered, I explained the situation, she quickly burst in, “He’s left, and he is on his way.” Bollocks, Helen started to organise lunch peeling spuds. I rang Grindale again, expecting a negative response, but no it was lifting we were a go. Helen didn’t feel that same sense of excitement, as she started throwing the spuds and saucepan at my head as I shot through the door. I met Brian in the field, we made our way to the office, there now was another problem, the bloody wind. If the wind blows at more than ten knots, it’s a no go it was now 15 knots, there was nothing for it, but to hope the wind died down, it was now about two in the afternoon. Brian amused himself with his seven iron up and down the field knocking his golf balls, I noticed he kept going into his inside pocket of his jacket, he offered me a slurp from his bottle of scotch, I declined warning him if they found out he would be grounded. Christine Dennis and Clare, Marge and Duncan, Helen and Katie arrived, it was a nightmare as the wind was still blowing. Helen and the family decided at five o’clock, they would have to leave as the bairns would need their feeds, they hadn’t got out of the field when the office called for Close, Hart and the young men from Bradford to go to the rigging bay. We were going, they were explaining in detail how the chutes were packed and we would have to pack ours when we got back.

The wind in my opinion was as strong as it had been all afternoon, the chutes were distributed, the guys couldn’t get over how big a fellow Close was, the chute they gave you reflected your size, they were PX 19 chutes the round ones, once inside the aircraft we had to fix a clip onto a static line, the line was attached to your chute, the idea being when you jumped the line fed your chute out. With the wind being still on the breezy side, they explained they were going to drop us a mile away from the drop zone and hopefully the wind would carry us to the target, if they had calculated correctly.

We were all kitted out, I'm sure feeling and looking a little anxious, Brian was a little pissed if the truth be known. I imagined what it must have been like at Arnhem during the last war. We were taken to our waiting aircraft, which was piloted by no other than Ginger Lacy a hero of the Battle of Britain, spitfire pilot extraordinaire, those were the boys who withstood real pressure as the great Keith Miller once announced whilst addressing young cricketers, 'Ya don't know what pressure is until you have a messershmitte up your arse.' Keith Miller had been a bomber pilot during the last war, they were debating 'Pressure within a team' situation

Brian would be number one on the door I was number 2 with the young man from Bradford number 3, the idea is whilst gaining height say at 250' that's the height you turn into the wind and prepare to land and roll, everything has to be tucked in for a safe landing, there's no way you can judge the ground coming to you, you have to relax and when you feel the ground roll over-amen.

The jumpmaster checked all clips and bellowed 30 seconds, I tapped Closey on the shoulder, he turned smiled without his teeth, he was green, he sidled his arse halfway out of the door, the jump master tapped him on the back he was gone I was next on the door, pat on the back go, it takes four seconds for the chute to deploy it seemed like an hour, then it pulled you up short I looked up, there she was I was screaming, 'you beautiful f***ing parachute. Everything happening so quickly.

I caught a glimpse of the coast all the way to Hull, amazing. I looked down Closey was heading straight for a hedge that straddled the field and I was following in his wake howling at Brian to get his f***ing legs together, he was falling like a sack of s**t.

It was total exhilaration now, the adrenaline rush, really enjoying it, time to head into the wind. Closey was down being pulled across the ploughed field with men running trying to catch his chute, I was travelling at approx. 25mph when I felt the floor, collapse and roll made it, then wow I was being bowled along I couldn't resist the wind in the chute. Eventually someone stopped the thing, I stood up shaking still trembling still under the adrenalin influence, Closey ran towards me, his face was a picture pure elation, we hugged each other it got a bit emotional.

We made our way back to base, Colin Hurd from the club I remember had stayed to witness the event. Closey shook my hand he was shooting off, he had been an absolute pleasure, and I'd enjoyed his company over the last two seasons, learnt a lot about the game from a master. I think he appreciated this day, like me you learn a little bit more about yourself. It was then when the rush began to wear off, in no time I was feeling absolutely knackered, I was about to have a swift half with Colin, but decided to head home instead. We had been presented with a certificate of our endeavours. I was just entering Scarborough down Filey Road when out of nowhere directly behind me a blue light flashed and a siren sounded, it overtook me then stopped just in front, I wound my window down, "Now then Nicky Lauda in a rush are you?"

I was thinking of a reasonable excuse when I looked down and clocked my certificate. I actually recognised the officer, he lived down my road quite close, 'Sorry officer, I'm just a little excited, I've just had my first jump.'

I had a feeling that he thought I was being a bit clever, then I produced my certificate, I believe he was a tad impressed as he went to his car for a torch, he checked the certificate happy with my explanation. I mentioned that he lived just down from me, I praised the work he was doing on his house, 'yes,' he said 'he had been an electrician before joining the force.'

He then shook me by the hand, and commented, you can't do your neighbours, can you?'

I eventually arrived home, what a day. I felt as though I had been to heaven and hell and back, all my emotions had been tested, there's no doubt. We made close to a thousand pound for the new build, quite a sizable amount in 1980.

Chapter 9

First Class debut and Hadlee ... Martyn meets Sue ... Rebel Tour and South Africa

On a balmy September evening in1980, history was in the making. A Brian Close X1 v Scarborough CC not to take place at NMR or any other local cricket arena, but under floodlights at the Athletic Ground. Home of the 'Boro' or Scarborough Football Club. Don Robinson, the entrepreneur and successful businessman, was Chairman of the Football Club. He was a local man, born just round the corner from North Marine Road. His love for everything Scarborough was so apparent within the town, his enthusiasm and new ideas within the Football Club helped them to achieve four FA Club finals at Wembley in the 70's, running parallel with the cricket club, an amazing achievement from a small seaside town on a limb hidden away on the East Coast of England. This was another first for the town, cricket under a set of lights they had just been installed from monies collected locally from donations from business and local clubs and social outlets.

Closey's international X1 included the Australian legend, Denis Lillee, one of the greatest opening bowlers ever to grace not only the Athletic Ground but grounds throughout the world...that's fact!! It was risky organising a cricket match in the evening in Scarborough in September, but to everyone's delight the weather was unseasonally kind, a warm balmy evening welcomed the 2,000 supporters who turned up to witness the event. A polyurethane strip was laid down for the wicket, the outfield had been manicured to resemble a cricketing arena. Luckily for the Scarborough X1, the playing surface was low and slow. Denis Lillee being a typical Aussie had not just come for the ride, he ran in with his usual fluency and control, not forgetting 'pace'. The crowd loved it, as a local lad to me it was a special evening, both the Cricket and Football Clubs commemorating those incredible successful years of the 70's and early 80's. Closey's X1 went on to win the match by 26 runs. An auction was held after and the game and a local publican paid 200 pounds for Denis Lille's sweater (Priceless)

A few weeks away from cricket now time to spend some quality time just the three of us, four counting Sally.

I had an idea to build an aviary on the end of my garage. I fancied a few canaries and cockatiels. Dad came up and we measured up the plot, Dad was a competent DIY man handy with a saw hammer and nails, he set on in earnest digging holes for the posts, ordering the wire etc. it took us a few weeks probably six to complete the run and housing for the birds, which included a water feature with fountains. We travelled far and wide buying our stock, which included canaries, cockatiels, weavers and a cock golden pheasant. This particular day as I was driving past our local pet store, they were advertising terrapins at 50p each.

I collected my terrapin he was placed inside a plastic bag, he was only small the size of bar of soap. I gently placed the bag down in the passenger well, as I was driving home I happened to check out the plastic bag, no terrapin, shit, checking my seat, my leg, the back seat no terrapin.

I arrived on my drive in a bit of a lather, where was the bloody thing it couldn't have vanished, then out the corner of my eye I clocked him sat in the back window nodding like one of those dogs. I clicked him then carried it to the pond and released him.

From that day to this, I never clapped eyes on him again. It was worth it all the expense and effort erecting that aviary, listening to the cock canary's singing as we relaxed in the garden, was a wonder to behold. Helen would invite Dad and Willy Maw up for lunch on a Sunday. Katie was taking notice now, crawling around chasing Sally getting into the usual mischief the two of them. Willy brought up some postcards one Sunday, they were from his brother, sent from the front during World War 1, written in pencil, they told of the horror and hardships they had to endure to survive every single day. Willy told us that his brother had been killed by a sniper the day after armistice was announced, all very sad and dramatic, but really very interesting, how grateful our generation should feel, being born after the austerity and hardship of both World Wars.

Susie, Helen's sister had lost that little girl tag and was now sixteen and very pretty, she had a bubbly personality which rubbed off on all around her.

On occasion Sue would accompany me with Sally, Katie and the pushchair, walking on the beach or over the cliffs, I would try to encourage and help to guide her along, the usual issues that involve young lassies seemed to be prevalent, we would discuss these openly, I felt Sue trusted my judgement and to this day we are very close.

Bill Pincher returned to Scarborough CC in 1981, as well as playing he would be taking over from his Father in law Bernard Pearson as Head Groundsman. Bernard was from the old school, treated the ground as his own, and for thirty three years, he cut and managed that outfield and those exceptional wickets with devout and loving care. A new kid on the block had also been headhunted another from Hull CC, Adrian Dalby a shy unassuming young man, but we would soon change that Adrian was an attacking all-rounder, very capable with bat and ball. Another young man from the East Riding also entered the fold an opening bowler, Paul Ellis, he bowls with very low trajectory difficult to score off, these boys were made very welcome, another young player, steadily attracting attention, a young farmer David Byas, a forceful left hand bat, making his debut season within the first team ranks. There's a definite buzz around the club with the influx of the new talent on show.

After the disappointment of losing out in last seasons Semi Final, we were raring to put the record straight. The first bank holiday Saturday we were up against a strong Harrogate side, Harrogate had two of the finest league cricketers ever to don whites. Peter Chadwick opening batsman of the highest order, pundits from all around the county were in total agreement that he would have gone onto reach the top as an opener, stylish, balance, correct technique all the assets required, but Peter loved his job, loved Pately Bridge in rural Nidderdale, a rural man, a shame that he didn't go onto fulfil his true potential, but credit also to a man who knew where his loyalties lay. Peter Kippax another good friend and Foe, started playing for Leeds CC, an opening bat who bowled leg spin.

If he didn't score runs, he definitely took wickets, a great character on the field. Competitive, loved to talk to batsman in his own charming way. Played a lot of minor counties games for Northumberland, his highlight was bowling Vivian Richards with the wrong un'. Without a doubt a great player who loved the game, an inspirational character, we recorded a stunning victory over our rivals that day a positive sign for the future.

Steve Coverdale the Harrogate and Yorkshire 2nd, wicket keeper approached me in the bar after the game, he was keen to notify me of possible developments within Yorkshire CC. Apparently Phil Carrick the County left arm spinner was having a dip in form and rumour had it, Doug Padgett the county coach was coming to check me out. I thought yes and pigs will fly, I told him it was a windup, I was thirty four for god's sake it's a young mans game.

Doug Padgett did ring me, he explained the position regarding Fergie Carrick, and would I be prepared to play under a short term contract, I accepted with relish their offer then with immediate effect arranged a meeting with Plaxtons who were very supportive and agreed to allow me time off to play. I mentioned to Doug Padgett or Padg my feelings regarding my age, surely there was an up and coming young bowler available. Padg replied I had been highly recommended, and it was experience they were looking for short term, so that was that.

Padg and Colin Johnson the skipper were fantastic, they had a great rapport with the young team, who from an outsider looking in, were a credit to our great county I was made most welcome from day one, even though I could have been their dad, I was accepted as one of the boys my nickname soon materialised 'Alf', very fitting. I have to thank CW, Atthey for that piece of genius. We travelled the length and breadth of the motorway system, playing cricket and getting paid for the privilege, down to Swansea up to Marske, over to Liverpool. Liverpool now there was a story, Colin Johnson and myself met Padg at Headingly, he then drove us to Liverpool in his navy blue Ford. It was only a couple of days since the toxteth riots you could smell the acrid smoke with burnt out buildings either side of the main drag. We were all dressed in our blazers and ties resembling a scene from The Sweeney.

Padg then realised he was lost, we were looking for our digs the Excelsior a B&B gaffe, Colin noticed a black lad walking the footpath and asked Padg to pull up alongside, the lad checked the car and occupants, then he just legged it obviously he thought we were the Sweeney. You could feel the tension, that look in people's eyes it was a little intimidating to say the least, we were glad to leave that part of the city behind. We eventually found the digs, all the boys had arrived. The weather forecast for the next three days was rubbish according to the met office and sure enough the following morning damned cyclonic, with no break in sight it was decided to call it off for the day.

Padg and Colin invited me to accompany them to Liverpool Crown Court, this was their usual course of action if weather was inclement. We arrived at the court, Padg picked a trial at random in we strode into the public gallery, we couldn't have timed it any better, and the gallery was called to its feet as the judge made his entrance. I was enthralled with all this drama, this was a million miles from Scalby, Helen and Katie.

The defendant a young man of nineteen had murdered his best mate, then tried to burn him, by putting his body onto a bonfire in his garden. The gallery was packed to the rafters with the family of the victim, and the family of the defendant next door neighbours, amazing stuff.

Women with curlers in, fags on and slippers, fellas jostling, sledging, working each other up. Padg was loving it. Colin was with me, I felt we were intruding on these two families at war. The judge ordered quiet or people would be ejected. The jury had come to their verdict, it was pure theatre you could have heard a pin drop. GUILTY was the call from the foreman, the place just exploded into total chaos, we sat their rigid, not showing any allegiance to either side, calm was again called for, now the judge donned a black cap and put on black gloves, he stared at the defendant, then told him slowly that he would go to prison for life, the gallery again resembled a bear pit, the young defendant then turned to the face the gallery with a brutal look on his face, he snarled out to all and sundry, 'FUCK OFF'. The judge then ordered the defendant to be taken down. I wondered about that young man for years after, he will be out now going about his business. One would hope a reformed character.

The weather refused to stop raining, therefore the next day we were back in court, it was a less dramatic situation but even so, we witnessed the brilliance of the barristers for the prosecution and the defence going hammer and tong at each other.

The case was to do with fraudulent dealings, it was clever how the barristers tied the witness in knots, with their very use of words they really earn their coin, what a total out of the box experience this had been. I wouldn't have missed it for the world, the cricket became incidental we played the final afternoon session more as a practice exercise.

As the weeks passed I felt more relaxed with the squad and was picking up my share of wickets. I had a couple of five wickets hauls in the bank, I was bowling as many as 40 overs each innings. The old spinning finger was becoming very sore, finding time for recuperation was difficult therefore a couple of days off for weather was welcome.

Kent were our next opponents, a long drive down to Canterbury the weather was set fair it was late June by this time. The Kent countryside sparkled in beautiful sunshine. The garden of England with all those houses portraying the Elizabethan theme, majestic buildings with the intricate brickwork, this for me was a real pleasure.

The ground at Canterbury was very typical of Kent in general, serene, easy on the eye everything and everyone in control. Both the Cowdrey brothers were playing Chris and Graham, I was looking forward to the challenge ahead. And the tree I had read and heard about over the years, standing majestically on the ground within the playing area. It was interesting measuring peoples preferences regarding the tree, I came out with a 50/50 split.

I personally had an excellent three days in Kent; the season for me had been improving steadily week in week out. I took ten wickets in the match five each innings. I found it a dream wicket to bowl on, turn and bounce I could have rolled it up without a doubt. We were having a de-brief after the game. Padg was pleased with the performance to win by ten wickets was regarded a hammering in anyone's book. Padg then got out the team sheet for the next game it was now 18.30 Friday evening. He told me I had to report to Harrogate at 08.30 the following morning, as I had been selected in the first team to play Surrey. When the lads picked me up off the floor, there was back slapping hand shakes. I was totally numb overjoyed and a little emotional. Padg looked me in the eye, 'you deserve a crack, just go out if you get the chance enjoy it. It's only a game', yes I said and I won't have a messerscmidt up my arse either. No mobile phones in those days, I ran round to the secretary's office, I phoned Helen told her the news; she was delighted ecstatic in fact.

I asked her to phone Dad, and tell him to please pick me up at York station where Colin would drop me at midnight. As we were driving up the M1, my mind was in a spin, the weird thoughts; I was rolling back the years, all the old mentors who had steered me onto this path. Eddie Wilson from my Primary school, George Welbourne of Seamer CC, Simon Smail and Tom Singleton, Junior Leaders and last but not least my dear old dad, these men, I'm sure will be delighted for me, living my dream.

Colin wished me good luck with a solid handshake, Dad was there at the station, to Scarborough don't spare the horses, he was pleased as punch with my selection. The morning dawned with a glorious red sun climbing out of the sea, let's hope it would be a fair omen for the day ahead. Julian Vallance met me in the car park behind the dressing rooms, he offered to carry my bag. I knew most of the boys, and was introduced to the ones I hadn't met. They were great as I knew they would be, Chris Old the skipper, 'chilly' as he was known.

A genial lad from Middlesbrough from a family full of sporting talent. Eric Brailsford the North's equivalent of Arthur Mullard, he was very physical a Rugby league man. He thought cricket was a ponces game, he had us round the ground at a gentle pace then a stretching session, that was it in those days nothing like the physical abuse they go through today.

John Hampshire led me to the bottom corner of the ground for some throw downs, it felt good to get the ball in my hand. The ground at Harrogate looked totally different, they had erected all the temporary stands, the crowd began arriving in numbers the old heart rate began to race a little.

Chilly won the toss and without hesitation stuck Surrey in, Ray Illingworth our team manager strode over whispered in my ear that I was to play, brilliant I made my way to the main stand found Dad who was sat at the back anonymous, I put my thumb up to him he'll be thrilled I thought. Cup of tea and a team talk followed, Illy was of the Closey ilk forgotten more about the game, than we knew, he drilled into us the importance of bowling straight with no extras if possible, backing up the throws, the usual pre game build up. The highlight of my entire cricketing career climaxed within the following couple of minutes, walking out of the dressing room at Harrogate as a Yorkshire Cricketer how good did that feel.

I was sent down to fine leg for the first over to be bowled by Arnie Sidebottom, then up to mid off for Chris Old. As

I stood at fine leg, I could hear and sense the mutterings around the crowd. People wondering who was this new face. I don't recall there being any tannoy system, on that first morning I felt like turning round to face them and bellowing 'I'm Phil Hart from Scarborough CC'. As I walked into my position at mid off Jack Van Gelhoven the umpire came across shook my hand and congratulated me on my selection. Jack was another great character of the game, loved nothing more than with a pint in hand relive his memories of his glory days, he was the last player to do the double a thousand runs and a hundred wickets never to be done again with covered wickets according to Jack.

Graham Roope and David Smith were the Surrey openers, experience in abundance, both went on to represent their country in one form or another Smith on all accounts was renowned for winding the bowlers up, big time, this was my first morning and I was about to witness these antics first hand, we had only bowled half a dozen overs when the Surrey Physio had to be called to attend to Smiths back pain on went the magic spray, all seemed to be well. Chilly ran and bowled beat the bat up he goes arms akimbo expletives explode at the end of his follow through.

Smith stands his ground (six feet six) then lifts his head and tells Chilly in no uncertain terms to pick the fucking ball up and bowl. This was new territory for me enthralling stuff. I glanced at Jack he made a gesture to the batsman to tone it down a little. This encounter caught the imagination of the players who I think thought it was amusing, Chilly ran in again grunted as he put a bit more into this delivery, he was bowling superbly without any luck, again he went through Smith who didn't seem able to cope with the amount of movement both ways, he again gestured to Chilly to get on with it instead of fucking whinging, it was then as I was walking in towards the stumps we both made eye contact where upon he with hands on hips told me I could fuck off too. Bill Athey who was at short leg with a smile on his face put Smith in the picture explaining to him be careful with Alf, he's been in the SAS I quickly responded to this outburst picking up on Bills link. I told Smith in no uncertain terms that I would break his fucking back, with that he guffawed you better get a fucking ladder and when you come into bat to have a lid on. I couldn't believe what was happening he'd certainly got everyone wound up. Jack luckily kept the lid on the proceedings and I'm positive no one in the crowd knew of this little sideshow. Eventually after all the ranting and raving we got the breakthrough Arnie trapping Graham Roope, LBW. At twelve thirty or so Chilly came to me, have an over at this end next Alf, bloody hell the adrenalin was kicking in now, my hands were damp with sweat the last thing I wanted, then we had another interlude, the Surrey physio advised David Smith he thought it best if he left the field for treatment. Apparently Illy had agreed to allow this on a temporary basis until lunch. In strode Intikhab Alam and Chilly handed me the ball, we set an orthodox field, my first over was nip and tuck, the batsman facing had never seen me bowl therefore treated it all in a respectful manner, a maiden.

My second over Intikhab facing, Chilly placed Neil Hartley at extra cover I held my second delivery back a little, Inti went for the drive on the up, as it was a little slower he didn't get full purchase into the shot instead of clearing Neil at extra it cannoned into him waist high, he took the catch to my sheer delight a great catch. During that spell before lunch I bowled seven overs seven maidens 1 wicket, I walked into the dressing room to a rapturous reception, thinking what was all the panic about, that first morning play was definitely the most interesting few hours I've ever spent on a cricket field.

During that lunch break interested parties from within the game were keen to speak to me about my history, the usual run of the mill stuff. One gentleman who implied he was doing a piece for Wisden the professional cricketer's bible asked me for my details. My age was my Achilles heel, therefore rather than telling him the truth that I was thirty four I told him a porky telling him I was twenty nine. I didn't feel I needed to be that precise, many years later an acquaintance who enjoyed collecting cricketing stats and memorabilia found a booklet portraying all the naughty boys who had mislead this highly respectable organisation, there was a list as long as your arm and I found myself amongst them. Also whilst on the subject of ages Bill Frindall brought out a publication quoting exceptional performances on first class debut, I'm also mentioned in there under bowling. P.R Hart bowled forty two consecutive deliveries without conceding a run. That is the morning I will never forget, 4th July 1981 American Independence Day.

Lunch over, the five minute bell, David Smith resumed after lunch I bowled another seven overs in the day ending up with 1for22. We got into them early on, the seamers doing all the damage dismissing them after tea. We were then well placed going into the second day. John Hampshire and myself were the only two to be staying in digs, if you lived x amount of miles from the venue you then qualified for lodgings, we were staying at the Old Swan a rather quaint Edwardian hotel. After the debrief it was time for a pint. I met up with Dad, he had enjoyed the day he was pleased with my performance, he wouldn't be able to get for the rest of the match due to work committment. I was very grateful to him for being there on this day, it meant a lot to me and I knew how much it meant to him he'd be telling 'em all at work tomorrow.

The ground was buzzing with Yorkshire members, having a drink chewing over the days play. I found myself wedged into the corner of the Tetley beer tent having a swift one with Capt Desmond Bailey, who ran the commercial side of the operation. After the third pint with my new buddy I began to wonder if this was a good idea drinking in public on my debut. John Hampshire arrived in the nick of time and we both legged it into Harrogate to find some food, I was starving.

Day Two, another lovely day, full Monty Breakfast of the highest standard, taken with the Daily Telegraph then a pleasant walk with Hamps back up to the ground. Mr Joe Lister the Yorkshire secretary met me and to my astonishment in his office was a heap of telegrams and cards congratulating me on my debut, from Cricket Societies and members. All this acclaim for me I was staggered, it is distinctly true when people comment on the generosity of Yorkshire folk, it took ages but I did thank them all for their kindness.

We went on to win the game quite comfortably the Seamers did all the damage, Arnie ended up with ten wickets and Hamps scored a magnificent ton to set up the first win of that season. I was very excited as Yorkshire were again taking on Surrey in the Sunday John Player league at Scarborough. Unfortunately for me, Illy made me 12th man which was disappointing but understandable. Apart from the cricket there was another battle taking place. Internally Yorkshire CC were having problems, the members under the guidance of their spokesman Sid Fielding were at odds with the committee all to do with the role of Geoffrey Boycott, it was an embarrassing time for the players being caught up washing their dirty linen in public. During that game on Sunday the contracted players were instructed to vote on this issue. As an outsider in the dressing room, I was at odds with it all. I did notice it became very interesting how the boys reacted, human nature I guess, but all the South Yorkshire lads assembled together, as did the Wessies, as did the rest, in times of crisis you stick together obviously.

Put all that political stuff to bed, leave it to the people who have the common touch, and common sense to move it forward. It was lovely to see the family. Helen and Katie, catching up with the local gossip and enjoying a proper nights sleep in my own bed. Scarborough CC were enjoying another great season heading the league, and going well in the Haig trophy, the new lad Adrian Dalby was proving to be a class act, Tony Moor and Chris Stevenson were breaking records for runs accumulated, to be honest I missed the boys, but I knew I would never get this opportunity again to sample the game at this level.

I was selected for the trip to Cardiff, Sofia Gardens I travelled down with Bill Athey and Neil (Tommy) Hartley, we met up at Bills in Bradford, where there was a real buzz around the city as the previous evening Peter Sutcliffe the Yorkshire Ripper had just been arrested. We arrived down in Wales after a musical extravaganza listening to the Abba album 'Super Trooper' still a great sound.

The digs were just outside the city and we were the last to arrive, Bluey Bairstow had some interesting news for us, Chris Old was injured after the Surrey game, John Hampshire had been made skipper but he had just gone to hospital with palpitations of the heart, therefore Bluey had been promoted to Skipper. My room mate on this trip was a young man making a big impression on the game, having scored a century on his debut. Martyn Moxon a tall graceful right hand bat, he was a grand lad from Monk Bretton, Barnsley. Our evening apparently had been organised we were to appear at the local Bass Brewery to take part in a sports quiz, Geoff Lister a rep for the brewery and a Yorkshire member had put it altogether.

I'm sure Illy had his reservation about the night ahead, and I do remember him warning us against having too much to drink. I can honestly say that if a young man couldn't consume a gallon of ale safely he was no use in the Yorkshire 1st XI. During this period if there had been a county championship for drinking no contest. A social evening to savour, shiny aluminium buckets of Bass Best bitter passing between the two teams on a regular ten minutes service inviting hilarity amongst the audience.

It was a fine bright morning to follow the excesses of the night before. Eric was waiting for us, Illy must have warned him off, he had his rugby league head on that morning, he had this masochistic streak in him. The mining community of Yorkshire were fantastic supporters, I was amazed that morning how many made the journey down to Wales, the car park was full of expectant fans. The team talk was the usual Illy rant, we had lost the toss and had been inserted. It was a nightmare scenario from the first ball after ten overs we were three down, then there was utter panic another wicket has fallen, but there was no Jim Love, Illy's having a thrombie where the fuck is he, he's having a crap manager came the reply.

Tommy Hartley quickly strode out to the middle, Jim appeared from the bog totally oblivious to the situation. Illy was beside himself, we are going to have to do something about this crapping. I go after breakfast he then went round everyone individually asking when they went for a crap, another wicket we were dropping like bloody flies. I wondered whether last night had anything to do with our performance, someone suggested we may have been slipped a mickey fin. John Hampshire had been passed fit and was holding up one end even though he had electrodes attached to his chest to monitor his heart, I was number ten, I made my way to the wicket at 12.15 on the first morning, as I marched to the wicket Javed Miandad the Pakistani legend made fun of my new batting gloves, they were jaguar gloves from a sports shop in Scarborough, looked a little ungamely, but there was no need for his sarky comments. John Hampshire gave me some encouragement, the West Indian Ezra Mosley had done all the damage, he was sharp as I found out when this blur nearly took my head off.

I settled down and played an anchor role, Hamps was going well, now the shine was off we got to lunch, I was on eleven. The first over after lunch I went onto the back foot to cut this ball a foot off the ground through gully, Rodney Ontong took off and caught the bloody ball to his left what a catch. I couldn't believe it that was a statement to say welcome to the first class game. It was a poor batting display. I felt sorry for all those fans who had motored down for the day.

The second day things didn't improve much Glamorgan were building up a lead, Miandad was batting he had just come in when I was given the ball, my first over went ok, the first ball of the second over ended up in the river Taff, two quick strides down the pitch and bang, the second ball also went for a swim things were becoming serious now. Miandad was ruining my career big time, smiling at me as he did so. The next delivery, it tucked him up a little, he played an uppish on drive straight to Kevin Sharpe who clung on to it, I lost my cool I'm afraid to say, Mr Budd the umpire had to warn me, as my conduct flouted the rules of the game. When Kevin pouched the catch I ran down the wicket and politely told Mr Miandad to 'FUCK OFF'. The adrenalin got the better of me, I did apologise to him at the close and we shook hands, I honestly did lose control which worried me a little bit, I thought of Keith Miller and there wasn't a Messerschmitt in sight.

That was my only wicket, and I had a bit of bad luck batsman chipping the ball between fielders, but that's cricket. Our new skipper Bluey even took the pads off and bowled, we lost that game by ten wickets not the greatest preparation, as we travelled up to Trent Bridge to tackle the championship leaders Notts. My spinning finger by this time was like a piece of raw meat, I guessed this was going to be my swan song. Therefore I kept it to myself, Trent Bridge an elegant Test venue built in the old Victorian era, the pavilion with its balustrades and staircases much to be admired you could sense that aura of empire, those days when they put the Great into Britain.

Eric had us jogging for a couple of laps, a few stretches he was struggling after pulling a hamstring climbing into Illy's Saab. I had shown Raymond my finger he advised me to try some plastic skin.

He swore by it, I'd tried that already it was no use once the skin was broken, the only remedy was rest, but I wasn't recommending that. Kevin Sharpe was 12th man for this match, he was suffering from an in growing toe nail, Eric had him in the treatment room, he was now in his element. It didn't take long before the screams were echoing around the corridors and chambers. It was blood curdling stuff it put us off our tea and biscuits. Two of us opened the door to the treatment room, got a glimpse of Kevin he was chewing on a lump of wood in total agony shouting and cursing at Eric, who was calling him a baby it's only a toe nail. Kev was in real pain you could see it etched on his face, Eric in his own benign manner bellowed to us to bugger off and leave him to his work.

It was like watching King Kong thread a needle. Eventually the patient appeared, his bandaged toe resembling a King Edward on the end of his foot. Kevin was really upset, suggesting Eric shouldn't be allowed anywhere near a first aid kit, he should have been a butcher. It was an amusing incident for the non participants, it eventually faded into insignificance as we won the toss and were preparing to bat.

The lack of confidence among our top order batsman, was there to see, Richard Hadlee the legendary New Zealand all rounder was finding in roads.

Early on only Neil Hartley offered any real resistance, scoring his maiden century. I was relegated to no. eleven and entered the arena just after the tea interval. I was facing the great Hadlee, in he strode up to the wicket gave me a ball of full length which I confidently dispatched through the legs of Clive Rice at silly mid off to the extra cover boundary. I recall the ball thudding against the wall. I stood tall ready for the next delivery. I thought this will probably come to me at throat height as he delivered. I was on the back foot, in no position to defend the leg stump Yorker, that sent my leg stump cartwheeling, I then got that Hadlee stare and pointing to the dressing room told to piss off.

Alan Ramage had been drafted in to shore up the pace attack, Alan was a boisterous young man from Middlesbrough had a lot of potential as probably the next England quickie, we all struggled to be honest, Derek Randall and Clive Rice got at us both scoring hundreds. I went for a gallon, which in bowling slang meant I went for 100 runs. We lost that encounter by an innings; the boys were feeling really down, time to go home recharge the batteries.

Phil Carrick was back to some kind of form, he never looked back after that interlude and went on to captain the side.

I arrived home feeling my age even though thirty four is comparatively young; to be competing on the first class cricket stage it's creeping up to the veteran level. I came away with my two wickets and sixteen runs, not as I would have wished, but more importantly I came away with priceless memories, and I salute all those people who offered me that opportunity.

I spent the next week at home, enjoying our young daughter learning to walk and allowing my finger time to heal. I met Chris Clifford at the nets in Scarborough, he asked me if I would be interested in going to South Africa to coach in a college for the winter. I was excited at the prospect, I had been made redundant from Plaxtons and my letter arrived while I was away with the county. I talked it over with Helen and the family, they needed more details about accommodation salary, etc. The college was St David's Marist College in the Northern suburbs of Johannesburg. Chris had arranged for me to ring the headmaster Brother Timothy a Marist monk. The phone call answered the questions, the accommodation was for one only, and the salary was decent it was for six months October to March. I wasn't happy leaving without Helen and Katie.

I told Brother Timothy I would ring back in two days with a definite answer. We decided that I would go with the view to finding accommodation as soon as possible to get Helen and Katie over with me, we dotted the I's and crossed the T's and my future was assured for another winter. It was now the run in for the honours Scarborough were unbeatable in the Yorkshire league and won it in a canter; they also reached the final of the Haig trophy for the fourth time up against another London side Blackheath.

I played a couple of games for the Yorkshire 2nd's, my final game was at Derby a most unattractive venue, so exposed as the wind raced in over the racecourse. Martyn Moxon and Arnie Sidebottom were also performing, I had the privilege of meeting Martyn's Mum and Dad, Audrey and Derek. Derek was a cricket fanatic played and coached most of his life, was very supportive of his son, and had guided him to become a confident well mannered young man, any mother would be proud of.

Audrey had the task of feeding these two men of hers, and she did it with aplomb the picnic hamper brimmed with chicken legs, ham cobs, pasties of all descriptions a cricket mum of distinction. I was bowling that day into the wind, when the batter drove the ball straight back at me, I tried for the catch the ball striking the little finger of my right hand, it soon became apparent through the swelling that appeared, that the local Hospital awaited my arrival, after an examination taking an age it was diagnosed as a crack to the finger, and some tendons had been severed which threw the top digit of my finger inwards 45 degrees to resemble a crabs claw. I have to thank Molly Staines for wet nursing me on that day; she drove me to the hospital and back. I had the pleasure of meeting Molly often during that season; she was a soothing influence to all the young players and fulfilled her role on the Yorkshire committee with solid commitment. I missed my lunch, whilst at hospital but no worries up to the plate came Mrs Moxon with those savouries aplenty.

A couple of weeks later, shock and despair hit the Yorkshire club, Neil Lloyd a sixteen year old lad with a very promising future died from an obscure virus, we were all devastated and in total shock. Neil had been one of the fixture and fittings of the 2nd xi a left hand bat of great potential, who was being touted as a future test player. Neil's father, Dougie was a very well known league cricketer a competent wicket keeper for many a year, we had played together for the Yorkshire cricket association.

The funeral took place at Ackworth, it was one of the saddest days in my memory, nothing prepares you for such tragedy. Having all your friends and colleagues together at that time of deep sorrow helps to lift the burden, I'm sure we all helped Dougie a little on that awful day. Rest in peace Neil.

I was walking on the beach with Katie and Sue, we were taking Katie for a ride on a donkey. Sue was a little down she had blossomed into a stunner, she had no need to be in low spirits and asked me if there was any decent lads in the Yorkshire Squad, I told her not to worry, love would arrive when she least expected it. It was the cricket festival at North Marine Road. I had arranged to meet some of the boys for a drink after stumps. During a pee stop in the gents at North Marine Road I happened to mention to Martyn if he would be prepared to take my sister in law out for a drink, I gave him all the relevant details, the ones he would be interested in, yes he would be delighted.

Sue was beside herself I told her not to worry he was a decent young man, she had her own car and it was arranged for her to meet him outside the Durham Pub the following evening. They both looked happy as they rode off into the sunset together a match made in heaven.

The Haig final had arrived another army of Scarborough supporters were making their way to their other adopted ground, Lords! What a record three wins, going into the fourth final. I must also mention the Scarborough Football Club at this point, as they were helping to put Scarborough on the sporting map. They had won the F.A Trophy Final 1973 to 1976 at Wembley, the Scarborough folk knew their way to London alright.

The Blackheath side weren't to be intimidated by the three time winners, they had organised with a professional agency to have a video filmed during the game. Scarborough batted first with only Adrian Dalby and Tony Moor getting a start, they bowled Scarborough out for a paltry 157. Blackheath must have felt justified by there decision to film the event., but as any old sweat will tell you it's never over till the fat lady sings.

The Scarborough bowlers took the fight to Blackheath, their bowlers recording amazing figures in the process. Paul

Ellis 8 overs 5 maidens 4 runs 2 wickets, M. Shepherdson 8 overs 5 maidens 8 runs no wickets, AJ, Moor 8 overs four maidens 10 runs 3 wickets. Blackheath were sent packing 100 for 9, what does that tell you of the amazing character of an amazing club side, four wins in four appearances some record.

My next adventure was gathering pace, my passport was still in Liverpool at passport control, there was total public servants strike at that time which meant we all got a board the car, had a family day out in Liverpool. I was excited about going to South Africa, but I wasn't happy leaving Helen and Katie for six months. I was going to do everything possible to have them with me. Dad agreed to look after the aviary which took pressure off Helen. We had a little family bash before I left, the weather was closing in I wasn't sorry to be leaving the winter behind. I was flying from Heathrow to Johannesburg; Richard Lumb was to meet me at the airport he lived out there.

After what seemed a long flight, I arrived quite knackered Richard was there it was great to see a friendly face. On the way into the city we drove adjacent to the Alexander Township, a slight shock to the system, families having to live in such squalor, small wooden dens barely big enough for a dog. Before Richard dropped me at the college, he pulled into the Wanderers sports complex more or less next door, he informed me that the wanderers was the largest private sports club with the largest membership in the world.

We enjoyed a couple of beers on the stoop overlooking the cricket ground very impressive. Richard then tried to impress on me, how this apartheid works, he told me to be wary and not to enter the black areas, he maintained there was a problem, but nothing for me as a guest to worry about I bid farewell to Richard, he said he would call on me later. Brother Timothy was a charming man, very knowledgeable about the game in general. He gave me a guided tour of the facilities. Fifty seven acres of cricket Rugby and soccer pitches, the campus was massive.

He then introduced me to my hosts, the family I would be living with during my stay, the McFaddens. Tom was a jovial Irishman who taught maths and history, Margaret his wife, Connor and Brian their two boys. Connor aged eight Brian eleven, they lived in what in England would be considered a listed building, before the college was set up all the land was farmed. Tom's house was the old farm house, with a thatch roof, lovely garden with fig trees. Tom was very outgoing, friendly a bit like a long lost brother. In fact he used to be a brother which meant he had taken the vows and become a monk, he then had a change of heart for he left the brotherhood.

That first evening after I had settled in, we had a couple of beers on the patio outside, Tom told me about the ghost in my bedroom and that I should not worry as she would not harm me, that was it, can you imagine I tiptoed up to bed climbed in pulled the bloody covers up over my head, I honestly don't think I had a full nights sleep ever in that room, and I never clapped eyes on this women either.

After a week or so I was finding my feet all the staff were very helpful and friendly. Osborne was my groundsman he provided the wickets as required. I met him one morning as he was preparing a wicket with a push mower, no engine he said it took him all day to prepare a wicket. Apparently the last powered mower, had been pinched by the locals it was a problem throughout the college, pilfering.

The college employed up to twenty black workers, to do all the menial jobs and with their families lived in a compound on sight. They got their pay at the end of the month and for a day or two after it was carnage at times, they used to brew their own type of booze, there were tribal fights, stabbings very violent goings on, the compound was well policed nothing spilled out into the college, even so it was a little different to life in Scalby.

After deliberating with Brother Timothy it was decided the college could afford another powered mower. Tom, Osborne and myself made the purchase, and my grounds man was back in the 20th century. When I arrived at St David's all the grassed areas were as brown as snuff, it had not rained all winter only the squares were green where the sprinklers had done their job. Then after a nights rain the fields just changed from brown to green within a couple of days incredible stuff grass.

What I hadn't catered for was how cold it was in early October, I didn't bring any winter woollies thinking it would be warmer, there was frost on the windows in the morning, bloody freezing. One evening after work, Tom and I were having a beer on the patio when there was an almighty crash and bang by the college gate. I quickly ran up to assist whoever or whatever, it was a young lady, her car had been hit by another car the driver had driven off leaving her in shock quite dishevelled, we rang her parents, sorted the car, then brought her down to the patio. After a while her parents turned up, it turned out she was the great granddaughter of the Yorkshire and England spin bowler Hedley Verity, how weird was that.

I was really missing Helen and Katie, accommodation was really tight, it was going to be a problem finding somewhere but I would still be trying. I had met all the boys who made up the different sides, they went up to 16 years they were very keen to impress, which was a good sign.

The discipline within the college was quite strict much different to the liberal attitudes of home. The parents were very supportive towards the college, at a parents evening I attended they were keen to meet this Yorkshireman, the new cricket coach. I had decided not to play cricket at the weekends, I committed myself to the job of standing umpiring the college games, I felt I owed them that after they finally offered me the post.

Another evening after work, Tom and I were in a local bar having a beer a friend of Toms introduced himself, we got chatting I mentioned to him that I was trying to get Helen and Katie over but it was proving difficult.

He was a janitor a local primary school and he and his wife were going on a cruise for three months, and he was looking for someone to look after his property. It was like a bolt out of the blue. Tom took me to one side explaining that the guy might be bullshitting me. When we arrived back at the farmhouse we discussed it again, I wasn't sure how kosher the story was but he knew how much I wanted the family with me, another impulsive moment, I phoned Helen told her the news she was delighted, the problem was Sally our Labrador, after a few days organizing herself Helen rang back to say she had found a new owner for Sally, we both thought it a little sad to be giving her away, it was a done deal.

Helen had booked her flight with Katie to arrive in ten days. I was beside myself fantastic she would love it here the weather had improved it was really warm now. Three or four nights later Tom and myself were having a beer after work, and there was my janitor friend but he was out of it pissed. I was thinking the worst scenarios now. I decided there and then to drive him home and confront his wife about the cruise, he sidled off to bed leaving me in his lounge, his wife was out would be back soon, I hadn't met her she wouldn't have a clue who I was, how bloody odd was that, at last she arrived home with her daughter they got a bit of a shock seeing me sat at the table.

I explained myself to them and told them the story, apparently it happens quite often he makes up these stories, she was very apologetic. I thought what I am going to do now. Helen would be on her way expecting a house to live in, my world was crashing down around me, Tom and Margaret were very helpful we decided to give the first team cricket pavilion a make over, it had all the usual facilities water, heating, gas. Someone lent us a bed and cot for Katie curtains were made and erected, it looked very homely thanks to the lovely parents who chipped in. I had a little smile to myself, I thought bugger it, they are coming we'll manage move on. A teacher lent me her car to drive to the airport to pick up my beloved passengers.

I remember watching the jumbo land cheered when it touched down, in arrivals I was shaking with nervous tension, then little Katie appeared she spied me crying daddy then ran into my arms, tears were streaming down, Helen also ran to meet me it was a profound moment, one in a million. What a feeling to have my wife with me. We never stopped talking all the way back. Helen was taken aback a little when we reached our new abode but she quickly realised how much work had gone into setting it all up, I didn't care we were back as a family. Priceless.

Margaret fell in love with Katie from day one, she would have loved a daughter, Katie was now 2 and half years old, got on with the boys Connor and Brian as if they were her brothers, plus the new addition to the McFadden household the new boxer puppy Finn. In the grounds of the college was a very attractive swimming pool. Helen would walk Katie over most days and it wasn't long before she was swimming without her arm bands. Helen grew to love South Africa, we were based in a pretty affluent area known as Sandton in the Northern suburbs. She would go off pushing the buggy down to the new shopping mall known as Sandton City. She was the only white lady who used to walk, most would use their Porsches or 4x4's.

Marge and Duncan were missing us all, apparently, the weather at home had gone rapidly downhill, snow and ice in abundance, here the weather was improving the Jacaranda trees were beautiful with their blue blossom, it was odd to think that we were living at 6000 feet above sea level, that's a long way higher than Ben Nevis or Snowdonia, the storms we encountered in Sandton, were frightening, the lightening then the thunder horrendous claps really scary. The hailstones also the size of golf balls, so intense they dented the bodywork of vehicles and stripped the paintwork.

Early in the New Year of 1982, a rebel cricket tour had been organised, it was for three tests matches and three one day internationals. There was international condemnation, the players, all English county and test stars, were immediately labelled the 'Dirty Dozen', with Graham Gooch and Geoffrey Boycott accused by the Labour MP Gerald Kaufmann as selling themselves for blood covered krugerrands. Desmond Tutu, the Archbishop of Johannesburg stated 'It's not a glorious chapter in their history, they ought not to tell; their kids they came'. Personally, this was an interesting few weeks, my view has always been that politics and sport do not mix. Arnie Sidebottom and Chris Old signed up for the tour, they had been with us at Richard Lumb's house on Christmas day, no mention then of the rebel tours. I recall receiving a call from the touring party a couple of days before the first test at the Wanderers, asking whether I would be prepared to bring along my first X1 bowlers to bowl at the tourists in the nets.. I put the request to the boys and their response was that they would be delighted to have the opportunity of removing Gooch or Boycott's middle stump. They were raring to go and arrived at the ground which was subject to a few local protesters. The police managed the situation in their usual subtle way!! The outcry at home had become more hostile, it really got up peoples noses that these international sportsmen had sided with this ailing regime, they had found it immoral with no ethical justification. My thoughts at that time as I was actually 'there', was that the press and media really seemed to hype up the story, with the public and politicians at home totally over reacting. Those cricketers were at most a little naïve, they did not realise they were being used as political pawns. They play their game within a multi cultural umbrella, dismissing racism and are definitely against Apartheid and discrimination. I am certain the attraction of the financial rewards on offer glossed over the political issues being played out. These county players would earn in a month what it would taken them five years to earn on the English county circuit. In South Africa, segregation in sport had been the norm long before this Nationalist Government was elected.

Another strange phenomenon are the bees, we were having net practice one day, when on the horizon what looked like a rain cloud turned out to be bees. Somebody shouted "down" within seconds we were all on the grass in the prone position.

We are going into some alternative accommodation shortly, a colleague has a friend who wants a family to move in and share the property. It turns out while he was away on holiday his maid got her family round and they cleared the place. Every household employs a black maid to do all the washing cleaning looking after the kids etc., this guy was of Africaans stock called him Greenwold, he worked away every day so was happy to have us look after the place. We spent Christmas in his bungalow. On Christmas day we were invited to Richard Lumb's ranch where all the Yorkshire boys who were over playing congregated. Kevin Sharpe, Arnie Sidebottom, Neil Hartley, Chris Old and Peter Ingham. It was marvellous to catch up with them all again. It was a red hot day, seemed strange carving the turkey with all the trimmings in such heat. We had a lovely day Richard and Sue, his lovely wife were the perfect hosts, Helen and Katie were having a ball, both had a deep tan by this time, Katie was beginning to talk with a South African accent. Our stay at the bungalow petered out quite quickly this Greenwold guy was pain in the arse; he upset Helen more or less treating her like a bloody maid. When he went off to work this day, we just packed up our stuff, pinched all his apricots off his tree for the monks at college, left him a note, then buggered off. Someone offered us a caravan which we parked on the campus very cosy it did the job a treat.

The Christmas break lasted much longer than England something like three weeks break. Alan and Val Ashby, a family who invited us regularly to their home to relax by the pool very kindly asked if we would like to accompany them to Durban for a week's holiday. It was a marvellous opportunity to see a little of the country. Alan had a big ford galaxy, with his two kids and us three it made seven for the ten hour drive to the sea, I drove most of the way there, we travelled overnight, I remember driving up over the Drakensburg mountains, it was like a three lane highway, it was quite foggy at around three in the morning, I was doing about 60mph when this giant petrol tanker bloody massive, shot passed me as though I was stationary. When the sun came up, the view over the rolling plains of natal was magical absolutely endless, on passed the Zulu battlefields, Rorkes Drift with its plaque by the roadside.

Val and Alan were Lancastrians there was red and white friendly banter on-going. They had two kids, Craig who I coached at college and Maxi who unfortunately had downs syndrome, she was lovely and bubbly the star of the show and Katie loved her. Eventually we arrived at our cottage by the sea in a district named Margate. It was furnished with a maid, and all mod cons.

During the week unbeknown to us just round the corner in the next bay was the launch party for the boats taking part in the world Marlin championships.

Every morning at dawn we the boys would head over to check out the rigs, they were fantastic beautiful sleek machines on the back of these trailers pulled by monster tractors, big chevvies and dodges. What luck to find this going on, on your doorstep. The weather stayed warm for the week, we had a couple of excursions into Durban, there was apartheid in your face, white's only beaches.

Back at college a bombshell was about to break, Brother Timothy who had been head master for years was to be moved on to the Cape, to take up another post. The College was in shock, parents were unhappy, teachers also, I must admit he had been ideal to work for, kept his distance, but was on hand to lend support if needed.

I was enjoying my work, the sides were performing well, I made some controversial changes to the first team, which made a couple of players jaws drop in despair, but that's what happens when a new broom arrives. It was suggested to me that money was being made available to bring me back next year that put a spring in my step. Helen was delighted, apart from the accommodation, which would need to be sorted.

Katie had started nursery, I remember taking her that first morning with her little bag, the first steps to who knows where, priceless. Helen had passed on the information to Marge and Duncan about our plans for returning, Duncan was far from happy, he thought politically South Africa was a worry, if I had to be honest I also had the feeling things would become worse, before it improved. Ex Pats were in a very precarious position, there was no way they could afford to return to the UK because of the pound v rand situation.

Also anyone leaving South Africa could only take 2000 rand out of the country. The new headmaster arrived from the UK, he was an Irishman. Mr Murphy an ex Featherstone

Rovers Rugby League Player, what a combination, the teaching staff within the college were a little non plussed, the headmasters appointment seemed a trifle mysterious to say the least. Tom as he was Irish became an ally of Murphy, but after a few meetings, Tom thought the man was a joke. I came to the conclusion early he had no idea or knowledge of the game of cricket therefore I became less involved, in fact the money sanctioned for the cricket coach the following year was scrapped in favour of a Rugby Coach.

To be honest I was delighted I couldn't imagine working for this pleb. Tom and I played a few rounds of golf together when possible; there were some superb courses around the district. The black lads would set out from their townships very early to caddy for the players, they were very knowledgeable around the course, I remember one such morning, it was beautiful warm, the fourball in front all Africaans big and loud the young black caddy described the shot his player should attempt, when he made a pigs arse of the effort, he then grabbed the lad who was totally intimidated and abused, this happened regularly, it did for me. Tom used to grab me, warning me not to interfere the whites lived in cuckoo land with no regard for anything black. No wonder there was tension in the city.

I'm not saying all the blacks were blameless; they had their law avengers also. I arrived in South Africa with an open mind, but I would leave with a heavy heart, I could see no winners, there was so much hatred on all sides. It's the most amazing naturally beautiful diverse country, shut off from the real world.

One Sunday I was invited to play cricket for the old boys. It was on the outskirts of Sandton, against a club side Helen and Katie came along, I borrowed the college mini bus, we took our picnic had a lovely day. After the match, we all socialised with a beer and nibbles, they were a friendly squad good fun, made a fuss of Helen and Katie, then it got dark quite early. I remember when we set off home, a storm broke, it absolutely hosed down, thunder and lightning. Then the bus just packed up, stopped dead no power, luckily we had just left the ground, I had to run back to the club house, Helen and Katie were terrified. I locked them in and then legged it. I arrived back at the club, entered like a drowned rat, the boys were brilliant hurried to the mini bus, and it was black dark the girls had been hysterical with fear. The main fuse had blown, one of the boys took the silver paper from his fag packet connected it in the fuse box and hey presto ignition, amazing.

Helen and Katie relived that night for many moons after, Tom and Margaret and the boys asked us all round one evening, they very kindly invited us to join them on a Safari to the Kruger National Park, how exciting would that be. We would be taking the college combo and driving., taking our own food and drink, the girls organised the food.

Steak, bread, biscuits, eggs, bacon and all the trimmings. Beers for the boys, coke usual soft drinks for the kids, it would take us a full day and night to reach the park it stands on the border with Mozambique, its massive, about the size of England. Tom booked our trip it was all pre-paid, to last four days, we would be sleeping three nights in designated camping areas, in round houses, known as Rondevals.

I was so looking forward to going on safari, and having Helen and Katie to share the experiences, priceless. Tom drove the first day. I took over during the night; I remember we stopped by the roadside at dawn and cooked our bacon and egg, the real outdoors. Early morning we checked into our first camp. The accommodation was sparse, a bed a fridge and a barbecue outside, they were also air conditioned as it was hot hot hot. They were comfortable, practical, all you desired. We unloaded our gear quickly, showered then totally refreshed, climbed back into the combo to spot our first animal of the African plain.

Katie was loving it, there was giraffe, Kudu, Springbok, Elephant, Zebra, really mind blowing, after a couple of hours we headed back, lit the Barbie, relaxed with a beer, this was paradise.

Tom had visited the Kruger previously he suggested the two of us should leave at dawn and visit the large water hole, it was close to the camp. It would be interesting to see what turns up to take on water. It was a totally fascinating place, birds of all descriptions all the stuff I had watched on telly, it was my David Attenborough moment. We set out in the combo, the gates were opened at dawn, they keep the camps secure and safe from the large predators, I was driving slowly along a track with a Banana plantation on the driver's side we were heading for the waterhole, a hippo was running alongside us on the passenger side, they were physically very powerful and could run quite quick.

I stopped the combo suddenly but kept the engine running, the banana grove was swaying up in front like it was out of control, only a few metres then out of the cover of green, strode this bull elephant, it towered over the combo, a giant, bloody massive. Tom tried to reassure me, keep calm, don't make a mad dash, what seemed like an hour, it was marvellous wild, and I was in my element loving it. Eventually the monster decided he'd seen enough and carried on his way to the relief of two rather inferior beings. At the water hole we were hoping to catch a glimpse of probably a lion or cheetah, there were other visitors too in their vehicles so that obviously put paid to the big cats on parade.

It was full of hippos having a great time wallowing enjoying the cool of the day. After breakfast we struck camp our next night's sleep was a fifty mile drive through the reserve, the terrain was diverse as you would imagine, metal roads ran through the centre with branch tracks leading off, we had a map, which was pretty straightforward to follow. Herds of zebra were crossing our path forcing us to stop, there were hundreds of em. I noticed one had an injured foot struggling to keep up. We all commented that he would probably become the lion's meal that evening.

I've never felt happier and relaxed as I was on that trip to the Kruger. Another interesting incident happened on that afternoon. We were desperately hoping to spot the big cats, when a passing warden lifted our spirits, intimating that they were close, we decided to stop and make a brew. In the distance heading our way I could make out a shape resembling a large dog like creature, it just kept coming along the same route which would take in our kettle boiling, as it got decidedly closer we got decidedly nervous and bundled everyone into the combo, it was a dog hyena with its head down it was onto a scent, a warden told me later that nothing would have kept the hyena from its scent, and we took the right course of action, moving out of its way. It looked really powerful with massive jaws, there was probably a kill in the vicinity, and he fancied some. That evening was magical, the camp was laid out around the perimeter of another water hole, this time the bathing was taken up by elephants, two or three families, matriarchs aunties and juveniles, we cooked our meat with a beer on the side, then relaxed to the sight and cacophony of a mixture of mammals and bird song, incredible on the ear and eye. Perfect. No luck next day regarding spotting big cats but the day was magnificent our final resting place was close to our original campsite we had more or less gone round in a circle.

Our final evening we had a mega Barbie, we took far too much meat with us on the trip it was heart-breaking throwing prime rump steaks into the bin before we left. That trip ranks as one of the finest we have ever taken together as a family, I would recommend a safari holiday with young children, it leaves you with a feel for survival in the confines of a true wilderness. Tom and Margaret had been the perfect hosts, we were now thinking about returning home. The boys from the cricket teams put on a leaving party for me, Helen and Katie, we had become quite close to the boys and their families. South Africa with all its problems is very much family oriented with weekends on the whole spent with the family, the climate tends to lend itself to family entertainment, playing sport, watching sport or barbecuing, of which they are currently the world champs, probably the Aussies would care to differ in that regard.

After our adventure on safari I volunteered to take the first fifteen rugby team for pre-season fitness training, we had three weeks before we returned home, the idea was for the boys to arrive at college at 0530am, all kitted out in overalls and boots, with a pack on their back full of bricks, they would also bring their breakfast, as we had kitchen staff on hand, it gave us the opportunity to train for an hour or so then enjoy breakfast before college, the lads were really keen this was thinking outside the box, something new. It was dark when I left our caravan and made my way kitted out and excited, I organised them into three ranks, we were going to walk or powerwalk for an hour no running, they thought it was to be a doddle, the college was in possession of an army assault course similar to the ones at home, I was to make use of the eight foot wall splitting them into teams.

At 0600 we set off at a good pace this brought back memories my army days back at Bovington power walking under a little pressure is a great way to keep fit, all was going well, the boys were trying really hard to keep in formation, I had a slight problem with a lad, and I knew I had to nip it in the bud, this little twat was imitating every command I gave, so without any more crap, I halted the group, straight in amongst them pulled the little prick out in front of the rest, I slapped him round the kisser in front of his mates, slagged him off for being a pillock there wasn't a sound after that to be honest, I was a bit severe with him, it was a calculated risk I was prepared to take, I thought they were the first fifteen therefore would appreciate character, and a bit of moral fibre. The boys completed the walk, we had casualties, blisters being the biggest culprit the boys realised they had some way to go, and there was more to walking than they realised.

The wall was another first for them, I split them into teams of three, instructed them on how to clear the obstacle in the quickest and safest manner. They then went against the clock, they absolutely loved the competition each team working hard, after about twenty minutes I brought them altogether, praised them on a great first mornings work. I could sense by their faces how much they had enjoyed the session; it was all in the swimming pool for ten minutes then up to college for a hearty breakfast. At the end of college that day the young man I had dealings with in the morning, came to me doffed his cap, he apologised for his behaviour and complimented me on how I dealt with him, he was full of remorse, but he really wanted to carry on with the sessions, I told him we both probably learned something from the incident, I was impressed by his honesty and told him so, he was never any bother after that, I bet he grew up into a top man.

We completed nine sessions before I returned home after the final session which comprised of twenty lads that's how popular it became, we had a few beers and nibbles. I then came face to face with a few anxious parents one father came to me explaining how he had set off at three in the morning to get his son into college for 0530, I was flabbergasted, I thought I bet they were glad I was going home.

It was quite emotional especially for Helen and Katie, Margaret and the boys were tearful as we bid farewell our South African adventure behind us, never to be forgotten we had grasped the nettle, out of initial adversity our six months literally blossomed into the most interesting educational, stimulating time of our lives. Priceless.

Dad holding a beautiful young fox destined to become a fashion accessory.

Mum posing in Peasholm.

Mum and Dad looking resplendent at Uncle Tom and Auntie Joan's wedding at Weaverthorpe.

Dad upon his beloved Norton 500, in the Libyan desert helping to win the war.

Me and little brother Bill, with Auntie Joan's son Gordon in the background.

Primary school aged 6 years old.

Grandad, Arthur Armstrong.

Passing out parade, I'm the smart one on the right.

Receiving my Cricketing award from the General during the Passing Out ceremony.

Junior Army Champions 1964

Selerang Barracks 1967

Scarborough at Lord's in 1976, celebrating victory in the Haig Trophy Final.

Back row (left to right): P. Woodliffe, M. Davison, B. Rennard, M. Heath, A.J. Moor (Captain), K.C. Stockwell, C. C. Clifford, M. Shepherdson
Front: S. P. Glaves, P. Hart, R. C. Sherwood, D. Kneeshaw

Brian Close and Phil Hart before their sponsored parachute jump at Grindale in 1980.

Wedding Day 18th March 1972

left to right: Dad, The Groom & Bride, Duncan and Marge.

Winning the game with a six into the Tavern bar at Lords 1976.

Helen, Christine and Marge bringing Katie home.

With brother Bill at his Wedding

Just How Old Are You?

by Philip Thorn

The interesting article by Keith Booth (Spring Journal) raises the general point as to the year of birth of first-class cricketers bearing in mind that Ted Pooley tried to hide both his age and his birthplace.

It is clear from our researches that many cricketers pretended to be younger than they actually were but it is only over the last 30 years or so that many details that had been accepted as correct have proved to be wrong.

As Keith Booth says, dates of birth that appeared in *Scores and Biographies*, *Lillywhite* and *Wisden* were taken as set in stone but these sources had little option other than to accept whatever dates of birth were put forward by the cricketers themselves.

The official records of birth, marriages and deaths were kept until recently at Somerset House in the Strand and the system up until the mid 1960s was that one had to apply at the entrance desk for a search form and after paying one shilling and sixpence one was then allowed to search for a selected person for a period of five years only. This was rigorously enforced by the officials and Peter Wynne-Thomas recalls being severely reprimanded for trying to look up his own birth without having paid an extra fee. This made looking for deaths over a long period very expensive and was also a deterrent in trying to check the birth details for the thousands of first-class cricketers born in England or Wales.

In about 1966 this system was relaxed and I began searching for details of 'missing' cricketers, mainly in an extended lunch hour, up to 1971 when I moved from Surrey to Nottinghamshire. Since then Philip Bailey has done a great deal more research to the point where most cricketers have had their year of birth checked although there are still a good few who for one reason or another have not been found in the birth records. Kit Bartlett in London and Lionel King in Birmingham have also given valuable assistance with our research.

In addition I sent several thousand forms to cricketers for them to complete and this also revealed much new information in particular in the places of birth it being found that many cricketers had merely given the nearest large town to the cricket press.

Several hundred cricketers were found to be older than thought from the original published age and whilst no doubt some of these may have been due to misunderstandings with the cricket press, in most cases it seems a deliberate action to appear younger to their County Club and therefore more likely, other things being equal, to be taken on the staff.

Most of these were from one to three years older but those, excluding tourists, who were four or more years older than their correct age are listed overleaf:

Difference	*Name*	*Represented*	*Original Birth*	*Correct Birth*
-10	W.Wilkinson	Nottinghamshire	1869	1859
-8	D.D.S.Taylor	Warwickshire	1918	1910
-7	G.W.Brook	Worcestershire	1895	1888
-6	B.Blomley	Lancashire	1885	1879
	T.A.Brown	MCC	1869	1863
	S.Hadden	Essex	1883	1877
	S.Lowe	Nottinghamshire	1873	1867
	L.Radcliffe	Lancashire	1871	1865
	O.L.Williams	Warwickshire	1938	1932
-5	B.T.L.Watkins	Gloucestershire	1907	1902
-4	G.J.Carver	Surrey	1883	1879
	F.L.Cole	Gloucestershire	1856	1852
	W.Cuttell	Yorkshire	1839	1835
	W.East	Northamptonshire	1876	1872
	H.Elliott	Derbyshire	1895	1891
	F.H.Farrands	Nottinghamshire	1839	1835
	J.Flint	Derbyshire	1844	1840
	P.R.Hart	Yorkshire	1951	1947
	P.T.Mills	Gloucestershire	1883	1879
	W.Padley	Nottinghamshire	1846	1842
	D.Sullivan	Surrey/Glamorgan	1887	1883
	R.Thomas	Lancashire	1871	1867
	H.Watson	Yorkshire	1884	1880
	W.C.Wheeler	Middlesex/Surrey/ Hampshire	1845	1841

George Brook is an interesting case as he was engaged by Worcestershire when they thought he was 34 when in fact he was 41 and in six years for the county took 461 wickets at 27.85. Lees Radcliffe, the Lancashire wicket-keeper knocked six years off his age and this was repeated by his successor Ben Blomley.

Finally during our researches we discovered than no less than 47 England Test cricketers claimed to be younger then they actually were.

Katie with her pet gosling, Cook.

Martyn with Sue on their Wedding Day,
Arnie Sidebottom and Jim Love paying their respects.

Darren Harland in the drivers seat with Adam Lyth up front, Chris Batchelor in the rear, on their way to net practise.

*Working with my junior squad.
Headingley Test England v South Africa.*

Graduation Day, very proud.

Our trip to the Barrier Reef on board Ocean Spirit 1997.
Katie, Charlotte, Susie, Jonny, Helen and Martyn

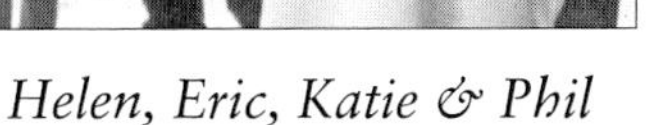

Helen, Eric, Katie & Phil *Jonny & Charlotte Moxon*

Martyn, Helen, Phil and Susie at Katie & Eric's Wedding
9th June 2007

Proud moment with Adam Lyth after Yorkshire CC win the Championship

Posing with 'Neptune' another Yorkshire Legend.

Chapter 10

Diggers ... Martyn for England and Sue ... Family life ... a competition win and a funeral

As we ghosted into arrivals Marge and Duncan, Christine and Susie were there to welcome us home, it was good to see everyone looking so well, Katie was amusing. I think she had forgotten her Nan and Grandad, and was a little coy, she had a strong South African accent, with her long blond hair, and deep tan, you would have taken her for a Springbok. It was a crush fitting us all in the car, with the luggage, nothing beat Duncan and he arranged it to fit. It was March now back home in 'blighty,' it took us a few days to recover from the jet lag, then it was back to it, back to the bank for Helen part time, Katie started Primary school down the road in Newby, and I had an interview at the Scarborough cricket club, as commercial manager.

I took the job on a temporary basis, I got to work with immediate effect, travelling the area flogging perimeter advertising, North Marine Road is a sizeable stadium and in no time we were filling it with boards representing a vast array of businesses from all over the area; these people were keen to become involved with the club, with its reputation as a provider of world class cricket.

After my interesting season with the county, it was back in the saddle with my buddies at North Marine Road, we were looking very formidable as a unit, the young boys were maturing into a class act with the bat, the dependable duo of Moor and Stevenson were still getting us off to a solid start, Adrian Dalby, Bill Pincher experience personified, these two would have a major say on how the season would evolve, not forgetting the skipper Brian Rennard, who with his strategic planning and total belief in his players, and his ability to stifle the opposition, we had the right combination for another successful season. My other team in the office were also formidable people, Lt Com Harry Wood secretary, a wily Scotsman, with a dry sense of humour, loved the game of cricket, he came from a naval background and served in the Far East during the time I was there. Mrs Pat Hanby, a keen supporter of Yorkshire cricket, Pat enjoyed her job as receptionist at the club and she radiated warmth as she welcomed members and guests to the club, another asset young Colin Adamson had just starting out on the secretarial ladder, a staunch Methodist, who in his spare time takes on the role of cub leader within the Westborough Church.

It was a pleasure working with this illustrious band of dedicated people. On the field that summer we won the Yorkshire League setting up another double as we reached the final of the Haig trophy for the fifth time, amazing. It wasn't a straight forward campaign, there were many heart stopping moments on the way. The Harrogate game at North Marine Road where we tied the game, but went through by having lost the least number of wickets. Peter Chadwick was in great nick that day for Harrogate, he was then given run out, which was very dubious to be honest it was nothing more than embarrassing. The semi-final was another nail biter against Old Hill CC from Birmingham, real drama. Tony Moor caught a blinder of a catch on the edge and we won by three runs.

It was back to Lords for the fifth time in ten years, a decade had passed since the initial victory in 1972. An inspirational moment came to me as I sat in the office one afternoon, I would ring Burton the tailors with a sponsorship idea. I rang the head office in Leeds explaining my plan, we had won the National knockout trophy at Lords on four occasions, we were heading down again, five times in ten years, how would Burtons feel about fitting the players out in the Blazers and Grey Slacks, the gentleman on the end of the phone apologised,I was dealing with the wrong department, I should ring the Oxford St branch in London.

They were delighted to be of assistance they were looking to sponsor a successful team. Over the phone that afternoon we designed a Blazer badge on the lines of Seagull sat upon crossed cricket bats, nothing too elaborate we only had a month to play with. The Burton team were great, they reassured me that it would work, my next job was to ring all the players, each individual had to go into his nearest Burton Branch to be measured, then all the measurements to be sent to London, it sounded straight forward enough, but the lads didn't believe me they thought it was a wind up, what a performance convincing them, but eventually all the numbers were sent. The club committee were quietly impressed and kindly invited the Burton executive to Lords for the final.

Three days before we set off for the capital, the player's new attire arrived at the club, it all looked very professional. Navy blazers, grey flannels with a gold badge, I felt a great sense of relief to see it, the boys arrived; there was only one cock up. Chris Clifford's outfit needed some adjustments just a minor blip. And to this day the Burton Tailors equip the finalists for their encounters at the Lords cricket ground.

We were to play Finchley, another London team in the final, we were staying in the usual hotel over the road from the ground, and we all looked immaculate on the morning of the game. We were to have a photo shoot, Fred Robson a committee member had arranged for the process to take place after breakfast. Adrian Dalby, myself and Helen struggled to finish and pay for our breakfast; therefore on arrival at the ground, we missed the opportunity to say, 'cheese'.

Fred was most apologetic, I thought all the bloody work that went into tarting the players up and I missed out, no worries we were here to win a cricket match not a frigging beauty contest. Over in the nets, we were stretching, running the brecky off, and checking the opposition out. I was bowling to Dave Byas, he drove one back at me, it came like a shell, I stuck out a hand to pouch it, but it took my thumb instead Bollocks!! I knew straight away, another broken digit, the boys couldn't believe it of all the places to fuck up, Brian Rennard, the skipper had to deal with it, three of the senior players and Fred Robson held a meeting to select my replacement, the young boy Nick Tubbs was down on the sheet as twelfth man but they went for a lad who they felt had more experience at this level John Precious, he would play. Nick Tubbs was very upset at being left out which was understandable, and it affected him for a long time. I guess it was my stupid fault as I trudged off in a taxi with Helen to the Royal Free Hospital. I spent a couple of hours waiting to be seen.

After the x-ray I was then bandaged up before we returned to the game. The Scarborough innings suggested it had been full of drama, Bill Pincher had run a couple out before staging a blitz on the bowling, he ended 61 not out, there were four run outs in the innings which totalled 150 for 7, it was definitely going to be nip and tuck. The Finchley innings got off to a fair start without loss at tea,

Helen and myself were invited into the Mayor's box, which was full of nobs. I was feeling pretty pissed off at this point, our only chance was an early wicket after tea. That's exactly what materialised, Chris Clifford making the breakthrough, they needed five runs per over, Bill Pincher removed the other opener game on!! No one else in the Finchley Team reached double figures and they ended up with 146 for 9 incredible. Apparently the cheques had been signed off at the tea interval with Scarborough CC bearing the losers cheque, what a turn around, it's never over until it's over. Marge and Duncan had made the journey down to support us, only to meet me with my arm in a sling. It had been a truly strange day; you never know what's round the corner.

That day ended the domination of the National knockout for Scarborough cricket club, it had been the most glorious ten years, I'm sure never again will one club go on to win the trophy five times, people came up with superlatives going back to those days, to be frank it was about honest, hardworking amateurs, playing the game with professional values, sustaining the highest level of team spirit. After the drama's and highlights of the Lords trip, it was back to work, it was the Cricket Festival at North Marine Road, I had organised a balloon race. The balloons to be set free after the final session, we were busy blowing up the balloons with helium in a caravan on the popular bank adjacent to the wicket area. Geoffrey Boycott was taking strike as the bowler bound into his delivery stride, a bloody balloon decided to die with a loud bang as if a bomb had gone off. You can imagine the impact at the wicket, Boycott turned his back to the bowler raising his bat in the air, the bowler by this time had released the ball which sent a stump cart wheeling along to the keeper, the crowd turned to the caravan, all eyes on me, it was surreal, then some wag mentioned the war and the popular bank exploded into hilarity, the umpire signalled dead ball, Boyc's looked up, face like thunder, pointing at the caravan, I stood outside, bowed to the crowd acknowledging my mistake then moved on.

Plaxtons were taking on staff again at the factory, I enjoyed my brief few months with the cricket club, but I needed to be earning more money, therefore I took up my old job, all the old buddies were back it was strange catching up with them, we all had plenty to talk about.

Katie was back in the groove, South Africa a distant memory, we had started taking her for swimming lessons, with Clare, they joined the Kingfishers swimming club, swimming two nights a week. I enjoyed taking them and watching them develop, it was certainly hard work all those lengths, but hard work did no one any harm. Clare was the stronger swimmer, naturally more coordinated, Katie was a trier, and she had tenacity never a quitter. I remember the day they were swimming a mile for their badge, I think I was more nervous than the girls, Clare powered away lovely breaststroke action, they had to swim sixty five lengths, I was swimming every length with them. Eventually Clare completed her mile and climbed out, Katie on seeing Clare got out also, I ran down to urge her on only ten lengths left I informed her, poor lass she looked all in, with a tear in her eye, she applied herself stretching out again, I was so proud of her. She struggled to the end but she completed the mile, I grabbed her it was amazing we got some sweets on the way home. I tried to instil in Katie that it was a great feat to complete that swim, no way could any person do that without the training and commitment.

We had seen some puppies advertised locally, I took Katie up to the kennels to have a look, they were Westies crossed with a poodle bonny little dogs, we both fell for the same dog, he looked a character full of himself, I made the decision and we all went up the following week to pick him up. Katie chose the name 'Digby', he turned out a terrific dog, he had the Westie coat therefore shed no hair just the job. We would walk thousands of miles over his lifetime.

After a silly altercation at the club I had another impulse and decided to leave, we were going through a bit of a transition we had lost the bulk of our incredible team, which would be almost impossible to replace, significantly it was money that had crept more and more into our game players were demanding ridiculous amounts. Scarborough being out on a limb had steered clear, but the inevitable was upon us, I didn't want to think I was leaving a sinking ship, I felt I needed a break. I was going to join Cloughton CC in the local Beckett league. Alan Readman was skipper at Cloughton, a good friend it would be fun joining forces helping to bring the young lads on. Cloughton was one of the few villages that still retained its heritage, the locals supported the village in all its endeavours, especially the cricket club, they were my kind of people. Apart from cricket, there was another pursuit that ticked my box, sea angling, Alan and Barry Wood were keen anglers and they were keen to get me started, as we lived by the sea it made sense, it was also a great way to keep fit up and down those cliffs. I spent a few weeks following the boys learning to dig bait, lugworm being the most popular, there was more to angling than you would think, tides tables, high and low water marks, wind direction it made for key decisions being taken, where to fish to gain the maximum result, all the gear required. Rod's, waders and lamp for night fishing,

All weather suit, it took me weeks to gather it all together. Alan was a bugger you had to keep an eye on him, he caught a billet one day, this is a fish you would normally throw away, when I had my back turned he threw it in my bag, it was there for a week. When I got the bag out the following week it absolutely reeked, full of maggots, there was hilarity throughout the group. We also spent quite a lot of time in the local pub, the Blacksmith Arms enjoying the ambience getting used to the ale. Helen apart from being a cricket widow now became an angling widow. I really got into the hunter gatherer scene. I mention this as I translate a couple of interesting fishing stories.

I had been down to Cayton Bay, spent all morning digging bait, tomorrow was the Bridlington fishing match £1000 first prize. I shared the bait among Alan and his brother Mick, another icon of the village. Sunday dawned, Alan picked me up in his van, we were off down the coast to Brid. It was a very popular occasion, there were hundreds of anglers on show, therefore you had to arrive early to find a decent mark to fish.

All those hours digging bait, it never guarantees you will catch fish, and this day was no exception, neither of us caught bugger all, not to worry we would make our way to the spa for a pint and the prize giving. It was dark, there were cars arriving from all directions, out of the corner of my eye I noticed a small Jack Russell dog. Thinking no more about it we made our way to the bar. One of our local anglers Steve I'anson was winning prizes, he was the top angler, knew the game inside out, totally committed.

Dave Medd was another a former school mate of mine, he also lived for pulling codling out of the sea. Running round our feet was that little dog again, she was a bitch in good nick lovely coat, but had the dreaded blue eye, which meant she was blind. She seemed to know her way round the joint, after a couple of pints we decided it was time to leave, hungry knackered and fishless ... priceless.

We found the van and bugger me there was that dog again, it was dodging cars, it was a worry. There were lights all over the place, we looked at each other.

I made the decision snaffled the bitch, there we were on the way home, nothing to show for our endeavours but a whimpering little Jack Russell.

Alan dropped me off, I was struggling with all my baggage. I knocked and Helen opened the door, there I was with my rod in one hand and a dog in the other, look what I've won. I gestured, a blind Jack Russell. Third prize on the tombola, bugger off was the reply, Digby our westie cross thought he'd won the raffle when he caught the scent of my new friend, it was plain obvious she couldn't stay with us, I would have to take her to the police station in town, I gave her a saucer of milk in the lounge, she then thanked me by pissing on the carpet. Poor little sod what would happen to her, I know where the police send the strays, a kennel up on Irton Moor, it would be hard enough with full eyesight, a nightmare without. At least I had prevented her being knocked by a car, that I thought was my salvation.

The desk operative at the station as you can imagine was a tad confused, as I tried to explain, I had been fishing in Bridlington where we found this blind dog dodging traffic, he let me ramble on sharing no interest whatsoever. Take the dog into the back, he informed me into the kennel, she'll be taken up to the dogs home on the Moor, let's hope someone reports her missing. She was trembling and whimpering as I left her, I felt bloody awful, but there was no other solution. Alan was keen to know what had happened to the Jack Russell, he was busy organising the Cloughton Cricket Dinner for the coming weekend. It was quite an occasion the cricket dinner, a definite highlight on the village calendar, popular amongst the members. In the eighties most village clubs organised their individual end of season dinners, and presentation evenings.

Alan had organised a coach to pick up members in Scarborough, to transport them to the Raven Hall, a beautiful hotel up on the coast at Ravenscar. Saturday arrived. Alan was sat on the coach with the driver, awaiting the passengers, the coach was hired from a firm in Bridlington.

He started to relay the story of the dog we had found, the previous weekend, the driver quickly chipped in, that it was his mates dog and he rescued it after reporting it missing last Monday, he explained how the little Jack Russell had escaped, she had a big Alsatian as a brother who knew how to open the gate, after following the brute out through the gate, she made her way down to the spa, and the rest is history. It was marvellous to hear the outcome, a story with a happy ending that makes a change.

During this winter I was fishing two or three times a week, I found it more productive after dark, I remember one evening in March, fishing off the Undells platform round the corner from Cloughton Wyke, it was a beautiful moon lit evening very bright, the tide was on the ebb. I had a couple of decent codling in the bag, as it was around eleven o'clock I cast in my last bait of Lug worm and mussel, there was a full moon, it was quite eerie, ghostly and still. I was standing about thirty metres away from the cliff, I was holding my rod, completely away with the fairies, when all of a sudden without warning a vixen fox stood up on the cliff above me and howled like a banshee, I nearly bloody died with fright.

That was it fishing over, my only problem, I had to climb that cliff to the path that took me to my car, as I struggled up the incline, I kept whistling as I reached the top, there they were, two beautiful foxes playing and rutting in the field adjacent to the path. As I turned inward with my head lamp I got their eyes reflecting back an intense yellowy glow they were following me. It's crazy really what goes through your mind, I was scuttling along the path imagining these foxes as ferocious predators, when a mouse scuttled across my bows on the track, I jumped out of my skin, a bloody mouse for god's sake. I kept looking in the field they were still there, escorting me to the car.

I arrived at my car sweating profusely, quickly climbed in after stowing my gear then locked both doors safe at last, its strange how your mind plays tricks on you, when I settled down, I thought how privileged I had been to witness such a display from a very shy and cunning animal of the night. Digby was growing into a lovely dog, he would sit at the front gate for long periods, he made many friends with all our neighbours, having a word with all and sundry who passed by.

Dad would spend most weekends visiting us often with Bills daughters Becky and Nick, they were growing up fast how time flies. Dad had found a new lady, Robbie she was a lovely warm caring old girl, great sense of humour, they were a formidable pair on the whist drive circuit, bringing prizes home most weeks. He was very happy with life it was plain to see, I was pleased for him no one deserved it more than Dad.

I had put a goose egg under a mate's chicken and before long we had a gosling in the aviary. Katie, Helen Dad and myself put a name into a hat and hey presto, the name that appeared in Katie's hand put a smile on our faces Cook the goose was his name. The kids loved our new addition, he would follow me everywhere, I would be chatting to friends at the gate, with Cook at my side gibbering on, he grew rapidly from a bundle of fluffy down to a full size moody gander, his sense of hearing was amazing anyone just touching the gate handle would be confronted with gander abuse. He spent less time out of the aviary as he would eat all the plants and mess on the lawn. I remember when we were going away for the weekend. I had to make some preparations for Cook, as no one would dare to enter the aviary with his food. Phil Mainprize a fishing buddy lived on a small holding close to us with a chicken run, I arranged for him to pick Cook and myself up in his pickup truck, it must have looked weird, me sat in the back with my goose, holding his neck with one hand and his body with the other a bit like a ventriloquist dummy, I recall those days with a smile, Cook was great fun, it was a novel way to introduce the kids to wildlife..

The new cricket season arrived a totally different kettle of fish, I was now playing in the 'B' division of the local Beckett League. At least the travelling to and from games enabled me to spend the morning at home. I was welcomed into the team, I knew most of the lads quite well, they were a noisy bunch, plenty of banter, which was my way, therefore we gelled from day one, they were a decent unit, experience and youth, Alan and Mick Readman were useful players definite characters icons of the village. John Boyes the keeper renowned throughout the area for his ability behind the stumps. And a youngster Jonathon Malthouse was showing promise.

Martyn and Sue were by now an item and totally loved up. He had become a run machine. Fluent in all aspects of the game the only downside, he was plagued with injuries. He got selected for England the previous summer, only to suffer a broken rib playing for Yorkshire he was very unlucky, but with sound advice and perseverance he eventually got his chance and was selected for the first test at Lords against New Zealand, as a family we were immensely proud. Derek, Martyn's Dad had been diagnosed with a brain tumour ,another bombshell to hit the young man.

Duncan rang me the evening before the test match, he had decided we should be there to support the lad. We set off at 0600 for London, it was a beautiful morning when we arrived at the Westmorland Hotel just over the road from Lords, memories again of our stays there. We parked the car, and then legged it to the ground. Play had been underway a short while we could hear the crowd applauding not having any idea on proceedings who was batting or bowling, we entered and amazingly there was Martyn and Graham Gooch in the middle, how lucky was that. He played ever so well, looked every bit at home opening the batting for England. The ground was full it looked superb, a little different from the three or four thousands that were there for our games with Scarborough CC. Martyn was bowled just after tea for 76, a good delivery from the great Richard Hadlee, it was a positive display on his debut, the crowd rose to him as he walked off.

Duncan and myself made our way to the pavilion, we got a message to Martyn, he was delighted to see us appreciated us making the journey down. We were introduced to his captain Mike Gatting who made us most welcome, Duncan bought a round of drinks for the team, he was so made up with the occasion, after an hour or so after another drink we decided it was time to be heading home. Duncan had consumed a couple of large whiskies, I was a little concerned about the driving arrangement, he assured me he was fit for purpose. We hit the M1 traffic was light, we pulled into the Woodall services had a coffee, reflecting on a marvellous day, another hour up the road I noticed we were swerving all over the bloody place. I looked at Duncan he was asleep, frigging hell, I pulled the wheel over shook Duncan he woke with a start "Christ", he shouted and pulled over to the hard shoulder, it happened so quickly we were so lucky another second or two we would have been into the central reservation. I took the wheel feeling a little guilty we arrived home no worse for wear, we kept our little incident a secret, no one was ever the wiser.

Showing promise, John Dudley, Alan Thraves, Jim Lawson great servants to the club. We had a successful summer winning the league, we also won the premier competition, the hospital cup, and it had been ninety years since the club had last won this prestigious trophy. We beat local rivals Flixton in the final at North Marine Road, a night to remember, back in the village it was a marvellous atmosphere. All the locals enjoying the success a momentous evening, bought memories flooding back of our heroics at Lords.

As well as Katie's swimming on Tuesdays and Thursdays, Helen came up with the idea of giving her the opportunity to try her hand at music, we enrolled her for piano lessons, Mrs Beatrice Horsley a well-known teacher of piano welcomed little Katie as I dropped her off for an hour on a Monday evening, I would then take Digby for a run up on Oliver's mount. I picked her up after an hour. She had enjoyed her first lesson. I must say I envy anyone who can sit and play the piano; it was a gift that evaded me I'm afraid, I took the French Horn home from school once, drove the family to distraction. Duncan and Marge adored their grandkids they were really pleased with their progress Duncan had spotted a piano for sale

Up to Boroughbridge sixty miles away, he took a works van with me to pick up the instrument. It cost £100 including the stool, Duncan was not the smoothest driver on the planet, we had the bloody piano tied and secured in the back. I was also in the back of the van when he just stood on the brakes, the piano just slipped its moorings then hurtled across the van pinning me to the side, I only cracked a rib which was agony enough, I was really lucky the heavy piano didn't decapitate me. Eventually we arrived home, what a performance getting the object into its final resting place we both forgot our ordeal as Katie gave us a rendition of her repertoire... priceless.

The summer had slipped by very quickly, we all had busy agendas balancing work with out of school activities, the girls were now enrolled into the local brownies, it kept us all busy, but I guess we wouldn't have wanted it any other way. Martyn and Sue, Helen and yours truly took a well-earned weekend away in the Lake District at a hotel in Ulswater, Martyn was cock a hoop he had been selected to tour India with England. It was also a celebration to announce their engagement; we were all delighted by the news.

Duncan was retiring from his post as Managing Director at Plaxton Builders, he had been an inspirational leader, during these years after the war, and had built up the business into a nationally recognised company, winning contracts to transform buildings all over Great Britain. Plaxtons organised a night to honour his achievements, friends from all walks of life were there from labourers to consultants it showed the power of the man. Over the years Duncan had become friends with Robert Luff, the impresario. Robert owned the Futurist Theatre in Scarborough, where he brought the famous Black and White minstrel show to town. Plaxtons builders had renovated the theatre in the sixties for the Luff Empire and they became firm friends, he would occasionally stay at Marge and Duncan's as he enjoyed the solitude and Marge's cooking. They had both served in the war with distinction, Robert in the Black Watch, they enjoyed swapping their stories and I enjoyed listening to them, I believe it was the man to man contact with Duncan, away from all the theatrical types and luvies that made his stays more enjoyable. Robert had sold the Futurist Theatre and became the new owner of the Royal Hotel in Scarborough.

Robert's nephews both suffered from that debilitating disease, cystic fibrosis, he then set up the Royal Hotel as a charitable trust, and all the profit went back into the charity raising funds to combat the disease, and bring public awareness to the fore. Duncan was to partner

Robert on this mission he was to play a similar role within the hotel, IC of all maintenance and new building work that was in the pipeline. Duncan enjoyed his new role, no more motoring up and down the motorways his days in the fast lane were over.

We had a family dinner at Marge and Duncan's to wish Martyn a successful tour on the sub-continent, he was a little anxious thinking about the meals he would be dished up in India, therefore he made the most of the food on offer, ex-players who had toured India had been pulling his leg on the issue of the grub, tapeworms were mentioned, cats and rats also, I'm sure there would be no problem staying in five star accommodation. Sue had been busy making preparations to join him for a while over Christmas, she also had joined Duncan at the Royal Hotel, taking on the role of receptionist, it was a busy quite pressurised job, but with that lovely smile polite manner, Sue had all the necessary attributes any aspiring receptionist should need.

Plaxtons the coach builders were slowing down with new customers difficult to find, therefore they were laying people off our department was no exception, our days were numbered. John Ness, a mate from work and myself were made redundant, we knew it was coming, but it was still difficult to take in. Duncan came to our rescue offering us both a job at the Royal Hotel, John was a dab hand as a decorator, I knew one end of the paintbrush from the other, we were to make an enterprising partnership. John was a good reliable bloke, enjoyed a laugh and a joke, he was a bloody solid grafter, we also fished together and played five a side.

We got the very sad news that Derek had died of his illness it was now November, Martyn was on his way home, it was a tragedy we were all stunned. All the families rallied round, the support shown for Audrey and Martyn was clear to see, the funeral took place in Monk Bretton the church was packed with mourners from Derek's work place the Pilkington glass factory, plus all his many friends and colleagues from Yorkshire cricket, Harold 'Dickie' Bird was a friend of the family, and shared some lovely memories of Derek with the congregation, I consoled my close friend, I knew how it felt to lose someone so special, who had always been there to steer a true course. Derek was only 50, a young man no age, he had so much to live for, he was as proud as punch of his son's achievements, I remembered the day Martyn was presented with his first team cap at Scarborough, he was batting in his new cap and sweater, Derek through his illness had become blind, it was so sad, life can be cruel it certainly was on that occasion.

Martyn after coming to terms with his sad loss made the journey back to India, I know he was worried about his Mum, but she had genuine caring people around her offering support. Sue flew out in December for a welcome break and to offer some comfort to her fiance. We were busy organising another Christmas ho, ho, ho, Clare and Katie were performing with the brownies at the local village chapel, the annual carol concert. Helen, Chris and I really enjoyed that evening it brought the families together to celebrate the real values of Christmas and the kids singing their hearts out hitting the high notes.

Sue arrived back in Scarborough, she had stories to tell, the trip of a lifetime, she was accompanied by other girlfriends and wives, they all got on and enjoyed the lavish lifestyle, there was tension in India during the tour apparently Mrs Ghandi the prime minister had foiled an attempt on her life, England were playing in that city, all the players and entourage were escorted by armed guards wherever they went, Sue said it was very dramatic quite scary at times, a little different from day to day life in Scarborough.

All our livestock was thriving, we hatched our first pair of Cockatiels, the girls were genuinely interested and embarked on a project for school with information and drawings of the birds in the aviary, where they live in the wild, their types of habitats, diets, nest building rearing young it was quite extensive. As parents we were chuffed to bits with their tenacity towards the subject and felt building the aviary had become a positive project on their behalf. Children were being denied access to the childhood we had as kids, running around in the fresh air hunting for birds' nests, fishing for sticklebacks, gaining a knowledge for types of trees and wild plants, these childhood pursuits had been passed down for centuries, only now there was a tangible change taking place, the electronic era was in its infancy and upon us. Katie at least could hold a newly hatched chick, knowing exactly where it had come from.

Martyn arrived back from his travels across India he was lean and tanned and glad to be home. He and Sue had set a date for their wedding, October the 12th at St Laurence's Church Scalby, with the reception at the Royal Hotel, Katie and Clare were to be bridesmaids, they were delighted and excited, Martyn then invited me to be his best man. I grabbed him and proudly said to him that it would be 'an honour' and a 'privilege'

Over a period of three weeks two very good friends of ours, Willy Maw and Milly Stephenson died. Milly was the instigator of Katie's christening held at the church in Staintondale. She happened to be in the wrong place at the wrong time this particular morning. A glass bottle fell off a lorry as it was passing Milly in Cloughton Village, it shattered on the pavement close to Milly cutting her leg quite badly.

The poor lady never recovered as complications set in, and she died on our anniversary 18th March. Willy went into hospital, we tried to lift his spirits, he was refusing his medication therefore it was only a matter of time, and he also died on 4th April what a tragedy brought on by sheer bad luck. We as a family had grown very fond of these two lovely people, they were from an age far removed from the throw away society that was emerging today. It had been a great pleasure sharing cherished memories for only a short period of time, Amelia Stephenson and brother Willy Maw sadly missed.

Duncan had accompanied Martyn and Sue looking for a house, they came across a property which ticked all the boxes in Wetherby, it was situated close to the A1 strategically ideal for all the miles cricketers clocked up throughout the season. It was quite a large house in a quiet cul de sac known as Deerstone Ridge. It needed a lot of work on the inside, new kitchen, new bedroom furniture, a new fireplace, the usual cosmetic changes, Duncan was again in his element planning his campaign.

All the family could talk about was the ensuing wedding, invitations, dresses, menus, the girls were oblivious to much else, I found escape cricketing at weekends with Cloughton and fishing the odd evening down on the shore where I could think about my speech. All the legalities regarding the house went through. Duncan had signed me on as his labourer, stroke painter, we arrived on the Monday and left on the Friday, this arrangement lasted for about eight months; it was a long haul cooking our meals sleeping on lilo's, just like being back on manoeuvres. Eventually it began to come together the final phase arrived to coincide with the stag night celebrations not the greatest timing really. The do had been arranged to kick off at the Tetley brewery in Leeds, all the Yorkshire staff were there, I can honestly say with hand on heart, I have never drank a finer pint of Tetley bitter ever, before or after. It was the usual stag night, good company good ale good buffet, I don't remember much after that, I do remember ordering coffee and spilling it down Martyn, managing to concentrate the spill around his nether regions, he was groaning in agony rolling around expletives being aimed at me as I could only see the funny side of this predicament after checking for blisters, he realised his tackle would survive we boarded the train home.

At last all the painting was finished the touching up completed the house looked amazing a tribute to Duncan's design skills, his all round DIY abilities were on show for all to see. We had worked nonstop for weeks, but had some funny moments on the way, fast asleep, we both slept on lilos, one night I awoke to the sound of heavy breathing, I honestly thought Duncan was having a heart attack. I shot up expecting the worst and there he was blowing his lilo up, it sounded dreadful, I then curled up laughing what a relief.

Or the night a young lad knocked on the door, he was dressed in fancy dress looking like a bloody skeleton in black, he looked at me and shouted 'trick or treat,' I had no idea what the silly little bugger was talking about. I ended up giving ½lb of our sausages that had reached their sell by date, he didn't seem to mind, but I wondered if my tyres would be still up in the morning. Oct 12th dawned it was fine no rain forecast, my old buddy Bill Foord had prepared a piece for me to recite at the reception, he was a genius with words, especially poetry, it was called a match for all seasons, which incorporate all aspects of the beautiful game of cricket. Intertwined with the story of how a couple met, fell in love and married.

It was a packed church players, friends, colleagues, presided over by the Rev Chris Tubbs, Sue looked beautiful as she walked in on the arm of her proud Dad. The bells were relaying the message to all and sundry, that they were man and wife, as they made their way through the lych gate into the waiting limo and down to the Royal Hotel.

The bloody photos took what seemed like hours, everyone looked splendid in their finery, Katie and Clare were loving all the limelight it truly was a special day. I was sweating up a little bit like a thoroughbred before the Derby, it was a nerve tingling few minutes standing up before so many distinguished guests, but once in my stride, I got the job done. Sue and Martyn jetted off to Rhodes for their honeymoon, I think we all had such a fabulous day we all wanted to jet off with them. But it was back down to Earth, music on Monday, swimming on Tuesday, back to the realities, waiting for the next special day to arrive.

As a family we all got back into our routines, Dad was happy with his new life with Robbie, they travelled all over the country, enjoying each other's company, Scotland to the Isle of Wight, they were in their element, they both had a positive outlook on life up for any challenge. We had now reached 1987, I was now forty years old, reached the apex, bloody hell how scary, now on the slippery slope of life bollocks, I'm here forever.

I remember this particular day, the car had been playing up, needing money spending on it, we were busy at the Royal changing the heating system, and it was hard graft. Knocking walls down, heavy work. I was feeling a tad negative, not on any occasions have I mentioned negativety in these accounts, but this day was an exception, I finished work and Helen picked me up as she had picked the car up from the garage, the bill for the repairs depressed me even more. Helen organised our tea, whilst I was checking the aviary, Cook our goose was nibbling away at my clothes it was a form of friendly greeting, no one else dare go near him he was a big softie really. Helen came out and called me in for tea, with a smile on her face, which was odd. She had gone through the mail, and there it was a large brown envelope, she had won the holiday of a lifetime. Let me explain she said, a few weeks ago I entered a competition sponsored by Embassy cigarettes, the idea being to collect coupons attach them to a card, when the card was full then send it off to the Embassy cigarette company.

The title of the comp was the Embassy wonders of the world holiday of a lifetime, when you sent in the card you had to prioritise your choice of destination, the options being the new world I.e. United States of America, the ancient world i.e. Rome, Athens, Jerusalem Cairo, cruise down the Nile, Luxor to Aswan or the Asian world i.e. India following the silk route, Thailand to China ending on the Great Wall. Helen had always fancied a cruise down the Nile, therefore she ticked the box Ancient World. Also included in the package, £400 spending money per couple, there were to be fifty couples on each trip. I read the letter in total shock over and over again; I didn't want it to compare with the Readers Digest Competition. Where they have you believe you're a winner. We were definitely one of the fifty couples, how bloody exciting was that, how weird I'm down in the dumps at five o'clock, and end up on cloud nine at 6. The trip was to depart Heathrow 17th September, we were to travel by train in first class to London Kings Cross, there transport was laid on to ferry us to Heathrow, we were booked into the Hilton Hotel where a champagne reception awaited us, how fantastic we were both absolutely made up.

Our travel bag arrived with the Embassy logo emblazoned all over it, I would feel a little bit of a prat carrying that around I thought. After arranging for the goose, the birds the dog and Katie to be looked after, we arrived at Scarborough station to catch the 10.10 to York, Duncan arrived on the platform to wish us bon voyage, it was exciting, Heathrow here we come.

Along the route to Kings Cross, I spotted three embassy travel bags stood on the different platforms, our buddies for the next 17 days.

The Hilton reception looked quite formidable as we both entered, no need to worry there was embassy staff there to greet us, sort us out with our entitlements, and make a fuss of catering for all our needs. We were then taken to our rooms to freshen up and relax before the reception to meet our fellow travellers. During our relaxation period I went through the itinerary, it was really very impressive, visiting places I could only have dreamt about.

When all the guests had been ushered into the suite, we were introduced to the group of travelling experts, whose job it would be to make our trip exactly what it said on the ticket, the holiday of a lifetime. The two of us mingled with others who like us were a little nervous. I noticed little groups beginning to form, I suppose it's quite difficult getting around everyone in such a short space of time, we met a couple from West Yorkshire Rawmarsh, they were a welcoming duo and he was a cricket grounds man that broke the ice straight away.

Another fact that came to my attention made me think not everyone on the trip were a true cross section of British Society, fifty couples one hundred people, but they were all white. It was an early start next morning, up at dawn, we were presented with our pocket money and cigarettes, and then we boarded our flight to Rome. We were staying for four days in this beautiful city, at the Cavalieri Hilton, the most prestigious of Hotels, the rooms were massive, with beautiful marbled bathrooms, typically Italian full of panache and style.

As we entered the enormous foyer and lobby after our coach trip from the airport, we sank into leather settees and armchairs, whilst savouring a glass of chilled sparkling wine, we were on nodding terms by this time with our fellow guests. Our representatives gave us our orders for the rest of the day, we were to meet in the foyer at 8 o'clock, where we would be bussed to a typical trattori outside space for dinner, taking in some of the amazing sights of Rome by night, I kept pinching myself was it really happening. We got a couple of loungers and joined a group of our new friends round the pool. Helen was loving it, seeing her so happy sorting out her wardrobe, having a hair do, it meant a great deal, sharing all our adventures, there's no substitute for that, we had a little luck on the way, but I believe you make your own luck.

That evening early whilst Helen was wallowing in beauty products, I decided to head down to the piano bar for a pre-dinner drink, I had arranged to meet her in the foyer, what happened next rates as one of my funniest observations ever, this hotel was the height of chic, beautiful ladies stylish young men, there was a guy tinkling the ivories somewhere in the distance, as I made my way slowly, I eventually arrived staring down into a sunken bar, it was busy, active, full of Italian passion as people were remonstrating on their day.

I took a seat round the bar ordered a dry martini shaken not stirred, it cost an arm and bloody leg equivalent to six quid, I was enjoying the moment taking it all in, bottles of champagne at forty quid a throw, I was way out of my league, these punters were probably footballers, or even Mafioso, who cared. I then noticed a couple of older lasses making their way to the bar, they were from our party, from Leeds, bless 'em they stood out from the Italian beauties, as they peered into the pit making eye contact with the slick professional barmen.

'Aye up cock, whose ale is it', was the cry, that got the bar staff into a flap, they had no bloody idea at all how to counter or answer that question. Whose ale is it cock, I made my way back up to the foyer to meet Helen that incident never to be forgotten.

Our meal was a great success, lovely Italian food with fine wine, interesting how many Japanese tourists were in

Rome at this time, Japans economy was enjoying massive growth they were a leading player on the International Stock Markets. We were bussed the next morning to St Peters Square, where we were introduced to our guide for the day, the person in question was a lady, dressed in a gaudy patterned dress carrying a large umbrella for obvious reasons, we wouldn't lose her. There were thousands of tourists within the square, getting lost would not be a problem. We were to be shown round Vatican City, it is incredible but the place has its own rules, economy, police, even army, it's a micro country within Rome. It's head of state being the pope. For anyone who has the opportunity of visiting the Vatican do not delay, it is spell binding our guide was of the top order, she worked her socks off, there must be more gold per square mile in these corridors, lavishly gilded rooms ornate, in great detail, then we were taken to stare in amazement up at the ceiling of the Sistine Chapel, we were extremely lucky as it was in the process of being cleaned, the first time for four hundred years, we had the opportunity of seeing how it looked before, but then just a long the ceiling how it gleamed at you after the operation. With all the centuries of grime removed, the figures stood out as though it had just been painted. Michael Angelo took years to complete his masterpiece, laid on his back, sheer brilliance. There's no doubting the fascination of the Vatican, the sheer opulence, the power, a great start to our trip, it was a full day. I was quite knackered, how some of our party were coping, god only knows.

The next day we visited Tivoli gardens, another historical location, filled with water features all designed to work by gravity, the weather had played its part so far, it was glorious, warm and sunny, we had our evening meal in the grounds of the gardens under the stars all very five star. The Embassy staff along with the tour company, were doing a fabulous job, they engaged with everyone as muckers all with that Dunkirk spirit.

We said goodbye to Rome, a stunning suave city, looking forward to Athens, another city that never sleeps. Unfortunately the Greek Public Service workers were on strike the day we needed them. No worries our team were one step ahead of the game, and quickly solved what could have been an embarrassment for them. They hired private transport to ferry us up the Parthenon, probably the most historic site in Athens, it stands overlooking the arena that facilitated the first ever Olympic games. Our group were now taking on board this entire mind blowing Ancient culture with certain aplomb, even the old lasses from Leeds had a smile on their faces.

Our adventure was to take a change of course due to the strikers in the city, we were to be taken on a cruise of the Greek Islands, we embarked the next morning climbing the gangplank onto the deck of a resplendent sailing cutter all one hundred of our crew. I personally was feeling very unwell, as I had par taken of one or two too many the previous evening. Helen was far from happy with my behaviour, therefore I had to crawl a little for forgiveness, she was justified as I had not got to bed until 0330, we had to be up on parade at 0530, it was going to be a long day, when will we, or I, ever learn.

We boarded from the jetty on Aegeana, and sailed for a couple of hours it was a bonus, and it soon brought me round all that sea air, the beautiful blue Aeagan Sea crystal clear, we had dolphins gliding along with us at the bow, perfect!! Land ahoy was the cry as the first tiny island came into view. Hydra very typical, very pretty, as we approached the harbour.

All the waterfront properties pristine with their new whitewashed walls, the small houses all had colourful pots plants and herbs, picturesque to say the least a small cove lay to one side of the harbour with a little sandy beach, there were a few tourists visiting with their long pigtails and beads trailing, these were the fellas obviously nothing had changed since San Francisco, and flowers in their hair, a hippy commune, then we all got a whiff of the baccy. Yeah man!!

We had an early start to catch this voyage, therefore a chance to stretch ones legs and sample the local coffee and pastries was a delight. The sun was high in the sky, it was pleasantly warm. Helen was soaking it up, she loved nothing more than a restful sunbathe. All good things come to an end and it was all aboard, our next stop on our days cruising Poros, this was another hour away.

Probably a little busier than Hydra. Great views again as we entered the harbour, I remember there being a couple of massive cruisers anchored, real gin palaces fit for kings and footballers. We enjoyed a leisurely lunch here, superb crab, fresh fish and salad. Everyone had found their sea legs, which was incredible really, the group were revelling in the sunshine, relaxed now, and I'm sure feeling very privileged to be here. Aegena re-appeared on the horizon, we all disembarked, thanking the skipper and his crew for a wonderful day, it truly had been another one to remember.

We had dinner in the hotel followed by a dance, after my indulgence the previous evening, we decided to step away for an early night. We had the day off tomorrow, some sun bathing, relaxing round the pool. Another warm day greeted us, Helen had been down to the pool and arranged the loungers to suit, there was six of us in a little group all very cosy, there was the usual banter, you know the stuff, when the lasses get together look at her, what is she wearing I wouldn't come out looking like that,and did you see him last night, and how bloody stringy was that squid!!

Passing the time of day they call it. I was having a game of table tennis with Howard, when I noticed one of the young lads on the trip, he had been laid out in the full glow of the sun, and was turning pinker by the minute. I decided to go over, I was a little concerned for the lad, he was a quiet young man, I had noticed him a few times on our excursions. Howard and I coaxed him into the shade, where the lasses were bleating. Nick was his name, he was a hotel porter from Bournemouth, the lad had dabbed a small amount of cream on his person, not enough to stop the irritation of sun burn, we got some water into him and he slowly recovered, I can't imagine how he would have fared without our intervention, probably ended up in the local hospital, all's well that ends well.

Nick was grateful for our actions, and became another buddy. The days seemed to be flying by, another early start for the airport, on another bus, we were having a tour of Athens on route, the guards guarding the presidential palace, how odd they look in their uniforms, strapping soldiers in tutu's with pom poms on their slippers, they look like characters from the Night Garden how bizarre, there again I wouldn't want to be the one to tell them. Goodbye Athens hello Jerusalem.

As we landed at Tel Aviv Ben Gurien Airport, I looked out of our window, and there before my weary eyes on the tarmac outside the airplane was a military tank, and everything was pointing at us. It made us feel very welcome I'm sure, but this was Israel, this is the hub of the ancient world as far as I was concerned. Jerusalem was very busy, traffic and traders going about their business, we were heading for the Hilton Hotel, our guide was highlighting the route, calling out names of places we had all heard and read about, The Gardens of Gethsemane, and of course Bethlehem. We were to be here for three days, the itinerary stated all the sights our guide would be visiting we were going to be busy, busy.

Breakfast in Israel is regarded as the main meal of the day. We were treated to a momentous meal for brekky set us up for the day. Our first port of call was the old town, the ancient part of the city, following the route Jesus took with his cross, arriving at the place he was crucified which is now a church. We witnessed the money lenders in the street still plying their trade, nothing had changed much in that area, the hustle and bustle of the shoppers in the market,

You could imagine this man being prodded and pushed out of the way by people not knowing his plight, unaware of who he was, and what he stood for, as he struggled along the route. All those years as a kid at Sunday school, the bible readings, I was actually here standing on the spot where reputedly Jesus also had stood, quite moving really.

After lunch we were taken to Bethlehem to visit the birthplace of Jesus, to be honest I was a little disappointed, I had been looking forward to this visit. I had it all mapped out in my mind how it would look, the place was overrun with gift shops, selling the same old tat. The actual area he was supposedly born, probably had stood the test of time, I tried to visualise the kings on camels, and that guiding star.

The Wailing Wall was our next port of call, difficult to describe really, we were segregated from the women, they had their own area. Men of the real Jewish faith were reciting prayers, as they nodded towards the wall, they looked totally committed, offering up their thoughts real earnest, very powerful. On the way back to the hotel I noticed at every public bus stop there stood an armed guard. It brought it home, the struggle for power and control of their respective lands that was taking place, between the Arabs and Israelis. Fortunately for us it seemed we had picked a reasonably calm few days, that said, it was in the back of your mind what if.

This evening we were going to the Hassan Effendi, an Arab restaurant for dinner. As we entered the restaurant, I noticed how bloody dark it was, it was busy, bustling in fact, Big Arab men smoking their hubba pipes, I mentioned to Helen that I wasn't sure about the menu, all that goat, spices, and sheep's eyes to see you through the week. Helen replied she was sticking with the chips. As we were such a large number, we were ushered into a separate suite, where we found the food laid out in the buffet style, typical of our group, they piled in without too much fuss, who could be first, usually it was the same faces at the front, I wondered how long had it been there, frigging flies all over it. Luckily they did bring some chips in and Helen filled a plate, and that was it. After the meal we were entertained by a belly dancer, what a performance the bitch got me up to help her with a few moves the less said the better.

The next morning rumours were rife of people being struck down with stomach problems. We were heading down to the Dead Sea, due to people being stuck on the toilet; our numbers on the coaches were noticeably reduced. The Dead Sea is the lowest point on the planet and it took us forty five minutes of travelling non-stop downhill to reach this wonder of the world. As we travelled we passed many kibutz, a farm stead housing young people travelling, supplementing their incomes helping to bring in the produce, all nationalities, colours and creeds. We were told about the Dead Sea, how salty it is, we had brought our swimming attire, I was looking forward to relaxing in the water, the guide made a point of stressing how important it was not to splash the water especially close to the eyes, people should not enter the water, if they had open wounds or suffered from piles, this brought a chuckle but the guide was deadly serious. We arrived at the coach park. Helen had decided not to bother.

We quickly got changed, then made our way to some indoor baths, as we entered the bloody smell, sulphur like rotten eggs hit you, 'Jump in!' this wrinkly old bugger shouted, I tentatively entered, it was quite warm, the old guy told me how invigorating these waters were very good for the complexion and sexual appetite, I said I didn't have a problem with my appetite, he replied he didn't either and said he had just celebrated his 96th year, I thought bollocks to the sea, I'll stay here all day.

They were marvellous old liars the boys in the tank good fun; I made my way outside, just as they were dragging one of our group down to the first aid station. He was screaming in agony. On entering the sea his initial act was to rinse his eyes with water, we all had a wry smile, it was not the first incident of this nature this complete nob head performed, as they say in Israel, you can't educate pork.

The sea was just as I imagined it would be, warm relaxing, very buoyant, it was an honour to be here. After our swim we covered our bodies in the silt or mud from the bottom of the sea, this supposedly had qualities to extend one's life.

It was great fun a real treat. On showering and changing, we travelled a short distance down the road to the site of another incredible story, Masada. The Israelis regard Masada as there bench mark, after the holocaust of the Second World War, never again would they suffer that same fate without a fight.

King Herod built his temple, hundreds of feet high upon a hill known as Masada, he felt very insecure, his own people detested him, and the Romans who were the occupiers of the land did not trust him either, he therefore built his palace to escape from both factions. It was the most enchanting place, most of it was in ruin, but you could get the sense of peace and remoteness, up on the steps the breeze was cooling very refreshing, the swallows were busy darting about the sky collecting the bugs for their young.

The Romans who controlled the land with an iron fist, brought a legion of men from Briton, they needed to storm the palace at Masada, and make an example of the Jews. It took two years to build a ramp, and set a catapult in place to batter down the walls. The Jews who resided in the palace, burnt all their books, leaving nothing for the aggressors, then decided on a plan of mass suicide. Men drew lots, they then administered poison to the remaining families, and the last man standing then fell on his sword. The Romans eventually battered down the walls, and entered to find everyone dead and their belongings burnt a very courageous story. Our guide was quite emotional, as we stood there imagining the reality of their actions, one could understand why? Another breath taking day, nothing prepares you for the moving experiences, the genuine anguish, these lasting impressions of Jerusalem, and Israel will stay with us probably forever.

Up in the air flying to Cairo, this is our fourth flight, some of the old lasses are struggling with pressure problems like dizziness, the main topic of conversation is of a toilet nature, that meal in the Arab restaurant had knocked over fifty per cent of our party for six, the one thing it has done is bring the group closer together, everyone is helping each other, I remember this flight, looking back to the rear of the aircraft, it seems strange now but all that hit you was the blue fug of ciggie smoke, a hundred people all puffing away, how times have changed.

The check in staff at Tel Aviv airport must be the most vigilant; they go through the baggage with a fine toothcomb. We had a drama as one of the cases was exciting the x-ray machine. One of the lasses from Leeds, who I had met in

Rome was distraught, as the suitcase she had borrowed to come on the trip, arrived on the desk in pieces, the top had disappeared, and disintegrated exposing all her worldly goods, she was very upset bless her, no problem, we were round the gang with a hat, a quick whip round, it took ten minutes for another lass to nip for a new suitcase, job done, smiles all round well done team.

Arriving at Giza the sight of the largest pyramid, they are giant tombs, built by the pharaohs, as their respective burial chambers. Helen fancied a ride on a camel, there was no shortage of aerial transport, a dozen Arabs were touting for business. We embarked upon our beast, a real ugly fellow with hateful eyes, he would have taken pleasure in hurting us I'm sure.

We both made our way across our strip of the desert from the coach park to the entrance of the largest pyramid, Giza where our guide was to give us another history lesson on the incredible stories that surround these people from Ancient Egypt, we were then allowed to actually visit the tomb of the pharaoh at the top of the pyramid, this meant a climb up duckboards for at least fifteen minutes, it was hard work, and only a couple of us accepted the challenge, it was really warm in there not much air, eventually we came upon the chamber, and inside the stone tomb the sarcophagus, it was a bloody con really, the guide at the top explained everything in the chamber, and the tomb, had been stolen centuries ago. The actual size of the blocks making up the pyramids were enormous, hundreds of tons apiece, it made your eyes water, imagining the work of hauling and pulling them into position.

We arrive Cairo at eleven o'clock in the evening; our body clocks are all over the place. I'm not complaining in the slightest I wouldn't have missed this for the world, all I'm saying is we have some quite elderly folks on board, keeping up with all the travelling, sight-seeing, the bustle, they must be a little knackered.

We were staying at the Rameses Hilton, very posh on the 27th floor, most impressive views of the City, the city seems to be divided by the great river Nile. Our side of the city looks very affluent, whereas on the opposite bank I'm staring into buildings that resemble nothing more than slums. It's very busy, and noisy, motor horns piercing the still evening air nonstop.

Here we go again early start in the morning, we are to be bussed at 0930. I have to keep pinching myself, it still seems like a dream. Helen is looking more like a native every day, she has the skin that turns mahogany, she looks beautiful, very fit, and this life obviously suits her. Luckily we both have steered clear of the bug, more have gone down with what is apparently a form of dysentery. It's certainly causing a stir amongst our operators, they've had a meeting, and thank goodness we are to carry on as normal.

As we drove passed the sphinx, I'm sure it winked at me, the old face is a little worn now, not bad though for it is three thousand years old, they were erecting a stage for a musical extravaganza to be enjoyed that weekend.

Another early start we are flying to Luxor in the morning, being called at 0300hrs to fly at 0500, as we will be returning to the Rameses Hilton after our cruise, therefore we are advised to pack one suitcase between the two of us, this is to save space on the boat. Helen has gone down with flu like symptoms, sore throat a bit chesty, I wrapped her in a blanket on board made her as comfortable as possible, it was only an hours flight, everybody was a little grumpy on this leg as you can imagine, I met a couple of locals on the flight, it was interesting as they spoke good English, explaining how they relied so heavily on tourists, they appreciated our visiting them, I reassured them, by commenting how beautiful their country was, with all its treasures on view, people will visit in their millions.

Helen was quite groggy by now and needed medication, our gang were having breakfast in a cafeteria. we declined I found a young man with a pony and trap type contraption, the poor looking bloody pony looked like it was on its last legs, I offered him five Egyptian pounds to find a chemist, 'No problem, sir.' And off he galloped. Helen laid in the back, me up front with the driver. Arrived to find the shop closed, 'no matter, sir. I know another' ...off we go, whip cracking we left the metal road, as we sunk into the interior of Luxor, the complexion of the place had changed the shop again was closed. Helen was now beginning to panic thinking we were going to be taken hostage.

'One more try sir', the boy interjected, we needed the medicine off we trotted again further into the interior Helen squeamish, as we passed meat hung up outside a butchers shop. It was like a clip from Indiana Jones as we arrived at the chemist. I jumped down entered the shop, having to duck my head as it was tiny. The staff inside were all dressed in smart clean overalls, as my Egyptian is very limited, I mimed like a charade, explaining my requirements.

A sore throat. The chemist turned to me and in perfect English explained what I needed. I felt a right prat, the medication the very same as I would purchase in the UK. Our intrepid young man and his pony had saved the day, we were both grateful, Helen looked better already as we were dropped off at the side of our cruise boat; it was very posh, aligned to the Sheraton group. Our luggage was sent to our cabin, they were very snug, beautifully furnished, space was of a premium but one soon got used to it. Luxor was bustling with tourists, their boats tied up along the river, the town was in the process of a building boom, new hotels going up all around, we were warned not to venture far alone, as muggings had been reported the previous evening. That made Helen wince as she recalled our adventure earlier.

We enjoyed a leisurely day on board our boat, with a few drinks round the pool, looking out from the deck, the banks of the Nile so green and fertile, for probably a half a mile either side, then the barren desert takes over, obviously the majority of the population make their living from the banks of the river, and the river itself, farmers and fishermen ply their trades. Tourism also plays a big part in transforming many lives in these parts. Today we visited Thebes and the Valley of the Kings, as a group we were waiting for our guide by the gates of a temple it was very hot. Nick the lad we befriended in Athens, came rushing up to me in a bit of a panic. He needed a toilet, the lurgy was still prevalent amongst us, as I scanned the area there was a café type building away off, I told him to make a bee line for it. Off he went only to pull up after a few yards, out of control, the poor lad just shat himself. To be fair no one in the group took the mickey, they just rallied round, I asked for a pair of clean shorts and someone threw a pair of Bermuda's. I then took the lad to the toilet block we had passed earlier got him cleaned up, as I mentioned earlier the group, reacted with a sense of togetherness, Nick was one of ours, there was a strong sense of team spirit, the group reacted brilliantly to this young man's embarrassing situation, nothing beats the 'Dunkirk' spirit in us Brits.

We were then ferried across the river and up to the Valley of the Kings. This for me was going to be the highlight of the tour. The tomb of the boy king Tutankhamen. As we approached the site it was swarming with tourists, out in the middle of nowhere. The entrance to the tomb was very dramatic, we descended a flight of steps, before arriving inside what I can only describe as an entrance resembling a mine shaft, we were not allowed to take pictures as the flash would damage the beautiful hieroglyphics, which told the story, adorning the walls in fresh tones of reds and gold as though it had been painted only last week ... amazing.

I was trying to imagine being Carter on that day in 1948, stumbling across this treasure trove of incredible beauty. It took your breath away on entering the chamber emblazoned with figures of animals and birds. The majority of antiquities from the tomb are in the museum in Cairo, which we will visit on our return. Another truly momentous episode.

To cap a wonderful day, we visited the temple at Karnack in the evening to experience the sol illuminare, an amazing laser light show, illuminating the historic temple, those dulcet tones of Richard Burton and Diana Rigg as King and Queen reliving scenes from their illustrious past. Our cruise begins as we awake from our slumbers there's a sensation of movement, the slight vibration of those engines taking us along the historical River Nile, the journey to Aswan will take 3 days terminating 21st Sep how time has flown.

We are to visit truly another wonder of the world, after breakfast the group are bussed to the temple of Edu. Over the past ten years Russian Scientists have overseen the dismantling of the temple, every majestic pillar, every stone block, some weighing hundreds of tons, and then rebuilding it to its original state. A remarkable fete, thousands of workers, showing a commitment never bettered. The reason for all the upheaval, the Aswan Dam, artefacts such as the temple would have been lost for ever once they flooded the land.

Because of our numbers on board the H/S Anni, dinner is served in two sittings, Helen and I have gone for the second sitting, for that gave us chance to have a little pre dinner drink and experience the fantastic sunsets on board.

It's so relaxing up on deck, checking out the fisherman in their Feluccas, shooting their nets by hand. Waving at the kids on the river bank, all the people residing by the river do appear to lead an enriched happy life. The food on the boat is first class, buffet style, a varied menu to tempt all palates.

We arrive in Aswan tomorrow, Aswan is renowned for its granite, all the great obelisks around the world will have begun their journeys from the river at Aswan. The massive granite structures were cast in one piece, drilling hundreds of holes along the side then filling the holes with lime, the granite would then crack into the shape required, I'm sure the operation was more complex, bit it gives you an idea of how it worked. When completed the obelisk would then be floated along the river to start its journey.

It was quite emotional checking out of our floating palace, it had been a memorable experience, life will never be the same back home. It seemed months since we left and we wondered how Katie and all the family were faring. We arrived back in the Rameses Hilton, just one day and night left of our trip, it was a free day, we decided to visit the museum, after climbing down into the boy kings chamber, I wanted to check out all the marvellous antiquities they buried with him. Tutankhamen must have been a really powerful young man, according to the diverse paraphernalia they found with him. You have to see it to believe how much space it all takes up.

We were really pleased we had taken time out to visit the museum. Our final dinner was a special affair, aboard the Nile Pharaoh floating restaurant, on the river in central Cairo. It was primarily Seafood, very good beautiful squid, sea bass, prawns, washed down with bottles of chardonnay, how very civilised.

We had speeches from the team, complimenting us all on our teamwork, our behaviour under difficult circumstance at times. We all started swapping addresses. I just sat taking it all in, thinking ships that pass in the night. I've tried to express the flavour of our wonder of the world holiday, its difficult finding the words, for a couple we truly found the experiences of the last couple weeks, very humbling in my book, there's no substitute for travel, mingling with the different cultures, their customs, incredibly diverse from the coliseum in Rome, to the Temples of the Nile, it's been an absolute pleasure.

We arrived home after a long day travelling, initially flying from Cairo, we were sat on the tarmac for two hours, as they tried to free the brakes on the plane, and then the rail journey from Kings Cross, eventually we made it home, Katie was excited as we were to see her. It took us a few days to find our feet, and then it was back to the Royal Hotel, with a paint brush in my hand. The new gas central heating system was completed in the hotel, therefore there was loads of work up grading the rooms, and Duncan had been very busy overseeing all the transformation taking place, Marge was a little worried as he had been complaining of headaches.

It was unusual for him to mention any ailment. Not only had he been busy at the Royal he had just installed a new Greenhouse in his garden, a massive undertaking with its own heating system, sprinkler system, it had marble tops that were heavy, I know as I nearly pulled my pin out helping to lift and carry them into position. Martyn and Sue were very happy in their house in Wetherby, enjoying married life. Marge had been visiting them one day in her car, she had noticed on arrival in Wetherby that the clutch seemed to have a problem.

She immediately phoned Duncan, who then gathered me up, rope and all, we were going to tow her back. On arriving at Deerstone Ridge we found the clutch to be knackered, Duncan throughout his life has been renowned for his attitude to a problem, its simple there is no problem. I mentioned the fact that it could be illegal to tow a car along the A1M, 'we should be ok, at this time of day', was the reply. Martyn was shaking his head and rolling his eyes at me, as Dunc was attaching the tow rope, I thought we've done some stuff in the past but this takes the biscuit, with a wave and a good luck from Martyn and Sue we were off, Marge sat with Duncan in his car, with me steering Marge's Golf. Trying to keep the rope taut was a problem we were stop starting through Wetherby.

Onto the A1 I was sweating cobs, bloody great lorries overtaking us blaring their horns as we trundled on at 20mph, we had around three miles of the A1 before we hit the Bramham turn off onto the A64, where were the coppers, I couldn't believe the luck of the man. On we motored the rope was holding, then just before Whitwell Hill he stopped in a layby, he looked to be enjoying himself, joking all the while; he also thought it strange we hadn't come across the law. Marge was a nervous wreck in the car, as we set off once more. Part way up the hill there was a crack, the rope had snapped, bollocks was the cry, we had a right performance making it to the top, having to move from a standing start, Duncan's car struggled for momentum screaming in first gear. I imagined Marge having a do.

Eventually we made it to the top, to the delight of all the passing traffic who gave us the horn all the way up, it was plain sailing now, and we drove into a garage that Duncan used in Commercial Street without a care in the world. This had been typical Duncan or Jack Slack fearless and competitive, with men like him you could understand how we won the war.

I was absolutely buggered when I got home, Helen and Katie were relieved to have me return safely, they imagined the three of us locked up in a police cell. I relived the journey with them and we rolled about laughing. The days became shorter and the weather turned very autumnal. I remember I had been fishing, it was a Saturday, I arrived home early evening, when the bombshell struck. Our bungalow was deserted which I thought was odd. Helen had written a note, I found it on the kitchen table, Duncan had suffered a stroke, Marge who the previous year, suffered a slight stroke but after a few weeks she rallied and made a complete recovery, Helen felt it was probably all the worry Duncan had suffered over Marge being ill that lead to his downfall. We as a family were shocked to the core, this was definitely not in the script. Duncan had refused to go into hospital, his philosophy in life did not include hospitals, and becoming a burden this was typical of the man. Christmas of that year was one of vigil rather than celebration, he loved his granddaughters to bits, it was really sad and not easy for the girls to understand. Duncan had lost his speech, but he took hold of my hand, gripping so tight, expressing in a way I understood to look after all the family. He was easing his suffering by putting his house in order, he was immensely proud of his family, as we were of him, in all our eyes he was a true giant of a man.

On the third of January 1988 at ten past five, Duncan died in Helens arms.

This truly was the end of an era, the only saving grace being that we knew it was coming, the family had prepared themselves for the outcome, which on reflection made it a little easier to bear. Helen took it on herself to organise the funeral, it was to be held at St Laurence's Scalby, with a celebration of Duncan's life to be held at the Royal Hotel.

Duncan was one of six brothers and four sisters, he originated from the village of Wadsworth near Doncaster, the family were butchers by trade, Eddie, Duncan's eldest brother had stayed in contact, he and his family attended the funeral, friends and work colleagues from labourers to chief executives, filled the church in Scalby. Raymond Stockill his deputy from Plaxtons spoke with true sincerity, dignity and warmth, telling the tales of their many exploits together.

Duncan was a self-made man, successful, resourceful, a workaholic, not one to shy away from a challenge, he knew every trick in the book, and that is what endeared him to his loyal workforce, he was not averse to picking up a shovel on sight, shovelling concrete for a couple of hours to help keep the job on track. Definitely a man's man. But his greatest love was his family, it meant everything to him taking his wife and kids and grandkids on holiday, for his two weeks in the sun.

It was a sombre few weeks after the funeral for all the family. Marge was beginning life without Duncan, she had many friends, who supported her tremendously, going out to lunch organising coffee mornings. The garden was a bit of headache, she employed a local gardener Ken Gill to take it on, Ken kept it very tidy, a pleasure on the eye.

Chapter 11

Magical Orlando ... Douglas Bader's Wingman ... Killingbeck Trek and Injuries

I had gone back to play cricket at Scarborough, David Byas had taken over the reigns as captain, it was great to be back, as I thought I still had something to offer, back in tandem with my spin twin Chris Clifford. I also intended to become more involved on the coaching front, helping Bill Foord the club coach with the juniors. Many years previously Ray Bloom my old buddy, was the areas cricket coach he ran a level 1 coaching course of which I gained my badge. Over the years it was never a problem inviting players to play at Scarborough, we had such a marvellous set up at North Marine Road.

Modern facilities, including one of the best playing areas outside County Cricket. Now times were changing, that constant flow of eligible young players began to dry up, therefore we had to start looking at the idea of preparing more of our local youngsters, and turning them into talented cricketers, we had the pedigree at the club to ensure its survival, people like Bill Foord whose life had been dedicated to teaching kids, gave his time generously making sure all the local lads had the opportunity to shine. There were local boys who came through the system and went on to become very good players. Tim Watts the Gormely brothers, Andrew Wood, The Woodhead Brothers, to name but a few, we now had to take the conveyor belt system forward producing our own talent, keeping cricket at the hub of our community.

I was satisfied with my contribution back in the Yorkshire League, meeting old and new players from around the county again was magic, and I soon realised how much I had missed that buzz. David Byas had grown into a strong leader, he had developed in stature as a player, I'm sure he was destined for success with the county any time soon.

Katie had reached the grand old age of ten, she was very busy with piano, swimming, brownies, and now she had enrolled into the St Johns ambulance brigade, turning up every Wednesday evening learning basic first aid, how to apply dressings bandages etc., Helen and I were pleased with her work ethic, she was showing maturity above her years, therefore with all the grief of the previous months we decided as a reward, we would fly off to Florida, Disneyland to introduce our lovely Katie to Mickey Mouse. Helen who never seems to get the credit she deserves, is a magician when it comes to booking holidays, we were all booked in and ready to leave in October.

We had always taken our annual holiday abroad usually the Canary Islands, we always enjoyed our breaks together, hiring a car and exploring wherever we were staying, great fun, such precious memorable times. This would be our first long haul trip as a family, how exciting.

Orlando Oct 1989 after an enjoyable long flight around ten hours, didn't disappoint, hop on the mono rail to pick up the luggage, taking in the welcoming spiel en route, all incredibly Disney, futuristic, brilliant. Arrive at the Alamo car centre, pick up our motor for the duration, how slick.

Once aboard with the luggage stowed, I had to remember we were driving on the right. I thought the bloody car was a little sluggish, until I realised the hand brake was actually down by my left foot, I thought to myself I bet there's more pricks like me, get done with that one. We checked the map, we were heading for Altimonte Springs, it was early evening as we tentatively made our way along highway 4 through Orlando, and it was extremely busy, stop start rush hour traffic, plenty of room on the four lane highway.

Katie was gushing with excitement, 'Look at that Dad, did you see that over there?' My eyes were focused on the traffic, trying to get used to drivers overtaking on the outside, as well as the frigging inside. Altimonte Springs was a small working town about thirty five miles North of Orlando, it took us going on for an hour to eventually arrive at the turn off. On our map it told us to head for the water tower which stood above everything else in the vicinity. Days Inn Lodge came into view our home for a week, it resembled a travel lodge, with its own swimming pool. We had an initial problem with our room, the one they ushered us too was full of ants, crawling up the walls over the beds, into the bathroom, to their credit they quickly sorted the problem moving us into a superior room. After a long flight and the excitement and exhilaration of finding our lodgings, it was a quick snack and bed we were all done in. It was an early start next morning, we decided to have breakfast on the hoof so to speak. Helen popped into the Delhi next to our apartments, we merrily tucked into our pancakes and fruit juice on Highway 4 heading back south.

We had more or less organised our itinerary before leaving the UK, taking advice from people, who stressed there was no way you could do and see all the Disney attractions in the week. Therefore on our first day we were going to take it easy heading round Sea World, taking our time to acclimatise, I must admit driving down to Orlando that first morning just the three of us in the Florida sunshine felt so good.

To be there as a family, as the father I felt so proud giving Katie this opportunity to visit all these iconic attractions. I'm sure all the families who have witnessed the same, know how I was feeling, very special.

Highway 4 was very busy, the hustle and bustle with the odd incident of vehicles coming together en route. The speed limit has to be adhered to the traffic cops are very keen, its around 65mph, after an hour we arrived at the entrance to Sea World, another mile or so then the car park absolutely enormous, acres and acres of parked cars, it's so important to remember the line you're in, the chance of finding your car without that knowledge would cause a big problem.

We head to the end of our line and climb into the little train that ferries us to the entrance, this park and ride system is very slick, moving thousands of people very efficiently. Sea World as you can imagine is full of creatures from the deep. Aquariums full of exotic fish, sea birds, penguins, pelicans, every creature that lives in the sea or by the sea has a place at sea world, it is a labyrinth of beauty to be enjoyed at ones leisure.

The climax being the show in the aqua arena, Shamu the killer whale, dolphins travelling at amazing speeds with trainers on their backs, soaking all in the front rows with a splash of their majestic tails, the arena bursting at the seams, the screams of sheer joy and amazement, as Shamu brings the house down with his monstrous size beating the water into a crescendo. Katie is screaming delirious, the place is a cauldron of sheer delight, what a start to our holiday, after selecting a suitable tea shirt in the shop, and pin pointing the car, it was back up to Altimonte Springs for a shower before dinner, Tony Roma's steakhouse here we come.

We were to be staying in Altimonte Springs for a week then heading down to Miami for our final week, all very exciting. Tomorrow Magic Kingdom, Cinderella's Castle, Mickey Mouse and all the Disney characters, Katie is in seventh heaven thinking about it.

Another early start breakfast en route, another beautiful Florida morning, Magic Kingdom awaits us as we arrive at the car park another monstrosity; we have an option of how to travel to the entrance. A mono rail or a Mississippi steam boat, a show of hands suggests the boat as do the majority, Walt Disney and his team were very clever he was a true genius, delivering these passengers and transferring them in the blink of an eye into Fairyland, young and old transformed, from serious wrinkly old souls, into fun loving young at heart teenagers. When the boat clears the bend and the castle comes into view, this is when the transformation takes place.

It is difficult to contemplate such an act, but again all the millions of people who have had the pleasure of this event will know where I'm coming from. On gaining entry you just stand in total awe, the sounds, the cleanliness, the pastel shades, the characters, the sun bringing out the best in everything and everybody. The railroad with its beautiful old engines, which travel the perimeter of the park on the hour all day, passing the plaque of the great man, Walt Disney how he must look down with total satisfaction his dream put in place for future generations to marvel at. Looking down Main Street with its horse drawn bus service, people milling around planning their route for the day, the aroma coffee, doughnuts, jelly beans it is the perfect main street, how you would imagine heaven.

Another day in paradise, Katie and Helen I've never seen them so happy, Splash Mountain, the runaway train, the haunted house, Pirates of the Caribbean, people walk miles in the day, covering distances they would imagine impossible. Lunch takes in burger, chips and a milk shake and a welcome sit down. Pluto and Donald Duck appear from nowhere, Katie makes a beeline, there's no stopping her a cuddle for them, outcomes the camera again, more film required.

Of all the incredible places we have visited as a family over the years, that one day, that initial day in Magic Kingdom. Florida has to be the one, I suppose it's how you prioritise those pleasurable experiences, everyone has different ideas but that day did it for us.

As the week progressed the driving, became easier we were finding our way around. I remember visiting a park in Orlando known as boardwalk and baseball, it's not there anymore, it closed down in the early nineties, I got talking to a guy who operated a ride, he was getting on in years, been doing the same job for decades, all he was looking forward to was living through the millennium. I've often thought about him, that's the first time I ever registered the millennium, as it was another eleven years hence.

The space shuttle was due to be launched on this day, we all found a place to watch as people told us what a spectacle it was, climbing up from Cape Canaveral into space. Forty minutes from launch, it was cancelled for some obscure reason, which was disappointing to say the least. We enjoyed a relaxing day around the swimming area known as typhoon lagoon with water rides aplenty.

Our final day we saved for Universal Studios, with all the white knuckle rides plus King Kong, E.T and Back to the Future, another memorable day. The week had seemed to fly by. We had stuck to our itinerary; no way could we have done any more. We had tasted the delights, and the three of us were very impressed with Florida, the locals were genuinely pleased to see us, the theme parks were of the highest standards. Orlando with all it had to offer had wetted our appetites for returning in the future.

On our way down to Miami, we stopped off at a place known as Alligator Alley. This area is known as the Everglades, Central Florida is made up of swamplands, where local tribes of Indians lived, and still live. Katie and I took a trip aboard an air boat. We travelled into the swamp checking out alligator, the boats, travelled above the water on a cushion of air, at tremendous speeds the noise of the engine and the speed of the boat gliding just above the water was really exhilarating great fun. It was a little daunting the thought of driving into Miami, we were looking for Collins Avenue, I was imagining something like London, and it would be like finding a frigging needle in a haystack.

America's road system is designed to make arriving at ones destination relatively simple. No bloody oneway streets or roundabouts, just blocks of streets aiming North South or East and West. Collins Avenue ran beside the sea, we entered the Miami limits travelling all the way down to the sea, turned right bingo!!! Piece of cake. A few minutes down our street our hotel Beach Harbour, a pretty pink building right on the beach perfect!!! It was a pleasant family hotel, with a great location, after the hustle and bustle of Orlando, chilling out on the beach, checking out the bikini's! Magic!

On the second morning I arranged to go deep sea fishing. Helen and Katie were happy to sunbathe whilst I got picked up by the crew, early and taken to the boat, we were sailing from the port of Miami as the sun came up. I was given a rod with 6 lures attached, as I cast into the ocean within seconds 6 mackerel were hooked, this we did until our tank was teeming with fish, they would be our live bait. We steamed for about an hour, before the skipper decided, by checking his high tech aids that we were above our quarry, six of us were fishing including a lady from Sweden, it was great fun kingfish aplenty, they are a predator fish, with a long streamlined body, ferocious teeth, built for speed. I had brought along a six pack of beers, what a perfect way to spend a morning. The crew were brilliant, really made it enjoyable. Everyone caught fish, our lady actually hooked the prize specimen, a farmer fish it was bloody enormous she couldn't land it, her boyfriend managed to haul it on board we reckoned it weighing round 40 pounds, a very rotund fish great to eat apparently, more great memories.

Miami was a very interesting city, at the top end of Collins Avenue, all the hotels have been preserved and brought back to life, all painted in their periodic pastel shades of the art deco style, prominent in the fifties. A trip to Star Island, majestic houses, and properties owned by such names as the Bee Gees, Gloria Estefan, Michael Douglas and Barry Manilow.

On our penultimate day we decided to take a cruise to the Bahamas. We had to be ready to be picked up at 0630, and then transported to our cruise ship. It was going to be a long day, but interesting no doubt a first for us. Helen and I had cruised down the Nile, but never on the open ocean.

It took a couple of hours to clear immigration, before we were allowed on board, all that malarkey was soon forgotten as we tucked into a hearty American breakfast. At last, as we stood on deck taking in the view of Miami's skyline, the propellers were turning, we were making headway. The sea was unbelievably rough, all due to the eventual shuttle launch. The experts reckon it changes the weather patterns for a time, the yanks weren't too keen sailing in rough weather.

They had their sick bags at the ready. We were to sail for four hours over to Freetown, and then disembark for a couple of hours, just time to buy a tee shirt, have a swim, then back on board for our return journey. A message came over the tannoy system, one member of each family to make their way to the main lounge for a briefing on safety aspects of the cruise. I arrived to find hundreds of people milling around in what was the ships theatre.

The old boat was rocking and rolling on the high seas, the breakfasts were coming back, and people were moaning and groaning. Then the music struck up, it was only 09.30 in the morning when to the amazement of us all, this knobhead appeared dressed in a white tux and bow tie trying to keep his balance as the boat was lurching in the stormy seas, he then attempted to sing a jaunty Rick Astley number, what a pillock. This gathering of gut wrenching sickly individuals, quickly shouted down our star turn, who disappeared without trace. Helen and Katie arrived wondering what the fuss was all about, apparently the sun had come out on deck, which had lifted the spirits somewhat.

After an hour or two the sea seemed to lose its ferocity, we were reflecting on our holiday as we sat in our loungers, all three of us agreed what a brilliant place Florida as a holiday destination has proved to be. We were planning to return to make the most of all the amazing facilities on offer. The one subject that intrigued us all was the size of the people, absolutely bloody massive, fat men and women, obesity in its infancy, gluttony unrivalled, the size of the meal portions in the restaurants was staggering. The bell then sounded bringing us out of our reverie, it was time for lunch, look at them go, like a stampeding herd of fattened prize cattle.

After all the snouts had been ploughed from the troughs, Freetown appeared on the horizon. As we entered the harbour, we noticed all the taxis queuing, must have been ½ mile long. Our cab driver bundled us in to his very lengthy shooting break, there must have been twelve of us bundled in, Katie lying on the luggage in the boot. It was a typical bounty advert type island very pretty, blue water and white sand, we enjoyed a swim and a beer, just time to indulge in some serious bartering for our tee shirts, before heading back to our boat. Our taxi driver was actually quite a knowledgeable young man, we had some friendly banter on the route back, and he was staunch supporter of Mrs Thatcher and her policies. The highlight of this long day was our entry back into the Port of Miami. It was around 10:30 in the evening, the impressive colourful neon of the city was then cast into shadow, as a magnificent firework display erupted on the skyline.

I thought what a welcome for us as we entered the Port, only to be told that Miami was hosting a travel agents convention, and this was the grand finale, it certainly was it took our breath away. We all slept like logs that night ...priceless.

After our breakfast, it was the usual sad farewells my comment on these occasions "until the next time", back up to Orlando, to the airport drop off the car, all very slick it works very well. People appear in the airport lounge, you vaguely recognise from the flight out. Everyone seems happy, all looking tanned refreshed in their new shell suite, flip flops and tee shirts.

Helen and Katie agree Florida had been a wonderful experience, we all have been infected by its magic, we certainly will be back to sample more of the sunshine state. As 1990 dawns, I feel a sense of trepidation, only ten years to the millennium, how extraordinary to be born at a time when hopefully we will straddle into the next one. How will it play out, no doubt the media will be on hand to enlighten us, to keep us on our toes, bring it on!!!

Martyn has been appointed skipper of the Yorkshire 1st XI, it's a role he definitely deserves, I'm sure he feels it a great honour to lead the county, and I'm sure with his meticulous preparation and eye for detail, the Team is in good hands. Sue might have a point when she thought his timing was slightly awry. She gave birth to Charlotte Louise Moxon on 13th March a beautiful daughter, whilst he and his team jetted off to Barbados on a pre-season soiree, the family were delighted with the arrival of Charlotte, another granddaughter for Marge. Helen, Chris, Katie and Clare and their chauffeur, yours truly made the journey to Harrogate to visit Sue and the baby, Katie and Clare for some obscure reason were not allowed in to visit, they were upset as you would imagine, bloody stupid rules!!

I also have been asked if I would skipper the first XI at Scarborough CC. I was delighted and honoured to take up the role. David Byas is now a recognised contracted player with Yorkshire, and good luck to him, he's been a tremendous league player, re writing the record books with his powerful stroke play, I'm positive the next stage of his career won't phase him. At Scarborough CC we have an array of talent, it's mostly made up of local lads, which is testimony to the strength of local cricket throughout the area, to add to our squad I brought in two lads from Pickering, Neil Cowton and Dave Greenlay, both all-rounders, I'm sure the Scarborough wickets will suit their game, as I've mentioned before, mediocre league players were being paid throughout the Yorkshire League. Up to this point it really hadn't affected us as we were out on a limb so to speak, but as we travelled around Yorkshire, match fees and expenses were being muted around, hundreds of pounds for a weekends cricket, our boys ears were pricking up at that sort of rhetoric, it was to become very difficult to keep the lid on this new phenomenon.

June 1990 and Helen was about to celebrate her fortieth birthday, as it is an important milestone on lifes highway, we decided to help her enjoy the moment in Tenerife. It meant Katie taking time out of school, but you are only forty once!! Whilst waiting in the Airport for our flight to the canaries, Katie had found a new friend, a young boy, very cute with his 'Ninja Turtles' bag on his back, the two of them putting the world to right, she was eleven and he was about four!!

Our row of seats on the plane included this young boy and his Mum and Dad, to be honest I don't normally get involved with other passengers whilst travelling. As I was reading, the young man and his Mum were watching 'Fools and Horses' the excellent BBC comedy. They were giggling and wondering who the miserable so and so was next to them. Then a line from the show set me off laughing, that broke the ice, and we all introduced ourselves, Phil and Libby Wigginton and their son David. They are from Nottingham, and as if it was meant to be they were staying at the same hotel. The hotel was very chic, and only just opened. As we had booked a last minute deal we found ourselves allocated a room in the depths of the hotel. Helen as is her want complained to the reception desk, and Phil and Libby who were watching told us later that they thought they would steer clear of this mad woman. Katie got on very well with David, and was a surrogate nanny for him during that holiday involving taking him to the toilet and wiping his bottom...happy days.

Young David had just celebrated his fourth birthday, and Helen was adamant she wanted no fuss for her big day...that's not her style. Flowers from the local florists and a suitable card ticked all the boxes. We all got on famously, our new friends enjoyed the same interests, the Sun, a beer or two and a laugh. Phil was a keen sporting type playing cricket and squash and was also a keen Nottingham Forest supporter!

To this day we are the best of friends, and in fact we regard them as our extended family. As I write this piece it shows how time moves on a pace as David and his partner have just given birth to their first child, a baby girl called Willow.

Setting up the cash line lottery within the Scarborough boundary meant a lot of time out on the road, my initial thoughts were of dread, I used to hate selling raffle tickets for the annual Christmas draw, therefore this project would be really going against the grain, lottery's had just become vogue, as our own National Lottery had just taken off, people were in that mind-set. Our top prize of £500 didn't compete nationally, but it still wetted a few appetites. After a couple of weeks of hard slog. I managed to bring on board a hard core membership of 800 -1000 depending on peoples circumstances. After the initial feeling of despair, having to go off every week chasing pounds, I can honestly say that throughout this period I met some remarkable people. The lads from Filey, keen to restore Filey CC, Chris Hodgson, John "Pinball" Heaton, Jack Cammish and Keith Crawford.

Pinball and Jack were fishermen, negotiating the North Sea every morning in their cobble, taking in their stride all the hazards on offer, Keith was the tractor driver who laughed and retrieved them with his rusty old Nuffield, and their anchor Chris ran a shoe shop in Filey, Goody two shoes. These lads were literally the salt of the Earth.

We became good mates, their commitment and drive, involving wonderful support from the town of Filey, enabled the club to go forward and prosper, they developed a junior section, of which I got involved with their coaching and development. Another group of characters, who impressed me, were from a totally different background, the local rangers club, that's the Glasgow Rangers football club, Scarborough Branch. These boys were geniune, generous and funny, as you can imagine extremely loyal to their cause, headed by a lovely man Dougie Syne, he is an interesting bloke, very intelligent enjoyed all sport and local interests, and very kindly donated a trophy to be presented to the SCC junior player of the year.

Over in Kirby Moorside a village on our western border, another interesting human being lurked, Steve Colling, who ran a rather posh hostelry, the George and Dragon along with his wife. He was an avid Yorkshire supporter. He used to organise cricket themed dinners at the pub, inviting celebrities from the game to rock up and relive their memories. One day whilst I was visiting he offered me the chance to accompany him to the National sporting club in London, the Aussies were touring that summer and this was to be the inaugural luncheon.

Without hesitation I accepted his offer, I'd met up with Craig White, who was at this time just making a name for himself as a Scarborough player, we were having a net on the eve of me heading down to the smoke for lunch, he asked me to have a word with a mate of his in the Aussie ranks, a new protégé the two had been working at the Ashley Mallett School for spinners and became buddies, a Mr Shane Warne I said no worries mate, and buggered off to London.

I met Steve at York, we boarded the 125 express, it sped off for Kings Cross, we sped off for the buffet car. It doesn't take long now to reach the metropolis, a couple of hours not like the four it used to take when I was a boy soldier. It was kind of exciting, the both of us had consumed a couple of beers on the journey down, therefore we were ready to take on the world, Steve was quite au fait with this way of life, dining with the knobs in private gentlemen's clubs was another notch on my belt, we made our way by cab, arriving in good time, before luncheon, Steve arranged for us to partake of refreshment within the sacred walls of this select club, the East India Company. The paintings, the leather upholstery, I was in total awe, I could imagine Lord Nelson, or the Duke of Wellington making an appearance, it was very similar to the long room at Lords.

The same nutty, leathery aromas, I was totally captivated by all this historical paraphernalia. It was time for lunch the sporting club was across the street, I remember Bob Willis directing people hither and thither, we eventually found our table. The Australian boys were presented to us as a group. I quickly made my way over to this blonde quite tubby young man, I passed on Craig's good wishes, where on he shook my hand with a strong wrist I do recall, and a 'Thanks mate, good on yer, how is chalks? Good I hope, 'What a cool dude' I thought, I wonder if he can bowl!!

The Aussie players were then ushered to separate tables to sit with the punters, we got the very popular Merv Hughes, with his hang dog look and drooping moustache. I have to be honest he was a miserable prat, and it took a lot of hard work to register a nod let alone a word.

These boys have an obligation to themselves and their fellow countrymen as ambassadors, not to rock up totally disinterested knobhead! After the meal an auction took place of old cricket memorabilia, Steve paid £400 for a painting depicting some cricketing encounter from Lords. We carted this bloody thing around London, and how it survived not being nicked beats me!!

By the time Steve and myself separated at York, we were both blathered and in high spirits. I thanked him for an unforgettable day and wonderful experience. I found my train for Scarborough and duly entered. When people are in high spirits they seem to hide their inhibitions their self-consciousness, I'm no exception, on the train minding her own business sat a blonde lady, I sat opposite giving her a full account of my day, with not a care in the world I rabbited on, she seemed to enjoy my stories, as we made our way to Scarborough I found out she lived on the same road as myself. I was being picked up at the station, therefore it was only common courtesy that she could share the transport.

Helen wouldn't mind an extra passenger or would she??? My new friend was not all that keen on the arrangement, I said rubbish it's no problem. As I introduced our neighbour and explained the circumstances, I could feel the knives between my shoulder blades sinking further in, it was a long journey to Scalby. I was sobering up really quickly, and the atmosphere in the car well you could imagine, I see the lady occasionally and wonder if she ever remembers that day, I often smile as I pass her house, priceless memories.

Five minutes from my bungalow in Station Road, there's a group of retirement flats with their own community centre. One day I called into the centre during their coffee morning, offering them the opportunity to join our Cash line Scheme, they were keen to support anything to do with keeping youngsters off the streets, Muriel Pipe who was an ex school secretary, took over the reins collecting the monies each week, I found it a pleasure meeting groups like the Danes Dyke community, after a while they seemed to take me under their wing, some wonderful elderly characters none more than Mr Norman Cooper, one of the brightest stars I've ever encountered very knowledgeable, determined strong willed, incredibly lucid an absolute credit to his species. Just to elaborate on a couple of Norman's outstanding achievements. One of his claims to fame, he joined the RAF and during the Second World War was based at RAF Scampston and became Douglas Bader's wing man, he loves to tell the tale how Bader was the quickest of all the pilots to get is kite off the ground, after Norman had strapped him in. Even though he had artificial legs.

Norman was a mine of information marvellous historical facts of his time during the war, he recalled with some relish a story, when the pilots were strapped in ready for take-off, they had to run the engines up to temperature so to speak, whilst carrying out this procedure someone from the ground crew had to hang on to the back of the tail to keep the kite stable. This particular day one of Normans buddies was hanging on to the Spitfires tail as it was warming up, when it started to move, Normans recollection was one of panic, he knew the ground crew member was a woman a WAAF, there was only a handful of women actually working as ground crew, and this was one of them, once the kites started to move, they gathered pace and momentum very quickly, he recalls the pilot had a person hanging from his tail, he will have noticed her through his wing mirrors that something was seriously tits up at the rear of the aircraft. Norman chuckled as he remembers how the young pilot just nonchalantly after a circuit came back into land, very gently to allow his passenger to disembark. You can imagine the banter, the leg pulling in the bar after that sortie, amazing stories to warm the cockles during an uncertain period, from our chequered illustrious past.

He also remembers the bombers returning from the Dambusters mission, how foggy it was on their approach, all available personnel lining the runways with flares to illuminate the flight path, and how three of the bombers crashed on landing. After the war Norman married, he and his bride who was a member of the local bicycle club they rode to the Dales for their honeymoon, he even remembers the name of the farmstead where they spent their first night together. It's difficult to imagine today, how reliant we have become on easier modes of transport that's progress I guess.

Having the opportunity to meet such interesting characters like Norman who are so inspirational makes me I'm sure a more rounded gifted person, and I thank all the generous lovely friends of Danes Dyke community centre for their friendship and warm welcome.

Martyn had been contacted by Mr Duncan Walker the head of the surgical team at Killingbeck Children's Hospital, doing a tremendous job saving a high percentage of lives. Youngsters suffering from different heart problems, kids as young as three weeks old would go through very technical and complex procedures.

Martyn along with Wayne Morton the Yorkshire physio, after a visit arranged by Duncan Walker round the wards, were affected greatly by the marvellous work he and his team were doing under critical financial restraint. It was decided after the visit to do something to help their cause, a plan was put into action and a team prepared. Duncan Walker was an eccentric Scotsman to say the least, that year he had been voted Yorkshire man of the Year, an accolade voted for by Yorkshire folk, therefore as a Scotsman to achieve this adulation he must be a remarkable guy.

He was without doubt a totally one off individual, amazing energy levels and very charismatic, with an eye for a beautiful lady that makes him your average surgeon I guess!!

Gary Mcallister the Leeds United skipper waved us off on our epic adventure.

The idea was to walk three hundred miles round the county, taking in all the major towns and cities, starting in Leeds. Duncan, Martyn and Wayne, with Duncan's mate Norman, an SAS veteran would be doing all the foot slogging, my involvement was that of the town crier.

On arrival at the start, in the Asda car park at Killingbeck, I was presented with a Saab convertible car and a loud hailer, I should mention at this time that Asda the supermarket giant, had agreed to help sponsor the walk and were holding fundraising events in their stores along the route. I must also include two very important members of our logistics team, Debbie and Joan they would be supplying rations, I.E water, glucose, bandages, a shoulder to cry on, keeping the teams spirits up would be crucial in the initial few days. The walk was to take two weeks, 300 miles in 14 days, that involves some hard slog, and I was hoping my voice was going to last out.

My job was to go on ahead of the walkers, into villages and town centres, proclaiming to all and sundry of the arrival of our heroes striding out raising funds which would help save the life of a sick child, the local radio stations were involved also, delivering our message over the air waves which helped enormously, it was a little strange at first, the initial reaction of folks, as I wailed through the hailer, I must have reminded some of them of the air raid wardens of the last war. I remember one old lass during that first day, I was just packing up to move on, when I spotted this elderly lady struggling to make herself known to me, she eventually arrived at the car in a lather, clutching a plastic money bag, she had heard on the radio that we would be in her village, and she presented me with the bag full of two pence pieces, I could tell by the look in her eye what it meant to her, I've never forgotten that little incident, I was going to meet quite a lot of lovely genuine old ladies on this trip, it gets the juices running I can tell you. Brighouse Post House run by Mr Shaun Callaghan was the first night stopover, the boys were really knackered, absolutely buggered, Martyn and Wayne's feet were like raw meat, it would be touch and go whether they would continue, my car had ran well, my throat was a little sore, but on the whole I was sound, a swim in the pool, just the job after a hard day on the road.

The boys were really down about the state of their blisters, Norman the SAS man was in fine condition, remonstrating that in the mob he would probably be now involved in a fire-fight, as they had reached their objective, therefore taking care of the feet has to be number one priority, as they do all the work, Martyn and Wayne I'm sure weren't too impressed, but kept nodding in agreement with the old soldiers advisory comments. A wholesome evening meal and a couple of pints to follow marvellous, I don't recall any of the teams suggesting we might go clubbing that evening.

After the initial couple of days the boys were in control their feet were hardening to the task, our adventure was taking off, the local media were doing a great job in making Joe Public more aware of our plight, local celebrities were rocking up to walk a day with the boys, During the Barnsley leg we had the company of young pace bowler just making his name, a Mr Darren Gough, I recall the lunch time interval, Darren had walked for a couple of hours, he was knackered as well as sore around his arse and bits, we had to form a cordon round him as he applied the Vaseline, to the affected area. Members of the cast of Emmerdale also supported the gruelling event.

Another incident that stays with me during this stage of the trek, every morning I used to pick up a young Asian lad called Asif, he had suffered the tragic loss of a sister in Killingbeck, therefore he wanted to lend a hand to shake the tins so to speak, he was a bubbly lad, good fun to be around, we worked well together.

One afternoon we were travelling together in the car, through what resembled a one horse town, I noticed women entering an old cinema, I thought Bingo, and abruptly stopped the car. The Saab was covered in Killingbeck stickers, I was wearing a Killingbeck sweatshirt with a yellow bear on the front, something resembling the present day Pudsey. I confronted the manager of the bingo hall explaining what we were about, he looked me up and down, then asked if I had anymore ID, I was covered from head to toe in bloody ID, he then relented and allowed Asif and myself to pass our buckets amongst the crowd in the hall.

We had to proceed down a staircase into the main hall, when we entered and turned to face the crowd I nearly fainted, 2000 people were staring at us, 4000 piercing eyes glaring wondering what we were up to, I was handed a microphone by the caller, and presented our case with as much clarity as I could muster. It was quite daunting but we shouldn't have worried those lovely people were so generous, in twenty minutes we had filled our buckets, it was remarkable a little gold mine in the middle of nowhere.

As I recall these events I get a real sense of warmth, great community spirit, all we get rammed down our throats by media are the negatives, whereas the majority of our people in this beautiful land are good solid citizens, enduring a lot of hardship with dignity and pride. As the walk progressed it became more popular, people would be waiting for us in the Town Centres, it was quite harrowing at times listening to stories of kids that didn't make it, there was great affection for Duncan Walker he certainly was top banana in his field, it really gave us all a lift, the boys were strong now milking all the adulation of which they thoroughly deserved. The ASDA at Rotherham brings back fond memories, all the staff had been superb raising loads of cash for us. I arrived there quite early say 30 minutes before the walkers, I met a couple of the managers just to make sure a hot drink and a sandwich would be on hand for the walkers, I then mentioned to them in a kind of tongue in cheek way that Elton John, and George Michael, were doing this leg to the Rotherham ASDA, well that was it off they shot before you knew it, it was put over the tannoy system, the buzz in the store you could cut it with a knife, I went outside, there they were a smudge on the horizon, the store came to a bloody standstill, I could hear lasses shouting "there he is!"

Elton or George they were becoming very animated, it was time for me to take my leave, the boys told me afterwards there would have been a lynching at the Rotherham ASDA, and they hunted for me to no avail. Sorry to all those staff it was a cruel play, Sheffield brings back memories as I recall the city was in turmoil, they were in the process of installing the new tram system, it looked just like a bombsight, businesses were going to the wall, up in arms with the city council over all the disruption. I guess nobody likes change, it may be a boost for the city today, but back in those days people really suffered, Meadow Hall the shopping arcade had just opened that also had taken years to develop. It was on the route, we actually came through the centre of the retail park it looked really modern, clean, altering the skyline, a certain boost, I'm sure to the Yorkshire economy.

The people of Sheffield were amazing, all around them chaos, it didn't stop them donating to our cause, I remember standing outside City Hall with my megaphone accompanied by half a dozen volunteers shaking their tins, the locals were so generous and supportive, I felt really proud that day, priceless!!

We then headed for the East of the County taking in the Humber Bridge, we had left the hustle of the cities it was now a long slog up the coast to Scarborough. The walkers had really exceeded their expectations, talking to them at the end of the day, they were finding the physical aspect, the actual walking now comfortable, all four of them were in great shape, it was now more of a challenge mentally, the legs were long up the coast over 20 miles a day, rural countryside which proved a little boring, keeping the boys engrossed and focused became a priority. We arrived in Scarborough, down on the Foreshore late afternoon after a long slog from Bridlington, it was a pleasure to be greeted by Helen and Katie, it was lovely to see lots of friends had turned out to welcome our heroic band.

After an early start next morning it was off to Malton, the boys were keeping to the schedule, we were due, back in Leeds in a couple of days. The ASDA car park at Killingbeck was a picture, there was a band playing rides for the kids, it was packed with well-wishers a welcoming sight, brought a little tear to the eye, Helen and Katie were there, the boys marched in style really enjoying the last few hundred yards, what a magnificent performance, great will determination and discipline, without too much training beforehand I might add.

We all had a team hug at the end it had been a mind blowing experience, no question, we were witness to marvellous generosity, camaraderie work ethic of the highest order. I was privileged to have been associated with this gang of ordinary quirky good people. A few weeks later the team were reunited for dinner, a figure in the region of £65,000 was raised over the two weeks on that Killingbeck trek, that speaks volumes in 1991 that was a lot of cash, donated on the whole by decent working class citizens, who really do care about their fellow men and children in need.

Duncan Walker was as you would imagine very appreciative of the efforts he had been an inspired leader, it's just a shame he has to walk three hundred miles round Yorkshire to help finance his hospital.

During the summer of 1992, I had this gut feeling that the game of cricket was trying to tell me something. Early season playing at home, we were fielding, it was one of those situations where two fielders attempt to catch the one ball, I was one of the fielders involved, the batter in question loved to play his shots through the on side, that's the leg side to the uninitiated, as a skipper I arranged the field accordingly, with myself tucked into mid-wicket, it was not long before the batter went for the bowling, and sure enough the ball was propelled with some power straight up, a skier as it is known in the trade, I could hear Dave Greenley running in from deep mid-wicket as I was travelling backwards trying to keep my eye on the ball. As Dave was also directing his eyes towards the ball the inevitable occurred, bloody carnage, we made contact where as I wheeled round to face him my left wrist made contact with one of his knee caps at a rate of knots, I knew immediately my wrist was knackered as it hung limp.

With no feeling in my wrist, I duly walked off the field, passing instructions to Tim Watts to take over as skipper. In the A and E department luckily I didn't have to wait too long to see the Doc, he did a quick synopsis checking this and that then came to the conclusion I had a Collis fracture of the left wrist, which meant that my wrist joint had been pulled up into my forearm. They were going to give me an injection, then after ten minutes or so, he would then return with a couple of strong nurses to hopefully pull the wrist back into place. For the next ten minutes my mind was full of negative thoughts of butch nurses heaving and pulling. I perspire at the thought!!

After what seemed bloody ages, they all appeared round the bed, the Doc in charge explained the procedures and hopefully the wrist joint would be back in situ within seconds. They huffed and they puffed with no success, the Doctor conceded as it was my left wrist it was my strong arm, therefore his team were unable to gain enough purchase to succeed, without further delay I was duly transferred up to men's surgical, where I was quickly prepared for surgery. It was all a blur, the next thing I remember was being woken up on a ward on a drip with Helen peering at me. The operation had been routine, I was to stay in hospital overnight this was my first stay in hospital in England. I praised the staff for the efficient way they had dealt with me, it had been a slick operation I forgive the pun!!!

There was a funny incident occurred during the night, a drunken youth from Middlesbrough had been brought into the bed next to mine, he'd been scrapping down town and suffered a severe cut to his head, he had to stay in under observation. He was not a happy bunny as they eventually shoe horned him into his bed, he was cursing and ranting, they pulled the sides of his bed up so he couldn't fall out, it reminded me of a baby's cot.

All his possessions, clothes and all were left by his bed then everyone left, turning out the lights, there seemed to be no staff on the ward, our little room was adjacent to the main ward, therefore they just probably stuck their heads in now and again. It was around three in the morning, I could hear the lad talking to himself, 'I'm not staying in this shit hole a minute longer, I'm off, fuck 'em all,' he was adamant he was leaving, with that he hauled himself up and climbed, then fell out of the bed like a sack of spuds, he recovered found his clothes and quickly started to dress, he was still ranting at the way he'd been treated, bollocks he was having no more of it. As he pulled his trousers on all his loose change spilled from his pockets, rattling on the floor under his bed and mine, I was in a panic, as I didn't want him pulling the drip out of my arm, in no uncertain terms I made it clear to him to watch what he was doing. He was all akimbo scrambling under his bed for his money, he eventually satisfied himself he had regained all his cash, he then put on his shoes and jacket and buggered off. This incident must have taken 30 minutes in all, and not one member of the nursing staff appeared, it's difficult to imagine nobody had heard all the commotion, I found it a little worrying, the lack of security during my brief stay, but I'm sure now situations will be dealt with satisfactorily, due to the new technology on offer.

My arm was put in pot, I was to be six weeks side-lined, what a drag, I'm probably the worst watcher of cricket, it's amazing how you become the greatest player watching other players struggle with situations, I was glad to be back playing after six weeks with no adverse reaction from my wrist.

Towards the end of the season we were playing Castleford at home, I recall we had been having a really dry spell of weather, and North Marine Road was looking very ragged especially the outfield, similar to the 'Summer of 76' when the grass turned very brown, resembling a large slice of toast, we were in the field doing well keeping their score down to a reasonable total. With just a few overs remaining we had a defensive field set, I was on the long off boundary, sure enough the batter skied the following delivery, it went up for what seemed an age, I kept my beady eye on it.

On its descent, I realised I had got too far in front of the ball, I managed to cling onto the bloody thing, but the momentum threw me backwards, I landed on my arse with such force, it thrust my head back onto the rock hand ground. I didn't actually lose consciousness and I still had the ball clutched to my chest. I laid there for a while, my immediate thought process was just a jumble, and my head felt like it was in a spin dryer. The boys thought I should leave the field to get checked out

I was adamant I was ok, it wasn't long before I was forgetting to change the field for the left handers, the lads knew something was not right in my head, and therefore I was driven to the hospital for a brain scan.

The game was being aired on the local radio, the guy commentating must have mentioned I had gone off to hospital with a head injury, Katie had picked it up whilst working at Pacittos selling her ice cream, she then in a panic had contacted Helen and the two of them arrived at the hospital in a lather not knowing what to expect. I had a scan to find my brain, they found something resembling it, nothing sinister was detected, the Doctor reckoned I had suffered slight concussion and that I should rest up for a day or two, I returned back to the ground, entering North Marine Road just as we knocked off their total, there was plenty of leg pulling and piss taking over a couple of pints, the beer always tasted sweeter with maximum points under your belt.

Seriously now I was beginning to ask myself the dreaded question how long was I prepared to keep playing at this level, I analysed my two injuries, the first was bad luck, the second my own fault. Therefore I put it down to coincidence. I still had the drive to compete, I kept myself fit, my appetite for cricket was as strong as ever, I mentioned my thoughts to Helen, who without question or fuss made it plain I should be aware of how old I was and act accordingly, she saw no reason for me to change direction, which was a great boost and helped me conquer for the time being those irritating gremlins at the back of my mind.

I decided to make an allowance to ease the burden, I stood down as captain, handing over the reigns to Stuart Hardy our wicket keeper, he was an enthusiastic young man a gentleman farmer. He would blend a new group of lads together, putting his own stamp on the team. I was a little concerned with his team, I was a little concerned with his lack of experience at this level, but only time would tell, and he was certainly never short of a word a typical 'gobby' keeper.

I enjoyed the role of captain on the field of play, but chasing after players after some pillock had let you down, because he had to go shopping with the wife, or he simply forgot, was not my idea of fun. There was an element within the club, who would let you down at the drop of a hat, it's not easy putting into words, but standards had fallen, nobody wants to hark back to the past, but I found it difficult stomaching all the excuses for not playing. I also had become more involved in the coaching of the juniors, this was the way forward in my eyes, encouraging and selecting the teams for the next generation.

Helen, Katie and myself were flying back to Florida, for two weeks, it was now early May 1993, we had been advised after our first trip that the ideal time to visit the Gold Coast was during the first two weeks of May, all the American families have finished their holiday, and with the slow transition of Europeans arriving the theme parks are relatively quiet. We were going the whole hog this trip, a five centre adventure, taking in Orlando, Fort Lauderdale, Key Largo, Indian Shores and Naples on the Gulf Coast.

We were all really excited to be back in Orlando, we were staying much closer to the action not in the sticks like on our initial trip, the weather was warm with clear skies, we were to be here for five days. Universal Islands of adventure had opened since our last visit.

A remarkable feat of planning, design and engineering, Jurassic Park was the main attraction based obviously on the movie, it had everything to get the adrenaline pumping, ending with an amazing 100ft drop, simulating a massive waterfall, the girls loved it couldn't get enough, seeing is believing in all the parks, we spent five glorious days enjoying the weather, the food, soaking up the atmosphere, experiencing the whole place.

Next phase of our trip, took us to Fort Lauderdale, just up the coast from Miami, we were only staying for a couple of days in a Sheraton Hotel right on the Beach. The location was first class as you could imagine with a beautiful beach, and a clear blue ocean to bathe in. This location was ideal as it gave us a chance to catch our breath, and relax a little after the rigours of Orlando. It was here in Fort Lauderdale that we received the great news from home, Susie and Martyn were proud parents again, Sue giving birth to a little boy.

We celebrated in style, it had been on our minds we were expecting the news any day. All parties were doing well, he was going to be named Jonny or to his mum Jonathan. I took Katie out on one of those water bikes, we had 30 minutes to explore the bay.

They really do travel at the rate of knots, Katie was squealing on the back for me to slow down, as she hung on. I recall I got a bollocking from the guy, as I rode it up onto the beach blocking up the something or other, Katie was in stitches getting her own back. Onward, we were all looking forward to the next stage the Florida Keys, a beautiful clear morning as we set out, along the highway over the breathtakingly modernistic bridges that connect the keys or small islands, the flocks of sea birds. Pelicans, Eagrettes, Terns, Herons and Eagles, all waking and enjoying the fruits of the sea, hundreds of coves and inlets, natural harbours, providing safe and secure habitats for a flourishing and varied wildlife. This is what I imagined paradise to look like as I drove along it was breath-taking, Key Largo was one of the first keys, this would be where we were staying, we found the hotel, another Sheraton very nice, quite different from the one in Fort Lauderdale for obvious reasons, we were in a totally different environment, much more tranquil, more for the conservationist like myself.

We checked in to the hotel, it was palatial, designed to suit the environment, built mainly of timber, had a colonial feel to it. During our slumbers around I am in the morning someone was trying to enter our room, turning the door knob with rigour, we all woke with a start, Katie becoming agitated I recall. I quickly sent Helen to investigate.

No seriously I rushed to the door making whoever was at the other side clear we were occupying this room, it was quite scary at the time, Katie was imagining pirates carrying us off to walk the plank, it took a while to settle the two girls, Helen was furious she was up for confrontation in the morning. Over breakfast we were reliving our ordeal, Helen had arranged to meet the manager just to register the incident, she was keen to find out exactly what the problem had been, apparently after her meeting it transpired that a receptionist had double booked the room, this was food and drink for Helen, not good enough in her eyes, she was going for the jugular. Compensation that was the key word now.

The manager was typical American, quite charming very efficient, you could sense he had come across many irate customers in his career, after making Helen realise the genuine mistakes, he took her into one of the ladies outfitters and let her choose an article of clothing to make up for the inconvenience suffered, put it down to experience I thought.

Key Largo is famous for being the home to the African Queen, the famous old rust bucket pulled downstream by Humphrey Bogart in the film of the same name, we visited the dock she called home, there was a look alike Bogart tinkering with the controls, explaining how it all worked.

We planned to drive all the way down to Key West, and spend some time there, I would recommend the keys for a visit, it is a true wonder of the modern world, it has no parallel a truly magnificent one off.

What seems to be the first point of call when you rock up, is the red buoy depicting that you are standing at the Southern most tip of North America, only 90 miles from Communist Cuba, the area was full of tourists and who could blame them.

Whilst sat in Smoking Joes, a famous bar in the square we were soaking up the atmosphere, the rhythms the old musicians were creating it was electric, the fans in the ceiling coaxing up all that cigar smoke, the bubble and squeak of all the excited punters. I started to imagine Ernest Hemingway, Howard Hughes during those decadent years between the wars flying into the grassed airfield just across the street, or sailing on an ocean going schooner to this isolated paradise, ready to party.

"Anything goes" that was a great standard, I'm sure it applied to Key West. On every street corner the jazz was hypnotic, people were dancing in the street, the look on the faces of sheer ecstasy and joy, no doubt in some cases the drugs and booze were having an effect, but on the whole the majority were just sucked in by the amazing atmosphere and all that jazz.

It was quite sad leaving the Keys behind, it had been as they say,' a real blast'

We were now heading back up North to Indian Shores, a drive through town on the Gulf coast, we were to spend three days here relaxing on the lovely beach. We were staying in an apartment for this leg of the trip, it happened to be situated right next door to a Sea Bird sanctuary, how brilliant was that, at the first opportunity we went to visit the hospital for the sea birds. Pelicans, being the most numerous patients, they suffered from every affliction, volunteers would bring them in for treatment. The hospital was run by trained vets and volunteers, the monies donated by the public. One volunteer a man, who travelled down from Canada every winter to escape the cold these people were known as snow geese, they would drive thousands of miles in their camper vans heading South.

Apart from the pelicans, the hospital housed Herons, Eagles, Egrets. Gannet plus all the local Gulls and Terns, the local population were so mindful of their Sea bird neighbours always looking out for the well being, the most popular injuries involved fish hooks, which as you could imagine are lethal, fishing from piers and boats is such a popular pastime, that its obvious greedy birds like pelicans and gannets will come unstuck at some time. One sad but interesting incident occurred one morning very early just after sun up.

We were all taking our constitutional, as it was to us the best time of the day. We were walking towards a fishing pier some half a mile up the beach, walking through the surf before the throngs of tourists appeared was absolute heaven, marvelling at the sun rise another day on Planet Earth, we were soon brought back down to Earth, when we spotted just ahead a loggerhead turtle he was upside down, being driven in an out by the tide he was dead. He was the size of an average coffee table, covered in barnacles, I quickly with the help of the girls righted him, made him look more dignified, we were all upset, I sat for minutes just taking in the tragedy of it all, this mighty creature who would have travelled with the currents all over the Southern Hemisphere, thousands of miles. We were wondering what or why he had died, he looked very fresh as though it had happened not too long ago, there was no visual injuries apparent, it was at the sea bird sanctuary, the staff were keen to hear our chain of events they immediately sent a pickup truck to retrieve the turtle.

After the autopsy a conclusion was reached the turtle had died from a lack of oxygen, apparently within the Gulf of Mexico there is a phenomenon known as the Red Tide, creatures such as turtles which need oxygen to breath, get caught up in this tide, it seems they can't escape it, other mammals such as porpoises occasionally get washed up on the beach.

The staff of the hospital thanked us for our vigilance and care shown for the deceased turtle, what a bizarre state of events. Another amazing experience on our travels. Our final destination saw us rock up to the Town of Naples also on the gulf coast, I checked the mileage we had travelled over one thousand miles during our ten days, it was certainly a whistle stop tour no mistake but worth it in every way, having your own transport, liberates you to go wherever, whenever you decide, we still had a couple of days in Naples before we had to prepare for our flight home, Naples is a swish, manicured town very vibrant down around Tin City, with elegant restaurants and bars. Our hotel was touristy, but clean and the staff were typical, nothing was too much trouble, I found the waitresses and bar staff throughout Florida very efficient, switched on, appreciated the fact that us tourists were there spending money providing them with work. It was also interesting to talk to the locals. I've found wherever I've travelled people discuss more or less the same issues, apparently immigration was high on the locals agenda here, and guess where the immigrants were arriving from, you guessed it, the United Kingdom, they were saying there was a club set up in Naples for expats.

The weather had been kind to us, not a cloud in the sky for the duration of our visit, today we were heading for Busch Gardens, set in hundreds of acres not far from Naples, it's a theme park on the same lines as Disney up in Orlando, it also boasts a brewery in fact a world renowned brewery, the home of Budweiser bring it on!

Helen and Katie were having a ball together, they both adored the sunshine and were as brown as berries, Katie was developing into a beautiful young lady, vivacious with a lovely smile, I had been noticing the boys checking her out, ogling it's a strange thing but I felt for the first time very protective towards her, I guess it's a natural trait in fathers, throughout the animal kingdom.

Busch Gardens lived up to its billing as one of the top theme parks in Florida, we had a fantastic day, the roller coasters and log flumes brilliant, not forgetting the different species of wild animals from all around the globe, lunch consisted of a Busch Garden specialty, a turkey leg

BBQ with a special Cajun sauce, to be washed down with 'you got it' a bottle of bud.

That evening we drove down to the Sea front, parked in a quiet cul de sac, had a stroll to watch the sun go down for the final time, as we were flying home the next day, we were all in a reflective mood. Retracing our steps over the last couple of weeks, we just love Florida.

Helen and Katie went off to barter round the local mall, while I enjoyed another coke. We got back to the car, and there in the centre of the windscreen, a bloody parking ticket. I couldn't believe it "traffic wardens". Twenty five dollars traffic violation, I thought to ignore it, Helen being Helen thought otherwise. I mentioned it to the duty manager back at the hotel, she was adamant I should pay the fine, otherwise I may not get back into the US for another visit. Another incident to put down to experience.

It always takes a day or two to find your legs when you arrive home, this was no exception as it was the middle of May the weather was tolerable, the garden needed some TLC the lawns were in need of a trim. John Evans had organised the running of the cashline, he was a trusted mate, who could be relied upon, and that took a lot of pressure off. Helen was back at the bank wondering if they had survived without her.

Katie it was an important year of school, GCSE exams were not too far away. We were also thrilled as Katie and Clare had found employment at weekends and school holidays at Pacittos ice cream parlour on the Scarborough sea front, they would be clearing tables and washing up, the Pacitto family were renowned for their ice cream, Gene and Penny, with daughter Andrea and son Christopher, made up a lovely friendly family ideal grounding for the girls, as they start their working life, we were really chuffed and supportive of Katie, she was quite proud to be earning and making her own way.

The summer just seems to fly, taking the trip to Florida early in May had been the perfect tonic preparing us all for the rigours ahead. Our final Yorkshire league away game was versus Sheffield United at Bawtry Road, we were mid table nothing really to play for, it was a typical end of season day all round not many spectators, it was quite cold I recall.

They had batted, ended up with around 200 runs, but kept losing wickets. I was standing outside with my pads on to go in to bat at number 7, talking to some of my friends who had come along to watch. Another wicket, I was walking in to bat, to partner my buddy Gary Pickup, he was established, going well, we had a little chat in the middle, something on the lines of keep your head down, look for the single, good luck pal. I was taking strike after leaning on my bat for an over, I elegantly rocked back onto the back foot and punched the ball out to deep extra cover, I cried one, when crack someone I thought had just shot me through my calf, bloody hell I quickly glanced round wondering if the wicket keeper had kicked me, he was standing ten yards adrift of me, in the meantime Gary was sprinting towards me, as I had shouted for a single, my leg was buggered, I could not stand with my weight on my feet, therefore I hopped to the other end just making my ground.

I instinctively knew my plight, I had snapped my Achilles tendon, there was no pain, I was just helpless, if I had been a horse they would have shot me. I was helped off the wicket and Tim Watts kindly drove me to the Rotherham general hospital. An Asian doctor examined me, where upon I was directly sent to have my whole leg put in plaster. I had snapped the tendon, I would have to report to Scarborough hospital tomorrow Sunday, with a view to having surgery.

Travelling back to Scarborough with my leg in pot up to my thigh was no joke. I rang Helen from Tadcaster en route explaining my predicament. It would not have been too bad ...but we were flying to the Canaries on Monday for a well earned rest. Helen met me at the club, and was a little concerned at the sight of the plaster covering the whole leg. Sunday morning I was bedded down in Men's surgical ... here we go again I thought. The operation was a complete success. I was back home by Monday evening, wearing a plaster from thigh to foot, with a metal extension attached to my foot. This was to keep the pressure off my Achilles. It took some getting used too, I was to suffer this hideous contraption for eleven weeks. I returned to work on Tuesday. John Evans helped to run the cashline whenever I was on holiday, and he was a total brick, being connected to the club as a volunteer since 1949... one of the old school. He had been a school teacher, with Technical Drawing his speciality. John drove me around for over eleven weeks, collecting the cashline monies. He really enjoyed getting out and about, and with me only being able to walk in a fashion he was a life saver. Luckily the season had finished, and after eleven weeks the plaster came off, what a marvellous feeling it was to throw the pot into the bin. I had a few weeks of physiotherapy, the doctors were very pleased with the outcome and eventually discharged me, once again I was as fit as a butchers dog!!

In 1993 the first X1 finally won the Yorkshire League knockout competition, beating Hull CC in the final at North Marine Road. This was our first silverware since the heady days of the 70's and 80's. Our semi-final was against a strong Rotherham side, away at their Clifton Road ground. We travelled over to Rotherham from Cleethorpes, and stayed in digs on the Saturday night. The boys were up for the fight, we had an experienced squad on show, Dalby, Pincher and Cleaver to name but a few.

A few beers and fish and chips before a reasonably early night. Our digs consisted of an old Victorian house with two separate wings. Pincher and Dalby had teamed up with our very illustrious scorer Tony Jack. Tony deserves a chapter of recognition, he was by far the finest cricket scorer of his era. Yorkshire cricket league scorers are known for their dedication and total commitment. Tony started as a teenager, scoring for the second team making his debut for the first team in 1971, up to his tragic and premature passing in 2012. Apart from his scoring talents he enjoyed nothing more than mixing with the players, enjoying the crack after the game had finished. As cricket scorers go, he was a legend amongst his peers, his role will definitely be missed, and difficult to replace.

On this particular evening, after probably a beer too many, our scorer took it on himself to vacuum the landing after finding the Hoover in a cupboard, probably he could have got away with putting it down to youthful pranks, but to be hoovering stark bollock naked was a tad too much!!

Guests were not amused and it all became apparent at breakfast, the landlady was spitting feathers...we were a disgrace to be representing the town of Scarborough...she really laid it on thick!! The majority of the lads were in the other wing, oblivious to what was going on. We left with our tails firmly between our legs. Tony was full of remorse. Pinch and Dalby found it difficult to keep a straight face as they regarded our scorer as a hero...up there with Pete Townsend from the 'Who'. The incident did not affect our performance on the field. We outplayed Rotherham in all departments, as skipper I felt very proud of the boys, it was by far our strongest performance of the season. Back home around Wednesday, I was summoned to the Chairman's office, the landlady had written a scathing letter detailing the incident with the Hoover. Adrian Dalby, to his credit penned a delightful letter apologising profusely and taking full responsibility for Tony's actions. The incident blew over with no lasting problems.

In 1995 I ran into an old mucker from Plaxtons. He was keen to put me in the picture regarding the old employer. Apparently a worker had taken them to a tribunal regarding his hearing. It transpired that Plaxtons had not provided protection to adequately protect his ears, and he had successfully won his case. This opened the floodgates for hundreds of workers were claiming compensation. Men were receiving thousands of pounds, if they were able to prove that their hearing had suffered as a result of working in the Plaxton factory. He reckoned I should claim as I had worked in the top fitters, a very noisy environment. I mentioned it to Helen, I had left Plaxtons years before but this did not make any difference, and she thought I should pursue a claim, as I had nothing to lose. I made enquiries, and before I knew it, I was on my way to York to have my hearing checked out. The surgery was close to the centre, adjacent to the magnificent Minster. The doctor was a crusty old type, he was into hunting and fishing, he got talking about his exploits with gun, rod and line. We both very nearly forgot why I was there. Eventually I was put into a booth and had to press a button when I heard a sound. I thought I heard all the pings. Sure enough he explained to me that my left ear was down, probably as much as 50% it was a bit of a shock. A few weeks later, a letter arrived inviting me to attend a surgery in Sheffield, these people were acting on behalf of Plaxtons. It was chance to make a day of it so we contacted Libby and Phil in Nottingham and arranged to meet up at Meadowhall, the shopping mall. I was quite nervous as I entered the Surgery, as I felt I had previously put on a good show, but these were the enemy. It was a similar set up as York, I had to listen and register all the sounds. I had no idea how it materialised as no one gave me any idea about my performance. Whatever the outcome we had a good day with our buddies from Nottingham. It took months before I heard anything, (pardon the pun!!!!!!). In fact I am sure we had forgotten about it, when out of the blue a cheque for £5,000 arrived. It was unbelievable, there in black and white.

Chapter 12

Oz calls....Katie graduates looks skyward ...Ted and Cricket Management

1997 was going to be an important milestone on our journey, I was to be fifty, it was to be our silver wedding anniversary and Katie would be eighteen. Martyn and Sue `were discussing holidays...how about spending Christmas Day on Bondi Beach in Sydney Australia, ... the seed was sown.

I was going to be putting my new money to good use, Marge, the Mother in Law, was convinced that I had cheated the doctors over my deafness, that I would be paid back at some time in the future, and I could not dissuade her otherwise.

Philip Sharpe, the ex Yorkshire and England cricketer who runs a travel company, was asked to put together an intinerary for us, involving 21 days staying in top drawer accommodation. How exciting it was as we all climbed into our taxi in Wetherby, en route to Manchester Airport. We were catching a shuttle down to Heathrow. Sue had purchased a video camera for the trip, with a view to recording our adventures for all time. After an interesting flight on a BA 747 we touched down in Los Angeles. After standing in line for what seemed ages, to pass through immigration, they are so thorough in the States and seem to function on a permanent state of alert. Next stop was the carousel for the luggage. Incredibly one of our suitcases did not turn up and it turned out to be Helen's. After the long flight and delay at immigration and baggage collection, no one found it particularly funny. Helen, being Helen read the small print on the ticket regarding loss of luggage. It transpired that if luggage failed to turn up compensation of £$250 is paid. True to their policy, BA handed over the said amount to Helen and this went a little way to easing her burden. The staff were confident the case would turn up, probably on the next flight. Everybody was gathered up into a waiting taxi, we were heading for Annaheim, a suburb of Los Angeles where the original Disney theme park was built. The traffic was absolutely mad, no place for the faint hearted. En route our driver pointed out interesting and glamorous sights. We were passing Long Island, the home of the old Cunard liner, the Queen Mary, she was now a floating hotel. He stopped the cab, we took a closer look at the liner, the old girl really looked her age. I felt quite `sad, the millions of nautical miles under her belt carrying rich knobs around the world, to end up wallowing in this backwater. The Sheraton Annaheim appeared, very modern and swish in pastel shades. Our rooms were massive family affairs on the ground floor with the swimming pool just outside our doors. It did not take us too long before we were jumping in, the hotel did not seem too busy. The kids were ready for some fun time, Jonny was now four and Charlotte seven. Annaheim was just nailed on for these two, with Disney just around the corner. Katie was complaining of a stiff neck, unusual for her to create about being unwell. Helen and I put it down to the all night flight and the late nights back home with her friends. The hotel ran a deli and people would stock up with drinks and nibbles for the trips around the theme parks. We were visiting the deli on our return from the parks in the early evening. Sir Lawrence Byford and Lady Byford were there he was Chairman of Yorkshire CC. Martyn nearly fell over when their eyes met, how extraordinary, they were on their way to Australia, England were touring this winter, competing for the famous urn known worldwide as the Ashes. Our final day we decided to take a bus to Universal Studios, which were over the other side of the City. All aboard was the cry from our driver, a big black mama. She was really lovely, and she `handled the big bus with assured confidence, expletives singing out at other inferior beings. We travelled through the centre of LA, through all the touristy streets. The houses of all the stars she showed off to us, and made our trip very interesting, wouldn't have missed it for anything. She dropped us off at the` gate, 'Pick you all up here at five...have a nice day y'all' then she was gone. This was a working studio and was full of tourists enjoying the thrill of it all. Seeing is believing, the place was amazing with the iconic 'Hollywood' sign standing proud on the hillside. This had been a magical start to our holiday. Disney has a way of bringing out the child in everyone. We were all singing and dancing as we waited for our big bus to return.

Australia here we come, Los Angeles had been everything we imagined, warm weather, was in a great location and had interesting people. The flight to Sydney would be thirteen hours. We took off in the early evening, it was difficult to imagine that once you leave the coast of America, we will be flying all the way over water, thousands of miles, incredible. As I recall I am sure we also seem to lose a day, with all the time differences. As the Sun comes up I look down, the pilot has just announced below us the chain of islands that make up the Great Barrier Reef, even from 36,000 feet they look amazing. We are so lucky because the visibility is first class, providing us with a mind blowing experience. As we drive through the suburbs of Sydney, it looks a little scruffy and run down, a little different in that respect to Los Angeles, although to be fair we did not travel through the suburbs in LA … thank goodness!!!

Our apartments were in the centre of Sydney, Hyde Park, another superb location, Phil Sharpe was continuing to do us all proud, and the facilities were second to none with all mod cons, a swimming pool on the roof. The kids were again in their element. We had arranged to pick up a people carrier on this leg of the journey. With paperwork in hand, Martyn and myself set off to explore and find the garage. Martyn had visited Sydney before whilst on tour with England and he was keen to show us around. As we walked through Hyde Park, in the centre was a bronze statue of James Cook, another iconic Yorkshireman. I felt proud reading the inscription honouring the Great man who left such a legacy in these parts. Through the archway of Gum trees, three hundred years old, these magnificent relics, people come to seek shade and solace beneath their canopy. We pick up our vehicle and Martyn gives me the keys. It's an automatic and after a couple of minutes of settling the beast, the car not me, we motor off to the apartments … which way is that then?!

Christmas is upon us and the girls announced a few surprises for the kids. I was getting used to the traffic system, as we made our way to Bondi Beach for Christmas Day. Katie was still complaining of neck pains and feeling unwell, another paracetamol and it will go.

The surf was up on Bondi, the beach was packed, with the majority looking like tourists all wearing Father Christmas hats. It was a very friendly gathering and the old video camera was working overtime. Just to make things a little worse, Katie forgot to apply enough sun block and suffered burn to her shoulders and back. I took away great memories of Bondi that Christmas Day, a real privilege and pleasure. Martyn directed us to Watsons Bay, home of the internationally famous Doyles Fish Restaurant. It was not too far from Bondi, apparently Michael Parkinson, the television icon had introduced Martyn and his team to this renowned eaterie. After a plate of Fish and Chips, which were excellent, the gang began nodding, another cracking day, round the harbour tomorrow.

Boxing Day was another scorcher, not a cloud in sight. Temperatures in the high twenties. We all walked down through the park along through the fabulous botanical gardens, then you reach the water, turning left along the path, there in front of you another wonder of the modern world, the Sydney Opera house, so majestic and modern. We find our ferry for the Harbour cruise, Katie is really struggling at this stage, we are becoming a little concerned as it is so unlike Katie to be ill or moan about it ... another paracetamol??

On our penultimate day in Sydney, Martyn, Jonny and myself are off to visit Bowral, the home town of Sir Donald Bradman. I had brought some interesting photographs of the great man, when he played at North Marine Road for the Australians. He regarded the Scarborough wicket as one of his favourites to bat on, in fact in 1948, he scored a century before lunch. It was a two hour drive to the Museum, which was set up in his honour. They were delighted with the rare photo's, we got a guided a tour of all the paraphernalia and accolades he had accrued throughout his illustrious career. Bowral is a quiet agricultural area, similar to Pickering near Scarborough. Martyn told me the England touring teams initial game was usually here. He also mentioned that he had met the 'Don' during a game in Adelaide.

Koolangatta Airport, next stop on our adventure, a surfers paradise. Up on the East Coast, High rise apartments, very touristy, beautiful beaches, our accommodation and an Olympic size pool. I located a doctor and immediately took Katie for a check up, she was diagnosed with acute tonsillitis, poor lass, she had struggled long enough, and he prescribed antibiotics. It cost me £50, but that was cheap as it meant that Katie would be sorted and back to her normal bubbly self. 'I told you something was wrong' she was laying it on a bit thick as we made our way back to base. Two days later Katie was back to her normal self. In the meantime, Charlotte had fallen in love....with a kangaroo, Sue and Martyn took the kids to visit a local animal park and saw all the local species on show, as well as kangaroos, there were Wallabies. Saturday night in surfers paradise gets the juices flowing, we enjoyed a Chinese meal on the veranda, taking in the atmosphere of hundreds of tourists enjoying a beer and the hypnotic music. Then from nowhere, the boys and their toys, four litre coupes, roaring up and down the strip. They appeared to be in convoy, cars of all shapes and sizes and colours... what a spectacular sight.

Another flight up to Cairns, this was the highlight of the trip for me personally. I had been praying for decent weather, it did not disappoint. We were staying out of Cairns, at an exclusive resort, Palm Cove. If you can imagine the Rainforest creeping down to the White Sandy beach, another first class location, with our apartments beautifully appointed, leather furniture so relaxing. Just across the road was a friendly bar and Italian Restaurant. Saltwater crocs are prevalent at this time of year, therefore special areas are netted off for swimming, to hopefully keep out the crocs. I recall having a relaxing coffee in the Moxon's suite on our first afternoon, watching dramatic scenes on the TV of the Australian Navy saving an English man from his upturned yacht. I think his name was Tony Bullamore, he was a lucky guy to have survived that ordeal. I think he had a history within the yachting fraternity for being a bit of a risk, because he had been rescued several times before. We had booked a trip aboard the Ocean Spirit, a sleek catamaran, she carried 100 people max, we were to sail to Bird Cay, a sandy outcrop on the Barrier Reef, where the Brown Terns breed. This is where we would snorkel checking out the coral, fantastic, I have to pinch myself as this had been a lifelong ambition for me, and doing it with the family just put the icing on the cake. During the voyage to the cay, the girls applied sunscreen, it was to take us two hours sailing time. Eventually the shore line disappeared, the sun was warm, the breeze ruffling the hair, those that had any!! ...perfect. On arrival at the cay, the crew threw some edible goodies over the side and Wow, the ocean just erupted, total mayhem as the predator fish took hold, the crew making the point, not to enter the water with food

Helen was happy to stay on the little beach with Charlotte and Jonny, while the big kids donned their flippers and masks. Marine biologists were on hand to guide us over the coral, explaining how the eco-system worked. In many areas of SE Asia reefs similar to this were being ruined by over-fishing. Seeing is believing again, this place was as I imagined, similar to the Chelsea Flower show, but under the sea. Shimmering coral, amazing fish. The scientists stressed how even this pristine area covering thousands of miles, made up of the inner and outer reef were on a knife edge, with global warming becoming an increasingly important factor. A minute change in sea temperatures would mean the coral would begin to die. These points brought home how important conservationists and their tireless contribution to restoring the balance of nature is. After the lectures we were allowed to swim freely amongst the teeming life just below, brilliant!!

Back on the beach, Helen was there with the kids feeding the fish with potato crisps, no sign of the predator fish, thank goodness. On the sail back to Cairns we enjoyed a scrumptious buffet, followed by a raucous sing song, one of the crew had his guitar on hand, a great day enjoyed by all.

Our Australian adventure has one day left, tomorrow we fly to Darwin to board another flight to Bali, that seductive Island in Indonesia. It was Friday, and we flew to Darwin, en route we landed at the small town of Gove. Its actually an aluminium mine, employing thousands of people who live around the mine. The plane lands every Friday to pick up passengers on their way to Darwin. I recall we all got off the plane at this tiny airport of Gove. The only building, similar to the size of a family house acted as arrivals and departures. In the corner, a young girl was behind a counter selling knick knacks and sweets. I was interested in her predicament, living in such a desolate detached little town. What facilities did it offer her regarding leisure and sport. None was the reply, she was bored and could not wait to leave.

Inside the departure lounge of Darwin Airport Helen recognised a girl from home in Scarborough, who worked on the make up counter at Debenhams.

Five days left and we were all sad to be leaving Australia. It had been everything we imagined it would be, and more. We were all looking very tanned, Katie was back to full fitness, enjoying making fun of her Dad all too often. Bali was a totally different ball game. We arrived in late afternoon, and it was hot and very humid. The porters at the airport were annoying, as I insisted that I would carry my own case. Our accommodation was to the usual high standards we had experienced on this trip. We were staying in individual lodges, which gave you a feel of local décor and elegance. The lodges meandered around a beautiful sandy beach. Our last few days were obviously designed with relaxation in mind, and to gently programme us back to normal life back home. Then just with thoughts of returning, it started raining. To be honest, the thought of returning home and the rain dampened our spirits somewhat. To combat the rain, we hired a mini bus for a trip into the interior of the island. Our driver was an excellent guide, as we motored through the agricultural heartland. Mile after mile of rice paddies, built up on plateaus, stepped up into the hillside to aid irrigation. They were well irrigated, as we were getting plenty of rain. The driver was very enthusiastic, a man after my own heart. Into the centre of Bali our destination arrived at, appearing at a restaurant for lunch. Across from the eaterie, spewing out noxious gases and steam, was the only working volcano on Bali. Indonesia is home to a high percentage of the World's volcanoes, as they sit on the crack in the earth's crust. Our gang were a little sceptical to say the least at the sight of this natural phenomenon, they were not too pleased with the local menu either, if it didn't have chips in there, the kids were struggling. Some smart arse mentioned the fact that allegedly the locals eat dog as a delicacy. With dogs howling below the restaurant, as it was built on stilts that was it, the gang were back on the bus to get away as quick as possible. Personally I enjoyed the trip away from all the commercial hype, the locals out in the sticks endure a hard austere grind, to feed and clothe their kids. It was interesting to observe all the little food parcels being offered up to their individual Gods, to help to deliver a bumper harvest.

The next day we visited Kuta Beach, which is a renowned area for cool young surfers to congregate. Thousands of young Australians visit Kuta Beach each year, to be honest we were a little disappointed. In brief it was a total 'shithole', filthy litter strewn everywhere. I don't want to sound like Victor Meldrew, but as a pretty seasoned traveller, I could not understand its attraction. It was obviously a place for young guns to get laid, smoke some weed, get pissed, probably that's all they crave. On a more sombre note a month after we visited Kuta, a bomb devastated a night club, detonated by a group of jihadist nutters. Over 100 young people were killed.

It cost us an extra £28 each in airport taxes to leave Bali, they collected the money as you passed through immigration, putting it into a biscuit tin under the counter...corruption seems alive and well in this region!!

Back home the January winter very cold, but luckily everyone was fine. Chris had put on our heating and filled up the fridge for our return. A week later we drove over to Martyn and Sue to witness the first showing of 'the video' entitled ' Holiday of a Lifetime'. That it certainly was... until the next time.

In 1997 my brother Bill and his wife Christine sadly split up, their marriage reduced to history. Bill initially found it difficult to cope, travelling up to the Scottish highlands to find some solace and contemplate his future. Being of strong character, it did not take him long to come to terms with his situation, and he began to move forward. He came into contact with a lady who had gone through a similar episode. Pam Nicholls became Bill's best friend, and ally and in no time their future was secured. Bill said farewell to the McCain factory, his workmates wishing him bon voyage, to start a new venture with Pam in the form of a guesthouse, high up in Gairloch, amongst the mountains and glens of the Scottish highlands. This would be a totally new direction for the couple, dealing with the visitors from countries far flung, foreign visitors, making up a high percentage of feet through the door.

Beccy and Nicci, Bill's daughters were by this time self sufficient, making their own way in the world, enjoying the success of hard work. In July 1997 after our trip to Oz, Bill and Pam invited Helen and I to Scotland for a few days.

We took the train to Inverness, then picked up a hire car. The sun was shining as we drove to Gairloch, after a night in a hotel in Loch Ness. The mountains or Monroes were bathed in golden sunshine, the scenery was so impressive, just as you imagined it would be. The guesthouse stood prominently, a great location overlooking the local bay and across to the Isle of Skye. Inside the aromatic flavours of the evening menu, Pam seemed in her element catering for their guests, travellers from all corners of the globe. Unfortunately the weather played its usual trick, and we experienced all four seasons in two days.

Bill and Pam were the perfect hosts, our stay was very enjoyable, they were busy with bookings. I thought that Bill looked a little out of place, changing beds, cleaning toilets who knows…time will tell!!

In September 1997 after our invigorating trip to Scotland, it was back to the realities of life. Katie had achieved her grades required on the tourism course run from the Yorkshire Coast College over the last two years, she had pulled out all the stops to attain her diploma. The University of Central Lancashire had accepted her for a three year term. After numerous telephone calls eventually a room became available in Preston, her landlord being no other that Billy Bingham, the ex Northern Ireland soccer manager. After checking out the accommodation and meeting her new buddies, Katie was happy to sign on the dotted line.

Helen was putting a brave face on, as we loaded up the car with all the necessities, she was going to miss her little girl, big style!! I was also a little apprehensive, but also excited, thinking of Katie going forward into the big wide world alone, with all the encouragement over the years the day had finally arrived. Penny, Andrea and Chris Pacito had been preparing a box full of goodies, donated mainly by customers Katie had served in their shop, to wish her good luck, a lovely gesture of which we were truly grateful. With all the heartfelt wishes of good luck behind us, it was the M62 and M6 to Preston. Clare accompanied us. I always felt that Clare should have gone to Uni as she was certainly bright enough, and I feel it would have been the making of her. Clare was a very talented Arts and Craft designer, and it would have been interesting to see where she might have ended up.

Preston was bursting with students checking in, total chaos, the house was typical of a student let, very basic to say the least. The other girls were already there when we arrived and made us all, especially Katie feel very welcome with a team hug!! Sally would become like a sister to her and today they are still as close, swapping stories about their kids. After a couple of hours helping her to settle in to her new surroundings it was time to leave them to grasp the nettle!! I was thinking how lucky we have been as parents. It was a long journey home and we were all in reflective mood, and to Helen's credit there were no tears. I am sure we were the final intake to take advantage of the grant issued by North Yorkshire County Council. This was the introduction of the Blair years, where he championed that a high percentage of students should go to university, to rack up thousands of pounds of debt. Higher education for the masses. "Times they were a changing" as Mr Dylan would say!!

The year is 1998, and Dennis Harland a builder from Glaisdale, a village nestling within the hills and valleys of the North Yorkshire Moors, is father to a prominent member of the Scarborough first team Darren, who had worked up through the club's ranks. Apart from cricket, Darren excelled as a whipper at the local hunt. As a youngster he showed promise as a champion showjumper, soccer also played a big part of his winter activities, you could say a real all rounder. Visiting all primary schools in the district and introducing boys and girls to cricket gives me an opportunity to access the local cricket talent. I had the ideal place to bring these youngsters together. Fylinghall School, a private college nestling close to Robin Hoods Bay, over looking the North Sea. Paul Blackwell the head of PE at the college, an enthusiastic local player himself, gave me a tour of the Indoor Sports Hall. It was perfect with two cricket nets available. Paul was the most accommodating bloke, really keen, loving his job. Apart from the Sport he also taught Art.

I approached Dennis with a view to sponsoring a scheme I had in mind. I would invite the young players I thought showed promise onto a coaching course to take place every Wednesday evening. Dennis was a keen supporter of projects that included young local kids, anything to keep them occupied and off the street. He came up with the finance and got the ball rolling. Fylinghall were delighted to open their doors to local organisations. Peter and Claire White, the college administrators very kindly put on a brilliant buffet, as we launched the scheme. Martyn Moxon and David Byas came over from Headingly to offer their support and knowhow to the proceedings. Darren was the perfect role model, the young boys selected for the scheme all knew of his cricketing prowess, the two of us worked together shaping the youngsters into the next generation of cricketing stars.

A good friend of mine Mr Rod Gill, had just retired from a career in the insurance business, he had been a partner in a local firm of insurance brokers, Rod had been a keen sportsman in his younger days, soccer and cricket being his preference. He was solid at the back for South Cliff, in the local Scarborough and District soccer league, in the summer he donned his whites, representing Scarborough CC as a stylish right hand bat and occasional third change bowler, we had been mates for years always ribbing each other, he is very knowledgeable, especially on the subject of soccer a lifelong Leeds United supporter. I ran into him one day, explaining my role with the YCB. I invited him along one day on a school visit, Rod enjoyed his new role as wicket keeper during the quick cricket games.

From that day he became my buddy, we spent hours together travelling the Primary schools of North Yorkshire, he became a fixture and fitting, and I thank him for his excellent company and hard work, throughout our time together.

Scarborough 3rd XI captain this was my latest role, we were to be playing against lads just like me, who had seen better days, but still enjoyed the game, the majority helping to bring their local juniors on, it's a bonus for any club to have two or three decent experienced fella's to steady the ship. Martin North, my vice-captain, another who had reached veteran status.

Martin was a reliable lad, keen as mustard, couldn't have wished for a better man, he had played Yorkshire League cricket for Hull CC when in his pomp, he then moved to Scarborough to the join the Ridings XI. He has a young son Mikey, who became a competent opening batsman, who could bowl some tricky leg spin. This young man also had an alternative gift for acting, talking to him as a young lad, his ambition was to become a box office sensation, he is well on the way to living his dreams, as he secured the role of Gary Windass a young tearaway, in the popular soap Coronation Street.

Another milestone was about to be reached, Katie was to receive the key of the door, twenty one year's young. We booked the Scarborough Cricket Club for the celebrations, it was an ideal size to cater for up to 100 hundred people. Our friends Pam and Lyndsey Crawford from the Ellenby Hotel, agreed to prepare the buffet. Lindsey, Pam's daughter had just returned from back packing around the Far East, she was keen to show off her culinary skills. The fare they created would have adorned any table, it looked incredible, such a shame to carve it up. The Ellenby stands just up the road from the cricket ground, Phil my buddy from Nottingham and I spent most of that Saturday afternoon, transferring the food from one to the other. Katie arrived from Preston.

With all her room mates, and their boyfriends, they were dossing down at ours, it resembled a World War 1 clearing station. Marge made a big effort to look her stunning best, she was now eighty years old, being surrounded by young un's celebrating, put a smile on her face. The place was rocking that's for sure, family and friends coming together having a ball ... Priceless.

As skipper of the third XI, I laid down a few ground rules, if these young lads were going to represent Scarborough cricket club, they had to be prepared to act and dress accordingly. No matter which team you represented, these rules applied. One of the old Army sayings that stayed with me, 'Bullshit Baffles Brains' if you look the part, it goes a long way in winning the mind games, in my experience if a team rocked up in tee shirts and jeans, looking like a bag of shit, that's probably how they played. Pride plays a big part in life generally, but especially in sport. Pride in yourself in your performance in your team, getting these points across, is in my mind very important, these young boys were just starting out on their cricketing journey to who knows where, the majority probably 99% will only play club cricket, that's not the point, all will have been offered the same chance to shine, personally I think the game of cricket is not just a game, but a way of life.

Encouragement, guidance, early doors will determine in most cases, a proud individual who can leave his mark on the game.

Pam Crawford came to the fore one more time, as she sponsored the 3rd team by providing club ties to be worn to all games. We were to play our home games at the very picturesque ground of Hackness. The Lockey brothers, John and Tony had been the driving force at Hackness CC for years, Tony prepared the wicket. We were to share the ground with Hackness, who had a team in the Beckett League a higher standard than ours. It was a unique little ground, from the road you looked down on the playing area, as it sat by the river, surrounded by sheep and majestic beech trees, a very rural, peaceful, the perfect place to end my cricketing exploits. Graham Hall and his sons Ricky and Jimbo became good friends, Graham had played all his life for Whitby, where they lived, he had brought the lads down for coaching, Les Spedding another Whitby buddy, his lads Bob and Tom also appeared for coaching, Whitby lads played a big part in the initial Scarborough 3rd XI, Chris Dove, Dave Pearson, Ian Midgley, Luke Jennison, Jamie Ram, Ryan Swiers, Michael Dennis, Ricky Wilson, James Croft, Matthew Loades

These names formed the vanguard of the initial Scarborough 3rd XI, the majority of these had progressed from the Scarborough under fifteens junior eleven, there was the odd exceptions, Chris Bachelor came into the 3rd team only twelve years old. Another youngster who would make a big impact on the local cricketing scene, also from Whitby, Adam Lyth, Adam is the youngest son of Alastair and Christine, Alastair was a swashbuckling left hand bat playing for Whitby CC, a local legend in his own right, breaking the heart of many an opening bowler in North Yorkshire, their eldest son Ashley, another talented all-rounder, reliable left hand bat, who also had a knack and natural control as a medium pace bowler, taking wickets on a regular basis.

Ashley captained the Scarborough Juniors XI, he also had another string to his bow his first love being soccer, he represented the Scarborough Soccer academy at the different age groups, where he was spotted by a talent scout, he then signed as a professional for Leicester City, his good friend Richard Jackson had signed for Derby County, therefore the two were now on the professional ladder, a great coup for Whitby and also Scarborough soccer academy.

I met Adam at Airey Hill Primary School in Whitby, he was a rare talent at only nine years old.

Another man I've been privileged to call a buddy, Mr Adrian Grayson this gentleman, a very staunch North Yorkshireman, who has been coaching and guiding youngsters since before the dinosaurs became extinct. A decent all-rounder in his day. I remember as a lad reading about his exploits with bat and ball playing for Pickering in the East Yorkshire cup. A lovely man typical Yorkshire, who tells it how it is, he will be remembered for his dedication and commitment his fatherly manner, there's many a young man who today will secretly respect and admire that little piece of advice, which would improve his performance.

I remember Adrian becoming quite excited when he saw Adam Lyth and Chris Batchelor perform for the first time as youngsters. I would send groups of lads through to Northallerton for North Yorkshire trials where Adrian would cast his critical eye, it was always a pleasure for me to meet up with him to catch up with the gossip regarding Yorkshire cricket.

Adrian's eldest son Simon is now the manager of Leeds United, and his youngest son Paul, after playing cricket for Yorkshire, moved to Essex where he now holds the reigns as Director of Cricket. These boys are obviously testament to the love and leadership of a good man.

I recall an experience which has stayed with me, I was running a beginners course at the cricket ground in Whitby one evening, I was explaining some procedure or other, when from nowhere Chris Bachelor and Adam Lyth rocked up wearing their county tracksuits, Chris representing the under 12 years and Adam the under 11 years, there they were totally made up with their white roses blooming.

The youngsters were excited, I made the point that no matter who you were, from all backgrounds, with practice, hard work and dedication it was possible for any youngster's, boy or girl to go forward. I felt a ripple, stood there just a bit proud. Christine Lyth had to work this particular day, as she was the only driver in the family, getting Adam to Bradford for his first under 11 game against Glamorgan, was becoming problematic. I was keen to see how he would react and perform with boys at this level. Christine prepared a picnic lunch that would have fed the whole bloody team, she did say that young Adam had the appetite of a young horse; we hadn't got out of Whitby before he was into the sandwiches. Alastair had taken the day off, to support his boy,

Wild horses wouldn't have kept him away. We rocked up to the ground, it was a lovely sunny day, Adam looked very smart in his grey flannels, white shirt, tie and the navy blazer, there was all the built up adrenalin and nervous energy running through him, he couldn't wait to be with the rest of the boys, I thought how nervous I used to become before the game, I must admit I was a little jealous. Also in the team for this game a young Adil Rashid, Adam and Adil have come a long way since that initial encounter. Yorkshire won the game by nine wickets, Adam came in first wicket down knocking the runs off in fine style, it had been a long day, but worth all the effort, that's where it all began for this young, unassuming lad from Whitby, it wouldn't be too long before Adam would be making his mark in the Yorkshire League as a fifteen year old, he stylishly without fear scored a magnificent 94, nothing fazed the young man, if anyone deserved success, apart from Adam, it has to be his mum, who for years chauffeured the two lads from Whitby to all parts, to play cricket or soccer, practise or games, thousands of miles, that's team work of the highest order, devotion to duty. As the proverb states you only get out, what you put in. Another young boy who deserves a mention, he made his debut a few years before, Phillip Seed an exceptional all round athlete, with cricket and hockey his strong suits. Coaches were excited about his cricketing technique, very correct, good balance, all the attributes needed to make batting work for you, at sixteen Phillip was rated very highly on the county circuit, representing Yorkshire at that age. For some unexplained reason Phillip failed to live up to his billing. He was a cracking lad to work with, I guess the problems lurked inside his head, being able to counter mental pressures, the experts suggest that to become a successful 1st class batsman is down to overcoming 75% mental pressure 25% technique.

Of all the hundreds of young cricketers over many years, who have been guided and coached by myself, only the one has gone onto represent the county at the senior level. I sincerely hope he can kick on and make the squad at the highest level and represent his country.

We gained promotion from the C division winning the League in style, everyone had played their part, I found it totally exhilarating taking a back seat as the youngster displayed their talents in all departments of the game. During November Helen and myself found time for a few days in the sun, Gran Canaria, Maspalomas Princess to be precise, we had lovely weather the hotel and food first class,

We are the odd couple whilst on holiday, we would relax by the pool during the day, after dinner in the evening, we would change into our walking clothes, then set off up the hill to Playa des Ingles then back down the hill, to the hotel a night cap in the cocktail bar, it would be full of punters in all their glory diamonds and tiaras long frocks, they'd look at us when we walked in, tracksuits and trainers sweating like pigs we loved it. Priceless.

Martyn picked us up at the airport on our return, I knew there had been rumblings, he was having problems regarding his job as director of cricket. Apparently while we had been away the problem had come to a head and he resigned, this was so disappointing, but he was adamant, there were people at Headingly making life impossible for him, he found he couldn't work in that environment, therefore it would be best for all parties concerned if he quit his post and moved on. Durham CC, they moved quickly, they were keen to have him installed as their Director of Cricket, hand on heart, I regard Martyn more of a brother, than just a friend, he is a down to earth Yorkshire man through and through, he would be hurting, but he also relishes a challenge, he knew he could rely on his family and close friends to support him, he is a highly organised individual, determined respectful, a highly regarded coach throughout the first class game.

All I could say at the time, it was Durham's gain and Yorkshires loss. I was sure he was relishing the opportunity to prove his worth, he had a few weeks to prepare his strategy, to keep his powder dry. Then come out all guns blazing. Meanwhile Katie had been up to her neck in christenings and weddings, she was on work experience from University. The Hilton Hotel chain had taken her on, she was based at Garforth, near Leeds she actually lived back at home here in Scalby and travelled everyday driving to Garforth, it was a journey of around

75 minutes, she would be up and away by 6 o'clock each morning, then give us three rings when she arrived. As part of the junior management team, she set up and managed wedding receptions, christenings, this was all part of her Uni tourism management course. Katie amazed us by the way she got stuck in to this project, revelling in the prospect of working within a team structure, she made friends easily, always had done from being a kid, they were long hours, some days after a wedding for instance she wouldn't arrive home until the early hours. Then up again and away for 6am, they were certainly testing her stamina, and the money she earned was desultory, the Hilton Hotel chain were onto a good thing, getting the most out of talented young people, paying peanuts. It was a form of slave labour, I used to get so frustrated with the situation, concerned my daughter might even fall asleep at the wheel. We never let her know how we felt, but it was a worry, all we could do was encourage her and keep motivating her, insisting it will be worth it in the end. One particular incident caused us to panic she had broken down on the A63 after leaving work, it was dark by the time she rang on her mobile it was raining, she was upset to say the least. Something was wrong with the gearbox according to Katie, she couldn't change gears for some reason. This was a worst case scenario, Helen was beside herself with worry. I had told Katie to lock the doors and sit tight, we would arrange a rescue. I then rang the police giving them all the information, they transferred us to the area traffic police unit, who hopefully would be now scouring the A63. We then rang Sue in Wetherby, explaining Katie's predicament the distance from Wetherby to Garforth would take about twenty minutes to cover, we imagine Katie would probably ring Sue as that was where she was heading. Helen and I then spent an hour at the end of the phone, waiting for a call it was horrendous. I felt so helpless, after what seemed

like an eternity the phone rang, it was Katie she was ringing from Sue's just about to have tea, after we had rung, Sue had rung Katie to ascertain where exactly she was, she then rang the AA, luckily the AA arrived just as Sue did, he found the problem fixing it temporarily. Katie had been in a panic her phone had gone down, no charge, what a performance, it had taken all that time before we got the call. I then phoned the police explaining the situation, all's well that ends well, a few more grey hairs appeared, no bloody wonder. Katie said farewell to the staff at the Hilton. For her it had been a rewarding experience gaining her diplomas in Hotel management.

The hotel gave her a rousing send off with a party in her honour, back at Uni in Preston they were gearing up for the graduation, Katie had graduated with a 2.2 we were all very pleased and proud to be there as the Duke of Westminster presented them with their diplomas, it was a very posh affair, the girls had been together for years, and became very close friends, it was a tearful exit, but they promised to stay in touch. Back home Katie was back at her old ice cream parlour, selling those yellow tops, whilst applying for a job as cabin crew, she was creeping closer to living that dream. Being a graduate didn't seem to make much difference in securing a post, over a period of weeks Katie was up then she was down, interviews rejections it was having an effect on the poor girl. We were all feeling the heat it was definitely not through lack of effort, then her determination was rewarded. She had been accepted by the low cost airline Ryanair. This O'Leary guy, the chairman of Ryanair had definitely made the headlines with his brash approach and eccentric methods, people seemed to be backing his pioneering ethos, as the company was flying (forgive the pun). It certainly had a morale boosting effect on Katie, I recall taking her to Manchester to pick up her uniforms from a warehouse, skirts, blouses, trousers, full length coats, handbags shoes, and a hat. It was a squeeze stashing them into the car. It was an uplifting journey home Katie so excited, this was her springboard to who knows where, listening to her, she was pumped up so enthusiastic, I was like the cat who got the cream self-satisfaction written all over my face. I thought she deserved her self-acclaimed success, it had been a long frustrating road. We relived some of my old sayings with her, making the point of how important it is to keep both feet on the floor, and always be aware of your surroundings, these were my stocking trade lines which Katie had heard so many times, we both laughed as she finished off the sentence for me.

The 21st century had hardly materialised before it was blighted by the catastrophic outbreak of foot and mouth disease. I recall vividly one lunch time, I was up at Glaisdale having a cup of tea with Sue and Dennis Harland, from their kitchen window it was plain to see on the adjacent hillside the army of government vets initiating a cull of farm cattle. It was a tragic chain of events that affected all and sundry. Fires were raging throughout the country with farmers livelihood going up in smoke before their eyes. Hopefully never ever will we have to witness the barbarism of those awful days.

My older brother Derek arrived at NMR one Saturday during a match and it was great to see him and his wife Venerandah. It had been a few years since we last met. After leaving the RAF, with a pension, he settled in Gainsborough Lincolnshire. He worked for a few years as a civilian in the local police station office. He and Ven have four children, Leslie, Carmella, Fiona and Anthony and now live in Belgium, close to the Dutch border. They both love the outdoor life taking full advantage of their surroundings cycling most days. Derek is an avid photographer, and is well known locally for his handiwork with the camera. They are a close knit family enjoying their children, grandchildren and I am sure great grand children, whenever I talk to Derek or Ven they instill a pride in their lifelong achievements involving family. May it long continue, and one day I will get over to Belgium to witness their endeavours.

I was fortunate to find the time to be stood on the popular bank in North Marine Road on that final morning Yorkshire V Glamorgan, you could sense the relief in the crowd, the ground was very nearly full, as David Byas ex Scarborough buddy, and new Yorkshire skipper, fittingly caught the catch that sealed the County Championship. I recall the crowd surging onto the playing area and mobbing their heroes, this ground had been witness to many cricketing highlights, but this morning must rank up there as one of its finest moments. To win the championship at Scarborough was the icing on the cake for the old club, a most memorable day priceless.

I loaded up the car, we were taking Katie to Stanstead on Sunday morning early. Christine and Clare popped round as Christine and Katie were very close and they all enjoyed some girlie gossip.

There was certainly a strong bond between the two, it was a teary farewell on both sides of the fence. We then had to call to say cheerio to Marge or Nana as she was affectionately known. The strong family ties certainly seem to come to the fore on occasions like these.

After a long drive around 5 hours, we rocked up at the destination. A small friendly hotel, The Pippins, where Katie would lodge whilst doing her training. The couple invited us in they appeared warm and motherly, which I guess helped ease our tension, the place was full of young girls on the Ryanair course. After dropping off the luggage we decided to make for a pub restaurant I had noticed just up the road, as we were all in need of a meal.

Sitting in the restaurant Katie then recognised Jemma, a girl she had been on the selection course in Manchester with, she had travelled down with her parents from Liverpool, we all pulled up our chairs around one large table, we all got on like a house on fire, swapping stories of the trip down to Stansted. That was also reassuring, Katie having a buddy to share the load. They would be training for a month learning everything there was to know about the job, they would then get a weekend off before starting work. After another emotional farewell, we were heading North, and don't spare the horses. This was it, we were now in the club, another classic case of Derby and Joan.

Nothing braces you for sad news, we were all shocked to the core, to hear that Colin Oxtoby had terminal cancer. Here was a genius who enriched other people's lives with his warmth, his knowledge, his cheeky grin, I'm sure I speak for a multitude of people who were privileged to have him as a friend and a playing partner. It was a sad day. The day Colin hung up his boots.

Cricket enthusiasts would no longer witness a master craftsmen at work. It's regrettable that Colins memorable exploits were never caught on camera. I'm privileged to have probably his greatest achievements stored at the back of my mind. I recall the time I took Bill Foord and Tony Moor to the hospice in Driffield, our final farewell. His lifelong buddies Chris Kirby and Gordon Downes were with him when we arrived. We were all pals

Brought together over many years by the great game of cricket. It was a cosy room with glass doors that lead out onto a peaceful garden, Colin looked so well not as I imagined he would look. We spent a special hour retracing our steps over countless games together, sparring and pulling each other's legs just like the old days. Farewells don't come much tougher than this one,

I remember him so dignified, with that glint in his eye, never to be forgotten. A few weeks later came the sad news of Colin's death, his funeral was to be held in his beloved village of Weaverthorpe, the last time I was in this church as a page boy at Auntie Joan and Uncle Toms wedding fifty years previous. Bill Foord had been asked to say a few words on behalf of the Scarborough Cricket club, hundreds came, many having to stand outside. Bills words struck a chord with everyone, he delivered them from the heart, witty, funny, never downbeat, exactly as Colin would have wanted, even the joiner who built the coffin came up with his own subtle reminder of the great man, he had fashioned a miniature set of stumps on the coffin lid, a lovely touch RIP Colin (definitely priceless).

It was 11th September a grey uninspiring kind of a day, I was lying on the couch after lunch, Helen was reading the local rag, she roused me to check out the news bulletin being transmitted from New York. I was a little dozy as I watched the pictures, thinking I don't remember this film at all, I recall a journalist stood overlooking the Twin Towers as they collapsed, the thing that struck me was the controlled robotic dialogue, no panic or raised voices, all very alien and quite surreal. There were people trapped people actually jumping from offices to certain death, I guess everyone will remember where they were on 9/11, those dramatic images of the hijacked planes flying into the towers was murder of epic proportions.

The conspiracy theories were soon to follow the carnage, I personally like I'm sure thousands of other god faring human beings thought this act of barbaric cowardice would trigger the end of my world as I knew it. We all felt helpless, watching those poor souls struggle for survival. How powerful a medium TV had become, with their satellites beaming pictures into billions of homes across the globe. The two of us decided to switch the TV off, put on our walking boots and take Ted for a hike up to Hayburn Wyke, our usual haunt, while we still had the opportunity, who knows what's round the corner, I thought to myself, cowardly murdering bastards on the loose just as Katie starts flying, but I kept the thought to myself. Helen said she will be glad to see the end of this year, I agreed wholeheartedly for the times they are a changing. 2002 had us all looking for weapons of mass destruction the media, keeping us all on our toes, with scary innuendos, war with Iraq seemed inevitable all the major players vying for position.

Katie was now part of the Ryanair team working her socks off, it was demanding work. She was sharing a house close to the airport with a group of girls, socialising was on the back burner, due to rota problems the girls were either working or in bed. The rates of pay were above that of the majority of charter airlines, but as Katie acknowledged they earned every penny. The management team were rigid with the rules, clamping down hard on slackers, or misconduct of any kind. It all sounded very draconian, but Katie enjoyed the helter skelter lifestyle, I guess she was still young enough to cope, she reckoned if she could handle Ryanair, she could handle any airline, with that philosophy in place it must help to get through a shift.

The Yorkshire Cricket Board asked if I would be interested in managing the Under 19's during the season, I would be working alongside Mike Bore another respected member of the coaching squad.

Mike had started his career with Yorkshire CC then moved down to Nottinghamshire, where he helped win the championship, with his slow, to medium left arm bowling. The Under 19's side consisted of young players who had come up through the system, who had probably missed the boat, career wise, there was always the chance of a late developer, finding form something that can't be ruled out.

The format suggested we would compete in a three day game against local counties, eventually going forward to the final. Travel on Tuesdays, play Wednesdays, Thursday and Friday how the weeks just flew by, we enjoyed a memorable campaign, doing remarkably well, with what was regarded by some as a weak side, the support and spirit created by players, supporters and parents, was tangible and there for all to see, we went down losing to Sussex in the semi-final, it had been an absolute pleasure for me to have been involved, I thoroughly enjoyed the challenges brought forward through circumstance, to be involved in on the spot, against the grain decisions, how very different from the basic coaching drills with eleven year olds up in the Esk Valley.

As I drove home on occasions, I would analyse my situation in the scheme of things, within the big picture of life, diversity being the key, I felt at ease with myself, how lucky I have been, but then I thought you make your own luck. We had another successful season with the 3rd XI gaining promotion for the second consecutive season, we invited more youngsters into the ranks, maintaining the standards created the previous season. It was noticeable the impact the young lads were making as we travelled locally from village to village. Old cricket supporters were quick to point out to me, how smart they were turned out how they backed each other up in the field, comments like these put a spring the step.

A few weeks previous during a family gathering for lunch at our favourite local carvery, The Hayburn Wyke, I bumped into an old friend and ex cricket buddy Paul Sullivan, Paul was with his family, sampling the delights Sharon the landlady had on offer. The most welcoming of Country Inn's, a roaring fire, a fine selection of beers and a Sunday lunch to die for, oh for the simple pleasures.

Paul had worked hard building up his business over the years, he felt it was time to take life a little easier, his sons were now in a position to handle the everyday running of the operations

Paul had his boat anchored in Brittany, he explained how he spent his days relaxing, messing about on the water. La Trinite was a mariner's hideout, down the coast from Brest where the boat was anchored, in fact Ellen MacArthur or Dame Ellen the renowned round the world single handed sailor, spent long periods there preparing for her epic voyages.

Paul then invited the two of us to spend a week with him on his boat, just out of the blue we were both taken aback by his kind offer, nothing had prepared us for a proposal of this kind, we thanked him and as there was a lot to discuss we would ring him in the evening with a yeah or nay. To be honest there was nothing holding us back, Ted would go into kennels, Helen had leave in hand at the bank, she was a little unsure about how she would cope at sea. It would be something totally different a new string to the bow, the more we discussed the idea, the more exciting it became. Paul was delighted when we agreed to accompany him back to France.

We booked out return flights from Stansted to Brest for the following Saturday, we rang Katie with the news, there was probably a chance we could meet up with her at the airport. Paul lived in Seamer, my old stomping ground, he lived in Sid Greenwoods old farmhouse, where I used to deliver newspapers

When I was a young lad, Mrs Greenwood used to leave me a bag of goodies every Friday night, never missed. Paul was taking his car to Stansted, we would be travelling in style. We arrived after a pleasant journey, very comfortable in the Jaguar, with all the luggage unloaded I took the car and parked it remembering exactly where, as apparently I will be driving it home on our return next weekend, when I arrived back at the terminal Katie was chatting with Helen and Paul, she had a few minutes before she had to run, she looked a picture in her uniform, it was a lovely surprise seeing her in her glory. Time for a coffee and sandwich before the flight to Brest. Paul was really pleased to have us on board, he was really enthusiastic talking about how he was going to make sailors of us both, I was quite excited but a little nervous.

After an uneventful flight, Paul had arranged for us to be picked up by Limo, a black Mercedes was waiting, no expense spared it was a two hour drive down to La Trinite. The countryside was very similar to England very green and rural, with farmsteads dotting the landscape easy to imagine why thousands of English tourists head to Brittany for their rest and relaxation.

Brittany is very popular as a holiday destination, I believe the majority of tourist enjoy the delights of sleeping under canvas, camping holidays with the young children in particular, I guess the cost of holidays is the big issue for families, therefore destinations like Brittany cover all the angles and tick all the boxes decent weather, plenty to see and do and fantastic food.

The port of La Trinite looked very busy as we were dropped by the water. A quick sprint round the supermarket Paul needed to stock his wine cellar, then it was onto the jetty and into the dingy a floating taxi, which dropped us off at our pontoon, where tied up looking a little lonely our floating apartment for the week. She was a beauty.

Paul was keen to show us the layout our cabin with its double bed, storage space, very cosy if a little cramped. Paul had his bachelor pad up forward of us very swish, fit for a prince. There was toilet and shower, to flush the toilet you had to plunge a lever for a few seconds, this piece of equipment caught Helen off guard and we laughed till we cried all week the idiosyncrasy of that plunger I will take to my grave.

The lounge area with kitchen or galley very practical bench seats with table, plenty of drawers for stowing gear especially wine and spirits, Forward we had the drivers cab, or helmsmen, where the technical stuff like compass, sat nav and radio were all laid out on a glittering instrument panel. The boat could also be operated from a level above, we climbed a ladder onto the upper deck which consisted of the same instruments as below. She was powered by Twin-Perkin diesel engines, which sounded amazing and looked stunning encased in chrome. The first morning stood on deck, the weather sunny and calm, the whole bay looked a picture. Paul was busy setting a course, it was obvious the weather here was mainly sunny and warm, as he was as brown as a berry. Helen didn't take much encouragement before she was laid out on the upper deck. We were tied up to a floating pontoon in the middle of the estuary away from the main shipping lane, it was very busy with traffic, sleek racing dinghies passed by heading to compete, ocean racing catamarans with masts 90' tall filled the skyline, the place was a mecca for those historic maritime sagas, as I scanned the local promenade, straining to visualise the Lord Nelson, or Hyde Park pubs in the distance. Paul revelled in his role of skipper, he was a hard task master with high standards to uphold, I expected nothing less, I had trouble initially with the ropes, being left handed doesn't help. I've always had a hang up with knots since being a kid. But with perseverance, the two of us became competent crew. Paul was extremely generous throughout the week, allowing us both to take over the helm. We had our ups and downs, the second morning whilst trying to manoeuvre into a position between two other cruisers and not allowing for the current or wind speed, we had a slight head on, coming together, we came off slightly worse chipping the fibre glass at the bow of our boat, running repairs were on going. Paul was a bit prickly for an hour or two, realising he should have handled the situation with a little more panache. The following day, the generator for some reason had not been switched on, and the batteries were flat, not enough juice to turn the engines over, we sent for a man with some jump leads, while we strolled over to the café for lunch, another feast the crepes, the best I have ever tasted. I recall the night the wind freshened, we were tied up to our pontoon, we lay in bed listening to the bloody water hitting the side of the boat, all night just that few centimetres between you and the sea. A highlight of the week was when we sailed along the coast into an estuary, then up the canal to the old medieval city of Vannes, a place I had no recollection of. Very old, probably once ruled by the English around the time of Agincourt, quaint, beautiful red brick buildings leaning in old age. I recall a very long lunch with a couple of bottles of Côte De Rhône thrown in, we probably weren't fit to drive, I could now understand why so many people visited Brittany. I had never given the place a thought, we were having a brilliant few days, I will certainly be singing its praises from now on. Our final evening we went ashore, to treat Paul to a special evening meal, it was the least we could do after all his efforts in turning two landlubbers into decent sea faring crew, he had been very patient which I know is not one of his strong points, we hoped we had made his week enjoyable, we certainly had enjoyed something totally out of our box. Paul would be spending the rest of the summer relaxing. I think I mentioned something about him writing his memoirs, that would be an interesting read. The limo appeared and with a wave and a last look at the bay, we were off, back to Brest for our flight home. Due to a technical fault our flight was delayed for four hours. That just took the gloss off the last week a tad. I had the satisfaction of driving back home from Stansted in Paul's Jaguar, I guess that compensated a little.

We had been back from France just a week, with fond memories we were both delighted to have agreed to the trip. Another weird incident or coincidence had just taken place. Helen normally works on Thursday, for some reason that escapes me she was at home when the phone rang. It was a representative from British Midland Regional Airlways based at Leeds Bradford airport, they were recruiting cabin crew and wondered if Katie might be interested in applying. Katie had applied with them in the past, they had obviously kept her details, and how odd that Helen was on hand, she immediately got the message sent to Stansted. Katie had been with Ryanair six months already, from what I could gather the novelty had evaporated, if there was a chance for her to move on she would grab it. Ryanair run a very tight ship, scheduled turn arounds are on the limit.

I was positive Ryanair had been the ideal experience and good grounding for Katie, I'm sure it would stand her in good stead for her next assignment. I recall driving her over to Leeds/Bradford for the interview, I was amazed how street wise she had become, confident even clinical in her approach, we stopped off for a sandwich for lunch, plus a stiff vodka and tonic to stiffen her resolve. So I was informed. We had been in this position before, that feeling of being in limbo, all I could do was wish her well, but secretly I had positive vibes, if I had been a betting man, I would have taken her to succeed, she came out of the interview after twenty minutes, smiled to the next applicant wished her good luck, Katie was glowing, I am sure it went well. 'Bingo' didn't she do well. Katie was elated with the news, she had been selected from hundreds of applicants, also the girl who followed her in they became good friends, and still are today. Louise Steeples is her name, but not for much longer as she gets married in a couple of months. Katie worked a months' notice before leaving Stansted, Ryanair gave her a first class reference.

Another set of uniforms to pick up. Sue and Martyn lived in Wetherby, with Charlotte and Jonny and they had a spare bedroom, and very kindly offered Katie the opportunity to board with them. Amazing how things fall into place, Helen and I were delighted with the arrangement, I'm sure the Moxon's enjoyed having Katie around, the kids loved her to bits, I'm sure she would help with them when ever. Lee, Katie's boyfriend was based in Middlesbrough in digs, as he was at uni tackling physiotherapy, they would have more opportunity to share more time together, another decisive step within the saga.

Chapter 13

South Africa …

January 2003, it was the usual dark dismal post-Christmas blues period, with Katie now working for BMI she was entitled to travel perks. Family and friends could travel with nominated airlines at discounted rates, Helen and Katie got their heads together and came up with a very tempting holiday adventure. Travel Virgin from Heathrow to Cape Town at a very reasonable rate, that would also include Katie's boyfriend Lee. The package was flight only, we had to organise accommodation on arrival. As the Rand/pound valuation fell on the side of the pound, we agreed the cost of accommodation should fall within our budget. The duration of our stay in Cape Town would be ten days, with two days travelling. Katie had got to know the majority of the check in staff at the airport.

There was all the friendly banter as we checked our bags in, we would be travelling business class down to Heathrow, one hours flight, Katie explaining how everything worked, giving us a guided tour of the galley. It is a long flight to Cape Town, 12 hours, it takes four hours to reach North Africa, then another eight hours to fly north to South, it just amazes you the size of the continent, eight hours travelling at 550mph, it's a bloody long walk!!

We actually flew the majority overnight which helped us get some sleep.

On arrival we were all a little drowsy, trying to collect our thoughts and bearings after picking up the luggage, we made our way to a tourist information stand to try to find some accommodation. I was feeling a little negative, the lady was making the point that rooms were at a premium, like rocking horse droppings. When you've squirmed away in a plane seat for twelve hours that's the last thing you want to hear, then just like divine intervention she phoned the President Hotel asking for two double rooms to cover ten days. Two rooms had just become available that morning, "Alleluia lord". I was heard shouting in the foyer, they worked out at £35 per night. The Hotel shuttle bus was sent to pick us up, how lucky was that? A faint heart never won the lady.

The rooms were massive, deluxe with king beds, all mod cons, Katie and Lee's was superior to ours with a sea view, we were just thankful to be there. The hotel was of the colonial design, just had a makeover, and was re-opened by Nelson Mandela not too long ago. It stood at the end of sea point a brilliant location, we spent that initial day round the hotel pool, the sun shone all day the temp around 25 degrees Celsius, just right. After a few hours relaxation, we decided on walking round the point.

We were heading for the Victoria and Albert Quay, the old dockyard, which had been transformed into restaurants, bars and shops. As we were on a bed and breakfast tariff, we had been recommended to check out the quay for dinner. Walking round was not dissimilar to strolling round the Marine Drive at home, but on a much larger scale, all of Cape Town is dominated by the majestic mountainous skyline, Table Mountain is exactly as the name suggest an enormous flat peak, totally dominating, standing over the city, most evenings fog rolls down over the edge, as you peer up it reminds one of a giant table cloth, the cable cars running back and forth, are so minute against the backdrop. I can't wait to make the journey to the top another definite wonder of the world.

It was 6.30pm, a really warm, balmy night by our standards, if you can imagine the sea wall, then the footpath adjacent of that was a green strip of grass, I guess twenty metres wide, and then the busy highway, it was an absolute pleasure to be here sharing this very popular amenity, joggers of all shapes, ages and sizes endless line of them, families picnicking on the grass playing games, ie cricket, soccer, it was a joy to witness this coming together of a multi-cultural society, Black, Brown, White probably not in that order, it was a long hike to the quay, we passed Robyn Island out to sea about three miles off, Nelson Mandela spent many years of his incarceration there, it's a popular excursion with the tourists.

After an hour of steady yomping, we finally reach the Victoria and Albert Quay, a cacophony of vibrant rhythms, and people, everyone's so absorbed, enveloped, sucked into this vibrant atmosphere. Lee noticed a bar close to the water, we headed there, the music was fantastic, the South Africans love to sing and dance, it was hypnotic, certainly got the feet tapping and the blood flowing. The quay had been very cleverly transformed, one end was still a working dock, with vessels moored. The restaurants and bars were standing on the original wharf structures.

With the sea water running between, this was home to local sea creatures, the favourites being the seals, they enjoyed the titbits thrown by the revellers. It also boasted a shopping mall. Supplying Joe public with the largest hard wood gift, or the smallest diamond, or gold ring, it certainly was a hive of industry.

We were spoilt for choice eventually settling for a steak, Cape Town is renowned for its steak houses, we were not disappointed, our meals were of the highest standard, with a bottle of wine, the bill came to something equivalent to ten pounds per head, quite civilised really. We would definitely be returning to sample more of the delights on offer at the v/a. We found a bus that took us round the promenade dropping us close to the President Hotel, we were all feeling a bit knackered after an eventful invigorating first day.

Next morning after a hearty breakfast, I made for the car hire desk, after checking out the local map it became obvious that the majority of visitor attractions were no more than a couple of hours in all directions, therefore really a car was essential, again the rental costs were easily within budget, there should be no problems driving as it was the same as home, everyone drives on the left. The car arrived a brand new Honda, very comfortable and spacious, with the girls in the back and Lee navigating we set off to who knows where, just along the coast is the very desirable Camps Bay, the beaches looked so inviting, the properties here would knock you back a million or two, that's sterling not rands, all along this stretch of coast for a few miles, stand the beautiful apartments and villas perched on headlands with stunning sea views, we stopped the car just to ogle, we also had a walk on the beach, I was interested to dip my toe in the ocean, I was sure this far south it would be cold, again not to be disappointed it was bloody freezing. We were heading for the Cape peninsular, another hours drive, where the two oceans the Atlantic, and the Indian, have a coming together, the Cape of Good Hope, the actual tail end of this mammoth continent, where many a sailor has perished along with his craft in the deadly currents, and enormous seas created in this region. Before we actually reach the cliff edge, we drive through scrubland with grasses and small trees, this is Cape Peninsula wild life sanctuary, home to baboons, cobras and other small mammals of interest, they kept themselves to themselves as we failed to spot anything.

It was worth the wait, reaching the actual tip the view was absolutely stunning, my mind was racing. Imagining all the old sailing ships, the square riggers, the tea clippers floundering off the headland, those crusty old matelots earned their money, not half!! We had a glance at the map choosing an alternative route back to sea point, we travelled over Chapman's Peak a manmade route through the mountains, a massive engineering feat, with tourism really taking off here the new highway must be a boom to the economy, as well as making the route accessible to all and sundry. We were warned of possible problems with the locals, and to be on our guard at all times, especially in the rural areas, apparently stealing from cars was a problem.

On the return journey we stopped off at Hout Bay, here we enjoyed a coffee, whilst checking out the stalls on the jetty. Here you could charter a fishing trip, or for the extreme adrenalin rush you could go diving with sharks, there had been some opposition to this pursuit of pleasure, personally I cannot understand why anyone would want to be lowered in a cage to face a great white shark, what is the point of the exercise, sharks should be left to their own devices. A growing number of species are struggling, on the endangered list. Man again doing what he is good at, making a fat profit, without a thought for the consequences, disregarding the wellbeing of other less fortunate creatures. I enjoyed the non-commercial aspect of Hout Bay, this was a hardworking community, you could sense it in their eyes, their rugged weather beaten faces, men who had spent their working lives risking it against the mighty ocean. These fellas must totally resent these high rollers with their stupid pointless hobbies, rocking up to ruin the one thing these lads have helped to preserve for generations, their livelihoods.

Back to the hotel mid-afternoon, a dip in the pool, and an hour on the lounger. Helen has to have her sun allowance daily, it's all part of the deal, too much culture in one day makes for not a happy bunny.

Rather than walk to the V/A quay, the bus was the obvious choice, we all enjoyed our hike but the bus makes sense, we were acclimatising satisfactorily, getting used to our surroundings, a perfect winter retreat. We ate at the Hildenbrow Italian restaurant, a very friendly joint, the food was delicious, as were the staff, very entertaining, informative, offering local knowledge which would I'm sure be of assistance.

Up the mountain today, has to be the highlight of the trip personally, we stopped en route to check out the Newlands Cricket ground a very pretty picturesque arena, nestling beneath table mountain, picture that if you can simply sublime, I guess I couldn't have visited Cape Town without dropping in on one of the coolest cricket arenas on the planet. The parking area was chaotic, with mini buses, coaches, private cars, battling for parking rights. We've been lucky with the weather since arriving, the waiters in the restaurant told me the cable cars are regularly out of action due to climatic conditions, strong winds and fog being the main problem, that would have been really frustrating to say the least, but there again, you can climb up from the rear apparently, it's a long gradual ascent, lots of walkers do take that route up, thankfully we will do the riding. The cable car ticket was also very reasonable, I'm sure it was only a fiver return, when you eventually arrive at the station the actual cars look so tiny against the back drop of the mountain, it doesn't take long to reach the summit Helen was only too pleased to have the ground beneath her feet, we all followed a signed route to the viewing areas, on arrival words fail you, as we all peer down over the side.

This perpendicular piece of rock, rising 3 thousand feet into the sky, can be seen on a clear day by sailors out in the ocean as far away as 50 miles, incredible. People had wedged themselves onto the ledges, there was a sense of spiritualism, dominance, peace as I stood in awe gazing out over Cape Town, we agreed on a group hug.

Another remarkable place, the ground behind did gradually wind its way back down, people like ants coming and going, winding their way up and down the trail. Before a bite to eat in the station café, I have one last look down over the edge, down below me I spotted Eagles hovering gracefully, catching the thermals looking for a meal.

Whilst at Ryanair Katie became friendly with a girl from Cape Town, named Kirsty, they became good buddies, apparently we are going to meet her and her family tomorrow in the District of Melrose. Katie had kept in contact with Kirsty, she had travelled across from her house, and we followed in the car. Melrose was about half hour away, round the back of Table Mountain. What a spread, Kirsty's mum had prepared Yorkshire pudding and roast beef with all the trimmings, a lovely thought, a really nice touch.

The two girls were really excited about meeting up. We enjoyed our meal in their garden, delicious it was too. The wine was flowing, the girls were making up for lost time. I had to keep off the booze as I was driving. As the sun was going down, we thanked our hosts for a brilliant afternoon. Katie bless her was worse for wear, the wine going to her head, looks like an early night all round.

On our way to Simonstown along the coast from the peninsula, it used to be a Royal Naval Base, in the days when we had a navy and ruled the waves. About a two hour drive from Cape town, to get there we had to drive through the small town of Scarborough, it felt odd recognising the sign as we drove through, just above Simonstown is a small community known as Boulders Beach, in the old days it was a whaling station, as the name suggests massive boulders lay on the beach where the whales were hoisted up using the boulders as platforms, Boulders Beach today is thankfully rid of its whalers, and now is renowned for its penguins.

A pair of chinstrap penguins arrived here presumably from Antarctica many years ago, the locals took them to their hearts, allowed the pair to breed safely and before you know they have a colony on their hands. We parked in the allotted car park making our way to the beach. There were penguins everywhere, tame used to humans, females nesting, a remarkable story, also the boulders on the beach were as stated enormous, I was interested to have a closer look, you could see how the whalers had smoothed the surface of the massive objects whilst going about their grisly business. In Simonstown we made our way along the main street, the dockyard was on our right, the South African navy now utilise the facilities. We called into a bar fancying a beer, adorning the walls in all their glory were the Ward Room plaques, representing the names of those much loved ships of The Line HMS Vanguard, HMS Hood, HMS Ark Royal, to name but a few.

In those glory days Simonstown must have been rocking, it resembled a ghost town at present, a leisurely drive back along the coast, as we were now looking out on the Indian Ocean which apparently is noticeably warmer, I stopped the car and applied the toe test, definitely warmer, was the cry!!

It was a Dutchman who in the 1600's colonised the cape, I don't think there was too much resistance, as he sailed into local waters, he took his team of swashbuckler's inland setting up a fort and garrison, in a rural swathe of farmsteads which he named Stellenbosch, the Dutchman set about building a town with all the amenities that make up a thriving community.

In the region for one hundred years, the Dutch enjoyed life on the cape, the soil was very fertile especially for the growing of grapes. Vineyards began to prosper. It was at this time that Johnny English decided strategically the cape offered the ideal facility to counter any threat to his navy and empire, the rest as they say is history, here endeth the lesson!

Stellenbosch today won't have changed too much from those days long gone, it felt warmer inland, away from the stiff breezes that sometimes exist by the coast. The designs were obviously very Dutch, pretty houses, with their rounded gable ends, the Fort is now a museum with interesting facts on show. I remember in 1981, after playing cricket for Yorkshire, I applied for a coaching job in Stellenbosch, I'm still waiting to hear from them. From those early pioneering days, who would have guessed how important this place is to the South African economy.

Vineyards were visible as far as the eye could see, probably wine is the most popular drink worldwide, that's thousands of bottles drank every day. The pressure of producing the right product at the right price must be enormous, we were in for a relaxing day, thousands of tourists visit the vineyards of Stellenbosch, checking out the different brands, we had been recommended three vineyards to sample, as I was the mug again, the driver, I was restricted to a couple of small glasses.

We took lunch outside in the garden of this particular farmstead, it was a beautiful warm clear day, I recall we had Panini's filled with a selection of fillings beef, prawns, you name it, four large latte coffees, the relaxed atmosphere, the ambiance, I've never ever sat and enjoyed a finer hour ever, the bill eventually arrived six pounds unbelievable!!

Lee and the girls enjoyed the day, giggling and fooling around as I soberly drove back to base. This was our final sortie with the car, we would be returning it in the morning, having the vehicle gave us the chance to be independent, explore our own way around what is the most exhilarating captivating place, I would highly recommend Cape Town as a winter destination, its quite a long flight, but value for money, I'm sure there is no comparison.

We spent a couple of days just relaxing reflecting on the week I would definitely return to Cape Town given the opportunity, probably to watch some cricket who knows!! The flight is a long one, as we were travelling up the spine of Africa. I was thinking to myself there are a few countries down there I wouldn't want to land in keep going you big bird!!

Our adventure had a twist in the tail, we arrived back at Heathrow around 9 o'clock in the evening, we had missed the shuttle up to Leeds/Bradford. The next one being the morning flight 0900hrs. One option was to hire a car, with all the documentation in place, and seeing my credit card take another hit, I was presented with the keys to a Peugeot estate, this was something I hadn't planned for. We drove away from Heathrow at approx. 1045, arriving at Leeds/ Bradford 0130, it had been a trouble free drive, just over three hours, didn't hang around.

Katie and Lee had slept like babies all the way up from London, I still had another hours drive to Scarborough, in Katie's car, Helen kept me awake by talking non stop, I must admit I was beginning to drift off a little just before home, it had definitely been a long day and night.

Wherever you've been in the world, no matter for how long, the moment you land back home and get back on the road, it's as if you have never been away. After a couple of days jet lag life became routine again, Helen was in a state of shock, the bathroom scales can't be right, it was a case of joining weight watchers, I guess that's the cross you have to bear after all that value for money.

The cricket season arrived we were still playing at Hackness. Hackness cricket club had folded through a lack of players, it was a shock as they were one of the founder members of the local Beckett League. Tony Lockey the Hackness stalwart had agreed to prepare the ground this season, we were in the dark as to what will happen the following year. Jamie and Joel Ramm have left us to join their dad playing with Wykham CC. Val Ramm had been our scorer, she also acted a surrogate mum to the young boys in their hour of need, she will be missed, another young mum very kindly accepted the scorers post, Lyn Wilson, whose son Danny is a prominent member of our squad, Dad Nigel also deserves a mention for all his appearances as twelfth men. We resemble a young family, apart from a couple of crusty old dinosaurs, with mums and dads chauffeuring, umpiring, motivating and rolling the wicket, wouldn't want it any other way, you are all greatly appreciated.

My role at Headingly had changed slightly, this summer I managed the Under 17's, who are really the elite squad; these are the lads who were thought to have the capabilities to go on and represent their county. Last season was very much a learning curve for me, we had a relatively successful campaign with the under 19's, even though our squad was depleted, we created a competitive edge without prima donnas, who raised their level of performance with every game, winning is the main ingredient to restoring confidence amongst team players, which in turn develops that spirit needed to ensure success, the boys surprised many with the scalps they earned and deservedly so!

The under 17's on the other hand were expected to win all before them with the talent on show, Andrew Gale, Joe Sayers and Richard Pyrah were all boys groomed for the future. They have been prepared and groomed for the first class game, coming up through probably the finest cricket academy in the country, I was excited to be working alongside boys of this calibre, but the great old game they call cricket has proved so many times things never seem to go to plan, as I mentioned earlier a high percentage of the game is handling pressure.

If a batsman is having a bad trot, where will the next run come from, or a bowler struggles with his line and length, these are the gremlins that lurk in the head. The season didn't go as planned, losing to Leicester at Harrogate proved fatal, there is no question the boys can bat and bowl and physically play the game to a decent standard.

On reflection I can only assume, as these lads though at times were full of bluster, were still learning their trade, trying to cope with the pressures, some were I think naïve and lacked the steely commitment required. We analysed the Leicester debacle in the dressing room, trying to come to terms with the performance was difficult.

I sense I was more disappointed than some of the players which said it all for me, I rest my case. The last few weeks had stuck in my craw, the poor performances, I began to question my own commitment, did I show the dynamism these young bucks needed, was I becoming that old has been in a tracksuit and trainers, god forbid. Local cricket in and around Scarborough was flourishing, the courses we had set up and promoted were beginning to bear fruit. Lads, who have risen through the scholarships, were now promising members of their local sides. It gave me a boost and still does, when I check the results on a Monday in the local rag, totting up their runs and wickets. Oliver Stephenson, a youngster on the Filey scholarship, he's showing real promise as an opening batsman, he has all the natural attributes required, the next couple of years will be crucial in his development let's hope he can kick on and find that magic formula and fulfil his dreams and ambitions.

I still keep going to the centre at Danes Dyke, since the cash line ceased operation, I make a point of calling for coffee at least twice a week. Another winter has passed and thankfully all and everyone has survived, there's a real sense of community a strong bond, Norman still has that cheeky smile and dry sense of humour and his looking forward to the trips in the coach visiting interesting places throughout North Yorkshire.

I spent the summer of 2004 working with Tony Bowes, son of the legendary opening bowler Bill Bowes, Bill who took the new ball for Yorkshire and England is ranked up there with the finest. Bill Foord my Scarborough cricket club buddy made his Yorkshire debut, sharing the new ball with Bill Bowes who was playing his final game before retiring, BF stating it was probably the only occasion where both opening bowlers wore spectacles.

Tony and yours truly enjoyed the summer with the Yorkshire under 14's, up and down the motorways from Lincolnshire to Lancashire. I had found it very interesting being involved through the stages of development from 14 to 17 to 19.

There will only be a small percentage of the boys who make it to the top, but they all get the same opportunities, there's a hell of a lot of work goes into preparing the youngsters, one by one they find their own level. I'm positive the majority of youngsters who jump on the escalator at Headingly, or any other cricket academy, is a more rounded determined individual when they get off. As I mentioned before, it's not just a game!!!

I pop next door to wish Chris and Dennis bon voyage, they are flying to California for a two week holiday. This will be their second visit. They enjoy driving to different locations wherever they go. Yosemite National Park is high on their agenda this year. Chris works hard long hours, she loves her job at the doctor's surgery in Falsgrave, and it's one of the many plus points living next door to each other, no worries about the house.

It's a great time of year late September, cricket has finished the weather is still warm, Darby and Joan as it were spend most of our spare time walking up on the cliff top. Above the village of Cloughton, is the spot we visited on Millennium Eve, with its glorious views over the North Bay and Scarborough Castle. It's so naturally beautiful on a summer evening, the wife, the dog, the wildlife, then on to Hayburn Wyke for a pint, I think I've died and gone to heaven.

Chapter 14

Christine …

When the phone rings at 0730am, it certainly wakes you with a start, your first instinct is something's wrong. Helen answered the phone it was Dennis he wanted me, he was in a state of shock shouting down the phone, I told him to slow down keep calm try again, Chris had collapsed in the hotel pool, and Dennis had been at the other end when he noticed she was in difficulty. As it was high up in Yosemite the first aid capabilities were limited. Staff were quickly on the scene trying to resuscitate Chris and the next thing Dennis remembers was a helicopter arriving to transfer her to a medical centre. Dennis was then taken by the road to the town of Modesto, a two hour drive away.

In the hospital Dennis was befriended by a local pastor, who just happened to be visiting, Clifford Sexton was his name, Cliff realising how helpless and traumatised Dennis was at this shocking time took him under his wing. They spent what seemed to Dennis an age checking Chris out, it didn't look good when she was put on a ventilator which meant she couldn't breathe unaided.

There was nothing anyone could do but wait, Cliff then offered the use of his home and telephone to Dennis from where he called us. We were both numb, it hadn't really sunk in the tragedy of it all. I told Dennis I would organise with Martyn to bring Clare out immediately, we obviously had to acquire tickets. I contacted Martyn and Sue with the awful news, luckily Katie was on hand to organise tickets, there seemed no time to take in the enormity of events.

Helen and I both knew the hardest task would be breaking the news to Clare. Clare idolised her mother, how would she react. Clare had split from her former boyfriend some months earlier, she now shared a flat with another young man Alastair, they seemed happy together, he had just joined the RAF. I saw the look on Clare's face as the door opened, she had been washing her hair and it was still dripping. It was only 0830 in the morning.

We sat her down and explained what we knew of the tragic state of affairs, we all shed tears Helen was feeling the pain now, it was sinking in. Katie had done well in organising our flights, we would be leaving from Manchester airport on the 0830 flight to Chicago, and then onto San Francisco with American Airlines. How could this be? What on earth had caused Chris to collapse?

Sue and Martyn and the kids drove to Scarborough, as they felt they should be here to support Clare, I guess we were all still in shock trying to get our heads round the dreadful news. Katie had rung work, and they sent her home, she was also on her way, we had probably the hardest hurdle to overcome, breaking the news to Marge, with everyone present we entered High Mill Drive, the look of total surprise and confusion on Marge's face, she was a frail old lady, having to come to terms with the worst possible scenario for a mother, like us she found it difficult to take in how could it be, Chris was only young, always on the go, never complained never ill.

Sue and Helen, dropped the three of us off at the airport, we were all hoping for a positive outcome as we collected our tickets from the American Airlines rep. After approximately fourteen hours travelling we eventually arrived into San Francisco, Dennis was there looking worn out, "I guess you'll be Phillip?" I turned to face this mountain of a man, with those soothing dulcet tones, coupled with a crisp Californian accent, a full set beard and rounded spectacles, if I had to imagine a pastor, he was spot on. This was the start of a beautiful meaningful friendship. Clifford Sexton one extra ordinary man.

With the formalities over, Cliff pointed the way to the transport. I sat in the front with the genial giant as he drove us to Modesto a two hour drive. I was asking questions all the way. Dennis was at a loss, Chris seemed just her normal self, they were having a lovely holiday she never complained of feeling unwell, with the eight hour time difference, it was still relatively early, therefore we could go over and visit Chris, Clare obviously was keen to see her mum. Cliff was very knowledgeable, we had a riveting debate, putting the world to rights, all subjects from American politics to Yorkshire cricket, he was an inspiration. Modesto a modest town of 100,000 souls, the hospital Chris is in is renowned for its expertise in the cardio vascular field probably that's a positive omen.

Cliff's wife, Lin and son Caleb were there to greet us, how special it felt to be welcomed with warmth and love, into a stranger's house. Dennis had mentioned earlier how the Sexton's had taken him in, comforted him, allowed him access, gave him a bed, and now the same kindness was being offered to us, it was overwhelming, their Christian values shining through. Lin was an extraordinary lady, full of energy and vigour, softly spoken with an air of authority, the theatre her indulgence. All the family were heavily involved with their church, Lin directs plays and musicals, even performs on the boards with a heavenly voice. Caleb is the technical wizard, heavily into the recording and filming aspect, the perfect combination.

Their house is a typical American homestead, quite large detached property, with the quintessential porch on the front. Dennis had a bedroom, Clare also, Martyn and I shared a room with two single beds, it was ideal, after a shower Lin provided a cup of Yorkshire tea to make us feel at home. It was a five minute walk to the hospital, which soon bought us down to earth reminding us of the reason we were here. Dennis prepared us, explaining how Chris would look, she had tubes inserted working her organs, it was with fear and dread, the three of us walked into her room, poor Clare was physically shaking it has been such an ordeal for her, and to her credit she has been so brave.

There she was lying amongst an array of plastic tubes, monitors and screens, her eyes were closed, she was breathing with the aid of a tube inserted into her mouth, she looked so peaceful, Cliff made us all hold hands round the bed whilst he said a prayer. Dennis was urging Clare to give Chris a kiss and talk to her, Clare was obviously a little uncomfortable dealing with her emotions, we had to calm Dennis down a little, it was painful for us all. I just wanted Chris to open her eyes, smile at us, with her customary cheeky grin. Cliff, Martyn and myself, walked back to the house, leaving Dennis and Clare to come to terms with the situation. It had been a very long day, tomorrow we were to meet the consultant who would put us in the picture regarding the next course of action.

As we appeared from our rooms after an erratic night's sleep, Lin had prepared us a typical Californian breakfast, orange juice, eggs, pancakes the works, it was difficult not to imagine being on holiday, the weather was sunny and warm in the 70's

The consultant was very young I thought, looked more like a hippy than a doctor, I guess this was California, he didn't beat about the bush, the tests on Chris concluded she had suffered a heart attack, which had stifled the oxygen supply to the brain, leaving her in a coma, it is policy to place the patient on a ventilator with a view to monitoring their progress, he had come to a conclusion that he was sure Chris would never regain consciousness ..., she was clinically dead. He gave us the option, we could leave her on the machine, or have the machine taken away, he did make the point that however many beds they had in the unit it was never enough, as there was a constant stream of patients needing the facility. Cliff helped us to come to a decision, in all his experience which was vast he had been witness too many similar traumas, he made the point no one was influencing our decision, the consultant was just telling us how it is. In our heart of hearts we all knew what had to be done, it was down to Dennis and Clare to affirm that view. I recall it was such a moving period the female nursing staff were very caring, they are privy to these scenes on a regular basis. These people are so effective they give you hope, they always encouraged us to talk to Chris converse with her hoping against all the odds, a flicker of the eye a finger twitch would materialise.

Dennis and Clare did agree to have the machine switched off, again it was so moving, Martyn acknowledged the fact that he had never shed so many tears, he wondered if he would run out, but if that happened, he could have some of mine. Two o clock in the afternoon, we were asked to leave the room whilst the team dismantled the ventilator and all its plastic tubes, it took around twenty minutes and then a nurse invited us back in, explaining how Chris was now breathing unaided, she made the point of how strong her breathing was, as I looked at her without all the paraphernalia strapped to her, she looked totally normal, I found it so hard to come to terms with the fact that she was as they declared, clinically dead.

The time ticked by it was now eight o clock in the evening, Chris was still breathing with all the gusto of a healthy person, we were all thinking how can this be, Dennis and Clare looked done in, totally knackered, we suggested they should nip back to the house, grab a shower, it was only five minutes away if there was any change we would notify them A.S.A.P. Reluctantly they agreed, leaving the two of us on guard so to speak. With Dennis and Clare out of the way, I was keen to question the nurse on the eventual outcome. She pointed out no matter how strong the breathing was and she acknowledged it had been consistent for a long period, the organs will collapse, once one goes it compounds the problems until the heart expires and the breathing will stop.

I was willing Chris to prove this nurse wrong to go on against all the odds and recover, she looked so resolute and strong, I called Martyn over to check out her breathing it was now nine fifteen, I thought it had become less robust a little shallow, he agreed there was a definite change, we then phoned the house with the news, I held Chris by the hand it was now nine thirty. Clare and Dennis had yet to arrive, what was keeping them. It was all over so quickly, from breathing normally, the two of us witnessed her final futile breath, Chris had finally succumbed.

She was now at peace, a couple of minutes passed then Clare and Dennis appeared, what a day, we were both emotionally drained, Cliff arrived after hearing the sad news. He was a tower of strength a great comfort to us all, I wondered how Dennis would have ever managed, us also without this family's extraordinary kindness.

Now the work had to begin, to repatriate Chris's body back to the UK. Martyn with his organisational skills, took on this mammoth task, he worked tirelessly never off the telephone, cutting through the red tape, the British Embassy helped in some regard, they eased some of the burden. After another of Lin's superb evening meals, including her awesome brownies, we all sat down, it had been noticeable the lack of a television set, Cliff made a point of showing us the T.V it was hidden from view behind sliding doors, this came out if there was something interesting to watch. Caleb then produced a bottle of single malt whiskey, Cliff had been badgering Dennis before we arrived, I guess he was preparing the ground, having strangers in the house gave him the opportunity to enjoy an evening of getting to know you, to ease the tension, and curb nerves there's no firmer remedy than a wee dram or two or three, Cliff was keen to learn about Martyn, his career with England and Yorkshire. I'm sure he was thrilled to have such a celebrity staying within his four walls. We learned more about the workings of a local pastor. According to Cliff there was a lot of hardship, unemployment, drug issues domestic problems, California was going through a difficult period, he emphasized the importance for change, the divide between rich and poor was a gaping abyss, and had to be addressed. After a couple of glasses, I lightened the mood a little recalling some of my army experiences, it seemed to do the trick, we all relaxed, enjoyed each other's company it was great to see faces smiling again. On Wednesday we had to drive to Sacramento to pick up the death certificate, Cliff drove us in the people carrier Dennis had hired for the holiday. The countryside around Modesto is rural farm land, Almond groves abound, if you like almonds there's a good chance they came from the surrounding area, the landscape is quite diverse, hilly mountainous, with lush green valleys. Wine is also a mammoth industry in these parts, with Modesto being the main distribution hub worldwide. After picking up the certificate at the funeral parlour, we had a problem with the car, something to do with the brakes, first this pungent smell, then the smoke, on inspection the front discs were shot, red hot luckily the hire company had a depot in Sacramento, Dennis had the paperwork in hand, we gingerly drove into the depot there were hundreds of such vehicles on hand, Cliff in his suit and long mackintosh burst into the office, he looked every inch the perfect hoodlum, demanding to see the manager, towering above this scrawny little guy, Cliff stated his case, with the paperwork in order another vehicle was quickly made ready, we laughed as we exited the vehicle park, Cliff enjoyed his role portraying the heavy, he was definitely an all-rounder, a man for all seasons. Martyn was doing a superb job, there was more to moving a body than we realised. Dennis made the job more difficult, he wouldn't budge from the idea of Chris travelling back with him and Clare on Virgin Atlantic. We could understand him wanting Clare to travel with him. Everywhere Dennis had travelled long haul with Chris it had been Virgin Atlantic, nothing could persuade him otherwise, he felt Chris on her final journey should travel Virgin Atlantic, Martyn got clearance from the insurance company, they had been another fly in the ointment. He felt now he was over the worst. Cliff had planned another memorable chapter, he was driving us in the new van to San Francisco, his place of birth, this man certainly rocks, San Francisco is up there with the iconic cities of the world and it burst onto the scene in the 60's, the birth place of flower power and hippy communes. It takes approx. two hours, before you get the feel of the city, across a couple of bridges, then you get some idea of the size of the bay area.

It stretches as far as the eye can see, Cliff was brought up in the suburbs, enjoying his job as a postman in his early working life, he did suggest he may have hung out with the new kids on the block, "Hippies", during those heady days back in the 60's, we parked the van, down by the waterfront, Dennis was keen to show Clare the sights he and Chris had visited during their stay, we arranged to meet up in a couple of hours. Cliff flagged a taxi down, Martyn and I were going for a guided tour. First stop the Cathedral,

I had noticed it standing tall on a hill overlooking the city, very majestic, a very impressive building as we approached the massive oak doors, we were greeted by a couple of rather camp wardens in their matching purple cassocks, speaking with an effeminate high pitched California drawl 'Hi there, where have you come from?"

"Yorkshire" I replied, an octave lower than usual, "Wow Yorkshire, GP Taylor, Shadowmancer". When I told them GP Taylor lived on my street only 100 yards from my house, I'm sure a double orgasm occurred under those cassocks, as they shuffled forth, glowing with Christian pleasure. We lit a candle for Chris, holding hands, Cliff with total sincerity from the heart, recognising Chris within these holy walls with such beautiful words, as the sun shone through a magnificent stained glass window; again we were witnessing a memorable moving scene.

San Francisco is amazing, the hills it is built on, the world famous trolley buses running up and down the very steep gradients, China Town with its vast array of restaurants and shops, Cliff wanted to show us some dramatic photographs, they adorned the walls of a large hotel, they gave us an insight to life in the city after the earthquake in 1906, total chaos, the population showing great character and single minded resolve to set on and build the city again to be devastated in another earthquake in 1989.

Back to the van, Clare and Dennis had enjoyed their time together, Cliff had another icon up his sleeve, I guess we couldn't leave San Francisco without travelling along the Golden Gate Bridge, the traffic was heavy as we motored to the far end of the bridge to the tourist park to take some snaps.

Just along from the bridge we also visited the relics of World War Two, old gun emplacements built to repel any attack from the Pacific by the Japanese, it was a stark reminder how important these positions were during those hostilities, many years ago. Cliff drove with consummate ease, handling the vehicle with an assured air, he drove down the routes of the famous movies that kept San Francisco in the spotlight, 'Bullet' starring Steve McQueen comes to mind. Chris, Dennis and Clare would be returning home on Friday, Martyn and myself on Sunday. As far as Martyn was concerned all the paperwork was in order, he had done a tremendous job. Dennis and Clare were very grateful and thanked Lin for her kindness, for all the meals and support. Cliff drove us again back to the airport, Martyn organised Dennis and Clare with check in, for some obscure reason the check in staff were not aware of Chris travelling in the hold, chaotic scenes ensued, Martyn normally a phlegmatic character, began to put himself about, out came his paperwork, his notes of authority from the embassy staff.

On hand to offer any assistance and convey their condolences to Clare and Dennis. Eventually after what seemed an age, the problem came to light, lack of communication, the left hand not knowing what the right hand was doing. Confirmation that Chris was in the hold came through smiles all round, Cliff said his farewells to Clare and Dennis, Martyn was wreathed in smiles, he admitted he was "shitting himself", imagining they had lost Chris in transit. All week we had been in constant touch with the girls back home, they were missing us by all accounts, we passed on the information that Clare, Dennis and Chris were on their way. The body would be transferred to Leeds Bradford from Heathrow, travelling with B.M.I regional and "guess what" Katie's rosta pin-pointed her as crew on that flight carrying the body of her auntie, another macabre coincidence to this saga. Katie asked to be rescheduled onto another flight. It had been a rollercoaster ride all week, up and down emotionally draining, strange circumstances, coming to terms with the sad loss of a dear friend, it had not been all doom and gloom out of the flames of adversity our phoenix had risen, the family Sexton, they are a credit to their species their god, their country and themselves.

During the week the single malt had taken a hammering, this Friday evening was no exception as Martyn and I toasted our new found friends. We were both in reflective moods that night as we lay in our beds. Martyn and Sue had been invited to Matthew Hoggard's, the Yorkshire and England opening bowlers wedding tomorrow, but I am sure he will understand their absence in view of the circumstances. I had come to the conclusion, it was time for me to retire from cricket, and all that went with it, from playing and coaching, if I have to be honest I had been thinking of changing tack,it had been at the back of my mind, this week's ordeal has just put it in to perspective and pushed me over the edge. Cricket has been my life, giving me an enormous amount of pleasure, building cast iron friendships over many years. I felt I wanted to do something totally different with my life. I had played every summer, disregarding my army days since being eleven years old. We discussed many topics that night, laughing until it hurt, over the years we have created a very strong bond, the same ideals and sense of humour, this week has typified those close family ties. We also discussed inviting Cliff and Lin, Caleb and Evelyn his wife, to dinner in appreciation of their wonderful efforts, and as a tribute of our respect for their church and all the good it does in helping the poor and needy, we would leave a legacy. Saturday, a lovely clear day, Cliff dropped me at the bank to cash in some travellers cheques. He then took me to one side, staring at me with those piercing eyes, "Philip, look me in the eyes, tell me that money you have just drawn out is not for our services rendered." I made a point of copying his pose, 'No buddy, we've planned leaving a donation to your church, in recognition of their services to humanity". There was a standoff for a moment or two, then that smile appeared, handshakes and hugs all round. After lunch Martyn and myself decided to watch some ladies soccer, as in the states this is very popular, it was a very well organised event, the level of skills suggested these girls were above average, all the teams boasted two or three coaches, defence attack and fitness, we enjoyed the standard of soccer on show, providing end to end entertainment, being from England the home of soccer proved a big hit with the partisan parents, we injected some of our limey humour into the proceedings of which they duly appreciated "come on you reds."

Our farewell dinner, was a fitting end to a memorable week, Lin had booked the restaurant, one the family use on special occasions. With champagne, we toasted absent friends, and also the emergence of new friends, the food was first rate the ambience warm and friendly, a special evening, it had felt much longer than a week since we arrived in California, we were both ready now to be united with family back home. After what has been an extraordinary state of events. It was with a sense of sadness tinged with relief that we said our thank you's and farewells to Lin, Caleb and Evelyn, I discreetly left our envelope on the tray that housed the single malt, I was sure they would find it there.

Another trip to San Francisco for Cliff, he had been superb in his roles as the caring minister, the most infectious, enthusiastic tour guide and chauffer, we would miss this the most genial of giants. Priceless!!

Monday morning Manchester airport, its grey and raining, Sue and Helen were caught up in traffic, just what we wanted, it gave us a chance to grab a coffee. It was a very emotional reunion, Helen was upset, bless her, it was now kicking in the enormity of losing her sister. Sue drove us back to Wetherby filling us in with the local news.

Back home, Bernard's the local funeral directors had transported Chris to their headquarters in Scarborough, Martin Threapleton their director, a well known and respected gentleman had arranged with Dennis, Clare and the family for a meeting to discuss the data and details regarding the funeral. The funeral went ahead on a cold grey typical October day, she was buried at St Laurence's church Scalby. The church was full to bursting for the service, testament to Chris, she was a private individual in the main, who enjoyed the love and respect of her work colleagues and family. People were invited back to Marge's in High Mill Drive for a cuppa and buffet. It was a trying time for us all, especially Marge, we were going to have to keep a sharp eye out for her in the weeks to come.

Chapter 15

Retirement ... Railways ... Marge ... Boris and Singapore and Oz revisited

Helen, Katie and the family were shocked to say the least with my revelation of retirement from the game of cricket. They wondered if my decision had been probably a tad hasty, a knee jerk reaction, I assured them, that was not the case, Lee, Katie's boyfriend had finished University, he was in the process of finding a physio post, in the meantime he was working for Scarborough Council.

Lee has worked for the council during the summer holidays for years, working on the South Beach selling deck chairs, he came to me with some useful information, the council were looking to employ the right type of person as a guard on the North Bay Railway. This is a miniature railway, iconic to Scarborough, opened in 1931, a favourite tourist attraction with holidaymakers throughout Yorkshire.

Edward Lancaster was the chap who would fill me in. Helen had more or less grown up with Ted, I knew him from the cricket club, and he used to come up for a drink with his parents on a Saturday in the summer. Apparently the supervisor on the railway had died suddenly, he wasn't very old, Ted was pleased to welcome me, to have a look around, I had never been on the railway in all my life, like I mentioned earlier all the local summer tourists events, and attractions were alien to me, playing cricket saw to that.

It was quite exciting like starting over, thanks to Martyn the local council tourist and amenities supervisor, I got the nod, as the railway was council owned it was shut down and put to bed from Halloween to Easter, therefore I had a month or three to organise my departure from my coaching duties and cricket in general. I would definitely miss the challenge, the brilliant parents and kids, all the encouragement, support, friendship and success achieved over many years.

God bless the game of cricket and all who take part. Here's to cricket, from the HART.

It was now the week before Easter 2005. I had been asked to report to the Railway station at Peasholm. I was excited, and a little nervous this was a new beginning, Ted Lancaster was there to meet and greet, we were wedged into the ticket office, a relatively small garden shed, he was running through the order of the day. John Winn was introduced to me. John had started the previous year, he was a big lad, pleasant enough, and his job was to take the money in exchange for tickets, return or single. Ted showed me the ropes for the first week, and I shadowed him as guard making sure to clip all tickets, the role of the guard, be it on the main line or on a miniature railway is very important, passenger safety being paramount. Being in contact with the driver at all times, carrying a telephone, whistle and Red and Green flag at all times. After a couple of weeks guarding I was beginning to find my feet, the job is repetitious after 20 or so return journeys during a day you soon become aware of your surroundings.

The railway is situated within what is known as Northstead Manor Gardens, which incorporates the railway, a lake and the Open Air theatre. The stage of the theatre sits in the centre of the lake, with seats built up in rows resembling an amphitheatre. At the Peasholm end of the lake, another icon from those early years the very popular water splash ride, people can hire pedalos and enjoy 30 minutes relaxation watching the world go by.

The two engines who pull the trains have become celebrities in their own right, they were built specifically for the job, Neptune being the senior loco, built in Leeds at the Hudswell Clarke engineering works, she was built as a replica of the world famous Gresley Pacific loco, The Flying Scotsman, scaled down to one third of the size. People who ride the railway assume the engines are steam driven, but in fact they are powered by diesel engines. In 1931 Neptune was the first diesel hydraulically powered unit in the world, Triton of similar design appeared a year later.

To the keen railway enthusiast, these two locos enjoy pop star status, and the hours of TLC they receive keep them in the condition they have become accustomed. The council employ three drivers, Derek Thompson, the senior, Graham Hill and Geoff Boyes. Derek was a butcher by trade but hung up his apron when the supermarkets hit town. He now enjoys the fresh air and the adulation as a Casey Jones of the NBR railway. Graham Hill worked for years in the stores at the local Gas Board, his father worked on the railway before him, he is carrying on the family tradition, a jovial lad always `expressing himself in song. Geoff Boyes works as cover for the other two, another character employed by the Council for years, also renowned throughout the community for his contribution to the junior soccer leagues. The engines and the rolling stock are maintained by council employees who also help out during emergencies.

People buy tickets and board the trains at both ends of the line, therefore we have a ticket office at Scalby Mills, this is usually manned by a member of the Council's tourism team. I recall the first couple of weeks, I would wake up in the night in a lather, imagining I was on the train, on one occasion I had to put my hand to the floor of the bedroom just to make sure were weren't moving. I would then wake up and think 'stupid prat,' I was really enjoying the job, the banter with the public. I found this very important, we resembled tour guides, historians, Naturalists, a mobile information centre, all in a days work.

Helen Katie and yours truly were having a day out in London, Katie had an interview for a job with Emirates Airlines based in Dubai. We had booked our away day train tickets where you had to specify the actual train times you would be travelling on. We arranged our tickets which meant travelling back from Kings Cross on the 20.30. We thought it would kill two birds by giving Katie some moral support, and a few hours sightseeing for the two of us. It had been a while since we had been down to the metropolis. As it was only a couple of weeks to Christmas, I believe the girls had other pursuits in mind. I enjoy a train journey and find it a really relaxing mode of transport, we were rolling into Kings Cross after a couple of hours. The hotel the Emirates were using for their interviewing was in Chelsea. After wishing Katie well and arranging a place to meet the two of us explored the well heeled streets of this affluent Borough before reaching the banks of the River Thames. We followed the river bank up to Westminster, checking the usual tourist trail. We were enjoying the morning, the weather was bright but cold. The Palace looked magnificent, a state visit had just taken place and the Mall was decked out with flags from the Commonwealth Countries, you could not help but feel a sense of pride at being British. The old back suddenly became straighter, the shoulders pinned back, and I was digging my heels in.

Katie arrived at the arranged meeting place, a pub just across from Admiralty Arch, a pint and a sandwich, just perfect. The interview had gone to plan and Katie felt confident about the outcome. I have to admit she had pulled out all the stops and looked a picture. I felt very proud to be escorting two gorgeous ladies through the streets of London (reminds me of a song). After lunch they wondered if I would enjoy an hour or two Christmas shopping, I would rather have my teeth pulled was the reply. However, I knew this was on the agenda I had been ambushed good and proper, the girls made light of my objection, grabbing my arms and marching up Oxford Street. I do not think I have ever witnessed scenes like it, with hundreds of thousands of bloody people eight abreast on the pavement. I imagined I was on the receiving end of a full frontal assault at the Battle of Waterloo, mindless bloody people, all with miserable faces, spending money as if the world was going to end tomorrow. Helen and Katie seemed to relish this crazy atmosphere, ducking and diving, bartering to get the best deal. The clock had eventually dawdled to 17.30. I suggested to the ladies that my enthusiasm for retail therapy was somewhat on the wane, and to my amazement they agreed. With that we caught the tube back to Kings Cross where a train was waiting. Our tickets stated 20.30, we were knackered so thought we would swing it. The train was full to bursting, with only odd seats here and there. Helen took one seat and Katie managed to find another just along from Helen, and guess where muggins found himself, standing at the end between coaches. We had been travelling about an hour and I was beginning to think we might get away with our minor indiscretion, no such bloody luck. There he was the ticket inspector, who was making his way methodically through the coach, he was accompanied by a sidekick that looked like he was learning the job, I felt this might help my cause when I began to explain why I was travelling at this particular time. Helen was smiling and fluttering her eyelashes at the inspector, pleading total ignorance (being a northerner) to the fact that in accordance with details on the ticket we should be travelling on the 20.30 train. He took it, hook line and sinker and with a little wink for my benefit, she got away with it. When the inspector approached Katie, she turned and blurted out that 'I am with my Dad'. Being Dad I then had to try to wriggle my way out of the delicate predicament my daughter had left me in. The inspector suddenly became a different proposition and began to impress on the trainee the situation, and for my trouble I had to stand for the whole journey back to York, and he extracted a further £92 for the privilege. What had started as an enjoyable change of routine, a family day out had left a bitter taste and a dent in my bank balance. I suppose rules are rules, we took a chance and we were rumbled.

Katie had a three week wait to find out about the interview, she was not successful which left her very low as she had felt very confident about getting the job this setback knocked her confidence a little bit, rejection is tough for anyone, but we consoled her by confirming that it was not meant to be and felt that she was probably too experienced, as we thought they would be looking for someone with less knowledge to train up and pay less but from the look on Katie's face I could see she thought I was clutching at straws. Katie always seemed to struggle but always achieved her targets...in the end. She has always shown much determination, and I feel that this minor setback will be the launch pad to something more beneficial.

Qantas, the Aussie long haul airline were advertising for UK crew, the successful crew would staff flights from Heathrow to Bangkok, Singapore and Hong Kong. From these destinations the Aussie crews would take them onto Australia. Katie had applied as it had been her burning ambition to fly long haul, with her experience in the bag, she felt quite confident with her application. She had just changed her car, the Fiesta had never let her down but with the constant trips to Stansted and back she had really piled on the miles. She had a test drive in a Polo, from the local VW dealer, a demo model using diesel fuel. It was a smart little car, and it suited her so she closed the deal. Only a few days after taking delivery, the phone rang, it was Katie, in distress once again. She had just finished her shift and left Leeds/Bradford airport then filled her new pride and joy to the top with ... petrol!! The Polo managed to splutter to a stop in the middle of nowhere, she had telephoned Sue, who luckily was at home and she set out to rescue Katie. She was entitled to VW recovery under the warranty deal. I was summoned to meet the recovery vehicle, the local agent Des Winks played a blinder and flushed the tank out at minimal cost. I was very grateful to their team, and reciprocated by purchasing my next car from them. I am sure Katie was not the first and will jot be the last to fall into the petrol/diesel trap

Qantas replied to Katie, and she was called for interview. Everything seemed to be in turmoil at this time. Dad and Robbie were creating their own dramas, and it seemed that they were both showing early signs of dementia. Dad was becoming forgetful and confused, I was regularly taking him to the doctors as he was suffering with a prostate problem, compounded by a skin condition caused by years of exposure to the sun without any protection. I now had to collect their pensions each week as they were forgetting to do so. They were acting like young children, it was so sad to see this happening to Dad, who had been my hero through all these years. The worst day was when Dad was out driving and simply could not remember his way home.

He had driven Robbie to a local whist drive and poor old Dad could not find his way back. Taking the car away from my Dad was one of the hardest things I have had to do, as he had been driving for years and it was his love, his work his salvation. I for many years used Dad as a role model as far as driving was concerned, he taught all his sons well, he would be proud that we were chips off the old block as far as driving was concerned.

Lee had just passed his test so to help him get started on the road he took on Dad's car, his prized possession, the Nissan Micra.

Both Robbie and Dad were starting to deteriorate, this intensified when they both started hiding money. Robbie's daughter Margaret and myself would find money stashed in the strangest places, with plant pots being favourite, it had become clear that they were becoming a risk to themselves, with health and safety issues being of paramount importance. After meetings with Social Services, it was recommended that for their own wellbeing, they would need constant care probably within a nursing home. Eagleview had just opened on the edge of town, when we visited it was a bright modern place with all the facilities, including a shop and hairdressers. I guess it was unusual for a couple to come in together, and following a chat with the manager they moved into a room specifically designed for two.

Dad was 84, and it left me very frustrated to think his mind had let him down, as physically he was in good shape for his age. Robbie was a couple of years older. She had been a remarkable woman, an inspirational character, together they had enjoyed many years together, never happier, when they were watching cricket, or spending an evening with their many close friends. I recall the day I drove them to their new home, Margaret was there with her husband Reg. She had brought a collection of nic nacs and photographs to decorate their new room. I was a little concerned as to how Dad would react. I was not convinced he understood the fact he was actually going to be staying. We escorted them both to the lounge, it was full of Robbie and Dads new neighbours, the majority were asleep, the staff made them very welcome with the tea trolley just arriving. So we all had coffee and biscuits...good timing

I was dreading having to stand and leave as I was sure Dad would kick off. I got up and made my excuse to leave, when Dad, in a very loud voice shouted, 'I can't stay herewith all these 'old buggers'. Dad was quickly becoming upset and agitated. The manager, who must have witnessed this on numerous occasions, assured me that Dad would calm down, and that I should continue to leave, with that I winked at dad and was gone. It was very hard for me to leave but I was reassured by the fact that Robbie and Dad would be safe and secure.

Dennis had received the autopsy report on how or why Chris had collapsed and died. The report showed that Chris had suffered from heart disease, which came as a shock to all of us. It left us frustrated that we felt it ironic that she worked in the doctor's surgery unaware she had a problem. On reflection Helen mentioned that on the afternoon before flying out on holiday that Chris had complained of feeling dizzy and had to lie down for a while. I guess you think nothing of it at the time but that was probably a sign, hindsight is a wonderful thing but no matter how many issues Chris had with her health nothing will bring her back to us. I still expect her to walk through the back gate and into our kitchen just like she had done many many times over the years. It is particularly hard for Helen as they were really close, together for most of their lives.

We all got some good news as Katie had been accepted as Cabin Crew for Qantas, which meant another set of uniform. She was really pleased with herself, she would work her notice with BMI, and then a month's course at Heathrow learning all there is to know about the layout of a Boeing 747 Jumbo Jet. From being a little girl this had been her aim, she would be living her dream. The BMI regional crew room would become a quieter place when Katie left, as they had become a close family of friends, from the cleaners to the captains, Katie I am sure would have been torn and I had a little bird telling me that a certain first officer would definitely feel the loss of Katie ... more about Boris later

The doctors and staff at the surgery where Chris had worked had moved into a new surgery just up the road from the original site. A small room on the top landing of the staircase where the staff could relax if necessary was named after Chris, dedicated to her complete with photograph in pride of place in memory of her. The family were invited to attend the blessing, and formal opening of this facility. Another moving tribute to a quiet unassuming lovely lady who left her mark effectively on others. They say time is a great healer and everything moves on, with life taking on some sort of normality, whatever that is. Mundane tasks such as dog walking Ted again, Dennis had booked a singles holiday to some exotic island in the Caribbean. Helen and I dropped him off at Manchester Airport, this would be the first time he had ventured anywhere alone, this was probably the tonic he needed to get his life back on track. No doubt there are many people who have suffered similar losses, and as we left him at the airport I remember that he looked bewildered as he made his way to check in...alone

Marge was really struggling to come to terms with losing Chris, she never let her guard down in public being of strong character, but the loss of one of her babies took its toll. She became thin and was eating very little and quickly became a shadow of her former self. Carrying the burden of losing Chris became too much. Helen called the emergency doctor to visit Marge as we were both becoming very concerned. He arrived and checked Marge out and we fully expected her to be admitted into hospital. However, he said not and arranged to see her later. Before he reached the gate Marge was struggling into the kitchen informing us that she was alright, 'now lets be having you.'

The following morning Helen rang Marge but there was no reply. We drove the short distance to Marge's bungalow, I rang the doorbell several times but no answer…we feared the worst. We forced the door and sadly found Marge dead by the side of the bed. Nothing can prepare you for that, from the initial emotion of shock, I reflected that this was the inevitable outcome. I feel sure that she knew the score and did a deal with the doctor. This was another blow to us all, and in particular me, another one of my favourite ladies gone, the Matriarch…gone but never ever forgotten. This was turning out to be a terrible year, with another family funeral in such a short time. After a few days we were all coming to terms with the loss of Marge, when we realised just how ill she had become, therefore it was a blessing that she was at rest. She was well represented at the funeral, even though most of her contempories were now deceased. She was buried with her beloved husband Duncan, reunited, together again.

Since losing her Mum, Clare had set her stall out, working with steely resolve achieving the post of Team Leader at the Scarborough Building Society. Her and boyfriend Alistair, who was hoping to become a PTI in the Royal Air Force had forged a loving relationship, selling their tiny flat and moving into a stylish three bedroom detached house in Crossgates, a community three miles south of Scarborough, the two of them had found the formula for success, and it was marvellous to see Clare laughing again. In fact after such a dreadful year with all the despair and grief, Clare gave us the perfect tonic, when she announced she was pregnant. Baby Alex was born on 1 October, so here we go again on to the next generation, doors close and doors open. Mother and son were both doing well (priceless) The whole family were delighted for Alistair and Clare, and gave them their blessing.

Before the season kicked off around Easter, Helen and I decided to grab a couple of weeks in the sun. Egypt looked the best bet regarding guaranteed sun. All Inclusive at the Hilton, Sharks Bay, Sharm El Sheikh, sounded perfect. Five hours flight from Manchester found us arriving early evening just in time for dinner. The sky was clear blue and it was really warm. It all seemed very relaxed and civilized, as the waiter dressed in local Arabic costume, served up a selection to tickle the taste buds, soups, salads, local fish, racks of lamb, ribs of beef, breasts of chicken stuffed with cheeses and herbs, and a whole pig honey glazed with a large Jaffa orange between its teeth, all this meticulously arranged in perfect harmony to suit the eye. It seemed such a shame to ravage this fine array of gastronomic art. Not to be outdone, the pastry chefs were also amazing; this was the perfect start to our holiday. Egypt was becoming a very popular winter holiday destination, not without its problems, in some resorts guests were suffering serious illness, in most cases it was stomach related, the squits or the trots.

After our visit to Egypt back in the 1980's, Helen and I had witnessed scenes involving poor buggers with uncontrollable stomach cramps, there are issues of personal hygiene that have to be addressed, we decided to follow our own hygiene code then try to put the subject to the back of our minds. The rooms were quite basic, but spotlessly clean, the room attendants were all grown men, which is the case in Egypt.

The Red Sea is another wonder of my world, Sharks Bay, where we are situated has its own diving centre, and diving is a thriving industry all along the Red Sea, with thousands of participants of all sizes and ages taking the plunge from their chartered dive boats. Helen puts her priorities into gear early on in the first morning, arranging her sun bed into the perfect position to catch the day's rays. Cloudless skies with warm sunshine, these ingredients are all that is needed to propel my wife into her perfect environment. Wooden walk ways or pontoons have been built enabling the people to walk out approx. 50 meters onto the sea, ladders have been fitted into the sea.

Conservation is high on the agenda within all diving resorts, therefore it becomes obvious why the walkways have been designed to stop the public walking all over the beautiful banks of coral and grasses, habitats to the thousands of fish and creatures that take refuge within.

We made an effort and attended the welcome meeting. On the list of excursions was a day trip to Petra, that ancient historical city of three millennia passed, high in the hills of Jordan. We decided to book our seats, another adventure on the horizon. The complex was ideal for families, two large swimming pools, crazy golf, five a side soccer pitch, tennis courts, the amenities were first class, personally we enjoyed a couple of cocktails before dinner, relishing the fantastic sunsets out across the bay. We met a friendly couple from Yorkshire, Wakefield to be precise, Shirley and Malcolm. They enjoyed simple pleasures of relaxation whilst on holiday, topping up their tans, betwixt good food, and a couple of glasses of wine ... perfect. The day we went to Petra, sounds like a song title. It was an early start at 05.30 with transport to the airport. We boarded a light aircraft that flew us to Aqaba, approx. 50 minutes flight. From Aqaba it is possible to view three countries, namely Jordan, Israel and Eygpt, all from the same spot.

Our guide was on hand to greet us at the airport and he was a polished performer. I knew from the moment we came into contact, perfect English, dry sense of humour and an enjoyment of his job highlighted from the smile permanently creasing his face. In our experience tour guides can make all the difference, ensuring an average day, becomes and extraordinary day. Our coach was two thirds full as we pulled away from Aqaba airport. Aqaba had looked quite an affluent city, with leafy suburbs, two storey tenements and wide streets. We were going to be travelling for about two hours to reach our destination. The road wound its way through a deep gorge, the rock having a green tint to it caused by the metallic element within the rock, seeping through the fissures, reminding me of the veins which course through our body. Lawrence of Arabia had been active in this part of the world according to our guide. Large petrol tankers began to pass us on their way to Aqaba, they were returning from Iraq from the war. That seemed a poignant reminder to us all that trouble was only a short distance away. After an hour the coach pulled into a very convenient café area, a quick coffee followed by a toilet break, was just what the doctor ordered. It was becoming more and more mountainous, three thousand years previous, large caravans of camels would have been trudging the same route. We were very excited at the prospect of walking down the narrow passageways or alleyways that bring you into the main thoroughfare of ancient Petra, with its magnificent buildings. I remember some years earlier watching Alan Whicker, the famous TV presenter making the same journey bringing Petra into our living rooms, stimulating our vivid imaginations and giving us a chance to dream of the day we could become Alan Whicker ... priceless.

The rock is a salmon colour, it stands out and seems to glow in the sunshine, the buildings have been sculptured and chiselled out from bare rock. It seems impossible to imagine the hard graft, even more impossible the amount of time taken to create this fantastic sight. Families of stonemasons would start the buildings and in all probability would not see the project finished before they died. The next generation would carry on, much like in England with many of our great Cathedrals and Churches. It is so very clever how Petra is hidden away from view, you would have no idea it existed, in fact it was only discovered by westerners during the last century. Helen and I were blown away by the sheer historical intensity of this ancient site, all the countries that make up the Middle east have inter connecting trade routes, like a giant spiders web. We tend to frown upon the exploits of citizens from centuries passed, but by visiting Petra and identifying those incredible buildings you were left awe struck. The Town hall, the Banks, the Court Rooms and prisons, hotels, cafes, no doubt this had been an affluent and prosperous society at the heart of the trading world, a civilized law abiding community, who worshipped the Sun as their God ...very similar to Helen in fact!!

Egypt, Sharks Bay, Petra, snorkelling and the delicious food we had enjoyed, meant our stay had been brilliant. The bonus being no problems with our tummies thank goodness. Back home to Blighty, ... its time to get the passengers on the train, ... all aboard!!!

After such a traumatic year, it was suggested by Martyn, that we should take another trip to Oz. England were playing cricket down there for the Ashes, it was tempting to imagine spending Christmas day on Bondi Beach again. It had been rumoured that the railway was going into private ownership; the Scarborough Council was in negotiations with a partnership from Cleethorpes. Ted Lancaster and the team were left in the dark contemplating their future.

Katie was now based in London with Qantas, preparing for her maiden long haul flight. She had returned home for the weekend, her relationship with Lee by all accounts had run its course. They had been together for six years. Lee was a decent enough lad, but lacked ambition, had been a student for years. I personally never imagined Katie settling down and marrying Lee. It was a sad couple of days for the pair of them after the split, but as parents all you can do is move on and accept that it was not meant to be.

There was a positive buzz in the air regarding the trip to Australia for Christmas. Martyn contacted Phil Sharpe, the former Yorkshire opener who now specialised in organising trips. To sort out an itinerary, including family and friends. It would mean arranging rooms for 14 people, no easy task. Martyn's mother Audrey and his old school pal Neil Carr, would be joining us. Interestingly Katie's new boyfriend would also be making his debut. Eric Post is a first officer with BMI regional and according to Katie, only a work colleague she used to fly with. Helen, Sue and Clare seemed much more clued up than I was on the subject, apparently the romance had been simmering for quite a while. Helen was secretly delighted that her little girl had fallen for a pilot.

We had yet to meet Eric, by all accounts he was born in New Zealand in December 1973, after his family emigrated there from Holland in 1964. They lived in the suburbs of Auckland, where Eric's father Dirk worked in the printing business. On Eric's fifteenth birthday his Dad paid for him to have flying lessons, Eric's passion in life. He took to flying like a duck to water and the rest is history, as he is currently working for Emirates Airways and based with Katie in Dubai. All the family were looking forward to meeting the young man, I am sure Katie will be parading her new beau anytime soon.

Halloween was upon us again, how time flies when you are busy, particularly on the railway. This was the final week before the railway shut down for the winter. Ted Lancaster and I, were trying to drum up opposition to the takeover by the consortium from Cleethorpes. It just did not seem right, that our iconic railway should be taken over by outsiders, what was the Council thinking, it seemed at the time that the Council were looking to offload many of their amenities.

My first impression after joining the team on the railway stuck out like a sore thumb, all the thousands of people who rode the railway, had nothing to commemorate their journey apart from their ticket, enabling them to purchase some form of memorabilia ie a postcard, timetable, or just an ice cream, would have surely enriched their experience. I found the Council lacking foresight in marketing the railway and in many respects totally shambolic. Therefore more debate between Messrs Lancaster and Hart decided on a u-turn. They now felt that a new broom, new ideas would be just what the old railway needed.

We were very busy clearing the bungalow that Marge had lived in for 30 years. This proved to be a sad time, as all the family spent many happy occasions with Marge and Duncan over many years. The bungalow had seen three generations of the family spend Christmas's, birthday's and just amazing family times there. However, life goes on as they say and it was time to put the property on the market. Back to the railway, as Helen picked me up it was time to say goodbye for the winter.

To my surprise, I was greeted in the car by a stranger, a tall bespectacled young man, he looked every bit as I imagined a young pilot might look. He jumped out the car and grabbed my hand 'I'm Eric, very pleased to meet you. 'Delighted' was my response, 'That's my boy'. Eric came into our lives and from that day its been as if we have known him forever.

A friend from Filey passed on some very sad news about a good friend, Chris Hodgson BEM, had passed away. Chris had become a very good friend over the years ,with his contribution and hard work in connection with the Cash line scheme, which helped finance Foords CC and the setting up of the Filey junior coaching scheme. Chris was a larger than life character, who lived his life to the full, whether it was a round of golf, a pint of Guinness, surrounded by friends telling tales found him in his element. This planet is now a much duller place without the charismatic Chris Hodgson ... RIP Chris.

It was similar to taking the register on a school morning, as we all rocked up to Manchester Airport, 14 of us very excited, a bit like school kids having a day at the seaside. It certainly had all the ingredients required to test the resolve, as we set out on our family bonding extravaganza for three and a half weeks. We would be arriving in Perth, spending a day at the third test match. From Perth we fly up to Cairns, staying again at Palm Cove. Then onto Sydney for Christmas, the plan was then to fly to San Francisco to visit Cliff Sexton, our saviour from Modesto, who had very kindly offered to provide us all with bed and board. It was going to be a momentous challenge for all concerned. Eric and Katie would be flying to New Zealand, instead of going with the rest of us to San Francisco, Eric was keen to show off his new 'lady' to the family back home. Interestingly we stopped off in Singapore for three days, before jetting off to Perth. I personally was excited to be back in 'Singers', it had been thirty eight years since I had left the Regiment in Selerang barracks I was keen to visit the old stomping ground. On arriving in Singapore my first reaction was one of disbelief, travelling by taxi from the Airport. It had changed completely, out with the old and in with the new. I was a tad disappointed, but then realised Singapore had grown to become a high flier on the world stage. The temperatures were just as I had remembered, with very high humidity levels, it was not long before the gang were casting off their vests and woollies.

Martyn and myself booked a taxi next morning, as I was hoping to visit the old barracks. The driver was excellent, a mine of information, the perfect tour guide. I felt strangely emotional as we arrived at the barrack gates. The guardroom, the gates were just the same, the road down to the barracks, the road I had fallen asleep in the middle of, on the white lines, just as it was, Ray and Margaret Cornish's bungalow where I used to baby sit was still there, I was transfixed for several minutes. Martyn, bless him, must have thought I was a nut case, as I was babbling to him about incidents from the past. Apparently, the barracks is now home to the Singapore Rapid Defence Regiment, one young soldier made his way across to check us out. I explained my connection with the barracks and asked whether it would be possible to visit my old room. After consulting with the Guard Commander, he came back and explained that it was not policy to allow strangers inside military compounds. To say I was frustrated and disappointed was an understatement, on the one hand understanding their position, but on the other hoping they might relent … it was not to be. We stopped off at the world renowned Changi prison, just down the road from Selerang. It is a truly moving experience visiting this site. How the inmates suffered and the truly innovative methods they created to survive from their ferocious captors during those dark days. It seemed to put everything into perspective. We then rocked up at the Singapore recreational club on the Padang by the parliament building. This is where I got selected to represent the Club up in Kuala Lumpur all those years ago. It was off season, but the cricket square looked in good nick, I was hoping to show Martyn some proof of those days, via team photos, or some recognition, but unfortunately another blank. He would have to take my word for it, the old members were still there hammering down their majong dominoes in typically aggressive fashion. This was like a time warp, the last few hours had brought back many many memories ... priceless.

A beautiful morning greeted us in Perth, clear warm and sunny, which was a total contrast to the humidity we had experienced in Singapore. Our transport was on site to transfer us to our apartments. It was a luxury 50 seater coach, resplendent with its dark leather seating. The gang were chuckling, enjoying the thought of arriving in luxury. The apartments were palatial, only ten minutes walk to the WACCA, the famous test match ground in Perth. We were going to be based at the apartments for the best part of a week. Eric being an organised young man, had pre-booked the people carriers and we walked to collect them the following morning. With the weather set fair, it was decided a day on the beach was the most suitable way to relax and rid us of any jet lag. Now this visit to the beach was not any old beach, but in fact Scarborough beach which was in the suburbs of Perth. The Oz Scarborough retained the same street names and districts as back home. On arriving at the beach, it was stunning, with beautiful soft white sand and the rolling ocean in a vivid aquamarine colour ... just the same as the North Bay at Scarborough England! I was in need of a new pair of swimming trunks and found a shop full of the Billabong range. When I mentioned to the proprietor I was from Scarborough England, he knocked me off 50%, commendable for an Aussie I thought. Perth is a modern city, well designed sitting alongside the Swan River. It has a thriving ex pat society. One of the negative aspects to living in Perth is that it is very isolated. When flying over Western Australia, it hits you how vast it is, nothing but desert for thousands of miles, just as I imagine the moon might look. We took the ferry to Fremantle and disembarked for brunch. There were many little restaurants with tables and chairs along the wharf, accompanied by gift shops, bookshops, bars all plying for trade. The locals told us how the area changed at night, springing into life with a different set of people enjoying the beautiful surroundings and different types of music, ... it reminded me of Whitby. Back on board the ferry we were heading for Rottnest Island. Arriving by the Quay, this small community seemed to be buzzing, it was a unique little island named after the large rodent, the Rottnest, these creatures still roam around the place and according to the locals are friendly ... allegedly. A small catholic church greets you on arrival, with the bell tolling; the jovial Irish priest offers his hand in welcome. Bicycles are for hire to tour the island and check out the amazing little coves, or the alternative is a bus tour with guide. The majority of the gang chose the bikes. Helen and I joined Audrey on the bus, deciding a leisurely mode of transport suited out taste. Colourful chalets were dotted around the island, they were available for hire for up to a week. It was a naturally beautiful place, historically I think I recall it having a different tale to tell, probably something to do with the slave trade. The guide did enlighten us with an interesting tale, back in the early 1800's, a sailing ship laden with cargo of timber, left Liverpool headed for Rotness Island. In those days a journey like that would take up to six months depending on the prevailing weather conditions. This particular ship arrived off Rottnest just as a momentous storm blew up, three hundred yards from the quay, the cargo moved destabilizing the ship and it sunk. Many of the crew were lost, as was the cargo. What an incredible end to an epic voyage, having covered 12,000 miles only to flounder within sight of the land.

I recall the guide pointing out an Osprey's nest, the nest site of this particular family had been in existence for at least 60 years, an incredible stat. Rottnest Island was as the saying goes, a breath of fresh air, right up my street personally, could have booked one of the colourful picture postcard chalets for a couple of nights to soak up the atmosphere thank you's no worries it had been a great day.

The first day of a test match is always a special day, all the boys were up for it. The results on the tour for England had so far been disappointing, we found ourselves two down, with a potential whitewash on the cards. It was interesting to walk down to the ground with thousands of fans milling around outside. It had been estimated that 20,000 supporters apart from the Barmy Army had made the journey over from the UK, this certainly increased the tempo which can be described as electric. Trumpets were blaring out, with Jerusalem getting an airing. Martyn had done a deal with the England cricketer Paul Collingwood, who got us tickets in the Members stand just in front of the dressing rooms. Then another weird incident took place. I was sat at the end of our line with a spare seat to my right. Just before the first ball was bowled, a young man took this seat next to me. Steve Clark, who opened the batting for the Yorkshire under 19's looked my way and we both instinctively shouted 'Clarkie ... Alf'. Throughout the cricketing world I was 'Alf'. How amazing, with all the seat s in the WACCA, some 40,000 plus, that Clarkie ended up next to me. He was over playing for a local side, thoroughly enjoying his stay. His dad Tom had been visiting and had just returned home, which was a shame as far as I was concerned as I considered Tom to be a top bloke, and I would have enjoyed yarning with him for a few hours. We had a great day, England produced possibly their best performance of the tour, by bowling the hosts out for a meagre 230 and then ending the day on 45 for 1, we enjoyed some friendly banter with the locals, a couple of beers with Clarkie before he left ... a perfect day.

Neil Carr enjoyed all forms of sporting competition and close by the WACCA had spotted an unusual venue, it was a pony trotting arena, and there was a race evening that night. Neil was keen to go and add pony trotting to his list. With the form book under his arm he bode us farewell. Back at the digs we picked up the girls, who had spent the day visiting scenic locations, known as the local shopping malls. Another slight problem we were facing being such a large group was finding places to eat, with the restaurants being busy due to the influx of the many cricket supporters. Perth I am sure enjoyed an economic boom, albeit only short term.

On the flight up to Palm Cove we stopped off at Alice Springs, which provided us with a chance to visit the iconic Ayres Rock. We were not disappointed, with those shimmering hues of purple and pink as the Sun cast its spell upon this special place. Palm Cove offered the same glorious picturesque seascapes as it did on our previous visit, a rare treat indeed to be staying in the same apartments. Katie and Eric seemed so happy and content together, the feeling was we were in at the start of something a bit special!!

We spent the next day aboard the Ocean Spirit, the catamaran, another memorable day. Snorkelling on the Great Barrier Reef, Sydney for Christmas Philip Sharpe had excelled once again, we were staying in the World Towers, with the whole gang up on the 104th floor, which was not for the faint hearted. It did however provide a fantastic view over Darling Harbour, we could see for miles. Sydney in all its glory was amazing, and the sight of aircraft which seemed to be circling our hotel before descending. The hotel enabled us to look directly down to the street, it meant that traffic and people were like ants milling about. Bondi Beach on Christmas day was definitely the place to be as it was rocking, much more atmosphere than on our previous visit, I guess that the weather was more favourable, with the breakers crashing in onto the golden sand. All the kids were having a ball, Jonny, Charlotte, Katie, Clare, Alistair and Eric all enjoyed the day in the sun. Martyn had arranged to meet a young man he had signed to play for his club Durham back in England. Ben Smith and his lady rocked up, Martyn introduced us to his protégé. The Beach was full to bursting with all different cultures and quite a few Santa Claus's joining in the fun, which left me with a warm glow, feeling happy and content with my lot. Boxing Day saw the start of the Sydney to Hobart yacht race, which was a very important day for the locals. Being a Kiwi, Eric was keen on the yacht racing, as the Kiwis were in the ascendancy in this gruelling sport. The gang were not so keen and were more interested in heading for Manly Beach; this is another popular venue for surfers. Alistair, a prolific surfer, having just taken up the sport, was keen to show off his skills.

Along with Eric, I took the ferry to Watsons Bay, the home of the famous fish restaurant. It was regarded as the best venue to watch the boats, as they clear the heads out into the ocean. Sailing up towards us under full sail, was the replica ship so synonymous to Australia, Captain Cooks Endeavour. I felt proud, as she glided by to stand marker out in the ocean, she looked quite small, incredible to think that she had been in Whitby the previous year. The building of the replica Endeavour had proved an enormous success, historically and economically, as she sailed around the world visiting all those countries that had borne witness to her exploits of days past, under the watchful eye of her famous skipper, Captain James Cooke. I felt she should have been built at home in Whitby. This was my first taste of Yacht racing; the area around the competing boats was massed with vessels of all descriptions, with people coming and going, total chaos, then a gun sound which means five minutes to start. I was amazed how the place cleared in that time, we both had a good view of the start, the tension was there to see, hairs standing up on the back of necks ... Boom!!! ... they were off.

The razzmatazz had died down, it was down to business, with crews working their socks off, finding a favourable course to steer, the favourites were already powering ahead, as they glided past us out through the heads, amongst the strong currents of the open ocean. This race was going to end in tragedy for a couple of crews; serious injuries would be incurred as masts collapsed due to incredibly strong winds. It was a brilliant day and we enjoyed a typical Aussie lunch, Seafood Salad, seated outside in the sunshine. It was good to spend some time with Eric, getting to know him. He came over as a down to earth switched on young man, who enjoyed the normal healthy pursuits; it is and always will be a pleasure to have him on board.

Our third leg of the tour as we waved farewell to Sydney, and to Eric and Katie, who were heading to Auckland, Katie was excited at the prospect of meeting Eric's siblings. Another long flight to San Francisco, it was very noticeable to feel the drop in temperature when we landed. Cliff was there to meet us, with his two sons and their transportation. It was marvellous to meet up with Cliff again, to shake the hand of that big bear, he was genuinely pleased to see us again, if not a little confused. He reckoned on being ten of us, when in fact there were twelve, he whispered to me, who were the two extras. I introduced him to Audrey, Martyn's mum and Neil his school friend, without further ado Cliff was on the phone advising his wife about the change to sleeping arrangements. Helen and Sue were keen to embrace the big man, to thank him and his family for the tremendous kindness they had shown. We were all jet lagged, feeling a bit drunk, but without the drink!. It was very cold climbing out of bed, which was an ordeal in itself. Lin prepared a super brunch for the following morning, can you imagine for a dozen folk, such a talented lady. Cliff drove us to San Francisco, we visited the tourist areas. Dennis was keen to show Helen and Sue the places he had visited with Chris. Alistair, Clare and the young guns had found a fairground in Modesto and they were made up. On our final day Cliff took Martyn, Sue, Helen, Dennis and I up into the hills to an old cowboy film set. The old town of Columbia, the film set of High Noon, that gritty western starring Gary Cooper, it still carries that feel of those tough pioneers. We had photos taken dressed in Buckskins and Stetsons, the ladies in long dresses with hats and parasols. It is a brilliant memory of a great day. The visit to Modesto had been short and sweet, but we felt it was worth the effort in memory of Chris, the girls visited the hospital where she had been admitted, they felt some closure but much pain.

We travelled overnight on New Years Eve, another long haul back to the UK. It took a while to recover from the long flights, the different time zones and all this made the old body clock suffer. We all agreed it had been an amazing experience and although Australia is a long way to travel, breaking up the journey with a couple of days in Singers made all the difference. When you finally arrive down under you very quickly forget the hassle of airports. Australia has something to offer everyone, amazing scenery, history and a wealth of friendly hospitable people who enjoy the company of the old Poms, regardless of what you are led to believe. After OZ, San Francisco was a tortuous journey, but it enabled the girls to find out first hand and meet the Sextons. It gave them the opportunity to come to terms with their loss.

We had been home about a week, it was early morning and the phone rang. Immediately I thought ... what now!! It was Eric ringing from New Zealand, to ask my permission to marry Katie. Helen was at my side grinning like the proverbial Cheshire cat. Being me, I made out that it was a bad line, I had not caught what Eric had said and asked if he could repeat the question. Poor Eric recited his words, and after a pause, ... I said I would be delighted. Apparently the two of them were having dinner on the beach, without further delay Eric placed an engagement ring on Katie's finger. Helen said what a romantic moment, ... It was different in our day, was my response!!

Helen was beaming, I felt she knew that this was coming ... call it women's intuition, but whatever it was a marvellous day, something to shout about from the rooftops.

Spring arrived, Scarborough was waking up from its winter slumber. The railway opened the week before Easter, all the gang were wondering how it was all going to pan out. The Council big wigs arrived one morning explaining to us how the new operation was going to work. We were all to be kept in employment under the new management arrangements, with David Humphreys and Chris Shaw taking charge. They arrived on site, both had experience in running heritage railways, they were in partnership running the miniature railway in Cleethorpes, the one thing that struck us immediately was the fact you could tell they loved the heritage, they lived and breathed railways. We wondered what the plans for Scarborough were, when these were explained ,the ideas for the next two years made our eyes water. It included the development of the old shelter into a bistro and café, build a ticket office and retail outlet on site, together with uniforms for guards. The operation was to change the railway out of all recognition.

David Humphreys was a full time Nat West Bank manager and lived in Richmond with his wife and two grown up daughters, therefore the railway was his hobby. Kevin Wood a local railway enthusiast was brought in to oversee the maintenance side of the operation, volunteers were beginning to appear like rabbits out of the hat. It felt like all hands to the pump, this was the beginning of the assembly of a dedicated band of experienced individuals coming together to create a new brand, The North Bay Railway. The Council had run the operation on just bare bones, it appeared that not a lot had changed since its conception in 1931. In this day and age the paying public demand value for money, this was an exciting period for all concerned, and it resembled a Workers Co-operative. The team was expanding almost every week, with new faces appearing. Stella Larkin, the niece of Ted Lancaster arrived to work selling tickets, she brought vitality and energy, exactly what was needed. The plans for development were drawn up and readily submitted. The public began to voice their support in recognition of the forthcoming improvements. David Humphreys arrived with a small pasting table. This was our initial retail outlet and from the boot of his car he produced model engines, postcards, tea towels, badges and the wooden ducks and ducklings that proved to be such a big hit that first year. Stella quickly spied an opportunity for her daughter Jessica to man the table at weekends. David Humphrey's wife Leslie made her introductions, she came over as very friendly, a very elegant lady, it felt like you had known her all your life. The team was beginning to gel together and there was a sense of spirit amongst the crew. Great memories, priceless.

Chapter 16

Wedding Fever, Railway Politics

It was August 2006 Clare and Alistair were about to tie the knot. It had been a very busy summer so far, it was now August and everything seemed to be happening, the railway was busy enjoying its resurgence. Helen was set to retire from Nat West bank in October...how scary that felt. It was a welcome opportunity to have a knees up, family and friends were invited to attend the wedding of Alistair Johnson and Clare Chapman, to take place at St Laurence's Church Scalby, followed by a reception at Ox Pasture Farm ... delightful. Katie and Charlotte were bridesmaids and little Alex Johnson was the page boy. Dennis opened up his bungalow, to allow friends to drop in for drinks and nibbles and the weather was kind being a clear day. Phil, Libby and David made the journey from Nottingham. Katie spilt wine down her dress before proceedings. Dennis was cacking himself over his speech, all the usual drama before the five minute bell. A fantastic happy day was had by all, the night do was exceptional, the DJ worked his socks off ensuring most, if not all guests showed off their moves on the dance floor. I along with Eric took on the role of Patrick Swayze from the film 'Dirty Dancing,' totally hammered, but wouldn't have missed it for the world.

September arrived, I had arranged with Eric that we should visit the Air Show at Elvington Aerodrome close to York. I thought it would a great opportunity to take old Norman Cooper from the Centre, Norman being an ex wartime RAF legend, I'm sure would jump at the chance to see some of the old aircraft on show. I picked Norman up from Danes Dyke at lunchtime, he was waiting excitedly with his bag on his back. He told me on the way to York that he had spent yesterday preparing and baking and had a picnic lunch comprising Pork Pie, sponge cake, jam tarts and mince pies for the three of us. Norman was well into his eighties, a remarkable man. We picked Eric up on the outskirts of York, he and Norman got on like a house on fire. Norman began bombarding Eric with questions about flying. The sights and sounds around the airfield made for a special atmosphere. A Victor Bomber from the 60's opened his throttle whilst on the ground; the whole area just shook and throbbed, with such a deafening roar. It was so immense and hypnotic it seemed you were not in control physically for a second or two. The highlight of the show was a display by three Hawker Hunters; they were awesome, low level sorties. Amazing, reminded me of that day in Libya all those years ago. We enjoyed Normans pack up and thanked him for all his efforts. Eric really enjoyed his day, we dropped him off and the two of us enjoyed fish and chips on the way home ... another memorable day!!

Eric's Mum and Dad made the journey over from Holland, it was lovely to meet Carla and Dirk, we all enjoyed each others company and got on very well. Eric and Katie announced the date of their wedding the 9th June 2007, how exciting, the ladies were busy organising their outfits for the big day. St Laurence's Church in Scalby had been booked, followed by a reception at the Royal Hotel in Scarborough. Eric and Katie were also in the process of buying a house in Harrogate and were due to pick up the keys any day. It was difficult keeping up with all that was going on. As parents we were very proud, Katie to her credit had always managed to achieve her goals, there had been some disappointment and heartache on route, but sheer determination and self belief meant that she flourished. She was enjoying the long haul routes with Qantas, visiting the iconic cities and making the most of what was on offer.

Early in March 2007, the weather was typical, dreary and miserable, before the railway opened up for the new season under new ownership. Helen and I decided to take a couple of weeks away in the Caribbean and were lucky to get a last minute deal, booking a junior suite in a RIU Hotel in Ochos Rios Jamaica, RIU hotels are our favourite, they have complexes all over the world, beautiful hotels, offering the utmost in service. Everything you imagine Jamaica to be, you are not disappointed. I've always been a Bob Marley fan, like millions of others, the vibrancy as you step off the plane is there to see. Ochos Rios was a two hour drive, due to the fact that we landed in Montego Bay around evening rush hour, it was a stop start coach trip through the town, but also interesting, taking in the sights and sounds especially the Reggae music blaring from the bars as we passed. Our junior suite was ideal, on the top floor with a sea view overlooking Ochos Rios, where the cruise ships dock, in fact as we lay on our Queen bed looking out onto the be – jewelled glittering ocean, the Calypso of the Seas, one of the largest cruise ships silently glides by, bedecked in brilliant shades of light, making her way to the next port of call. I finish my brandy, taken from our personal drinks dispenser, before turning in, after another delightful day on planet earth. We both enjoyed a lazy two weeks soaking up the sun and also dodging the showers, as it was inclined to deposit heavy rain on most days, but only for a short burst before settling down again. The locals on the complex kept us all entertained, singing and dancing their way through the day, lovely people ... yeah man.

Week before Easter, return to the railway, another season is upon us, the transformation takes your breath away, the new shop and ticket office is up and running, the old shelter across the way is now a café and Bistro, very smart, the kitchen area is open plan with meals prepared to order. The dining bar area creates a rustic theme, with sturdy tables and chairs, reminiscent of a tapas bar in sunny Spain. During the day tables and chairs are set outside the whole length of the building creating a street café European feel in North Yorkshire. More staff have been appointed, Mr David Fardoe, a local lad has the enviable task of running the operation, Leslie Humphreys has taken over the reigns as Managing Director of the railway. It is made clear from the outset, as she sets out her vision and plan for the future, we are officially going places. Stella Larkin has been given carte blanche to stock and run the shop, which provides an opportunity for Helen to join the new family, along with Ted's sister and Stella's mother, Mura Elliot, the three of them responsible for the new retail emporium. Kevin Wood has been relieved of his duties as maintenance engineer, as you can imagine this post holds the key to the whole operation being successful. Step forward Mr Graham Duncan, another local man born and bred just a short distance from the railway, just loves getting his hands dirty. Graham spent years developing and expanding his knowledge of engineering at Wards of Sherburn, a large employer throughout the area. Graham is a man's man, played rugby for Scarborough Rugby Union club, then switched rules, to play Rugby League in Hull. He enjoys yarning and we get on like the proverbial house on fire. Another young man arrived on site to be taken on as the new apprentice, Stephen Johnson has been a long admirer of the railway, cycling down from his home in

Falsgrave most days, to sit down and dream of becoming a train driver, from being just eight years old. He befriended Derek Thompson, who was then a driver, learning all there was to know about the railway. During this time in the 90's, Scarborough, like all Victorian seaside resorts, was suffering from a lack of tourists. Tourism was in decline in England, the demand for new destinations such as Spain, Majorca, Tenerife, with guaranteed sunshine, highlighted the demise of the typical summer holiday. It was rumoured that the Council were going to close the railway down, this incensed Stephen, with the help and encouragement from the Scarborough evening News, his message became headlines and the rest is history. With Mark Butler arriving to take up the post of Head Chef and Debbie and Emma to manage the café and Bistro the whole gang was in place, bring on the public, we were now ready to rock and roll.

Wedding fever had been with us for weeks, Helen eventually had settled for a specific outfit, Eric's pal Phil Burridge was to be best man, his brother Reza and brother in law Geoff, were making the trip over with their families from New Zealand. A number of guests were staying at the Royal Hotel in the centre of town, as the wedding reception was to be held there. The wedding itself was taking place at Scalby, a couple of miles out of Scarborough. I organised a double decker bus, to ferry the guests from the hotel to the church and back for the reception. Hopefully this would mean that we did not lose any guests, plus it is a scenic route from the top deck of the bus. The weather to be honest had been a worry all week, with wind and rain, prolonged at times dampening spirits. There was no need to worry however, because whoever was looking over us that day 9th June 2007, had created a beautiful, warm day, with blue sky and sunshine, ideal for a family wedding. I had taken Ted to the kennels the previous day, the poor old lad had diabetes and had gone blind, he could not have coped with all the organised chaos and drama that families endure throughout their special day. We enjoyed a civilised breakfast with Katie; the tension was slowly beginning to build, with people starting to arrive, flowers being delivered, buttonholes for the groom and best man and ushers. Katie was whisked away to have her hair done and through all this Helen seemed to remain calm and in control. All I remember is how quickly the day was moving, before we knew it, the bungalow was teeming with family and friends. The bridesmaids arrived looking gorgeous, Clare, Charlotte and Sally ... what a picture. I eventually climbed into my suit; we were all in long coats with pink cravat. The groom, best man, ushers and myself were a flashback to the Motown groups of the seventies, very smart and cool without the silly dance routines!!

The official photographer arrived and started with photographs in the garden with Bride and Bridesmaids, Katie made her entrance from the bedroom, looking absolutely stunning. No bias shown of course. This was turning out to be a magical day, every parent who has been fortunate enough to witness those last few hours before their daughter leaves to start a new life as a married woman with a new name will know how I felt. One minute, the bungalow was heaving, with noise laughter people buzzing, then an eerie silence, with just Katie and I left. The wedding car and we arrived at the lychgate at St Laurence's, guests were arriving, people from the village who knew Katie were swelling the numbers, all to catch a glimpse of the bride. Katie was thoroughly drinking in the moment, laughing and joking, taking it all in her stride. I felt nervous, knees knocking, legs like jelly, wanting to take me in different directions. On entering the Church, the pews were full to bursting. A never to be forgotten experience. It was just a shame that Dad could not be there to see Katie looking so beautiful. The Reverend Marion Wright, the lady vicar handled the service in her usual friendly, sincere way. She is a lovely lady and is appreciated throughout the village.

Katie and Eric were united as man and wife, they made their exit from the Church, a wall of noise, cheering and clapping, followed by the usual storm of confetti. Mr and Mrs Post were being marshalled by the photographer for the next few minutes, with the amateur snappers eagerly pinching shots whenever they could. The guests were then herded back onto the old double decker bus, in brilliant red livery, pure nostalgia. It made its way through the little lanes, which looked magical in the sun, then along the Marine Drive, up through a bustling Saturday in Scarborough and back to the Royal Hotel. My brother Bill, and his partner Pam, were amongst the welcome guests, they had moved from Scotland to Great Ayton. They had sold the Guest house in Gairloch, Bill became a gillie, working on a large estate enjoying the outdoor life. Being a keen photographer, Bill recorded some very interesting scenes while culling Deer in the Highlands and probably would have stayed up there, but the very inclement weather became to much to bear.

The reception was a grand affair, guests had travelled from far and wide, from New Zealand, Australia and Singapore, to be there. The speeches went down very well, with the best man being very nervous and needing several pints of the amber nectar to help the words flow. He tried to wind up Eric, but to no avail. Before we knew it, after a memorable day, full of emotion, Helen and myself were on our own, with our cup of Horlicks!!

Looking back, not only on the day, but also reliving our personal memories of our beautiful daughter ... we are lucky indeed!! We had to have an early night, as next day we hosted a BBQ for Mr and Mrs Post, relatives, friends etc, which again we were fortunate enough to be blessed with glorious weather ... priceless!!

The anti climax we felt after such a busy social gathering, seeing friend's, relatives, making new friends over the weekend, suddenly left an enormous void for us both. I guess we were both tired, physically, mentally and most importantly, emotionally. However, there was a strong feeling of achievement and a satisfying feeling of contentment, in the fact that we had done our duty as parents, our baby girl had flown the nest to begin the next chapter of her life, leaving us to start yet another chapter of ours.

Mr and Mrs Post arrived and were greeted with spontaneous applause. They had spent their night at the Royal, in Royal fashion, in a four poster bed!! We were all still in party mood, we were particularly keen to welcome over Eric's family, and I am sure they took back with them to New Zealand many happy memories. Eric and Katie said their goodbyes to everyone as they began their first leg of their honeymoon to the Maldives in the Indian Ocean. When Monday arrived, the anti-climax arrived simultaneously, but there was no time to dwell on this as we had passengers waiting to board the train....all aboard!

A Match For All Seasons

(Phil Hart was to be Best man at his sister-in-law's wedding to Martyn Moxon. Help provided thus!)

This poem's a story of cricket,
A tale that I now will unfold,
It's the first time it's ever been written
And the first time it's ever been told.

Now cricket's a game for the Summer
Played out beneath blue skies and sun,
When the girls have an eye for the fellows
And boys think it's time to have fun.

But some earn their living by playing
And toiling all day on the grass,
So that is my story's beginning
About this cricketing lad and his lass.

Young Martyn, who hails from Monk Bretton,
(You can't blame the poor chap for that.)
Had come up to Scarborough for cricket
With his pads and gloves, helmet and bat.

He opened the batting for Yorkshire,
His job was to knock off the shine,
But he took a shine to Miss Susan,
And she thought his glances were fine.

Well, after the first introductions,
So both knew each other by name.
The partnership blossomed and lasted
It was more than a three day game.

Our hero, renowned as a fielder,
Knew he'd made the catch of his life,
And though he was not yet the captain
Declared – he'd make Susan his wife.

The match would take place in October
At a venue agreed by both clubs,
They thought of an umpire like Birdie,
But agreed upon Canon C Tubbs.

St Laurence's, Scalby was chosen
As the finest of wickets around.
And there they could lay sound foundations
After all – it is on the Lord's ground.

The fixture was publicised freely
On three Sundays before the date fell,
Crowd, umpire and one of the players
Were in place by the five-minute bell.

He stood at the steps of th'pavilion,
His partner was cutting it late,
He'd called and he'd hoped she'd come running,
But, like Geoffrey, she'd told him to wait.

His nerves were on edge, he was anxious.
He thought of the two-minute law.
But before there was such a dismissal,
Bride Susan appeared at the door.

At last they had both reached the wicket,
Together they took up their stance.
They'd an answer to every delivery
For they'd had a quick net in advance.

The umpire performed all his duties,
He knew all the questions and laws,
And the crowds of supporters sang loudly
When they'd looked on the boards for the scores.

The scorer had notched up two singles,
But after the umpire was through.
Having read from his wisden and signalled,
He changed the two ones to one two.

The umpire then called 'That's it over!'
Then both of the partners he took
To his own little room in th'pavilion,
To sign in his autograph book.

After that the proceedings were finished,
They emerged to some rapturous applause,
Just like it is out in the middle,
When he keeps hitting sixes and fours.

We saw then this happy young batsman,
Not wearing pads, helmet or gloves,
And this is one time he'll not carry his bat,
For his arm's round the girl that he loves.

They went off for a Royal reception,
Like a ream celebrating a win,
But knowing full well that tomorrow
Another hard game will begin.

For this match is a serious business
And as the Canon has fixed up the splice,
I feel I'm neglecting my duties
Without some well-chosen words of advice.

Married life is like cricket, my children,
At times it's a hard game to play.
But face it steadfastly together,
You'll find it much easier that way.

Carefully build up life's innings
As the world continues to spin,
Play straight, always back up each other,
That way you are certain to win!

Beware of the hook! Leave the wide ones,
And those not so true as they 'seam'.
Whatever you do your whole innings through
Remember you're part of a team.

There's nothing much more I can tell you
That the coaching books don't show
So may happiness, good health and good fortune
Be with you where ever you go!

Fathers speech at Katie's Wedding

Today I'm oh so happy,

Today I'm oh so happy,
Yet just a little sad,
For I've just realised – Today's
When Katie leaves her Dad.

She's found another fellow,
So handsome, young and spruce.
I ask you, 'If you had your pick,
Well, which one would you choose?'

My baby girl at a cricket match
In her carry cot she lay,
'Til Daddy was ready to take her home,
Waiting for close of play.

Such memories start returning.
I remember that first day
When Katie proudly started school,
First steps along life's way.

More education followed
At Comprehensive School
Where she enjoyed cross-country runs
And races at the pool.

The University at Preston
Bestowed a high Degree
To further her life's ambition
An air hostess to be.

r running the Garforth Hilton
:he experience she'd need
dreams she'd had in childhood
: ever to succeed.

r several applications,
ısals, frustrations and such,
ɜeverance paid off in the long run
ıen Ryan Air got in touch.

e'd landed the job she'd longed for
ɜr school-girl dream had come true,
ıe was going to fly and to travel
s part of a Ryan Air crew.

Today I'm truly happy,
And I'm not really sad
For though Katie's got a fellow
He's a really smashing lad.

He'll be a loving husband
And then there's one thing more
'Cos Katie has a husband
I've a welcome son-in-law.

My son-in-law is Eric,
A fine young Dutchman he
Who took off to New Zealand
And is now a proud Kiwi.

When four years old he'd promised
And started on his plan
That he would be a pilot
When he became a man.

University followed early schools
He set his standards high
For he was so determined
To pilot planes across the sky.

His aim, it never wavered
Interest in aircraft grew,
When only sixteen years of age
A trial flight he flew.

With great determination
He persevered until
The promise that he'd made when four
He did at last fulfil.

Now Eric moved to England
To further his career
He gained his A.T.P.L. and
A job while he was there.

He has left New Zealand's pastures
And the Dutch canals and dykes
And settled down in Harrogate
Among the Yorkshire Tykes.

We hear of friendships starting,
Strange places where folk meet
I suppose this friendship first began
At several thousand feet.

Folk talk of marriages made in heaven
But how close can you get?
Above the clouds, 'neath skies of blue
In a smoothly soaring jet.

And strange things happen way up there
As Eric and Katie found,
Though folk who know blame rarified air,
Those feelings persisted down on the ground.

Excitedly Eric wrote home to say
How contented he was with life,
He'd a job and a house and he'd met a girl
He would like to make his wife.

The rest is history, as they say,
What happened, I'll leave you to guess,
But we shouldn't be here celebrating today
If Kate hadn't said, 'Yes.'

For friendship turned to love it seems,
As friendships often do
So they pledged to stay together
To live their whole lives through.

All stories should have happy endings
As occur in the books I have read
The Hero and Heroine get married,
So Eric and Katie are wed.

The wedding took place at St. Laurence's
On the 9th day of June, – That's today
So that brings to an end my story.
But I've still a few more words to say.

May your flight path through life be turbulence free
With caring and sharing together, the key
Forget you're an I – from now on you are WE
And if you need help or advice just come and see me.

The North Bay Railway – 80 Years Young

by Phil Hart

On that May morning of '31,
hundreds gathered at Peasholm to witness a job well done,
The project started in '29,
up to Scalby Mills snaked that railway line.

Hauling the sleepers and rails into place,
the new shiny track put a smile on their face,
In went the points, the signals and frogs,
up went a fence to keep out the dogs.

The station at Peasholm was readied without failures,
the gardeners were busy with pansies & dahlias,
This icon was the work of visionaries unsung,
to bring in the tourists from countries far flung.

The 23rd of May dawned sunny & calm,
the railway was ready no need for alarm.
The coaches were spotless, pristine to the eye,
out in the open all that fresh air to try.

The nobs and dignitaries were called all aboard,
dressed to the nines with crinoline and cord.
The tension was looming as the engine appeared,
she was graceful & powerful as she was being steered.

This historic creation with the name of Neptune,
would become a true legend the talk of the toon.
The engine was styled on the Gresley Pacific,
the Flying Scotsman to be more specific.

At 10.30 precisely the train got the green,
another historic occasion the old town will have seen.
The journey takes in panoramic views,
thru woodland, to surf, to boats & canoes.

The Castle Keep on the headland the fisherman's guide,
been there for a millennium between low & high tide.
Thousands of flap caps and chokers, from Yorkshire & Lancs,
would wave at the train from valleys and banks.

Northstead Manor was transformed overnight,
to a theatrical creation of wonder & light,
Melodious music and songs from the shows,
Desert Song, Hiawatha, all sung by the pros.

Scarborough Council had created a wonder no fear,
it's eighty years since & that's why we are here.
Therefore, lets keep the stock rolling, the train on the track,
for another eighty years, and then we'll be back.